Ideology and Conspiracy
Aspects of Jacobitism, 1689–1759

Ideology and Conspiracy: Aspects of Jacobitism, 1689–1759

Edited by
EVELINE CRUICKSHANKS

Institute of Historical Research
University of London

JOHN DONALD PUBLISHERS LTD
EDINBURGH

ISBN 0 85976 084 7

The publisher acknowledges generous financial
assistance from the Twenty-Seven Foundation
towards publication of this volume.

Exclusive distribution in the United States
of America and Canada by Humanities Press Inc.,
Atlantic Highlands, NJ 07716, USA.

Phototypesetting by H.M. Repros, Glasgow
Printed in Great Britain by Bell & Bain Ltd., Glasgow.

Preface

THIS collection of essays is based on papers given to a conference on Jacobite Studies held in July 1979 at the Institute of Historical Research, University of London, which was designed to bring together scholars working in this field from Britain, Europe and North America. Our grateful thanks are due first of all to the Director, Secretary and staff of the Institute of Historical Research, whose help and encouragement made the conference possible, and to members of the staff of the History of Parliament Trust who gave up their time to assist in running the conference.

We are grateful to Dr. John Dinwiddy, Dr. G. C. Gibbs, Professor Ragnhild Hatton, Professor Henry Horwitz, Professor George Hilton Jones, Dr. John Miller and Professor W. A. Speck for chairing the meetings and presiding with skill and good humour over discussions reflecting diverse points of view. The essays have been revised in the light of these debates. An attempt has been made in the introduction to survey, as far as possible, further work in progress on Jacobitism.

The contributions of Pierre Burger, Professor Bruno Neveu and Professor Claude Nordmann have been translated from French into English by the editor. Hugh Murray-Baillie lent his bilingual expertise of archival terms to the translation of Professor Neveu's essay, and his wide knowledge of European courts to discussions at the conference. Dr. David Hayton has read most of the volume and has made a number of useful suggestions and corrections. Thanks go to Alasdair Hawkyard for compiling the Index.

Special thanks are due to the Twenty-Seven Foundation for their generous grant towards the publication of this book.

Notes on Contributors

Pierre-Francois Burger, *a Technicien au Centre national de la recherche scientifique (Institut de recherche et d'histoire des textes),* Paris, is working on a thesis on the abbé Renaudot.

Eveline Cruickshanks is Editor of the 1690–1715 volumes of the History of Parliament. She published *Political Untouchables, the Tories and the '45* in 1979.

Dr. Mark Goldie, a Fellow, Lecturer and Director of Studies at Churchill College, Cambridge, is completing a book on English political theory and party politics, 1660–1720.

Edward Gregg, a graduate of the London School of Economics, is associate Professor of History at the University of North Carolina. He is the author of *Queen Anne* (1980) and *The Jacobite Court in Exile, 1688–1807* (forthcoming). He is currently working on a two-volume history of the Jacobite movement provisionally entitled 'The Fall of the House of Stuart'.

Dr. Howard Erskine-Hill, Fellow of Pembroke College, Cambridge, is University Lecturer in English at Cambridge. He has edited Alexander Pope's *Horatian Satires and Epistles* (Oxford 1964) and is the author of *Pope: the Dunciad* (1972) and *The Social Milieu of Alexander Pope* (1975).

Paul Hopkins, King's scholar at Eton, read history at Trinity College, Cambridge and has been appointed Research Fellow at Peterhouse, Cambridge. He is engaged on a study of Jacobitism in the reign of William III.

Dr. Bruce Lenman is Senior Lecturer in Modern History at the University of St. Andrews. His published works include *Dundee and its Textile Industry* (1969), *From Esk to Tweed* (1975), *An Economic History of Modern Scotland* (1977), and *The Jacobite Risings in Britain* (1980).

Professor Bruno Neveu, *docteur es lettres,* is *Directeur d'Etudes* at the *Ecole Pratique des Hautes Etudes* in the Sorbonne on European diplomatic relations in the Seventeenth and Eighteenth Centuries. He has made a special study of the correspondence of apostolic nuncios in France under Louis XIV. His published works include *Jacques II médiateur entre Louis XIV et Innocent XI* (1967). He is now Directeur of the Maison Francaise in Oxford.

Claude Nordmann is Professor in Histry at the University of Lille. His published works include *La Crise du Nord au début du xviiie siècle* (Paris 1962), *Grandeur et Liberté de la Suède 1660–1792* (Paris, 1971) and articles on 'Louis XIV and the Jacobites' in *Louis XIV and Europe,* ed. Ragnhild Hatton (1976) and 'Les Jacobites écossais en France au xviiie siècle' in *Regards sur l'Ecosse au xviiie siècle,* ed. M. Plaïsant, Pub. Université de Lille III, 1977.

Professor Nicholas Rogers read modern history at St. Edmund Hall, Oxford, and obtained a Ph.D. at the University of Toronto with a thesis on mid-eighteenth century London politics. He is working on a book on the urban opposition to the Whig oligarchy with particular reference to London and Bristol.

Dr. L. B. Smith read history at the London School of Economics and wrote a Ph.D. thesis on Spanish support for the Jacobites, 1715–19. After a spell in the Cabinet Office, he joined the staff of the Eighteenth Century Short Title Catalogue in the British Library. He is engaged on a study of Spain's involvement with the Stuarts prior to the 1719 attempt.

Abbreviations

Note: all books are published in London except where otherwise stated.

Add.	Additional Manuscripts in the British Library
AECP	Archives étrangères, correspondance politique at the Quai d'Orsay
AEM & D	Archives étrangères, mémoires et documents at the Quai d'Orsay
AGS	Archivo General de Simancas
AHN	Archivo Historico Nacional, Madrid
Ailesbury	*Memoirs of Thomas, Earl of Ailesbury written by himself,* ed. W. E. Buckley, 2 vols., Roxburghe Club 1890
Ang.	Angleterre
Bennett, *Tory Crisis*	G. V. Bennett, *The Tory Crisis in Church and State 1688-1730. The Career of Francis Atterbury, Bishop of Rochester,* Oxford, 1975
BIHR	*Bulletin of the Institute of Historical Research*
BL	British Library
BN n.ac.fr.	Bibliothèque Nationale, nouvelles acquisitions francaises
Boyer	Abel Boyer, *The Political State of Great Britain,* 60 vols., London 1711-40
CJ	Journals of the House of Commons
Cruickshanks	Eveline Cruickshanks, *Political Untouchables, The Tories and the '45,* 1979
CSP Dom	*Calendar of State Papers Domestic*
CTB	*Calendar of Treasury Books*
Dalrymple	Sir John Dalrymple, *Memoirs of Great Britain and Ireland,* 2 vols., 1771-3
EHR	*English Historical Review*
Foxcroft	H. C. Foxcroft, *The Life and Letters of Sir George Savile, Marquis of Halifax,* 2 vols., 1898
Garrett	Jane Garrett, *The Triumphs of Providence, the Assassination Plot, 1696,* Cambridge 1980
Hatton	*Louis XIV and Europe,* ed. Ragnhild Hatton, 1976
HC	*The House of Commons 1715-1754,* ed. Romney Sedgwick, 1970
HJ	*Historical Journal*
HMC	Historical Manuscripts Commision
Holmes, *Anne*	Geoffrey Holmes, *British Politics in the Age of Anne,* 1967
Holmes, *Sacheverell*	Geoffrey Holmes, *The Trial of Doctor Sacheverell,* 1973
Horwitz, *Nottingham*	Henry Horwitz, *Revolution Politics, the Career of Heneage Finch, Earl of Nottingham,* Cambridge 1968
Horwitz, *Parliament*	Henry Horwitz, *Parliament, Policy and Politics in the reign of William III,* Manchester 1977
Howell	*A Complete Collection of State Trials,* ed. T. B. Howell, 33 vols., 1816-26
Jones, *Main Stream,*	George Hilton Jones, *The Main Stream of Jacobitism,* Cambridge, Mass. 1954
Kenyon	J. P. Kenyon, *Revolution Politics, the Politics of Party 1689-1720,* Cambridge, 1977
LJ	Journals of the House of Lords
Lenman, *Risings*	Bruce Lenman, *The Jacobite Risings in Britain 1689-1746,* 1980

Lüthy	Herbert Lüthy, *La banque protestante en France de l'Edit de Nantes à la Révolution*
Macpherson	*Original Papers containing the Secret History of Great Britain*, ed. James Macpherson, 2 vols., 1775
Mahon	Lord Mahon, *History of England from the Peace of Utrecht to the Peace of Versailles 1713-1783*, 6 vols., 1858
Marine	Manuscrits du département de la Marine, Archives Nationales, Paris
Miller	John Miller, *James II, a study in Kingship*, Hove 1978
NLS	National Library of Scotland
Nordmann, *Crise*	Claude Nordmann, *La Crise du Nord au début du xviiie siècle*, Paris, 1962
NSA	Niedersächsisches Staatsarchiv, Hanover
NUL	Nottingham University Library, Portland collection
PRO	Public Record Office
Recueil	*Recueil des Instructions aux ambassadeurs de France*
Riley	P. W. J. Riley, *King William and the Scottish Politicians*, Edinburgh 1979
Ruvigny	Ruvigny and Raineval, *The Jacobite Peerage*, Edinburgh 1904
SHR	*Scottish Historical Review*
SP	State Papers
SRO	Scottish Record Office
Stuart mss	Stuart manuscripts in the Royal Archives, Windsor Castle
Vat. lat.	Vatican latin manuscripts
W. R. Ward	W. R. Ward, *Georgian Oxford. University Politics in the Eighteenth Century*, Oxford 1958

Contents

Introduction

Eveline Cruickshanks

THE 'consoling legend' of Jacobitism, as Christopher Hill has called it, has been much cherished in a country that loves lost causes. Works treating Jacobite history as a form of escapism or as a saga in the Gaelic tradition abound. But serious work has been undertaken mainly in the areas of diplomatic or local history, and much of it in a political vacuum as far as English history is concerned. Because of the difficulties presented by sources dealing with Jacobitism, especially Jacobitism in England, many historians have either ignored the subject completely or have dismissed all evidence as unreliable, even when that evidence is confirmed by other contemporary testimony. Pargellis and Medley's standard *Bibliography of the Eighteenth Century 1715-1760* does not give a single entry to Jacobitism in its English section. History is generally written by the victors and little has been done to redress the balance of Whig rhetoric: Jacobites are always 'rabid', Whigs are always 'staunch'. There has, moreover, been deliberate suppression: Archdeacon Coxe had discovered and carefully copied from the Walpole papers the proofs of the Duke of Argyll's dealings with the Pretender in the 1740s,[1] but did not publish the evidence, presumably out of deference to Argyll's descendants. Similarly, eighteenth- and nineteenth-century county histories usually omit Jacobites from their accounts of county families. The tendency to accept the Whig interpretation at face value is at last being corrected, however, and Jacobitism is receiving proper attention as a significant force in diplomatic, literary, political, religious and social history. The present collection of essays, representative of various strands in this new and burgeoning historiography, is an attempt to make available the fruits of some of the most important current research into aspects of Jacobitism during the seventy-odd years of its lifespan.

The main source for the history of Jacobitism will always be the Stuart papers themselves. For the period before 1715, however, they have only survived in part. Historians will never cease to regret the loss of the Stuart papers kept at the Scots College in Paris. The late David McRoberts has recounted how during the French Revolution the three manuscript volumes of the original memoirs of James II were to be sent to England for safety, but were burnt at St. Omer in August 1793 to avoid suspicion, while on 3 July 1794, by authority of the French government, a certain Citoyen Deperthes seized and never returned most of the political papers at the Scots College itself.[2] Some papers from the college survived, such as the Leslie manuscripts, used below by Professor Neveu, and a copy of the five-volume 'Original Memoirs of James II' by William Dicconson, the treasurer at St. Germain: they are now in Edinburgh.[3] The Nairne papers from the college have been preserved in the great Carte collection in the Bodleian. Many of the papers now

1

missing from the Scots College archives were printed by Sir John Dalrymple in his
Memoirs of Great Britain and Ireland, published in three volumes in 1740 and in a
revised edition in 1771. Dalrymple realised, as he wrote in the preface, that his
work would provoke violent reaction, but thought it fitting 'that a man of a Whig
family should have been the first to expose to the public the intrigues of the Whig
party at St. Germain', adding that Lord Chancellor Hardwicke had encouraged him
to publish. James Macpherson, Member of Parliament for Camelford 1780-1796
and a protegé of Lord Bute, had visited the Scots College in earlier years and
published numerous documents from the College in 1775 in his two-volume
Original Papers. Whatever his reputation as a poet, Macpherson's transcripts of the
Nairne papers and of the Robethon (Hanover) papers now in the British Library are
accurate enough, so that there is no reason to suppose those he made at the Scots
College are less so. Another repository for Stuart papers in France was Chaillot, the
monastery founded by Henrietta Maria, Charles I's Queen, which was used for
retreats by Mary of Modena and often visited by James II. The manuscripts there
have survived in the Archives Nationales in Paris (Fonds Stuart K). Many have
been published either by Falconer Madan[4] or by Sir James Mackintosh, including
the account of the last days in England and flight of James II dictated by the King
himself.[5] The Gualterio papers in the British Library and in the Vatican archives,
again examined here by Professor Neveu, are very valuable, as well as Lord
Melfort's letterbook and the Middleton papers[6] in the British Library. For the last
years of Queen Anne, the despatches of the abbé Gaultier and the Marquis
d'Iberville at the Quai d'Orsay, which contain much Jacobite material, help to fill
the gap and have been widely used.

After 1715 the Stuart papers have, of course, survived almost intact, and the story
of the many misadventures they suffered before being acquired by the Prince
Regent and brought to England from Rome has been told in detail.[7] Their arrival
came at a time when the Romantic movement was at its height and Gaelic myth and
tradition a subject of fascination to writers. This and the subsequent Victorian cult
of the Highlands, fostered by the Queen, who was by no means unsympathetic to
Jacobitism, resulted in a great flowering of works on the subject. Sir Walter Scott
was one of the first to see the Stuart papers and made use of them in his novels.
James Browne, in his *History of the Highlands and the Highland Clans* (1832-3),
printed many documents from them, unfortunately often giving the cant names
rather than the true ones, which had been so carefully deciphered by James Edgar,
the Old Pretender's secretary. Victoria's own librarian at Windsor Castle, J. H.
Glover, edited the letters of Bishop Atterbury, and Lord Mahon also published
extensive extracts from the collection.[8] Since then most, but by no means all, of the
Stuart papers for the first six years of George I's reign have been published by the
Historical Manuscripts Commission. For the 1730s the Stuart papers may be
supplemented by the intercepted correspondence of the Duke of Ormonde;[9] for the
1740s by the Sempill and other papers at the Quai d'Orsay; and for the 1750s by
material in the Pelham (Clumber) manuscripts[10] now at Nottingham University
Library. Other Stuart papers, of less political interest, are in the Braye manuscripts
in the British Library.[11] Sir Charles Petrie used the manuscripts of the Duke of Alba

and published many letters from them in *The Duke of Berwick and His Son* (1951).

The easiest way of dealing with Jacobitism, and that most commonly adopted, is to concentrate on the Stuarts and their courts in exile, depicting the shifts, the poverty, the intrigues over ever-elusive prizes and the treasons which took place there. This had also, of course, been the predicament of Charles II in exile.[12] There were frequent and often justified complaints in Britain about the narrowness and incompetence of the servants of the Stuarts at St. Germain — Pierre Burger gives an instance of it — and later of the Stuart court in Rome, but the difficulty was that able and influential persons in these islands persistently refused to go and serve their masters in exile. It was a game in which the British government held most of the trump cards, buying information from Jacobite exiles with either money or hopes of pardon, posting spies round the Jacobite courts and bribing influential foreigners in exchange for intelligence or for blocking pro-Stuart projects.[13] This led George Lockhart to ask despairingly, 'What is proof against the money of Great Britain?'[14] British governments, however, were not uniformly successful: one of the chief agents employed by Portland, William III's Dutch favourite, John Simpson *alias* Jones, was, as Paul Hopkins points out, a Jacobite double agent, and there were 'moles' in Walpole's organisation too.[15]

The main historical importance of Jacobitism, however, was its effect on British politics and British foreign policy, its influence on the politics of other European states and the contribution made by the Jacobite exiles to those states.

One of the great and abiding problems of studying Jacobitism in Britain, especially in England, is the problem of identification, to discover who was a Jacobite. Because of the penal laws against Jacobites — these statutes should be prescribed reading for historians of Jacobitism — discretion had to be the better part of valour. Even in the comparatively lenient conditions of the later years of Queen Anne, a Jacobite agent admitted that there were persons in England who 'wish the King [i.e. 'James III'] well, who would not hazard their estates for him'.[16] The duc d'Aumont, the French ambassador, asked in 1712 to ascertain the numbers of Jacobites in England, reported:

> The King of England's [i.e. 'James III'] party has regained much of its strength over the past few years, and because of the divisions between the Tories and the Whigs this prince has won several friends among the former. But everyone is afraid to declare himself. No friend can be trusted when it is a matter of losing your head and property.[17]

Neither the Restoration of 1660 nor the Revolution of 1688 was brought about by popular risings, nor could it have been, given the presence in the country of a standing army, and because of the standing army the Jacobites had to seek troops and arms abroad, which incidentally enabled British governments to represent them as the instruments of foreign powers. Although the necessity of obtaining regular troops as a precondition of a restoration was generally accepted at the time, there were occasions when local sympathisers were asked to rise first and show their strength before foreign assistance was granted. Louis XIV insisted on an English rising in 1696 before he would send help,[18] as did Spain in 1715-16, as Dr. Smith shows in his essay, but this was in all probability simply a device to cause trouble in Britain without having to intervene directly. Lists of supporters such as that sent to France in 1696 (printed as an appendix to Pierre Burger's essay below), or the document brought to James in Rome in 1721,[19] consisting of the names of leaders in each county for a rising to be supported only by some Irish troops in the French and Spanish service, were meant as an encouragement to the foreign power to act. The length to which those named were actually prepared to go would have depended very much, to judge by previous seventeenth-century examples, on whether or not the attempt looked like being successful.[20]

It cannot therefore be assumed that the only Jacobites were those who rose in rebellion. This was recognised at the time and is now being recognised by historians, as, for example, in the case of William Shippen, perhaps the most notorious Jacobite M.P. of them all.[21] What indeed would Shippen have done, a lawyer and something of a windbag in Parliament, against redcoats and Dutch troops? Nor ought we to assume that every Jacobite would necessarily have corresponded at some time or other with the exiled Stuart court. This needed a special cipher or a messenger service, which few could have had access to, and which was actively discouraged by James Stuart, the Old Pretender, unless there was need. Clarendon's great-grandson, Lord Cornbury, a Tory M.P. and a friend of Bolingbroke's, wrote to James in 1732, 'I have hitherto not written, in which I followed your own desire to avoid unnecessary correspondences'.[22] And it would be even more naive, of course, for the historian to expect to find hard evidence of Jacobitism in a man's private papers: would someone whose personal effects were liable to be searched at any time be likely to leave proofs of treason? Jacobites did not, no more had the Whigs in the 1680s.

One useful way of identifying Jacobites is to find out those arrested on suspicion of high treason, who were detained during an emergency and released without trial once it was over: the real security risks. There are no court proceedings to consult, but the more important figures are usually mentioned in government sources. Much more difficult are the cases of those arrested on general warrants. Their names can very occasionally be discovered in private letters,[23] but normally contemporaries preferred to draw a veil of silence over the matter. Another obvious guide to the extent of Jacobitism among the nobility and gentry is the list of peers and M.P.s who refused at first to sign the Association of 1696,[24] though unfortunately this was to be a unique occasion for self-identification since, rather than be deprived of their seats in Parliament, most not only took the Association eventually but continued to take it at intervals until King William's death. The same applied to members of local commissions and corporations. Indeed, during the '45 known Jacobites took the Association and the subscriptions in order to avoid suspicion.[25]

There is a good deal of evidence for the many manifestations of popular Jacobitism, but its significance has been called into question. Professor Nicholas Rogers has done very useful work on 'seditious words' cases, as well as on the symbols and rhetoric of protest. He takes the view that these represented an expression of political consciousness rather than a genuine commitment. It might be thought interesting in itself that such expressions should have taken a Jacobite form rather than a 'Commonwealth' one. Tory voters, for instance, celebrated the defeat of both of Walpole's candidates at the Norfolk county election of 1734 by shouting 'No Hanover Succession, King James the 3rd for ever!'[26] A forthcoming article on Jacobite riots in Staffordshire in the late 1740s takes the view that popular Jacobitism was genuine,[27] while a thorough study of Jacobite engraved glasses has shown that they were English rather than Scottish in origin and were produced in 1743-6 rather than in the 1750s, and were thus a genuine political symbol rather than a nostalgic throwback.[28] The flourishing Jacobite publishing industry, producing large numbers of broadsheets, newspapers, pamphlets and ballads under George I, either out of personal conviction or in response to the demands of the market, is also now being studied in detail.[29]

To those brought up in the Cavalier tradition of hereditary right, non-resistance and Anglican monopoly as the only guarantee of peace and order, the very people who had opposed James II's policy of religious toleration, the Glorious Revolution came as a rude shock. Many, like some loyalists in the House of Lords, must have acquiesced in the legal fiction of the 'abdication' because 'there was an absolute necessity of having a Government' and there was 'no other way than this'.[30] Many West Country Tories who had joined William of Orange, apparently believing his Declaration that he had not come to seek the Crown, opposed the resolution to declare the throne vacant.[31] They eventually accepted William III as King *de facto* but not *de jure*.[32] The majority of those who remained in public life took the oaths, becoming what James Stanhope scathingly called 'the non-juring jurors'.[33] It was easy to scoff at the moral dilemma of political opponents, and it must be stressed that the concept of treason in the late seventeenth and eighteenth centuries was not ours. To great men like the 2nd and 3rd Earls of Sunderland or Marlborough, Kings and Queens were but pawns in the struggle for power. Most people had to go on living. This point was made by George Granville in a letter of 1710 written to his young nephew, the Earl of Bath:

> In a country subject to Revolution what passes for loyalty today may be treason tomorrow. But I make great difference between real and nominal treason. In the quarrel of the house of York and Lancaster both sides were proclaimed traitors, as the other prevailed. Even under Cromwell's usurpation all who adhered to the King were proclaimed traitors and suffered as such but this makes no alteration in the thing itself. It may be enacted treason to call black black or white white, but black will be black and white will be white in spite of all the legislators.[34]

In William's reign there were two types of English Jacobites. The 'Compounders' led by Charles, Lord Middleton, one of James II's two managers of the 1685 Parliament, who were for the most part Anglicans and included many bishops, disliked the new regime as illegal, frowning on the favour William showed to Dissenters and Dutchmen, and wished for a restoration on terms that would strictly safeguard the Church and constitution, with a general pardon and no further

B

measures to advance Roman Catholicism. The other, smaller group, led from St. Germain by Lord Melfort (who had previously ruled Scotland for James) believed that the exiled King should surrender none of his hereditary powers and that those who had rebelled should atone for their disobedience.[35] William's lenience to English Jacobites and his policy of employing all influential people did much to reconcile the Compounders, disillusioned as they were by James II's intransigence and the failure of the Jacobite plots of the 1690s. It was no coincidence that Sir Edward Seymour's contacts with the Jacobites were most frequent when he was out of office! The Act of Settlement produced another crisis of conscience. It passed by one vote in committee of the Commons, after many procedural delays, clogged with clauses either to make it unworkable or perhaps to sweeten the pill, and represented a triumph of parliamentary management for Robert Harley rather than a real expression of Tory belief in the Hanoverian succession. Shortly afterwards, in any case, the Tories were swept up on the tide of anti-French sentiment with the renewal of the war against Louis XIV. The accession of Queen Anne went much further to reconcile high Tory sentiment. Few Tories indeed would have wished to replace her with her brother while she was alive.[36] Work in progress on the Tory party in the last four years of the Queen's reign[37] shows how after Oxford's and Bolingbroke's failure in 1714 to persuade James Stuart to change or dissemble his religion, the Jacobite wing of the party became increasingly isolated in the face of the aggressive Hanoverian Tory wing and the 'fatal paralysis' of the bulk of the party.[38]

For the nonjurors, however, examined below by Dr. Mark Goldie, the issue was always clear: they believed 'that the established Church, born of the Revolution of 1689, was as illegitimate as the new political regime'. Comparatively few in number but including very talented writers, their influence was paramount in the ideology of Jacobitism. Jeremy Collier, quoted here by Dr. Howard Erskine-Hill in his essay, could charge Williamite legislation with resolving 'all Title into Force and Success' and making 'the Devil, if he should prevail, the Lord's anointed'. The nonjurors, as Goldie shows, played a central part in the defence of the rights and privileges of Convocation, asserting its independence from the Whig bishops, and in the Occasional Conformity controversy so vital to the politics of Queen Anne's reign. Deprived of all hope of office and paying more taxes than the rest of the community, nonjuring clergymen sought refuge as tutors and chaplains in Tory families and must have exerted on Tory thought the kind of influence ejected nonconformists had in Whig circles under Charles II.

A dramatic change in the political scene followed the accession of the house of Hanover in the summer of 1714. The role of the Crown had been that of arbiter between parties, but George I and George II chose to play that of tools of the Whig party. The proscription of the Tory party at national and regional levels was unprecedented and drove the party into the arms of the Pretender, not out of choice but because they had nowhere else to go. This does not mean that every single Tory became a Jacobite, but that the party looked to a restoration of the Stuarts as the only means of escaping from an intolerable predicament.[39] It has been argued that the Tories did not want office.[40] Why should a great political party which had fought tooth and nail for office under Queen Anne pass a self-denying ordinance in favour of their political opponents in 1715? There is a good deal of evidence that they would have taken office and abandoned the Pretender on the accession of George II in 1727[41] and again subsequently, but George II, who believed they were Jacobites, would not employ them.[42] Dr. Linda Colley, while regarding the Tories as a coherent and well organised party, appears to take the view that most of them were Hanoverian Tories.[43] This is to ignore the fact that the Hanoverian Tories, led by Nottingham, Sir Thomas Hanmer and Lord Anglesey, who were so influential in the last Parliament of Anne's reign, soon faded into insignificance under George I. The political scene is a fast-moving one and politicians cannot be studied in set attitudes, like butterflies in an album. For instance, Sir Henry Bunbury, a leading Hanoverian Tory in 1714,[44] had a year later become a convinced Jacobite.[45] In the late 1720s, Sir William Wyndham and his 'small band of followers'[46] took up the cudgels once again as self-proclaimed Hanoverian Tories, but this proved a blind alley, as neither George I nor George II would have anything to do with them.

Others have seen Bolingbroke's country party as the true home of Toryism. But whereas the country party of the 1690s was a coherent and effective political force, the country party of the 1730s existed in the pages of the *Crafsman* rather than in the world of practical politics. Generalisations ranging over half a century cannot replace a day to day study of real political situations. Incredulity has been expressed at the statement that it took a letter from the Pretender in 1730 to make the Tories vote with the Whigs in opposition.[47] A close study of the evidence reveals that the coalition, so painfully built up by Wyndham and William Pulteney, had broken down and that the Tories refused to vote with the opposition Whigs in division after division — much as they were to do before the fall of Walpole — until, upon the receipt of the Pretender's letter, there was a sudden and dramatic change in their voting. If there is some other explanation, what is it and where is the evidence? With an almost total lack of Tory papers for the post-1715 period, it is impossible to prove or disprove whether the party's rank and file were Jacobites. What one can prove is that *the leaders of the party were Jacobites and answered for the party*. Historians who declare the contrary are in fact seeking to know better than contemporaries: better than Oxford, Gower, Bathurst, Atterbury, Orrery, Cornbury, Cotton, Watkin Williams Wynn and Beaufort and better than Walpole.

It is true that, obliged to smother any expression of their traditional constitutional principles, and without their old rallying cry of 'the Church in danger' — with Convocation never allowed to meet under the Georges, a Whig majority in Parliament rendering futile the re-introduction after 1720 of an Occasional Conformity Bill or anything like it, and the Whig ministry thereafter cautious of provoking High Church anger — the Tories' political platform was very similar to that of the opposition Whigs, at least while the latter were in opposition. This was because the opposition Whigs adopted popular demands to secure Tory co-operation and ditched them as soon as they took office. Samuel Sandys, for instance, introduced place bills with Tory support year after year, but as soon as he was in office, opposed them! The point is well made in a dialogue by Sir Charles Hanbury Williams in which George Lyttelton, an opposition Whig, asks Edmund Lechmere, a Tory, why he is standing against one whose views appear to be the same as his own, to which the reply is:

> Because, Sir, you're a Whig and I'm a Tory.
> Howe'er with us you the same schemes pursue.
> You follow those who n'er will follow you;
> My principles to you I'll freely state
> I love the church, and Whiggism I hate,
> And tho' with you Sir Robert I abhor,
> His Whiggish heart is what I hate him for;
> And if a Whig the minister must be,
> Pult'ney and Walpole are alike to me.[48]

The failure of the '45 dealt a death blow to the Tory party because it was a Jacobite party. The agony was prolonged, there were Jacobite demonstrations and false hopes, but serious prospects of gaining power through a Stuart restoration had gone. This process led to the break-up of the whole party system and a complete re-alignment of politics, which has been studied in detail by Jonathan Clark, and which explains the transition 'between an age whose central political fact was the Jacobite threat and one in which Jacobitism was a harmless Oxford mannerism'.[49]

So much sound work has been done on Jacobitism in Scotland[50] and so much written about Bonnie Prince Charlie, that it need not detain us long here. Recently, however, a whole new aspect has been opened up by Dr. Bruce Lenman,[51] examining in a scholarly way for the first time the economic and ideological causes of the rebellions in Scotland. He has established that it was the Episcopalians — the Scottish equivalent of the English nonjurors — and not the Roman Catholics, who were the mainstay of Jacobitism in Scotland, playing a crucial role as tutors and chaplains in noble households, and has explained that the Union of 1707 handed over the assertion of Scottish national identity to the Jacobites, since they alone were willing to repeal it. In his essay below he draws on the private papers of 'fiery Alexander Robertson', minister at Fortingall, and of 'quiet, gentle Robert Kirk' of Aberfoyle and Balquidder, to show the ideas and loyalties which underlay the Jacobite cause. Further research into the material consequences of disestablishment for the Episcopalians, as well as their connection with the English nonjurors, is under way.[52] Dr. Lenman himself is now preparing a study of the Jacobite clans of the Western Highlands, concentrating on the Frasers and the Camerons of Lochiel, and bringing out their important links with the ministers in England under Queen Anne, while work in progress on the Atholl lands in the late seventeenth and early eighteenth centuries shows the effects on the tenants of the existence of two rival Dukes of Atholl, one a Hanoverian and the other a Jacobite, particularly during the '45 when the Jacobite Duke William regained control of his inheritance.[53]

After the final defeat of James II's forces at Limerick in 1691 and the subsequent confiscation of Jacobite estates in Ireland, which completed the massive seventeenth-century land settlements and further reduced the Catholic share to a mere 14%,[54] Ireland might have been expected to be the most disaffected part of the British Isles from the Jacobite point of view. It was in fact the quietest, so that Dudley Ryder, later attorney-general, was able to write in 1715-16:

Though the number of Papists is vastly superior to that of Protestants, yet the Protestants are able to keep them in order and prevent any trouble or danger from themselves, whereas we in England that have much fewer Papists here, are not sufficiently armed against riots, tumults and rebellions and popery.[55]

This was due to the huge numbers of troops permanently stationed in Ireland, not only to prevent rebellion there, but to screen the size of the standing army from English public opinion. Irish Protestants, even those who were Tories under Queen Anne, were almost without exception firmly committed to the Williamite settlement and thus to the Hanoverian succession, while the Presbyterians in the north, although excluded by and alienated from the Church of Ireland establishment, were vehemently anti-papist and in consequence inevitably anti-Jacobite. The Jacobite cause in Ireland was that of the Catholic Irish, but they had been deprived of their 'natural leaders' by the flight of the 'wild geese' abroad, while the Catholic gentry who were left either remained quiescent or actively collaborated with the new regime, many, because of the severity of the penal laws, even giving up their faith to preserve their estates.[56]

Without the support of a professional army like the one William of Orange had brought with him in 1688, a restoration of the Stuarts was impossible. There was always a possibility that some European power, usually France, might supply troops for the purpose, until Choiseul's attempt of 1759, examined here by Professor Nordmann, when Britain destroyed the French fleet and gained control of the seas.[57] This was a determining factor in British foreign policy, but one which has been consistently underestimated by historians. Work in progress[58] on the 1730s shows that the Walpole ministry, while discounting the possibility of a successful indigenous Jacobite rebellion, were very much alive to the need to prevent foreign support of the Jacobites, especially from Chauvelin, the bellicose French foreign minister.[59]

That foreign intervention in British domestic affairs would have been unpopular is undeniable. Many would probably have agreed with the 1st Marquess of Halifax, the 'Great Trimmer', who refused to subscribe to the Invitation sent by the Immortal Seven to William of Orange on the grounds that the people of England could settle their own affairs for themselves without recourse to foreign assistance or to force.[60] Nevertheless, foreign troops on British soil or the likelihood of foreign troops on British soil became a fact of life for a long time. Xenophobia was always a strong characteristic of Whigs and Tories alike, but each party hated a different set of foreigners. While Whigs forever praised the Dutch, anti-Dutch sentiment was a constant feature of Toryism: 'if you would discover a concealed Tory, Jacobite or Papist speak but of the Dutch, and you will find him out from his passionate railings'.[61] Tory attitudes to France varied according to the political climate. After accusations — unjust more often than not — of being under William and Anne the secret allies of Louis XIV, the Tories after 1716 became the severest critics of France, no doubt for what they regarded as a betrayal, the French being the closest allies of the Hanoverian government.

European alignments themselves did not follow the Protestant *v.* Catholic division of national myths. The Revolution of 1688 had been aided and abetted not only by Catholic Austria but by the Papacy:[62] as a letter, quoted by Professor Neveu, written from Rome by William Leslie put it, 'the Romans would crucify Christ again to be revenged of the French'. None the less, the stability of most European monarchies depended on the principle of primogeniture, and this obviously affected many rulers in their dealings with Britain. Louis XIV's attitude to James II, his guest and pensioner at St. Germain, was a complex one. Louis always convinced himself that his foreign policy and military adventures had a sound moral and legal justification, although he seldom convinced his enemies. His obligation to support James II was rooted in his fundamental belief in legitimate monarchy, the divine right of Kings and the truth of the Catholic faith. This did not mean, however, that he was prepared to intervene on behalf of the Stuarts unless French interests stood to benefit, and he was not disposed to assign troops, which were badly needed elsewhere, simply to help James regain his throne. In practical politics, as part of his plan to partition the Spanish lands and avert a succession war, he recognised William III as king of England *de facto* at the Peace of Ryswick in 1697. He then had to make a final choice on the death of James II when, after much heart-searching and against the advice of his ministers, he decided that his concept of kingship left him no option but to recognise James III.[63] This was, even so, a qualified recognition, which, in the words of Professor Neveu, 'could be applied either to the legitimacy of James III's title as King, or to his right to rule effectively over Great Britain'.

The Jacobites looked to other powers for help, besides France. In 1715, as Dr. L. B. Smith shows, an offensive and defensive alliance was concluded between Spain and James Stuart providing financial but not military assistance, although no Spanish help of any kind ever reached Scotland in the '15. Much of the material in the Stuart papers relating to the Spanish expedition of 1719 has been published,[64] and Dr. Smith is preparing a full-scale study of Spanish involvement leading to this attempt. Military assistance was also sought from Charles XII of Sweden, the great Protestant hero and a bitter enemy of George I as Elector of Hanover, tentatively in 1715, and more positively in the Swedish plot of 1717 when the English Jacobites actually sent money to pay the Swedish army,[65] but Charles XII never finally made up his mind whether to act on the promises made by his minister, Count Görtz.[66] Sweden's connection with the Jacobites continued in 1745-6 and 1759, as Professor Nordmann explains.

Although post-1716 France, first under the Regency and later under Cardinal Fleury, persistently snubbed the Jacobites, Louis XV's own attitude to 'James III' was very much the same as that of his illustrious grandfather. Despite his diffidence and indolence, Louis XV had a life-long attachment to the Stuarts, to Charles Edward Stuart especially. Attempts to restore the Stuarts and to preserve the independence of Poland were two of the few things he ever cared about. He took a personal interest, therefore, in Charles Edward's attempts of 1744 and 1745,[67] as well as in the 1759 expedition.

One of the most important aspects of Jacobitism in Europe and that perhaps most neglected by British historians was the contribution made by the exiles, 'the

Jacobite diaspora', to the armies and navies and to the economic and cultural life of their host countries, a contribution similar to that of the Huguenots in Britain. It was the Jacobites, for instance, who built up the Russian Navy under Peter the Great. Thomas Gordon, a Captain in the Royal Navy dismissed as a suspected Jacobite in 1715, entered the Czar's service, recruited officers for him from the Royal Navy, and was made an admiral.[68] Christopher O'Brien, likewise an admiral in the Russian Navy, returned to the Royal Navy but gave undertakings to bring his own ship over to Charles Edward in 1744.[69] These are but two examples. Austria and Sweden, as well as Russia, welcomed Jacobites. Frederick the Great sought them out. James Keith, brother of George Keith 10th Earl Marischal, was a major-general in the Russian army and governor of the Ukraine before entering Prussian service in 1747, becoming field-marshal and governor of Berlin, while Lord Marischal himself served as Prussian ambassador in Paris from 1751 to 1759.[70] There were Jacobite merchants in Spain, established in Bilbao, Malaga and Cadiz, and in the Baltic, in Gothenburg, Bergen, Danzig and Riga. France, however, was the greatest refuge of the Jacobite diaspora. Jacobites settled as merchants or shipowners in Dunkirk, Boulogne, Dieppe, Le Havre, St. Malo, Brest, Nantes, Lorient, La Rochelle and Bordeaux. One of the best known, Anthony Walsh, the great shipowner and slave trader from Nantes, provided the ship which took Charles Edward to Scotland in 1745, was in charge of French preparations for a descent on England in 1745,[71] and was again concerned in Choiseul's attempt of 1759. The famous financier, John Law, comptroller general of French finances in 1720, was also a Jacobite, even if an intermittent and a politically motivated one. Among many Jacobite bankers were George Waters and Son, bankers to the Stuart court, and Robert Gordon, banker and financier. The brilliant military record of the Irish and Scottish regiments in the French service speaks for itself. Many exiles also served in French privateers in the Nine Years War and, later, in the ships of the French East India Company with which John Law was closely connected. Horsebreeding and horsemanship in France was also developed by Jacobites, with horses smuggled in from England (Pierre Burger gives examples of this), while by introducing English looms into France, Jacobites made a significant contribution to the development of the French textile industry.[72]

Unaware of changing conditions at home, the Jacobite exiles inevitably became more and more out of touch. At the same time, their attitudes often perpetuated national rivalries in the British Isles, so that Scottish and Irish Jacobites tended to look upon a Stuart restoration as a means of achieving complete independence for Scotland and Ireland — Professor Gregg and Professor Nordmann both give instances of this. Eventually, however, as they settled and prospered, they became absorbed into the society of the host countries. The Duke of Berwick, James II's illegitimate son by Arabella Churchill, Marlborough's sister, put his own military ambitions before his half-brother's interests by refusing to lead the '15, and lived on to be a marshal of France. His descendants, the Fitzjameses, like the Dillons, soon became indistinguishable from the rest of the French aristocracy. It is ironical to note that the sons and grandsons of Jacobites fought on opposite sides in the American War of Independence, for while many in France went to America to fight under Lafayette, the descendants of the Jacobites settled in America remained loyal to George III against the rebellious colonies and had, as a result, to flee into Canada. But by this time of course the Jacobite cause was indeed passing into legend.

NOTES

1. British Library, Additional Ms. 9129 ff. 123-4.

2. See the *Innes Review*, 1977, vol. xxviii.

3. Almost but not quite identical to the copy taken from the Scots College to Rome and hence to England, which was published by the Rev. Stanier Clarke as the Life of *James II*, 2 vols. 1816.

4. *Stuart Papers* ed. Falconer Madan, 2 vols. Roxburghe Club, 1889.

5. *History of the Revolution in 1688*, 1834.

6. See G. H. Jones, *Charles Middleton*, Chicago, 1967.

7. See introductions to *HMC Stuart* i, and to Alistair and Henrietta Tayler, *The Stuart Papers at Windsor*, 1939.

8. In his *History of England from the Peace of Utrecht*, 7 vols. 1858.

9. *HMC 10th Rep.* i.

10. These were used extensively by Andrew Lange in *Pickle the Spy*, 1897 and in *The Companions of Pickle*, 1898.

11. See *HMC 10th Rep.* vi.

12. John Miller, *James II, a study in kingship*, (Hove 1978), pp. 6-28.

13. For Walpole's intelligence system see Paul Fritz, 'The Anti-Jacobite Intelligence system of the English ministers, 1715-1743', *Historical Journal* xiv (1973), 271-80 and *The English Ministers and Jacobitism between the Rebellions of 1715 and 1745*, Toronto, 1975; also Eveline Cruickshanks, *Political Untouchables*, (1979), 15-16, 23-24, 42, 57-8. Two highly placed foreigners who were bribed were Alberoni (Saint-Simon, *Mémoires Complètes*, ed. A. de Boislisle, 41 vols., Paris, 1923-30, xxx. 29, 36, 106, 119) and Bussy (Cruickshanks, 57-8).

14. *Lockhart Papers*, 2 vols., 1817, ii. 400.

15. Cruickshanks, 47.

16. James Macpherson, *Original Papers*, 2 vols. 1775, ii. 212.

17. *Recueil des Instructions aux Ambassadeurs de France, Angleterre*, ed. Vaucher, 126-7: this quotation has been translated into English.

18. Macpherson, ii. 541-46.

19. *The House of Commons 1715-1754*, ed. Romney Sedgwick, (*HC*) 2 vols., (1970), i. 109-13; Fritz, *The English Ministers and Jacobitism*, 147-59.

20. It has been argued, for instance, that Stephen Parry, who appears on the 1721 list, could not have been a Jacobite because he had a secret service pension from Sunderland (by W. A. Speck, 'Whigs and Tories Dim their Glories!' in *The Whig Ascendancy*, ed. John Cannon, 1981, p. 58; for the pension see *HC* ii. 325). This is to misunderstand Sunderland's policy. Nor were moderate or Hanoverian Tories in 1714 still necessarily so in 1721 (see Speck, *art. cit.* 58 and below).

21. Speck, *art. cit.* 58.

22. Stuart ms. 154/104. I am grateful to Her Majesty the Queen for permission to cite the Stuart manuscripts in this collection of essays.

23. For the arrest of suspects in Devon and Cornwall see Morice mss at the Bank of England: [Sir Nicholas Morice] to Humphry Morice, 7 October 1715, and Sir William Pole to Humphry Morice, 13 November 1715.

24. A. Browning, *Thomas Osborne, Earl of Danby and Duke of Leeds*, 3 vols. Glasgow, 1944-51, iii. 194-213, and *A Register of Parliamentary Lists 1660-1761*, ed. David Hayton and Clyve Jones, Leicester, 1979, 91.

25. Cruickshanks, 84-5 and Appendices I and II.

26. J. H. Plumb, *Sir Robert Walpole*, 2 vols. 1956-60, ii. 322.

27. Douglas Hay, 'The Last Years of Jacobitism in Staffordshire', in *North Staffordshire Journal of Field Studies*. Further work on the significance of songs and ballads and commemorative rituals, as well as 'seditious words' cases, is being done by Paul Monod of Yale University.

28. Dr. Geoffrey Seddon of Redditch, Worcestershire, has studied and dated over 350 of these glasses.

29. By Paul Chapman of Gonville and Caius College, Cambridge.

30. Cruickshanks, Hayton and Jones, 'Divisions in the House of Lords on the transfer of the Crown and Other Issues, 1689-94: Ten New Lists', *Bulletin of the Institute of Historical Research (BIHR)* liii (1980), 56-8.

31. Cruickshanks, Ferris and Hayton, 'The House of Commons vote on the Transfer of the Crown, 5 February 1689', *BIHR*, lii. (1979), 41-7.

32. For the triumph of the *de facto* theory see J. P. Kenyon, *Revolution Principles, the Politics of Party 1689-1720*, (Cambridge 1977), 21, 32-4, 64, 201.

33. Holmes, *Anne*, 90.

34. R. Granville, *History of the Granville Family*, (Exeter, 1895), 398.

35. Miller, 236.

36. See Geoffrey Holmes, *British Politics in the Age of Anne*, (1967), 89-90.

37. By Daniel Szechi of St. Antony's College, Oxford.

38. Holmes, *Anne*, 94.

39. See Cruickshanks and *HC* i. 62-78.

40. John Owen, in *The Rise of the Pelhams*, 1957, 214 and B. W. Hill, *The Growth of Parliamentary Parties 1689-1742*, 1976, 192-3.

41. Cruickshanks, 10-11 and *HC* i. 67.

42. In the course of his work on English politics and foreign policy in the early part of George II's reign, Jeremy Black of Durham University has found new evidence of the King's attitude on this point.

43. This is a tentative summary of her views, since it has not been possible to see in advance her book *In Defiance of Oligarchy. The Tory Party 1714-1760* (Cambridge, 1981).

44. Holmes, *Anne*, 274, 281.

45. *HC* i. 507.

46. Plumb, *Walpole, op. cit.* ii. 184.

47. Speck, *art. cit.* p. 59; for the Pretender's letter see *HC* i. 68.

48. *HC* ii. 202.

49. *The Dynamics of Change* (Cambridge, forthcoming).

50. See Pargellis and Medley, *op. cit.*, 406-409.

51. *The Jacobite Risings in Britain 1689-1716* (1980).

52. By Tristram Clarke of Edinburgh University.

53. By Leah Leneman of Edinburgh University.

54. See J. G. Simms, *The Williamite Confiscation in Ireland 1690-1703* (1956), 196.

55. *Diary of Dudley Ryder*, London, 1939, 144.

56. D. W. Hayton, 'Ireland and the English Ministers, 1707-16' (Oxford University D.Phil. thesis, 1975), 21-30. For a different view, see F. J. McLynn 'Ireland and the Jacobite Rising of 1745', *Irish Sword* xiii. (1977-79), 339-52.

57. On the Royal Navy during the '45 see F. J. McLynn, 'Sea power and the Jacobite Rising of 1745', *The Mariner's Mirror* xlvii. (1981), 163-71 and Cruickshanks, 98-103.

58. By Jeremy Black (see above, n. 42).

59. James Stuart did not send a desperate appeal to Walpole on 13 July 1732 as Dr. G. V. Bennett suggests (*The Tory Crisis in Church and State*, (Oxford 1975), 307-8). His draft letter to Walpole (Stuart ms 163/57) was one of several letters which were never sent, written to members of the British government, the Archbishop of Canterbury, the heads of the Universities, etc., designed to prevent civil war should France agree to provide troops for a restoration at Lord Cornbury's request (on the model of Charles II's letters from The Hague in 1660).

60. Lucile Pinkham, *William III and the Respectable Revolution* (Cambridge, Mass., 1954), 31-3, 67.

61. Shaftesbury to Van Twedde, 17 January 1706, quoted in J. H. Plumb, *The Growth of Political Stability in England 1675-1725* (1967), 153 n.1.

62. See John Carswell, *The Descent on England* (1969), 155-63; J. R. Jones, *The Revolution of 1688 in England* (1972), chapter seven; and Bruno Neveu, *Jacques II, médiateur entre Louis XIV et Innocent XI* (Paris, 1967).

63. In summarising Louis XIV's attitude, I am obliged to Dr. Roger Mettam for providing me with relevant sections of the introduction to his edition of Voltaire's *Siècle de Louis XIV* (forthcoming). For Louis' attitude, see also R. Hatton, 'Louis XIV and his Fellow Monarchs' and C. Nordmann, 'Louis XIV and the Jacobites', in *Louis XIV and Europe* ed. Ragnhild Hatton, (1976).

64. W. K. Dickson, *The Jacobite Attempt of 1719* (Scottish History Society, xix), Edinburgh, 1895.

65. *HC* i. 63.

66. *Ex. inf.* Claude Nordmann.

67. See Cruickshanks, and F. J. McLynn, *France and the Jacobite Rising of 1745* (Edinburgh, 1981).

68. John Charnock, *Biographia Navalis*, 6 vols. (1794-8), iii. 309-11; *HMC Stuart* vi. 331-2, 344, 346, 466.

69. Cruickshanks, 55.

70. *The Scots Peerage* (9 vols. Edinburgh, 1904-14), vi. 61-4.

71. Cruickshanks, 79, 96, 98.

72. The best accounts of the Jacobite diaspora are Claude Nordmann's 'Les Jacobites écossais en France au XVIIIe Siècle', in *Regards sur l'Ecosse au XVIII Siècle*, ed. M. S. Plaisant, Pub. Université de Lille III (1977), 81-100, and Bruce Lenman, 'The Jacobite diaspora 1688–1746', *History Today*, May 1980, 7-10.

1

The Nonjurors, Episcopacy, and the Origins of the Convocation Controversy

Mark Goldie

THE Nonjuring schism was the clerical counterpart of Jacobitism. The Nonjurors believed that the established Church, born of the Revolution of 1689, was as illegitimate as the new political regime. They stood beyond the pale of the Revolution and cherished a self-image of martyrdom to a purer Anglicanism, now perverted by an Erastian state. And yet their energetic churchmanship was not to run into the sands of the wilderness, for they exerted a profound intellectual influence over Augustan England. Time after time they traversed the boundary between the conformists and themselves and lent massive scholarly and polemical support to Anglican, Tory and Country opposition causes. One such campaign was the defence of the independent powers of the Anglican Church, a matter which predominated in the politics of the reigns of the last two Stuart monarchs, and a cause which, like Stuart legitimism, was ultimately to succumb to the Whig hegemony of Hanoverian England. In Nonjuror writings lies a crucial seedbed of the Tory leitmotif of the 'Church in danger', for in the 1690s the Nonjurors transmitted to the mainstream of Tory ideology the elevated view of Church authority characteristic of the High Church tradition.

In that decade there was much to alarm orthodox Anglicans: the Toleration Act, Occasional Conformity, declining church attendance, clerical poverty, the ignorance of the poor, and the apparent advance of licentiousness and immorality (a fear notoriously voiced in the Nonjuror Jeremy Collier's assault on the profanity of the English stage). In the early eighteenth century Queen Anne's Bounty, the London Churches Act, and the Society for the Promotion of Christian Knowledge attempted to cope with these problems.[1]

Most frightening of all was the systematic assault upon orthodox theology by the Deists. They sought to pare away doctrine to the barest minimum of rational natural religion, and coupled this with attacks upon the panoply of the temporal church, upon priestcraft, superstition and doctrinal censorship. In 1695-96 John Locke and John Toland published their treatises, *The Reasonableness of Christianity* and *Christianity not Mysterious*. It seemed too that heterodoxy was not confined to lay critics but had infiltrated the hierarchy itself: Latitudinarian churchmen entered the inner circle of the establishment with the elevation to episcopal Sees of such men as Edward Stillingfleet, whose Erastianism the Nonjuror Simon Lowth demonstrated to be derived from Hobbes's *Leviathan*. Not only were two Primates, Tillotson and Tenison, friendly with the notorious Unitarian, Thomas Firmin, but

Tillotson himself was publicly accused of Socinianism. In 1691 the Latitudinarian caucus founded the Boyle Lectures, an annual series devoted to the rational, scientific explication of Christianity against freethinking, but to High Churchmen the distinction between Latitudinarians and heretics was a fine one. The Nonjuror Charles Leslie believed William III to be elevating Presbyterians, fanatics and atheists, and although he genuinely feared the return to Romanist repression if the Restoration of James II occurred, he thought that preferable to England's impending collapse into complete irreligion.[2]

That these developments undermined the status of the Anglican Church as a communion co-extensive with the English state was epitomised in 1689 when Locke wrote that membership of a church was a voluntary and personal act with no more relevance for citizenship than joining a debating club.[3]

Throughout the seventeenth century Anglican divines had been prepared to assert the Church's authority against the encroachments not only of Puritanism and freethinking, but also of the civil Supremacy. The confederation between the Church and Stuart monarchs was a fortunate coincidence which tended to evoke from churchmen an exaggerated royalism. Yet this never obscured High Church principles less favourable to the crown. The High Churchman's persistent twofold message was the divine Apostolic origin of episcopacy and the Church's Godly responsibility for the preservation of true doctrine. Bishops were the *jure divino* heads of the visible Church, and the censorship of faith and morals and the ordination of presbyters derived from them. It was a view which potentially injured the authority of the Lutheran sacerdotal Prince. Jewell, Hooker and Whitgift, the early defenders of the *via media*, had been moderate in their claims for episcopacy, regarding it as necessary for good church government: bishops were jurisdictionally not intrinsically above presbyters. Higher claims were developed in the 1590s and under James I by Richard Bancroft, Hadrian Saravia, Thomas Bilson, George Carleton, and George Downame. In the middle and later seventeenth century the same tension existed in Anglican teaching. James Ussher's constitutionalist episcopalianism, unsuccessfully proposed in the 1640s to resolve the conflict of Anglican and Presbyterian, was moderate enough to receive the approval of the Presbyterian Richard Baxter. But after 1650 the stance of Ussher, Stillingfleet and William Lloyd was countered by Patristic scholars in their reassertion of Apostolic quasi-monarchic episcopacy: Peter Heylyn, John Fell, George Bull, Henry Hammond, Henry Dodwell and Simon Lowth, the last two of whom became Nonjurors. At the level of practical churchmanship, Archbishops Sheldon and Sancroft carried into the Restoration the Laudian commitment to the sanctity of the clerical estate and its moral and teaching authority. The strength of the political independence of this tradition was revealed by the Church's vociferous hostility to James II's Catholicising policies.[4]

The most raucous and protracted claim for the Church's autonomy was that made between the 1690s and 1717 by the High Church party's defence of the rights, powers and privileges of Convocation.[5] By the Act of Submission of the Clergy (1534) no Church synod could meet, nor Canons be legislated, without the crown's authorisation. Yet, under James I and Charles I, Convocation had become sufficiently assertive to arouse Puritan fears that it aimed to restore the Church's independence of the civil power. In practice the effectiveness of Convocation was limited: neither of the important sets of Canons of 1606 and 1640 was ratified, and the latter aroused a storm of protest in the Long Parliament. Although in 1662 Convocation undertook alterations to the Prayer Book, which were accepted by Parliament without examination, the institution began a long dormancy. In 1664 Sheldon, in a private agreement with Lord Chancellor Clarendon, relinquished the clergy's right to tax itself and thus obviated Convocation's regular meeting. When in 1689 the government sought the Comprehension of Nonconformists within a broadened establishment, there were fears that Parliament alone would rewrite the Prayer Book.[6] But Convocation was suffered to meet, only to be abruptly dismissed after the collapse of Comprehension through the implacable hostility of High Churchmen for whom true doctrine was not to be attenuated for the sake of a spurious Church unity. In the face of the government's indefinite suspension of meetings, the first phase of the great Convocation Controversy was the demand for a sitting and acting Convocation. It finally met in 1701 and, in the second phase, prolonged skirmishing between the Upper and Lower Houses was brought about by the High Church dominated Lower House's attempt to assert its independence of the Whig bishops in order to execute its programme of Church reform and heresy-hunting. In the final phase, the Bangorian Controversy of 1716-17, an astonishing flood of pamphlets (seventy-four in the month of July 1717 alone) brought about the Whig government's closure of Convocation in order to avert the formal condemnation of their champion, the notorious Benjamin Hoadly, Bishop of Bangor. Convocation was not to meet for business again until 1851.

Modern accounts of the Convocation Controversy almost invariably date its origin to Francis Atterbury's famous pamphlet of November 1696, *A Letter to a Convocation Man*, and the reply to it by the future Archbishop of Canterbury, William Wake, in his *Authority of Christian Princes over their Ecclesiastical Synods* (1697).[7] But contemporaries did not see it like this. Atterbury's *Letter* was not the dazzling novelty it has been made to appear. In *The Case of the Regale*, published in 1700, Charles Leslie explicitly saw Wake's book as an outgrowth of a much longer quarrel which had begun earlier in the 1690s. Indeed, he did not even trouble to mention Atterbury's pamphlet. One year earlier Humphrey Hody, the Whig author of a pamphlet called *Some Thoughts on a Convocation*, saw himself as drawing upon Wake's book and as attacking, not Atterbury, but the Nonjuror Henry Dodwell.[8] It is Hody and Dodwell who are the key figures in the origins of the Convocation Controversy.[9]

Although to begin the story of the Controversy in 1697 is to begin in the middle, it remains true that Atterbury's *Letter* was a brilliant piece of journalism which transferred the debate from the Nonjurors' camp to the established Church, and it is as well briefly to summarise its argument. Atterbury began by insisting upon the imperative need for a Convocation to deal with the horrifying advance of scepticism, Deism, Socinianism and contempt for the priesthood. He then proceeded to demonstrate that meetings of Convocation ought not to be occasional events subject to the pleasure of the crown, for Convocation was an essential part of the constitution: Convocation for the Church was exactly parallel to Parliament for the state and the two must sit together, the one legislating for the spiritual corporation, the other for the secular commonwealth. As Parliament might deliberate in freedom, so too might Convocation, in spite of the general legal view that it might not debate without royal licence. As Parliament required only the crown's consent to enact statutes, so Convocation required the king's consent alone, and not that of Parliament, to enact Canons. And as Parliament might act as a High Court, declaring the law, so Convocation might act as a spiritual court, declaring true doctrine and censuring heresy. Atterbury's rhetorical achievement was the linkage of the Church's claims to conventional claims for English liberties in Parliament.

Dr G. V. Bennett has said that Atterbury was deliberately innovative in using a constitutionalist argument, in preference to the deployment of any more abstract theological concept of the relationship of Church and state. This is misleading. As we shall see, the constitutional position of Convocation had already been debated in earlier years and, more importantly, Atterbury did explicitly base his argument on a theological foundation. At the transition of his argument from the topic of the suppression of heresy to that of the Parliamentary nature of Convocation, Atterbury devoted four pages to a summary of the ancient theory of the relationship of Church and state known as the doctrine of the Two Societies. He concluded that the 'Church then is a society instituted in order to a supernatural end; and, as such, must have an inherent power in it, of governing itself in order to that end'. Atterbury was succinct because the argument was familiar to contemporaries, but it is clear that his case stood squarely upon it.[10]

The doctrine of the Two Societies was the bedrock of High Church ideology and its roots must rapidly be sketched. Christian political theory necessarily provided an account of the status of the visible Church in relation to secular power. The agreed premiss was that because man has a dual character, body and soul, he has membership of two societies or kingdoms: a civil state for his earthly welfare and a church for his eternal soul. Church and state inhabited coterminous yet distinct spheres, and after the Christianisation of the Roman Empire the Church had developed an harmonic image of a universal Church and a universal kingdom, *imperium* and *ecclesia*. But the inevitable contention of the two later yielded two different and rival theories. In one the Pope assumed supremacy with the claim that the supernatural order, of which he was guardian on earth, was paramount over the mundane; it followed that to protect true religion the Pope might anathematise and depose kings. In the other, the claim was made that because the Church was a purely spiritual congregation of the faithful it had only the most tenuous claim to be a temporal corporation and that in all external matters the divinely entrusted civil sovereign was supreme; hence the temporal jurisdiction, wealth and coercive authority of the priestly order was held only by the Prince's good grace. The hierocratic doctrine dated from the early Middle Ages; the Erastian doctrine from Marsiglio and the Lutheran Reformation. In both theories the doctrine of the Two Societies tended to disintegrate, yet although in England the Henrician Reformation was predominantly Erastian in character, the idea of the Church as an independent society survived. High Churchmen domesticated Catholic theology: the doctrine was now made to refer to the national state and the national Church under the collective jurisdiction of bishops.

The doctrine is found repeatedly in the pamphlets of Augustan England. John Kettlewell, a Nonjuror, in his popular *Measures of Christian Obedience*, published in 1681 and four more times by 1700, explained: 'We are members of two great societies; one a society in things outward and temporal . . . which is called the state; and the other in things sacred . . . which is the Church'. In 1702 Henry Sacheverell declared, 'the civil and ecclesiastical state are the two parts and divisions, that both united make up one entire compounded constitution, and body politic'; the church, he said, is the soul and the state the body. In 1711 Atterbury, in *The Mitre and the Crown*, showed that the Keys of the Kingdom were given to the Apostles and their successors: the key of doctrine and the key of discipline belonged to the spiritual realm and not to the civil. The most extreme and eloquent statement is that of Leslie in *The Case of the Regale*, where he pronounced epigrammatically that 'the Western Church was (like her master) crucified betwixt the usurpations of the Pontificate on the one side, and the Regale on the other'.[11]

The doctrine of the Two Societies found its first post-Revolution restatement in Nonjuror writings in the early 1690s. The Nonjurors had good reason for having an early perception of Erastian threats to Anglicanism, for they were its first victims. Under the Act of April 1689 clergymen and office-holders were required to take the Oath to William and Mary by 1 August under pain of suspension and, after six months' grace, of deprivation. Nine bishops, including Sancroft,[12] some four hundred clergy and a number of Oxford and Cambridge Fellows refused the oath. The government was reluctant to bring about schism and delayed removing the bishops. This was prudent, for there was wide support for the deprived bishops. It was rumoured that they would be restored to their Sees and it was presumed that if they were removed the Sees would be left vacant indefinitely since, as Henry Maurice put it, 'it can scarce be conceived that any worthy men will be forward to accept these preferments and thereby shut the door against their predecessors'. The king's allowing the bishops to continue to draw part of their income was welcomed, and in the 1689 Convocation their absence was used as an excuse for not proceeding with liturgical reform, and there was a move to have them attend.[13] At the close of that year Bishop Gilbert Burnet was authorised to negotiate a deal — futile as it turned out — whereby the Nonjurors would be restored, without having to take the Oath, provided that the Comprehension scheme be allowed to proceed.[14] In 1690 the conforming clergy of the dioceses of Norwich and of Bath and Wells and the Grand Jury of Gloucestershire petitioned for the removal of penalties from the bishops.[15]

However, by the spring of 1691 William's ecclesiastical managers, Nottingham and Tillotson, believed that reconciliation was no longer likely, and — in the wake of the uncovering of the Preston Plot in which one of the bishops, Turner of Ely, was implicated — proceeded to fill the vacant Sees, with Tillotson as the new Primate. The plan received a sharp shock when four of the men offered bishoprics refused them and the situation had to be rescued by rapid rearrangement and bullying. John Sharp refused Norwich and was instead promised York for when Lamplugh should die. Wake refused both Norwich and Bath and Wells. Beveridge first accepted but then, after receiving Sancroft's counsel and angry letters from other Nonjurors, refused Bath, for which he was then dismissed as royal chaplain and publicly denounced in a pamphlet by Stillingfleet. Kidder refused Peterborough but was peremptorily instructed to take Bath, a decision which afterwards distressed him.[16] The Nonjuror bishops were inclined to resist eviction and took legal advice on their proprietorial rights; Sancroft did not leave Lambeth Palace till June when proceeded against at law for trespass. Bishop Ken made a solemn declaration of his canonical right from his episcopal throne at Wells, and Dean George Hickes, having refused to summon the Chapter at Gloucester to elect the new bishop, nailed an angry protestation to the cathedral door.[17]

The only schism in the history of the Anglican hierarchy dated from this moment. The substance of the Nonjurors' case was that the deprivations were both unjust and invalid. Unjust because the political crime of failing to swear fealty was insufficient cause for derogating a bishop from his holy function, and canonically invalid because only a Church synod was competent to depose a bishop. A temporal government — a usurped one at that — had invaded the spiritual realm. The Nonjurors had as early as autumn 1689 arrived at the conclusion that such deprivations would entail upon the conforming Church the guilt of schism and both sides, Dodwell in his *Cautionary Discourse of Schism* and Stillingfleet in his *Discourse Concerning the Unreasonableness of a New Separation*, had warned each other of the dire consequences. In 1690 an anonymous Nonjuror asserted that the bishops' case was 'not properly cognizable where their sentence was pronounced' and that Church history had never witnessed bishops deposed by 'mere laymen'.[18] The Nonjuror position raised immediately the issues of the propriety of summoning a synod and the deeper question of the relationship between Church and state in post-Revolution England.

It should be said that the Nonjurors never agreed on what the consequences should be of these invalid deprivations. Three views were taken. A few moderates, Bishops Ken and Frampton, felt no schism should ensue and that, whatever the improprieties of their own deprivations, this should not allow laymen to cease attendance at parish churches. Ken indeed was offered back his diocese in 1703.[19] Unfortunately neither bishop could be induced to express his views in print and it was more extreme arguments which received public airing. The stance taken by the most aggressive Nonjurors, Hickes, Collier, and Thomas Wagstaffe, was that the established Church was irretrievably schismatic and that the Nonjurors constituted the only true Church of England: the mass of Englishmen stood excommunicate. In 1691 Sancroft negotiated with James II for the consecration of new bishops, and in 1694 Hickes and Wagstaffe became the first of the new Nonjuror episcopate; consecrations continued, the last Nonjuror bishop dying in 1805.[20] A middle position was taken by Dodwell, who believed that the established Church was schismatic and that separate communion was a duty for as long as the rightful possessors of the Sees remained alive. As a result, in 1710, Dodwell and his followers returned to the fold of the establishment. He would not have sanctioned the perpetuation of the Nonjuror episcopate and it was kept a careful secret from him.[21] In the 1690s, however, the difference between Hickes and Dodwell was still academic and, in the absence of comment from Ken, the Nonjurors presented a united and hostile front to the Revolution hierarchy.

The government needed a scholarly defence of the deprivations. It was provided by Humphrey Hody, Fellow of Wadham College, Oxford. Oxford was a microcosm of the national Church, the training ground of future controversialists, Atterbury, Wake, Gibson, Kennett; and locked at this time in an inter-collegiate dispute over the heretical writing of Dr Arthur Bury, Rector of Exeter College.[22] Hody was Stillingfleet's chaplain and his pamphlets were dedicated to Tillotson. Inevitably the Nonjurors accused him of writing for preferment; inevitably they were right. In 1694 he became chaplain to Tillotson, in 1695 acquired a double rectory in the gift of Tenison, and in 1698 became the Oxford Regius Professor of Greek.[23] Another of Stillingfleet's chaplains was the young Richard Bentley and he and Hody, both of whom acquired early reputations as brilliant classical scholars, were working together on the Baroccian manuscripts in the Bodleian Library. In the summer of 1691 they published a document from that collection in Greek and Latin in a pamphlet called *Anglicani Novi Schismatis*, and in English translation in another, entitled *The Unreasonableness of a Separation from the New Bishops*.[24] Bentley's initials were appended to the preface of the English version but their identification was not made contemporaneously and this early foray into controversy has not been noticed by his biographers. Bentley in any case publicly quarrelled with Hody at this time over another issue and soon left Oxford for Cambridge, and it was Hody who carried the burden of the ensuing controversy.[25]

Hody surmised that his document was a thirteenth-century oration by the Constantinopolitan historian Nicepherus Callistus who, at a time of schism in the Eastern Church, wished to demonstrate that throughout Church history the intrusion of a new bishop in the place of a deprived one had not been regarded as proper ground for schism, provided that the new bishop was not a heretic. Hody argued that Nicepherus' precedents showed that even if a deposed bishop had been unjustly deprived and the new one uncanonically promoted, then the intruder was always accepted for the sake of peace and a united Church. A key example was that of St John Chrysostom who, upon his unjust deposition in 403, had apparently counselled against a breach of communion. Hody expanded his theme in two subsequent treatises in 1692 and 1693.[26]

Hody's argument was unfortunate, for it made no attempt to show the validity of the Nonjuror deprivations. He claimed to have argued *a fortiori* by establishing what conclusion must follow from the Nonjurors' own premiss that the ejections were invalid. Yet he slipped easily into regarding the new bishops' *de facto* possession of their Sees as their sufficient claim of right. He urged the 'reasonableness of submitting to the present possessor' and believed 'there was no custom or law of the Church so sacred and inviolable, but what they [the Church] readily sacrificed, whensoever necessity required, to the peace and tranquility of it'. Any other principle he regarded as mere 'theological pedantry'.[27] This shoddy disregard for Canon Law revealed that the argument owed more to secular politics:

it was a piece of ecclesiological Hobbesianism. Hobbes had argued in *Leviathan* that since peace and security were the highest good for a man, it was proper and reasonable in a case of civil contention to submit to superior force when 'the means of his life are within the guards and garrisons of the enemy'. In similar vein Hody asked — he hoped rhetorically — 'if the bishop of a frontier town will not own the authority of a conqueror, and is therefore deposed by that conqueror, I desire to know of our adversaries, whether the clergy of that town are perjured if they own that bishop whom the conqueror thinks fit to set over them?'[28] Hody's ecclesiastical *de facto* thesis exactly paralleled that which had recently been put for political allegiance to William and Mary by such polemicists as Stillingfleet, Burnet, Lloyd, William Sherlock and Edmund Bohun.[29]

Hody compounded his difficulties by outlining an uncompromisingly Erastian case for the supremacy of the crown over the Church which prefigured that presented later by Wake and Hoadly. He maintained that the civil power had always claimed, since the age of Constantine, the right to depose bishops by its sole authority as a necessary security for the state. Justinian in the sixth century had expelled the Patriarch Eutychius; the synod which had deposed Arsenius in the thirteenth century had been presided over by the Emperor Michael Palaeologus. The secular power, the Whig Hody reminded his High Church opponents, was *jure divino*, was historically prior to the institution of bishops, and submission to it was required by Scripture.[30]

The publication of the Baroccian manuscript elicited within a year several replies from the Nonjurors: by Thomas Browne, ejected Fellow of St John's College, Cambridge; Nathaniel Bisbie; Jeremy Collier; and by two men whose tracts the government attempted to suppress: Samuel Grascome, who spoke contemptuously of the 'factioni Tillotsonianae', and, more formidable than all the rest, Henry Dodwell.[31] Dodwell was a man convinced of his own infallibility and was dubbed by Bishop Frampton the Nonjurors' 'great lay dictator'. In 1689 he delivered angry letters to Bishop Ken upon hearing that he was wavering over the Oath; in 1691 he wrote to Tillotson and Lloyd solemnly warning them of the danger to their eternal souls should they accept episcopal Sees and incur the guilt of schism.[32] Until finally ejected from his Oxford history professorship in November 1691, he held court, pontificating on the issues of the day at a table in a coffee house 'filled with academics belonging to several different colleges'.[33] Although thereafter a frequent visitor to Oxford, he found a new home with Francis Cherry at Shottesbrooke in Berkshire, where he presided over an intellectual coterie frequented by Ken, Leslie, the devotional writer Robert Nelson, and the scholars John Grabe and Thomas Hearne.[34] Dodwell was universally respected for his scholarship — 'the learned Dodwell' as the antipathetic Locke conceded — and had, before the Revolution, established a reputation as a defender of High Church principles against Dissenters, Latitudinarians and Erastians.[35]

Hody was open to attack on several counts. In the first place, his scholarship was discovered to be unsound.[36] The Baroccian manuscript was shown to have been inaccurately translated and was proven not to have been by Nicepherus. The manuscript's authority was further limited by the fact that the precedents cited were confined to the Eastern Church and extended back no further than the fourth century. As a basis for a theological argument this was anathema to the conservative Patristic theology which had developed in the seventeenth century and of which Dodwell was a prime exponent.[37] This method rested on intensive investigation of the Church Fathers of the first three uncorrupted centuries as providing the only prescriptively valid precedents. On the subject of episcopacy Cyprian of Carthage was the unimpeachable authority. An examination of the Baroccian manuscript's precedents in the light of other sources revealed a more complex history than Hody pretended, and the Nonjurors discovered that a just cause, such as heresy, and a valid proceeding in a synod had always been deemed necessary before deprivation. The Cyprianic principle that *secundus* was *nullus*, and a host of precedents, showed that the early Church had not regarded as valid the second appointee to a diocese already canonically filled. In the case of Chrysostom, for instance, he had had the support of an outraged Christendom which had insisted upon his reinstatement. When Justinian and Michael Palaeologus sought the depositions of Eutychius and Arsenius they summoned synods because they knew their authority alone was insufficient. And, nearer home, in 1070 that other King William, the Conqueror, had sought the expulsion of Stigand, Archbishop of Canterbury — through a synod.[38] Hody's worst scholarly crime was the suppression of an appendix to the manuscript, clearly belonging to it, which contained ancient Canons expressly requiring synodical judgements as a necessary condition for a valid deprivation. These Canons, embodying the conventions of the ancient Church, were several times printed by the Nonjurors and the charge of wilful deception brought against Hody. The latter was stung into a reply denying any ill intent and weakly endeavouring to prove the Canons did not belong to the manuscript.[39] As a final blow, Dodwell triumphantly demonstrated exactly which schism had occasioned the manuscript, a fact Hody had failed to identify; and this too was a clear case of synodical not lay deprivation.[40] To argue the case for accepting the Revolution bishops, wrote Bisbie, 'for this cause only, that they are in possession, upon what reason and justice soever, of the said episcopal Sees, is very strange doctrine'. And Dodwell concluded his 1692 tract with an explicit demand for a 'just conciliary deprivation'.[41]

Hody's Erastianism provoked the Nonjurors' fiercest denunciation, for such a doctrine made it a practical possibility that the Church could be destroyed by an heretical, Socinian or Popish prince deposing orthodox bishops and intruding those of his own inclination, or indeed abolishing episcopacy altogether. It was pointed out that under James II Bishop Compton had been suspended from office by the Ecclesiastical Commission. Compton had rejected the Commission's jurisdiction because it was lay-dominated and the lawyers had upheld him. The case of Compton and James II was to be raised by Atterbury in his assault on Wake.[42]

In his *Vindication of the Deprived Bishops* (1692) Dodwell demonstrated not only practical but theological objections to Erastianism. The notion of secular deprivation gave the civil government the power 'to destroy the very being of the Church as a society'. The acceptance of this doctrine by the conforming Church as a whole, implicit in its acquiescence in civil deprivations, compounded schism with heresy: schism, St Augustine observed, generally ended in heresy.[43] Dodwell took as central to Christian teaching the Johannine concept of *koinonia*, by which partaking in the orthodox communion of the visible Church entitled men to share in mystical union with the Trinity.[44] The visible union of the Church, with the means of its own government and preservation, was the necessary channel through which sacramental grace was communicated and in the discipline of which all other doctrinal truths were preserved. Dodwell believed, with the Socinian writers in mind, that the truths of the Trinity and Incarnation were not 'revealed for speculation only, but purposely to oblige men to unite in it [the Church] as a society'. In a direct assault on Latitudinarian elements within the new hierarchy, Dodwell went on: 'it may perhaps be fit to be considered whether it be prudent to trust such persons with the management of the government of the Church, who have no obligation of principles or conscience to maintain it . . . or to suffer for it [under] a persecution'. The abandonment of the integrity of the Church would also remove any power authoritatively to excommunicate for heresy and to issue 'judiciary censures' upon error. The only alternative — and here Dodwell seems directly to refer to Locke's *Letter on Toleration* which argued for persuasion as the only weapon against heresy — was 'to reason with heretics concerning their errors, and [the only] means to reduce them are those reasons which can no farther prevail with them than as they may seem convictive in the judgement of the heretics themselves. But on that account they stand on even terms with the heretics, whose reasons ought likewise to take place with the ecclesiastics, so far as they also are in conscience convinced by them'.[45] The Apostolic authority of the Catholic Church would thus collapse into the indifferent pluralism of the debating chamber. If the Church was to survive it must excommunicate for heresy and ought in the first place to condemn those fundamental errors destructive of the Church as a society endowed with authority to preserve truth.

Hody replied to his adversaries with utter lameness by returning to the original theme of the Baroccian manuscript and devoting a substantial treatise to the historical case for the general practice of submission to the 'present possessor' intruded by a 'power irresistable'; he ignored all the larger issues raised by Dodwell. Dodwell thought it futile to pursue Hody's Hobbesian stance; the important issue was the extent of secular authority over the spiritual realm.[46] The narrow seam of Hody's mind was exhausted and his subsequent tracts had nothing new to say.[47] It was Wake who constructed in 1697 the positive case for the authority of Christian princes.

Meanwhile, from 1693-96 there was a hiatus in the controversy, both sides taunting the other for their silence.[48] In a show of magnanimity Hody, realising the Nonjurors' difficulties in getting books printed, promised to secure for Dodwell liberty of publication. Dodwell did prepare a new book, but at the beginning of 1696 relations were again soured. In the aftermath of the discovery of the assassination plot against King William, government agents seized the newly printed sheets of Dodwell's book. The Nonjurors charged Hody with treachery. Hody insisted he had had no prior knowledge of the seizure and that since hearing of it had tried without success to have his adversary's book released.[49]

This incident came at a peculiarly sensitive moment in Church affairs. In July 1695 Archbishop Tenison's circular letter insisted upon Church prayers for the lawful king and lawful bishops. In December the Socinian controversy reached a curious climax with the condemnation by the Oxford Convocation of William Sherlock's anti-Socinian doctrines as tritheistic, a decision then condemned by the crown's judges. Tillotson and Tenison both determined to use the royal Supremacy rather than Convocation to conduct Church government, and accordingly Royal Injunctions for the reform of clerical abuses and the restraint of theological dispute were issued in February 1695 and February 1696. They represented, according to one Church historian, a more extensive deployment of the Supremacy than any since the reign of Edward VI.[50]

Dodwell's new book, *The Defence of the Vindication of the Deprived Bishops*, was reprinted and published, this time without government interference, in 1697; but its preface had escaped seizure and was separately published in 1696 as *The Doctrine of the Church of England, Concerning the Independency of the Clergy on the Lay-power*.[51] These pamphlets unquestionably constitute the most important contribution to the controversy. Dodwell shifted the ground of debate significantly. Wishing to counter the argument that the precedents of the Cyprianic age were not relevant to the modern reformed Church, he turned his attention to the Reformation and the meaning of the Royal Supremacy.

He was stimulated to this by Edward Welchman's *Defence of the Church of England*.[52] Welchman had strengthened the establishment's cause by recognising that Hody's argument was an embarrassment and attempting a more constructive case. Welchman made two points. First, it was recognised by all that the Act of 1689 did not and could not remove from a bishop the essential character of his episcopal order, given him by the laying on of hands at his consecration. The state had merely removed the Nonjurors from the exercise of their jurisdictions and from the possession of their temporalities. Welchman explained that this was in keeping with Anglican doctrine, preserved at the Reformation, by which the *ordo* of episcopacy, its spiritual character, was inviolable, but that the *jurisdictio* belonged to the civil power. This was a compelling point: the Nonjurors were forced to the dubious counter-assertion that the diocese to which a bishop was attached had always been an essential part of the spiritual character of episcopacy and that this 'marriage' to a diocese belonged to the *ordo* and not the *jurisdictio*. The state was only entitled to remove diocesan temporalities. This was the Nonjurors' weakest shift, for if this argument were true it is difficult to see how even a synod could deprive a bishop.[53]

On a broader front, Welchman's second thrust was to deny the doctrine of the Two Societies, by maintaining that the Christianisation of the Roman Empire brought about the coalescence of those societies. Where the state is infidel the Church is necessarily a separate society, but in all Christian states Church and civil society are united in the same persons and under the same jurisdiction. Church and state were, as he put it, accidents subsisting in the same subject. In a later tract he showed that this was the doctrine of Whitgift, Hooker and Pufendorf.[54] Dodwell observed that here, and in some remarks of Hody's, was an incipient application of contract theory to the relations of Church and state. Since the dominant language of contract theory continued to refer to contracting corporations (rather than the individualistic contracts of Hobbes and Locke) it was not difficult to construe sovereign supremacy in Protestant society as the result of the contractual submission of the Church. This argument was to achieve its apogee in the well-known books of Matthew Tindal (*The Rights of the Christian Church*, 1706) and William Warburton (*The Alliance between Church and State*, 1736). Dodwell replied with some searching questions. If there was such a contract, why should the Church submit to the state and not vice versa, since the spiritual corporation was superior to the mundane? If the grant of authority to the Prince was irrevocable, what if the Prince should apostatise? A contract supposed that the participants were in possession of the powers they were revoking, but the Church's power was a trust from God and was inalienable, so that any putative contract was void. To argue for the Church's submission to the state was no better than Cardinal Bellarmine's converse argument that the state submits to the Church. The coalescence of the Two Societies would, Dodwell thought, inevitably lead to a dissolution of one or other: the Papal deposition of kings was the consequence of the Church's improper triumph; the secular deposition of bishops a consequence of the state's triumph. Dodwell was not, however, far off from the Papalist case, since he insisted that the temporal corporation is the greater gainer by Christianity than is the Church by the protection of the civil power. In a remark utterly alien to the Lutheran conception of Godly magistracy, Dodwell asserted that when a Prince is baptised 'he still remains, in reference to spiritual power, no more than a private person'.[55]

Not content with a general challenge to the Supremacy, Dodwell launched an assault upon Cranmer and 'that imperious and assuming Prince' Henry VIII. He despised Cranmer's Lutheran doctrines of the Prince's sacramental powers and his reduction of the clerical order to the status of officers of state. He condemned the king's brutal invasion of the church, the charge of *praemunire* brought against it, and the executions of Catholics for refusal of the Supremacy. He followed with an analysis of the Henrician Supremacy Acts: he saw the king's claims advancing in stages towards the final triumph of Cranmer's theories. The Act of Appeals (1533) had been modest, for in declaring the king's Headship of the Church it recognised the distinction of two concurrent jurisdictions. The Act of Submission (1534) went further: it established Chancery as the final court of appeal, and the powers formerly transferred from the Pope to English ecclesiastical courts now passed to the king. The Act of Supremacy (1534) translated all spiritual jurisdiction to the king, including excommunication. Yet even this Act might be construed favourably, for it held back from stating that the bishops' spiritual authority derived exclusively from the crown. It was an Act of 1545 (37 H.8 c.17) which finally committed heresy by explicitly declaring episcopal authority to be 'by, under and from' the king, a notion perpetuated in the Edwardine Act (1 Edw.6 c.2) declaring all spiritual authority to be 'derived and deduced' from the crown.[56]

It is strange that Dodwell selected the Act of 1545, for it was merely a provision to allow married Doctors of Civil Law to practise; but one modern historian has noted that its terminology did extend royal claims.[57] Dodwell's analysis is not dissimilar to that of recent historians who have shown that both Cranmer and Henry came very near to a denial of any necessity for episcopal consecration and to the view that the Christian Prince possessed the sacramental power of priesthood. Henry had replaced episcopal by royal Visitation, had forced bishops to take out patents for their Sees, and had given Thomas Cromwell the powers of Vicar-General: all of which Dodwell regarded as heretical and null. Yet ambiguity had been preserved, since the statutes held back from extreme Lutheran assertions as, for instance, in the moderating redraftings of the Act of Appeals.[58]

Dodwell now stood barely within the pale of the Reformation and he set about rescuing himself by a conventional eulogy of the Elizabethan Settlement. His interpretation of the 1559 establishment is open to question, but he was not incorrect in perceiving and exploiting its equivocalness. The Act of Uniformity ostensibly revived Henrician statutes but in practice, and in her Injunctions, Elizabeth made clear that she did not challenge the autonomous authority of episcopacy and did not revive the title of Head of the Church. The thirty-seventh Article and the second Canon of 1603 established, in Dodwell's view, a proper Supremacy which made no pretensions to royal authorship of the *ordo*. The doctrines of Apostolic succession and the indelible character of episcopal consecration were thus preserved. Powers the crown could not give it could not take away, despite the successive claims of Cranmer, Erastus, Hobbes, Selden and Stillingfleet.[59]

The Reformation Supremacy had been ambiguous not only because the extent of the powers claimed was left unclear, but also because the location of Supremacy, whether in the crown alone or in crown-in-Parliament, remained a source for dispute.[60] Dodwell was anti-monarchic in his claims for the Church against the crown, but pro-monarchic in his claims for the Church against Parliament. He asserted that the Supremacy lay exclusively with the Crown without the conjunction of Parliament. Crown-in-Parliament and crown-in-Convocation stood on equal footing and the Act of Supremacy had only levelled Convocation to a status equal with Parliament; Canons, like statutes, needed only the crown's confirmation. The meeting and acting of Convocation, like Parliament, depended upon the pleasure of the Prince, yet just as the regular meeting of Parliament was intrinsic to the civil constitution, so too was Convocation to the spiritual constitution.[61] Dodwell finally returned to the teaching authority of the Catholic Church. The Church ought 'to enquire into new opinions . . . that she may neither recommend heretics to the communion with foreign churches, nor receive them to her own communion . . . This will require frequent synods . . . But these cannot be had, if they must depend on the pleasure of the local magistrate.'[62]

The Baroccian controversy had begun with the Patristic case for and against secular deprivations, had proceeded to the larger issue of the theory of church and state, and then had focused upon the powers of the English Church and Convocation. By 1696 Dodwell had raised all the issues which became so familiar in the ensuing years. The original debate petered out and nothing new was said. Dodwell himself stopped here, not bothering to publish a tract he wrote in 1699, and in 1700 publishing simply an abstract of his previous arguments.[63] Ironically, in that year he began corresponding with Tenison on the subject of his re-admission to the established Church.[64]

Atterbury's *Letter to a Convocation Man* was a clever exploitation of High Church doctrines recently aired by the Nonjurors, and by 1698 a commentator was noting a conjunction of High Churchmen, Nonjurors, and Robert Harley's New Country Party.[65] Although apparently not a Jacobite before 1716, Atterbury's vision of the Church militant was never far from that of the Nonjurors.[66]

Both Atterbury and Dodwell used the appealing language of Bracton, of liberty, Magna Carta and the Coronation Oath. And, *pace* Dr Bennett, there was no 'startling novelty'[67] in Atterbury's assertion that the Reformation had not abridged the Church's right freely to debate its affairs. Just as Dodwell had traduced the Henrician Supremacy, so in 1700 the government called upon Chief Justice Holt to give legal opinion on whether Atterbury's doctrines were in breach of the Act of Supremacy. In the last resort Nonjurors and High Churchmen tended to discover, as any Papist might have told them, that the subsistence of the Catholic Church was incompatible with the royal Supremacy as defined in 1534. It is difficult not to conclude that the Act of Submission destroyed the Church's status as a separate *regnum*,[68] and this opened the way into a situation in which, as Nonjurors contemptuously remarked, 'through the midwifery of a vote or two . . . God's altar may be turned or overturned' and the Creed become 'as subject to a repeal as the Game-Act'.[69] After 1534 it was inevitable that the doctrine of the Two Societies would eventually fade away, as it did in the eighteenth century.

There was one important difference between Atterbury's and Dodwell's cases concerning Convocation. One of Atterbury's greatest mistakes was to contend that Convocation should meet every time Parliament met because Convocation was, he held, summoned along with Parliament under the *praemunientes* clause in the bishops' writ of summons. Wake showed the historical falsity of this. But Dodwell had already said, in his *Doctrine of the Church of England*, that whilst Convocation had originally been Parliamentary because of its function in taxing the clergy, it was now a distinct and separate body 'not confined to Parliament times'. This conclusion was part of Dodwell's case for Convocation's independence from Parliament and flowed naturally from the idea of the Church as a distinct society. Dodwell realised — and White Kennett was to make the point in 1701 against Atterbury — that the assertion of the Church's constitutional right of regular meeting need not and should not entail the yoking of Convocation to Parliamentary sessions.[70]

Although Atterbury's pamphlet shifted attention away from the episcopal deprivations toward heresy and the rights of Convocation, the subject of episcopacy did not disappear. It recurred in the writings of the Convocation controversialists, and in December 1702 the Lower House of Convocation produced a declaration in which it 'acknowledged the order of bishops . . . to be of divine Apostolic institution' and desired the Upper House's concurrence: the bishops demurred. Meanwhile, two other matters kept episcopacy in the public eye. One was the case of Bishop Thomas Watson of St David's, a Jacobite who had taken the Oath of Allegiance and continued in his See. The Whigs waged a long vendetta against him;

he was deprived on dubious charges of simony by an ecclesiastical court in 1698, but both he and Bishop Thomas Sprat denied the court's competence and he was not finally ejected until 1705.[71] The other matter was the assault on the crown's prerogative of episcopal nomination. During his reign, William had the unusual advantage of being able to make twenty-one elevations to the episcopate, plus seven translations. In 1701 a Bill was proposed to prevent the translation of bishops, presented to the Commons by Sir John Packington and supported by John Howe. This move was designed to limit the crown's freedom in clerical appointments and was rumoured to be partly designed to prevent Burnet from tripling his income by moving from Salisbury to Winchester. The Bill used the Nonjuror notion that originally the allocation to a See was an intrinsic and inviolable part of elevation to the episcopate.[72] In the Bodleian Library there is a draft of a more wide-sweeping proposal, probably set aside by the Tories in favour of Packington's more tactful scheme. This was drawn up by Anthony Hammond, one of the Tory MPs who succeeded in blacking his whole party as Jacobite in the 1701 election by having been discovered in conversation with the French Secretary Poussin. His proposed Bill aimed at nothing less than the repeal of that part of the 1534 Act of Annates which gave the crown the right of episcopal appointments. The proposal was that upon the vacancy of an episcopal or archiepiscopal See, Convocation would meet and draw up a list of six names, three offered by each House, from which the king must select within twenty-one days. If the king should fail to do so, the archbishop or senior provincial bishop would himself elect and proceed to consecration. And if Convocation should already be sitting when a bishop died, it would remain in session until election was complete, even if Parliament were prorogued or dissolved. This proposal, concluded Hammond, would restore to the Church the power 'it ought to exercise as a spiritual society and member of the Catholic Church'.[73]

Nonjuror ecclesiastical theory continued to be restated: by Leslie in *The Case of the Regale* (1700), a book reprinted by the Anglo-Catholics in 1838 and recommended to Atterbury by Bishop Trelawny in 1701;[74] by Thomas Brett in his *Divine Right of Episcopacy* (1708), by Collier in his immensely influential *Ecclesiastical History* (1708), by Mathias Earberry in the *Elements of Policy, Civil and Ecclesiastical* (1717), and by Hickes in his portentous *Constitution of the Catholic Church* (1716). This last was the tract, written partly in angry retort to Dodwell's apostacy from the Nonjurors, which provoked Hoadly and sparked off the Bangorian Controversy, the scores of pamphlets of which inspire only a sense of *déjà vu*. At this time two young Nonjuror clergymen wrote to Bishop Hough of Oxford seeking his advice on deprivations, schism and canonical obedience. Hough wearily replied that they were too young to remember the treatises of Hody and Dodwell and said, 'I believe it is hardly possible to say anything on the one side or the other which was not then said'. Predictably enough the Lower House of Convocation in 1717 found Hoadly guilty of tenets tending 'to destroy the being of those powers, without which the Church, as a society, cannot subsist'.[75] It was the parting shot of the High Church movement.

Whig assertions of the Crown's religious Supremacy were a significant element in the transition of Whiggism from Country to Court ideology.[76] Similarly the education of Toryism as an autonomous political movement independent of the Court, often assigned exclusively to Robert Harley's skills in forging the New Country Party in the 1690s, found its source in the long clericalist tradition of the Church's corporate rights. It is the vitality of this tradition which explains the response of the Seven Bishops to James II and of Nonjurors and High Churchmen to the Courts of William, Anne and George.

NOTES

For their help and comments I am grateful to Drs Eveline Cruickshanks, Linda Colley, John Morrill and Robert Williams. All works cited were published in London unless otherwise stated. Most contemporary works were issued anonymously and authorship has been supplied. Spelling in quotations has been modernised.

1. G. V. Bennett, 'King William III and the Episcopate', in G. V. Bennett and J. D. Walsh, eds., *Essays in Modern English Church History* (1966), pp. 112-116; Bennett, *The Tory Crisis in Church and State 1688-1730* (Oxford, 1975), ch. 1; Bennett, 'Conflict in the Church', in G. Holmes, ed., *Britain after the Glorious Revolution* (1969), pp. 155-175; Holmes, *The Trial of Doctor Sacheverell* (1973), ch. 2; J. Hopes, 'Politics and Morality in the Writings of Jeremy Collier', *Literature and History*, VIII (1978), 159-174; D. Bahlmann, *The Moral Revolution of 1688* (Yale, 1957).

2. M. C. Jacob, *The Newtonians and the English Revolution 1689-1720* (Hassocks, Sussex, 1976); J. Redwood, *Reason, Ridicule and Religion* (1976). Leslie: Northampton R.O., MS Buccleuch 63, No. 7, pp. 2-3; I owe this reference to Mr Paul Hopkins. Leslie, *The Charge of Socinianism against Dr Tillotson* (Edinburgh, 1695); Lowth, *A Letter to Edward Stillingfleet* (1687), pp. 43-46.

3. John Locke, *Epistola de Tolerantia: A Letter on Toleration*, ed. R. Klibansky and J. W. Gough (Oxford, 1968), pp. 71-73.

4. E. T. Davies, *Episcopacy and the Royal Supremacy in the Church of England in the XVIth Century* (Oxford, 1950), ch. 1; W. M. Lamont, *Godly Rule* (1969), ch. 3; Bennett, 'Patristic Tradition in Anglican Thought 1660-1900', in *Tradition in Luthertum und Anglikanismus: Oecumenica 1971/72* (Gutersloh, 1972), pp. 63-87; D. Douglas, *English Scholars 1660-1730* (1951), pp. 250-257; N. Tyacke, 'Puritanism, Arminianism and Counter-Revolution', in C. Russell, ed., *The Origins of the English Civil War* (1973), pp. 119-143; G. Every, *The High Church Party 1688-1718* (1956), ch. 1.

5. The most recent account of the Convocation Controversy is Bennett, *Tory Crisis*, ch. 3; the most comprehensive is N. Sykes, *William Wake, Archbishop of Canterbury 1657-1737* (2 vols., Cambridge, 1957), I, ch. 2. For other accounts: Sykes, *Edmund Gibson, Bishop of London, 1669-1748* (Oxford, 1926), ch. 2; Sykes, *From Sheldon to Secker* (Cambridge, 1959), ch. 2; Sykes, *Church and State in England in the XVIIIth Century* (Cambridge, 1934), ch. 7; G. Cragg, *Reason and Authority in the Eighteenth Century* (Cambridge, 1964), ch. 7; Bennett, *White Kennett 1660-1728, Bishop of Peterborough* (London, 1957), chs. 2-6; Douglas, *English Scholars*, ch. 10; Every, *High Church Party*, chs. 5, 8; H. D. Rack, '"Christ's Kingdom is not of this World": The Case of Benjamin Hoadly versus William Law Reconsidered', in D. Baker, ed., *Church, Society and Politics: Studies in Church History*, vol. XII (Oxford, 1975), pp. 275-91.

6. B[ritish] L[ibrary], MS Egerton 3337, fo. 2: Mr Evans to Charles Bertie, 10 Apr. 1689; Every, *High Church Party*, p. 35.

7. Bennett, *Tory Crisis*, pp. 48-49; Bennett, 'Conflict in the Church', p. 165; Bennett, 'William III and the Episcopate', p. 128; Sykes, *Wake*, p. 81; Holmes, *Sacheverell*, p. 30; Cragg, *Reason and Authority*, p. 188. The title-page date of *A Letter to a Convocation Man* is 1697; the tract is still catalogued in many libraries under Sir Bartholomew Shower, the Tory lawyer; his was the initial inspiration: Bennett, *Tory Crisis*, p. 48.

8. Leslie, *The Case of the Regale and of the Pontificat stated* (n.p., 1700), pp. 74 ff., esp. p. 91; Hody, *Some Thoughts on a Convocation . . . with some Occasional Reflections on the Defence of the Vindication of the Deprived Bishops* (1699), *passim*.

9. Only one modern scholar has alluded to this: Every, *High Church Party*, pp. 73-74, 82-84. There has been little discussion of the Nonjuror theory of Church and state, but see L. M. Hawkins, *Allegiance in Church and State* (1928), chs. 2, 5; T. Lathbury, *A History of the Nonjurors* (1845), pp. 137-145, 182-183; Sykes, *Church and State*, pp. 286-290.

10. Atterbury, *Letter*, p. 19; cf. pp. 17-20; Bennett, 'Conflict in the Church', p. 166; Bennett, *Tory Crisis*, p. 48.

11. Kettlewell, *Measures* (1681), pp. 135-136; Sacheverell, *The Political Union* (Oxford, 1702), p. 9; Atterbury, *The Mitre and the Crown* (1711), *passim*; Leslie, *Case of the Regale*, p. 161; cf. Samuel Hill, *The Rights, Liberties, and Authorities of the Church* (1701), pp. 20-32; Kettlewell, *Of Christian Communion* (1693).

12. Six were ejected: Sancroft of Canterbury, Turner of Ely, Frampton of Gloucester, Lloyd of Norwich, White of Peterborough, and Ken of Bath and Wells; three died prior to the date for deprivation: Thomas of Worcester, Lake of Chichester, and Cartwright of Chester.

13. Maurice, *A Letter out of the Country* (1689), p. 6; cf. E. M. Thompson, ed., *Letters of Humphrey Prideaux* (1875), p. 151; George Hickes, *Reflections upon a Letter out of the Country* (1689); BL, MS Lansdowne 1018, fo. 18: White Kennett to Samuel Blackwell, Feb. 1690; White Kennett, *A Complete History of England* (2nd edn., 1719), III, pp. 592, 594; T. Lathbury, *A History of the Convocation* (2nd edn., 1853), pp. 329, 332, 341; Every, *High Church Party*, pp. 37, 45, 58.

14. H. Horwitz, *Revolution Politicks* (Cambridge, 1968), p. 101; D[octor] W[illiam's] L[ibrary], Roger Morrice's Entring Book, MS Morrice R, fo. 87; Bodl[eian Library], MS Rawlinson H98, fos. 93-94; Bodl., MS Ballard 27, fo. 88; G. D'Oyly, *The Life of William Sancroft* (1821), I, 456-461.

15. *How far the Clergy . . . ought to Communicate with the Non-swearing Bishops* (1690), p. 1; *A Modest Apology for the Suspended Bishops* (1690), sig. Blv; *The Case of the Suspended Bishops Considered* (1691); Kennett, *Complete History*, III, 614; E. H. Plumptre, *The Life of Thomas Ken* (1888), II, 50.

16. Bennett, 'William III and the Episcopate', p. 121; Horwitz, *Revolution Politicks*, p. 125; Sykes, *Wake*, p. 51; Lathbury, *History of the Nonjurors*, pp. 88-89; D'Oyly, *Sancroft*, I, 463; J. Stoughton, *Ecclesiastical History of England, I. The Church of the Revolution* (1874), pp. 172-173; H. C. Foxcroft, ed., *A Supplement to Burnet's History of My Own Time* (Oxford, 1902), pp. 358-359; R. J. Kerr and I. C. Duncan, eds., *The Portledge Papers* (1928), p. 109; Edward Stillingfleet, *A Vindication of their Majesties Authority to fill the sees of the Deprived Bishops . . . Occasioned by Dr B[everidge]'s Refusal of the Bishoprick of Bath and Wells* (1691); *A Vindication of their Majesties Wisdom, in the late Nomination . . . to the Vacant Arch-bishopricks and Bishopricks* (1691); C[ambridge] U[niversity] L[ibrary], MS Baker 40, fo. 90: Lowth to Beveridge.

17. *The Diary of John Evelyn*, 7 May 1691; *Portledge Papers*, p. 108; DWL, MS Morrice R, fo. 31; Hickes, *The Protestation of Dr George Hickes, and Claim of Right, Fixed up in the Cathedral Church of Worcester* (1691); D'Oyly, *Sancroft*, I, 467; Stoughton, *Church of the Revolution*, pp. 169-171; Hickes, *An Apology for the New Separation* (1691); Thomas Browne, *Some Reflections on a Late Pamphlet, entitled, A Vindication of their Majesties Authority to Fill the Sees* (1691).

18. *How far the Clergy*, p. 8; DWL, MS Morrice R, fo. 31; Kennett, *Complete History*, III, 594. Dodwell's *Cautionary Discourse* was circulated in manuscript in 1689; there is no extant copy, but it is summarised in Francis Brokesby, *The Life of Mr Henry Dodwell* (1715), ch. 20. See also: Samuel Grascome, *A Brief Answer to a Late Discourse concerning the Unreasonableness of a New Separation* [1691]; John Williams, *A Vindication of a Discourse* (1691); Grascome, *A Reply to a Vindication of a Discourse* (1691).

19. Plumptre, *Ken*, II, 135-137.

20. Lathbury, *History of the Nonjurors*, pp. 96-99; D'Oyly, *Sancroft*, II, 33-38.

21. Brokesby, *Dodwell*, chs. 36-38.

22. W. R. Ward, *Georgian Oxford* (Oxford, 1958), ch. 1; Bennett, *Tory Crisis*, pp. 26-34; Every, *High Church Party*, pp. 75-77.

23. *DNB*, s.v. Hody; BL, MS Lansdowne 987, fo. 179; C. E. Doble, ed., *Remarks and Collections of Thomas Hearne*, (vol. I, Oxford, 1885), p. 98.

24. Hody and Bentley, *The Unreasonableness of a Separation from the New Bishops: or, a treatise out of Ecclesiastical History* (1691, licensed 6 July); Hody, *Anglicani novi Schismatis redargutio seu Tractatus ex Historiis Ecclesiasticis* (Oxford 1691, licensed 25 July). The document is Bodl., MS Baroccian 142, Nos. 17-18, fos. 270-276; 'Exempla ex historiis ecclesiasticis eorum, qui praeter canonas ad thronum patriarchalem evecti sunt, viventibus adhuc legitimis patriarchis': H. O. Coxe, ed., *Bodleian Library Quarto Catalogues. I. Greek Manuscripts* (Oxford, 1969), col. 244.

25. The identification of R.B as Richard Bentley is in Bodl., MS Cherry 16, fo. 110r. On Bentley at Oxford, see J. H. Monk, *The Life of Richard Bentley* (1833), I, ch. 2; R. J. White, *Dr Bentley: A Study in Academic Scarlet* (1965), ch. 5.

26. Hody, *A Letter from Mr Humphry Hody, to a friend, concerning a Collection of Canons* (Oxford, 1692, dated 12 Dec., 1691); *The Case of Sees Vacant by an Unjust and Uncanonical Deprivation* (1693, licensed 1 Dec. 1692).

27. Hody, *Case*, pp. 1-2.

28. Hody, *Case*, p. 6; Hobbes, *Leviathan*, Review and Conclusion; cf. ch. 21; Q. Skinner, 'Conquest and Consent: Thomas Hobbes and the Engagement Controversy', in G. E. Aylmer, ed., *The Interregnum* (1972), 79-98.

29. J. P. Kenyon, *Revolution Principles* (Cambridge, 1977), chs. 2-4, G. M. Straka, *Anglican Reaction to the Revolution of 1688* (Madison, Wisconsin, 1962); M. Goldie, 'Edmund Bohun and *Jus Gentium* in the Revolution Debate 1689-1693', *Historical Journal*, xx (1977), 569-586; M. Goldie, 'The Revolution of 1689 and the Structure of Political Argument', *Bulletin of Research in the Humanities*, lxxxiii (1980), 473-564.

30. Hody, *Letter*, pp. 20-25, 38-40; Hody, *Case*, p. 106. (It should be added that although Wake's book of 1697 was regarded as embarrassingly erastian, his stance in 1716 was considerably more moderate than Hoadly's.).

31. Browne, *The Oxford-antiquity examined: Wherein is briefly shewn the Notorious Falshoods in the Greek Manuscript* (1691, Aug.?): this tract has hitherto been unattributed: Jean de la Crose makes clear that Browne is the author: *The Works of the Learned* (Sept., 1691), p. 54 (cf. pp. 54-8 and August issue, pp. 17-21); Bisbie, *An Answer to a Treatise out of Ecclesiastical History* (1691, Aug.?); Bisbie, *Unity of Priesthood necessary to the Unity of*

Communion in a Church (1692, dated 29 Sept. 1691); Grascome, *Epistola ad Humfredum Hody* ... *de Tractatu e Scriniis Baroccianis* (1691); Grascome, *A Farther Account of the Baroccian Manuscript* (1692, appx. dated 1 Jan. 1692[3]); Dodwell, *A Vindication of the Deprived Bishops, Asserting their Spiritual Rights against a Lay-Deprivation* (1692, Aug.?); summarised in Collier, *A Brief Essay Concerning the Independency of Church-Power* [1692]; Narcissus Luttrell, *A Brief Historical Relation* (Oxford, 1857), II, 543-544 (18 Aug. 1692).

32. BL, MS Stowe 746, fo. 116: Dodwell to Ken, 27 Aug. 1689; MS Stowe 746, fos. 143-144: Dodwell to Lloyd, May 1691. Dodwell's letter to Tillotson (Stowe 746, fos. 141-142, and Bodl., MS Cherry 22, fos. 8-9, 12 May 1691) was published by the (later executed) Jacobite printer William Anderton but is not now extant; it is reprinted in Francis Lee, ed., *A Compleat Collection of the Works of* ... *John Kettlewell* (1719), I, Appx. V, pp. x-xi, and cited in Every, *High Church Party*, p. 66.

33. Edmund Calamy, *An Historical Account of my own Life*, ed. J. T. Rutt (1829), I, 281-283.

34. On Shottesbrooke see: C. J. Abbey and J. H. Overton, *The English Church in the Eighteenth Century* (1887), ch. 2; J. H. Overton, *The Nonjurors* (1902), ch. 5; Brokesby, *Dodwell*, ch. 25.

35. Dodwell, *Separation of Churches from Episcopacy* ... *proved Schismatical* (1679); *A Discourse Concerning the One Altar* (1683); *Dissertationes Cyprianiae* (Oxford, 1682); *Dissertationes in Irenaeum* (Oxford, 1689); Brokesby, *Dodwell*, chs. 8-16; Every, *High Church Party*, pp. 11-16; Locke, *Third Letter on Toleration* (1692), p. 266.

36. Dodwell, *Vindication*, pp. 4-11, 16, 34-37; Bisbie, *Answer*, pp. 21-23, 29; Bisbie, *Unity*, p. 58; Grascome, *Further Account*, pp. 1 ff.

37. Bennett, 'Patristic Tradition'; H. R. McAdoo, *The Spirit of Anglicanism: A Survey of Anglican Theological Method in the Seventeenth Century* (1965), chs. 9-10.

38. Dodwell, *Vindication*, pp. 17-18, 34-41, 51-52; Bisbie, *Answer*, pp. 5-12; Bisbie, *Unity*, pp. 24-25; Browne, *Oxford Antiquity*, pp. 7-11. Cf. John Sage, *The Principles of the Cyprianic Age: with regard to Episcopal Power and Jurisdiction* (1695).

39. Dodwell, *Vindication*, pp. 45-46; Grascome, *Further Account*, p. 15; Grascome, *Epistola*, pp. 7-9; Bisbie, *Unity*, pp. 67-70; Bisbie, *Answer*, pp. 29-32; Hody, *Letter*, pp. 1-8.

40. Dodwell, *Vindication*, pp. 34-37.

41. Bisbie, *Answer*, sig. A2r; Dodwell, *Vindication*, p. 104.

42. Dodwell, *Vindication*, pp. 3, 32; Dodwell, *The Doctrine of the Church of England* [1696], pp. 58-59; Dodwell, *The Defence of the Vindication* [1697], pp. 26-27, 109; Bisbie, *Answer*, sigs. A3r-A4v; Grascome, *Further*, p. 16; Dodwell had sketched this argument in the *Letter to Tillotson*: above, n. 32. Atterbury, *The Rights, Powers, and Priviledges of an English Convocation* (1700), p. xix.

43. Dodwell, *Vindication*, pp. 3, 24, 32; cf. Bisbie, *Answer*, sig. A2v.

44. Dodwell, *Vindication*, p. 28. Dodwell used the notion of *koinonia* against the nonconformists in his *Separation of Churches* (1679): Brokesby, *Dodwell*, ch. 8; see 1 John 1:3, 6, 7. (The idea of *koinonia* is in fact usually associated with Paul rather than John.)

45. Dodwell, *Vindication*, pp. 28, 26, 29; Locke, *Letter on Toleration*, pp. 67-69, 121-123.

46. Hody, *Case*, sig. A3v; Dodwell, *Defence*, pp. 12, 4, 32, 35; Dodwell, *Doctrine*, p. 8.

47. Hody, *Reflexions on a Pamphlet Entitled, Remarks on the Occasional Paper* (1698); Hody, *Some Thoughts on a Convocation* (1699).

48. Hickes, *Some Discourses upon Dr Burnet and Dr Tillotson* (1695), pp. 85-87; Burnet, *Reflections upon a Pamphlet, Entituled, Some Discourses upon Dr Burnet and Dr Tillotson* (1695), pp. 52-53, cf. pp. 135-150; cf. James Tyrrell, *Bibliotheca Politica*, 13th Dialogue (1694), pp. 941, 963-8.

49. For accounts of Hody's promise of press liberty and of the seizure of Dodwell's book: Hody, *Reflexions*, pp. 2-7; Lowth, *Historical Collections Concerning Church Affairs* (1696), sig. A2r; Anon., *The Occasional Paper: No. VIII. Shewing the Necessity of such a Christian Discipline as is Consistent with the Civil Power* (1697), p. 3; Thomas Milles, *Remarks upon the Occasional Paper* (n.p., [1698]), pp. 2-3; Edward Welchman, *A Second Defence of the Church of England* (1698), sig. A3r; Bodl., MS Cherry 16, fo. 109r.

50. Stoughton, *Church of the Revolution*, pp. 203-206; Kennett, *Complete History*, III, 707 ff; Ward, *Georgian Oxford*, pp. 21-22; Every, *High Church Party*, pp. 79-81.

51. Dodwell's *Doctrine* and *Defence* present some bibliographical confusion. All copies of the *Defence* are dated 1695; most copies of the *Doctrine* are dated 1697 (this date is given in Wing *STC* and in Every, *High Church Party*, p. 68); a few copies are dated 1694 (CUL and Petyt Library, Shipton, Yorkshire). In fact, Hody in 1699 (*Reflexions*, pp. 2-7) and Welchman in 1698 (*Second Defence*, sig. A3v) make clear that the newly printed *Defence*.was seized at the beginning of 1696 and was reprinted and published, without interference, in 1697; but the *Doctrine* escaped seizure and was separately published in 1696, and possibly reprinted in 1697. Brokesby's statement in 1715 (*Dodwell*, I, 268; followed by Lathbury, *Nonjurors*, pp. 182-3) that it was the *Doctrine* that was suppressed and that the *Defence* escaped and was published first is incorrect. This point is important in establishing that Dodwell pre-empted Atterbury. Note also that the *DNB* (s.v. Dodwell) mistakenly says that the *Doctrine* was meant to preface the *Vindication* of 1692.

52. Welchman, *A Defence of the Church of England, from the Charge of Schism and Heresie* (1693, licensed 10 Nov. 1692).

53. Welchman, *Defence*, pp. 10-11; Dodwell, *Defence*, pp. 77, 80; cf. Burnet, *Reflections*, pp. 142-143; Welchman, *Second Defence*, pp. 9-10. The government made clear in 1691 that no claim was being made to degrade bishops from their spiritual character: Hody, *Letter*, pp. 26-27; Stillingfleet, *Vindication*, pp. 17-19.

54. Welchman, *Defence*, pp. 7-9; Welchman, *Second Defence*, pp. 12-15; cf. Hody, *Letter*, pp. 20-21; Stillingfleet, *Vindication*, p. 18.

55. Dodwell, *Defence*, pp. 95, 84; cf. p. 76-99; cf. Leslie, *Case of the Regale*, p. 7 ff.

56. Dodwell, *Doctrine*, pp. 3, 12-35. Dodwell might be said to be guilty of distortion since both 37 H.8 c.17 and 1 Edw. 6 c.2 refer more ambiguously to spiritual 'jurisdiction' not 'authority'.

57. Davies, *Episcopacy*, p. 63.

58. J. J. Scarisbrick, *Henry VIII* (Harmondsworth, 1971), pp. 499, 501, 535-539; G. W. Bromiley, *Thomas Cranmer, Theologian* (1956), pp. 50-52; Davies' account of Cranmer seems inconsistent: *Episcopacy*, pp. 17, 65-66, 70, 107-109, 121, 137; Dodwell, *Doctrine*, pp. 2-3; Dodwell, *Defence*, pp. 86-87, 104; G. R. Elton, 'Evolution of a Reformation Statute', *English Historical Review*, LXIV (1949), pp. 174-197.

59. Dodwell, *Doctrine*, pp. 39-44, 60-86; Davies, *Episcopacy*, pp. 73-82; A. G. Dickens, *The English Reformation* (1967), pp. 412-413.

60. Dickens, *English Reformation*, pp. 172-173; Scarisbrick, *Henry VIII*, pp. 510-513.

61. Dodwell, *Doctrine*, pp. 50-55; Dodwell, *Defence*, pp. 27-28; 103-104; cf. Bisbie, *Unity*, pp. 49-50. An early draft of the Act of Submission *had* included parliamentary consent for canons but this had not been proceeded with: Scarisbrick, *Henry VIII*, p. 513.

62. Dodwell, *Defence*, p. 103.

63. Dodwell, 'An Answer to Reflections on a Pamphlet entitled Remarks on the Occasional Paper' (1699?): Bodl., MS Cherry 16, fos. 96-118; Dodwell, *An Abstract of Common Principles of a Just Vindication of the Rights of the Kingdom of God upon Earth, against the Politick Machinations of Erastian Hereticks* (1700). There is also an unpublished

tract against Dodwell by White Kennett (c. 1698): Lambeth Palace, MS Tenison 806, item 12 (see Bennett, *Kennett*, pp. 21-22); and a further contribution by Lowth: *Eklogai, Or Excerpts from the Ecclesiastical History* (1704).

64. Stoughton, *Church of the Revolution*, pp. 381-382; Every, *High Church Party*, pp. 88-89, 92-93. In 1705 it was reported that Dodwell would not return to the church till it declared against civil deprivation: Hearne, *Remarks and Collections*, I, 69: 9 Nov. 1705.

65. Henry Horwitz, *Parliament, Policy and Politics in the Reign of William III* (Manchester, 1977), p. 238.

66. Cf. Bennett, *Tory Crisis*, pp. 206-7.

67. Bennett, *Tory Crisis*, p. 49.

68. Q. Skinner, *The Foundations of Modern Political Thought* (Cambridge, 1978), II, 85; Sykes, *Church and State*, p. 287; Bennett, *Tory Crisis*, pp. 54-55.

69. Bisbie, *Unity*, p. 49; Matthias Earberry, *Elements of Policy, Civil and Ecclesiastical* (1716), p. 49.

70. Dodwell, *Doctrine*, p. 51; Kennett, *Ecclesiastical Synods and Parliamentary Convocations* (1701), p. ix.

71. Lathbury, *Convocation*, pp. 380-383; *DNB*, s.v. Watson.

72. Horwitz, *Parliament, Policy*, p. 293; BL, Add. MS 30,000 E, fo. 75: Bonnet's report (he speaks of 'une polygamie spirituelle'); Bodl. MS Rawlinson A245: Anthony Hammond's Collections, fo. 24v; Leslie?, *A Letter from a Clergy-man in the Country, to a Dignified Clergyman in London . . . Vindicating the Bill . . . for Preventing Translation of Bishops* (1702): this pamphlet gives the text of Packington's bill. A similar proposal and similar arguments recurred in 1731: Sykes, *Gibson*, pp. 149, 214-215; *A Court Bishop no Apostolical Bishop* (1732).

73. Hammond was MP for Huntingdonshire and Cambridge University between 1695 and 1701. Bodl. MS Rawlinson A 245: Hammond's Collections, fos. 83v-84v: 'Some Thoughts about a Bill to be brought into Parlt. to make the Bishops less Dependent upon the Crown'. Also included was a proposal that poor bishopricks have their incomes augmented from parochial First Fruits so that all sees would be worth at least £1,000 p.a. Packington had asked the committee attending to his bill to consider methods of augmenting poor sees: *Commons Journals*, XIII, 560: 22 May 1701. Horwitz, *Parliament, Policy*, pp. 297-298.

74. Francis Atterbury, *The Epistolatory Correspondence* (1783-87), III, 51.

75. *Table-talk and Papers of Bishop Hough 1703-1743* (Oxford Historical Society, Collectanea, II, 1890), pp. 406-407; *A Report of the Committee of the Lower House of Convocation* (1717), p. 22.

76. I. Kramnick, 'Augustan Politics and English Historiography: The Debate on the English Past, 1730-35', *History and Theory*, VI (1967), 33-56.

2

The Scottish Episcopal Clergy and the Ideology of Jacobitism

Bruce Lenman

THE case for studying the mental world of the Episcopal clergy of late seventeenth and eighteenth-century Scotland is simple: their flocks produced the vast majority of active participants in every single Jacobite rebellion from that of Claverhouse in 1689 to the final fling which died on the battlefield of Culloden in the Spring of 1746. Now I am well aware that there is more to Jacobite history than counting those who stood upon a battlefield under the banner of King James VII and II or that of his son the Old Pretender, or 'King James VIII and III' (depending on your taste). There is the complex and important problem of the extent to which the parliamentary Tory party between 1714 and, say, the 1750s was motivated primarily by Jacobite loyalties. Dr Eveline Cruickshanks spotted some time ago, in the course of working on *The History of Parliament*, that a very significant proportion of the Westminster M.P.s of Tory loyalty can be shown to have expressed more or less emphatic Jacobitism to a surprisingly late stage in the eighteenth century.[1] This theme she has subsequently developed in an important new study of the parliamentary Tory party.[2] Nevertheless, I do think that in the last analysis those who did Jacobite deeds are historically more important than those who only wrote and uttered Jacobite phrases. In fact one of the problems facing anyone who tries to recreate the mental values of active Jacobites is that, by and large, those who wrote most did not act, and those who acted wrote little, if anything.

This is where the Scottish Episcopal clergy come in, for they were the most significant single group of men creating and transmitting articulate Jacobite ideology in this period. This is not to say that they were the only such group. However, all the others were much smaller. Take the Scottish Roman Catholics, for example. Their Jacobite loyalties were taken for granted by everyone. In a 'Relation du voyage du Sieur Fleming en Ecosse et de l'état present de ce royaume', written at the time of the abortive Jacobite invasion of Scotland in 1708 and preserved in archives of the secretary of state for war in Paris, the narrator mostly describes his contacts with a long list of nobility and gentry. However, he also says of the Earl of Erroll, his original host, and the Earl Marischal, who came to join them within a few days at Erroll's castle of Slains on the coast of eastern Aberdeenshire:

> Ils me firent ecrire le quatorze a Monsieur Nicolson Evesque Catholique de ce royaume pour l'avertir de l'etat present des affaires afin qu'il avertit les Catholiques du nord de se tenir prets[3]

'Monsier Nicolson' is Thomas Joseph Nicolson, son of Sir Thomas Nicolson of Cluny (later of Kemnay) in Aberdeenshire, and younger brother of Lord Kemnay. Ordained priest at a mature age in Italy in 1686 (he was a convert), he had been nominated one of the two bishops for Scotland by James VII just before the Glorious Revolution of 1688, during which he was arrested and banished. Consecrated, finally, in Paris in 1695, he started to exercise his episcopal functions in Scotland only in 1697. For safety, he based himself in a remote cottage at Preshome on the Duke of Gordon's estates in the bleak Banffshire district of the Enzie.[4]

Nicolson was Scotland's first Vicar-Apostolic, but by 1705 he had only some thirty priests working under him, and of these only four were active in the Highlands. This fact must be recalled when historians blithely state, as too many of them do, that the Highlands remained 'largely Roman Catholic' in the Jacobite period. Roman Catholicism existed in small traditional pockets well summed up by their Presbyterian enemies in the 1720s as consisting of part of the Hebridean Islands (Barra, South Uist, Benbecula, Canna, Eigg and Rum) and mainland areas to the west of Inverness (Knoydart, Morar, Moidart, Ardnamurchan, Glenmoriston, Glenurquhart, and Strathglass). By 1727 there was a Highland Vicariate as well as a Lowland one, but it was hard pressed to maintain services to existing communities of the faithful, let alone to proselytise. The aged Bishop Hugh MacDonald, Vicar Apostolic of the Highlands, was one of the first to go to see Prince Charles when he reached the Highland mainland at Loch-nam-Uamh in the summer of 1745. MacDonald tried to persuade the young prince to go home again. Rebuffed by Charles, the bishop had no option but to appoint several of his priests as chaplains to the Jacobite forces. They wore kilt, sword and pistol and ranked as captains. Father Allan MacDonald of Clanranald's regiment rode down the line blessing the men before they charged at the battle of Falkirk, the last major Jacobite victory gained in January 1746 as the Young Pretender's forces slowly fell back towards the Highlands for their last stand.

Nevertheless it is highly significant that the great authorities on the prisoners of the '45 say of the fifteen Roman Catholic clergymen captured during or after that rebellion:

These priests were treated with more leniency than the non-jurant Episcopalians.[5]

Practising Roman Catholics were a small minority even in the Highlands. That is clear, even if there can still be historical controversy over the religious allegiance of particular groups such as the MacDonalds or MacIans of Glencoe. Such controversy tends to generate more heat than light.[6] We do well to recall that Dr Alexander Webster, in his apparently remarkably reliable census of Scotland in 1755, gave the total of Papists in a population of 1,265,380 as no more than 16,490.[7]

Episcopalian Protestants, by comparison, were in the first half of the eighteenth century undoubtedly a vastly more numerous and influential body. To understand why this was so it is essential to go back to the era of the Restoration in Scotland, and to the Glorious Revolution of 1688-9 which brought that era to an end. The

D

Restoration in Scotland was very much a restoration of the traditional aristocratic leaders of the country. In Gordon Donaldson's words:

The nobility and gentry, like the king, were now to enjoy their own again[8]

Largely due to their own poor judgement in contracting the Engagement — a pact with the defeated and imprisoned Charles I in 1648 — the Scots nobles had experienced military, political and social eclipse between 1648 and 1660. They who had led the Covenanting revolution of the 1630s were routed by the sectarian hosts of the New Model Army; excluded from power by Argyll and the Kirk in an attempt to placate England; and finally, after the battle of Worcester in 1651, ground down by the iron hand and swingeing fines of an English occupation. The decision to restore an episcopal order to the Kirk by Law Established was taken by anti-clerical politicians in London in December 1660 but there is no doubt that one factor on which pro-episcopal royal advisers like the Earl of Middleton counted heavily when they told Charles II that it would be easy to restore episcopacy in Scotland was the social conservatism of the resurgent nobility. Bishops were restored as a symbol of hierarchy, order, and seemly subjection. These were no proud Caroline prelates of the kind which had so irritated the Scots nobility between 1625 and 1638. They did not normally hold offices of state and they were specifically warned not to offend the susceptibilities of the nobles.

Archbishop James Sharp of St Andrews, like his colleague Bishop Robert Leighton of Dunblane a former presbyterian minister, set a consistent example to his brethren on the bench in this respect. Sharp lived in very considerable style, with many servants and no fewer than three regularly used residences.[9] Yet he was always urbanely deferential and helpful to any member of the noble order. Sharp's father had been a sheriff-clerk in Banffshire and a factotum to the Earl of Buchan. The archbishop made no secret of the fact that on account of his parents' 'special dependence upon the late earl of Buchan' he himself 'would do any good office within my reach to this earl, his son'.[10] Nor was this a mere form of words, as Sharp showed in his relations with a near neighbour in the county of Fife, David second Earl of Wemyss. Sharp always stressed to Wemyss 'the great honour I pay your noble family'[11] and he displayed the practical side of that respect when it came to presentations of clergymen to parishes where the archbishop of St Andrews was patron. Despite his own proprietorial instincts, Sharp seems to have accepted that in any parish where Wemyss was a substantial landowner no presentation was sensible without the prior approval of the earl.[12] The murder of so judicious a primate by a small group of religious dissenters on Magus Muir, two miles west of St Andrews, in May 1679, merely confirmed the view of most Scots nobles that religious and political radicalism was but the prelude to social anarchy.

Some 270 clergymen were deposed between 1660 and 1663 for refusal to accept the episcopal settlement of the kirk. That was a little over a quarter of the total number of parish incumbents. However, the Restoration Settlement lasted for nearly thirty years from 1660 to 1688. During that period the universities were placed firmly under episcopal supervision. Sharp was Chancellor of St Andrews

University just as Andrew Fairfoul, the Archbishop of Glasgow after 1661, was by virtue of his office Chancellor of Glasgow University. This was understandable, for the five universities of Scotland (St Andrews, Glasgow, King's College and Marischal College in Aberdeen, and Edinburgh) were the nurseries of the ministry. By an act of the Scots Parliament of 1662 all university teachers had to take an oath of allegiance to the Crown and obtain a certificate from a bishop that they accepted the episcopal settlement of the Kirk. This statute was supplemented by legislative enactment by the Scots Privy Council which had the effect of extending the same obligation to students. By an act of Parliament of 1681 university teachers had also to subscribe the so-called 'Test', which was arguably self-contradictory but eloquent against 'Popish as well as Phanaticall doctrines', not to mention the National Covenant of 1638 and the Solemn League and Covenant of 1643 — the two emotive symbols of the presbyterian revolution of the 1630s and 1640s.[13]

Thus for thirty years the Scottish universities had as their main business the production of clergymen imbued with the conservative, royalist, and episcopal values of the Restoration regime. Acceptance of those values was made all the easier by two factors. One was the extraordinarily pragmatic outlook of the Restoration Kirk. Presbyterian ministers willing to accept the new order were not asked to undergo re-ordination at the hands of a bishop. Nor indeed were the structures of kirk session, presbytery and synod in any way disturbed by the re-insertion of an episcopal order. Bishops and presbyteries had worked well enough together before 1638. They cooperated perfectly well after 1660.[14] The second factor was that with the restoration of lay patronage after 1660 in the Church of Scotland any divinity student who was at all maladjusted to the aristocratic ethos of the at times very brilliant culture of Restoration Scotland was unlikely to make much of his career.

William of Orange, after successfully ousting his father-in-law James VII and II from his thrones, would undoubtedly have been happy to keep bishops in the Church of Scotland, as convenient servants of the Crown. It was the intransigent Jacobitism of the Scottish bench of bishops, most authentically conveyed to William by the maladroit Bishop Alexander Rose of Edinburgh, which forced William to hand over control of the Kirk to a minority of dedicated men for whom presbyterianism was an exclusive solution to the problems of ecclesiastical governance.[15] The price of this revolution was on a scale which made the upheavals of 1660-1663 appear relatively minor. By 1690 it was clear that over half the parish ministers of Scotland were disaffected to the new Presbyterian settlement. It was a remarkable tribute to the strength of the mental world of the Restoration, even at a time when positive enthusiasm for the Stewart dynasty was hard to find.

Here in the 5-600 episcopalian clergy lay the hard core of Jacobite conviction in Scotland. Attempts to estimate the precise measure of popular support for the rival episcopal and presbyterian camps have been made.[16] They are all basically misguided because not only is the evidence too frail to bear the weight of such an enquiry, but it is also the case that in a hierarchial pre-industrial society values were largely, though not exclusively, determined by the groups at the top of the vertically linked local groups which when aggregated together constituted the community of the realm. Of course, there is a crude regional pattern. Presbyterians were at their strongest in Glasgow and the south-west. They had formidable cadres in the Lothians, the Borders, and to a lesser extent in Stirlingshire and Fife. North of the Forth they were a small minority, though even in the Highlands there were clans like the Campbells of Argyll and the Munros and Mackays north of Inverness with a long tradition of hostility to episcopacy. In detail, even these generalisations must be qualified and evidence interpreted in the light of known social dynamics. Can a stone-throwing mob protesting against an attempt to insert a presbyterian minister into a parish kirk long held by an episcopalian and Jacobite clergyman be taken as evidence of popular devotion to episcopacy? In parts of my native North-East (the counties of Aberdeenshire and Banffshire) with its long history of outstanding bishops, the answer may be 'yes', but elsewhere the historian has to weigh the fact that during such a riot the local laird or the heritors (the principal landowners of the parish) can usually be found in the records not actually rioting, but overseeing the demonstration from a short distance away, with a look of warm approval on his or their faces. Had the laird been of presbyterian sympathies, the story might have been quite different.

It was precisely in their close relationship with the nobles and lairds that the strength of the episcopalian clergy, and their influence, lay. Crusted Jacobite lairds such as Sir William Bruce, 'Architect Royal' in Scotland during the Restoration period and latterly Sheriff of the tiny county of Kinross adjacent to Fife, bitterly opposed the 'planting' of ministers of presbyterian persuasion in parishes where they regarded themselves as the dominant influence. This was not invariably a sign of deep commitment to the ministrations of an episcopalian predecessor. In the parish of Portmoak in Kinross, for example, Mr John Bruce had been suspended from the ministry by the bishop and presbytery on a charge of scandalous drunkenness just before the Glorious Revolution and had made no attempt to recover let alone exercise his pastoral rights. Yet Sir William Bruce opposed any replacement even before the Revolution, as a petition by the heritors and parishioners to the Scots Privy Council in 1690 made clear:

> ever since Appryle 1688 Mr William Macky being called by all the paroch except Sir William Bruce and the Laird of Powmilne has their preached and performed all the other parts of his ministeriall functione.[17]

In his own parish of Kinross, where he had built his great new neo-classical mansion with its italianate gardens sloping down to Loch Leven, Sir William was even more intransigent. He refused to cooperate with the Presbytery of Dunfermline in installing a sound presbyterian clergyman. On the contrary, in the words of yet another petition to the Privy Council on which the leading signature was that of William Spens, the new minister:

> Further, albeit Sir William was charged to deliver the keys of the church to the presbytery, he has hitherto refused to do so, causing deprived and disaffected ministers to preach in it, nor are the keys of the manse delivered.[18]

It is hardly surprising that this elderly and very great architect-politician, the 'Inigo Jones of Scotland', spent much of his few remaining years in preventive detention. He was an unreconstructed Jacobite. However, for our purposes the significant point about the old man is the way his behaviour illustrates the increasing dependence of the episcopal clergy on their aristocratic patrons. Though the new presbyterian establishment faced the usual difficulty of producing enough graduate clergy totally to replace its episcopalian foes in the parishes, there was no question of its malevolent determination ultimately to do precisely that. First, the universities had to be purged to render them capable of producing clergy well-affected to the new regime in Kirk and state. Whigs in politics and presbyterians in religion were unlikely to be produced by teachers who were Jacobite episcopalians. The upshot in the University of St Andrews was traumatic. There the masters of the university had shown their usual lack of political prudence by combining with the Scottish bishops to issue a notably sycophantish *Address to the King* (i.e. James VII) shortly before he fell. When a Whig commission 'for visiting universities, colleges, and schools' descended on St Andrews in 1690 in pursuance of duties laid upon it by a Convention Parliament, it promptly dismissed virtually all the senior members of the university.[19]

How justified was this degree of ruthlessness, or, to put it another way, just what sort of minds were the university teachers of the Restoration sending out into the thousand or so parishes of Scotland? One way of testing the evidence is to examine lecture notes of the Restoration period, preferably in the light of the subsequent career of the student who wrote them. Examples are legion, so I have taken one close to hand in the shape of notes from dictates on ethics and physics delivered by Mr Alexander Grant, Regent of St Leonard's College in the University of St Andrews and written down by Alexander Robertson in the early 1680s. Alexander Robertson was subsequently minister at Fortingall deep in the Perthshire Highlands and at the mouth of Glen Lyon, arguably the loveliest of all the glens. Interestingly this clergyman later re-used this university lecture notebook as a commonplace book where he jotted down stray thoughts, occasional poems, and lists of books lent to other people.[20]

It is in fact the jottings of Robertson after he became a working clergyman in 1687 which are so revealing. In the midst of a collection of sermon-notes there are the beginnings of a summary of 'Observations upon the Arise and progress of the late rebellion against King Charles I in so far as it was carried on by a malcontented faction in Scotland under the pretext of Reformation by H.G.L.B.D.'[21] In short, the ideology of order and the cult of Charles King and Martyr were both alive and well and flourishing in Fortingall Manse in the late seventeenth century. So was the cult of the royalist, as distinct from the royal martyr. The Great Marquis of Montrose, leader of royalist risings in mid-seventeenth century Scotland had virtually been canonised after the Restoration when his body, quartered and beheaded after execution by vengeful Whigs, was given a great state funeral. His descendant, James Graham of Claverhouse, Viscount Dundee, added to this cult with his own sacrificial death on July 27 1689 when he was shot dead at the moment of complete Victory in the Battle of Killiecrankie, the one Jacobite triumph during the brief civil

war which accompanied the Glorious Revolution in Scotland. Him Alexander
Robertson eulogised as:

> A souldier devout, a statesman true,
> A courtier, yet a man of conscience too,
> As Hector brave, yet as Ulysses wise,
> Forward yet wary in his enterprise,

and his death he lamented in the words (which, of course, may not be his own):

> Don Dei thats a gift from heaven sent,
> To us alas but for a short time lent,
> Our sins oppos'd stopping this bold advance,
> Robbed him of life, us of deliverance.[22]

That there were contradictions in the episcopalian world view is clear. The
biggest one was the fact that the cause of episcopalian Protestantism in Scotland was
identified with that of the very Roman Catholic exiled Stewarts. Hence the poem's
somewhat embarrassed reference to the fact that Dundee was 'A loyal subject, yet a
protestant'. The statement was absolutely true. The dead royalist general was a
devout episcopalian member of the Church of Scotland, and his chaplain was by his
side throughout the crowded days of his last, fated campaign. Alexander Robertson
was himself staunchly Protestant, despite his rampant disaffection to the Revolution
settlement. That he records the loan of books 'To Mr Patrick Campbell brother
german to the laird of Monzie' is a significant example of the intellectual
relationship between the laird class and the ministers, but even more significant are
the titles loaned: 'The English discourse against poperie', 'Claud his historical
defence of the reformation', and 'Sherlock's judge of Controversie'.[23]

To test how common were Robertson's attitudes among his ecclesiastical
contemporaries, it is instructive to examine the mind of a better-known episcopalian
incumbent — the Reverent Robert Kirk of Aberfoyle and Balquidder. Born the
seventh son of a clerical father in 1644, he died at the early age of 47 in 1692 after
achieving a work of Gaelic scholarship which alone would make his name immortal.
He produced in 1684 the first complete metrical translation of the Psalms of David
into Gaelic. After helping to distribute copies of an Irish Bible printed in Irish
characters at the expense of the Hon. Robert Boyle *gratis* to Highland parishes at
the rate of one Bible per parish (in theory, but many were taken for private use),
Kirk buckled down, in the middle of the political turmoil of 1688-90, to transcribe
the entire Bible into roman letters and to revise his version for use in the Highlands.
For a hundred years it was the only Bible in the Gaelic culture of Scotland and it
richly justifies Kirk's epitaph on his table-tomb in Aberfoyle kirkyard:

> Robertus Kirk, A.M.
> Lumen Hiberniae Linguae[24]

Kirk also wrote an extraordinary book entitled *The Secret Commonwealth* which
was published posthumously as late as 1815 and which is a detailed account, by a

believer, of the fairy world and its inhabitants. Kirk did not regard his belief in fairies as inconsistent with Christianity, indeed he wrote his work partly 'to suppress the impudent and growing Atheism of this age'.[25] Incidentally Alexander Robertson's jottings include a poem on the fairies.[26] Such was the sweetness of character of Kirk that he was the one avowed episcopalian incumbent in the Presbytery of Dunblane who was not deprived after the Revolution. Politically, he was inactive. Yet it is quite clear from his private notebook that he remained unable to accept the validity of the Revolution of 1688 because he was steeped in the Restoration ideology of indefeasible hereditary right and in the belief that unchallenged monarchical power was an essential condition for right order in society.[27] What the quiet Kirk and fiery Alexander Robertson, who was actually deposed for Jacobitism in 1716 after the failure of the 1715 rebellion, had in common (apart from a sophisticated tri-lingual cultural background in English, Latin and Gaelic) was a commitment to a conservative world-view, ultimately providential and presupposing a quasi-sacramental view of authority. Neither man was simple. On the contrary, both appear to have been complex and intelligent. There is therefore nothing pejorative in the statement that both wanted to keep the quality of magic in the human view of life on earth. It is interesting that Kirk was intrigued by the evidences of faith healing, especially healing of the King's Evil, a feat not only performed by anointed monarchs, but also by seventh sons like Robert Kirk.[28] King James VII and II would have understood Kirk's obsession. Despite his much-denounced determination to organise a cumulative process of Catholicisation in England, that monarch gave only some £2,150 to Roman Catholic schools and colleges during his reign, whereas he expended no less than £4,000 on healing medals distributed when he went round touching for the King's Evil.[29]

There was little positive enthusiasm for the Stewarts in Scotland in 1688-9. Only 2-3,000 men rallied to the standard of Claverhouse. Even the bishops, ground under an extreme erastianism since the notorious Act of Supremacy of 1669, and more or less openly sold down the river by the Crown with its policies of appeasement towards dissenters, were 'the Kirk invisible' of Claver's famous sneer. Had events run smoothly under William of Orange and had funds been available to make a generous settlement with clergymen who could not conscientiously accept the new dispensation, one does wonder whether the old regime would not have faded away as it had done after the Reformation-Revolution of 1560 (when financial provision for unreconstructed Catholic clergy was generous indeed). But this was not to be. Scotland suffered acutely under William's reign. His accession was followed by a long sequence of wars with France, wars which lasted off and on until 1713 and which had a devastating effect on Scottish overseas trade and shipping.[30] He was a bad King of Scots, fundamentally uninterested in a northern kingdom which he never visited. It became only too clear that he regarded Scotland purely as a source of troops and funds for his endless European wars. His reign was stained by corruption and atrocity, of which the most notorious example is the Massacre of Glencoe of 1692. On top of all this, William was an unlucky king, for his reign included an appalling subsistence crisis, of a kind commonly experienced in Western Europe in the late seventeenth century but with absolutely no parallel in

English experience. It is indeed one of the most convincing pieces of evidence that England was already very different from her neighbours that English society was free of dearth in the 1690s when both Scotland and France were experiencing its sharpest pangs. 'King William's Seven Ill Years' in Scotland must not be taken too literally, for the chronology is twisted by the phrase to ensure an analogy with a tyrannical Pharaoh in the Old Testament. The crisis ran for four years from 1695, with peaks of severity in 1696 and 1699 and a relative respite in 1697-8.[31] Still, the propaganda which associated the crisis with William, like the barrage of propaganda over Glencoe, was itself an index of a rising tide of Jacobite sentiment. The final gift to the Jacobite cause came in 1707 with the Act of Union. That greatest of eighteenth-century political jobs was essentially a short-term response to immediate problems but it had inevitable long-term results, one of which was to hand over the leadership of any assertion of Scottish national identity to the Jacobites, who alone were prepared to use force to dissolve the Union.

In the midst of all this turmoil the episcopal clergy became more rather than less influential. As the presbyterian General Assembly, working through the power of the Scots Privy Council, struck out to deprive them of their charges, they moved closer to sympathetic nobles, whilst often retaining the affections of their flocks. George Garden, minister of the valuable charge of East St Nicholas in the city of Aberdeen, was deprived in 1692 for refusing to pray for William and Mary. In 1701 he was deposed from ministerial office by the General Assembly on a charge of heresy or more precisely 'Bourignonism', a form of mystical pietism of French origin. He was typical of many in the North-East, though he was forced out earlier than some. In the rural Presbytery of Alford, for example, Andrew Livingstone the incumbent of Keig, a former chaplain to John, Earl of Kintore, and himself the father of two future episcopalian ministers, was deposed only in August 1716, as a known Jacobite. Robert Norrie, minister of the second charge of the City Kirks of Dundee (the South Church) was deprived in 1689 for disaffection to the Revolution and deposed on 26 December 1716 for open disloyalty. He was prosecuted before the central criminal court in Edinburgh, the High Court of Justiciary, on 29 July 1717 along with others of similar views on charges of intruding into parish churches, leasing-making and praying for the Chevalier (i.e. the Old Pretender). He was only saved by a general pardon under an Act of Grace, which caused the diet to be deserted. His political views were unambiguous and did not change, for in 1724 he was consecrated a non-juring (i.e. Jacobite) bishop on the nomination of the exiled 'James VIII' who, like his father before him, named Scots bishops from lists submitted by the episcopalian leaders.

Many episcopalian ministers held on to their charges with aristocratic support until they died. The deposed and deprived either continued as pastors, supported by their flocks, or they became chaplains, tutors, or even on occasion architects to Jacobite families. Robert Edwards, Minister of Murroes in the Presbytery of Dundee, for example, was a distinguished geographer patronised by the Earl of Panmure. Deprived at the Glorious Revolution, Edwards seems to have retired into the circle of the Panmure family where his commonplace book shows that he not only offered his spiritual consolations but also helped to sustain a rich musical life embracing both folk tunes and the heritage of sophisticated court music left over after 1603. Edwards was fortunate, but not all Episcopal clergy were so lucky. Without aristocratic support they could be reduced to the level of poor Mr John Bruce of Portmoak, whom Sir William Bruce unsuccessfully tried to defend, and who was by 1695 recorded as receiving charity from the kirk-session of Scoonie.[32] This was the fate which most episcopalian clergy must have dreaded in their hearts. It is hardly surprising that by 1715 they had become the spokesmen for a Jacobite and anti-Union rising in Scotland so formidable and so widely supported that but for the phenomenally inept leadership of the Earl of Mar it would, in conjunction with the Jacobite rising in the north of England, surely have spelled the end of both the Illustrious House of Hanover and the Act of Union.

Ironically enough, one reason for the immensely influential position of the predominantly Jacobite episcopal clergy in Scotland in 1715 was the considerable support they had received in recent years from the social and political establishment in England. After 1710 Queen Anne's ministry was a Tory one led by Harley (later Earl of Oxford) and St John (later Viscount Bolingbroke). Baiting Scotchmen, especially Scotch Presbyterians, seemed to be one of its hobbies, and the case of James Greenshields, an Episcopalian minister of English origin and non-Jacobite views, provided it with an opportunity to deal a heavy blow at the Presbyterian interest in North Britain. For defying the authority of the local presbytery which had forbidden him to use the English Prayer Book, Greenshields had been imprisoned by the magistrates of Edinburgh, whose actions were sustained by the Court of Session. A controversial appeal to the House of Lords in 1711 reversed his conviction and led in 1712 to legislation restoring lay patronage in the Church of Scotland and to a Toleration Act freeing from all danger of persecution Scots episcopalians willing to qualify for toleration by praying for the sovereign. Queen Anne warmly sympathised in an indiscriminate way with Scots episcopal clergymen. Their bishops were free to move around and their primate, Bishop Rose, was even pensioned.

Undoubtedly an effort was made to exploit this rather woolly-minded English sympathy. Faced with trouble in an outlying province, Westminster is usually only too ready to assume that it is all the fault of local bigots and that the discontented minority is all eagerness to embrace the privilege of Westminster rule, provided a few reasonable, timely concessions are made. At the time of the wildly controversial Peace of Utrecht in 1713, the episcopal clergy of Aberdeen presented an address of congratulation to Queen Anne. To present it, George Garden of St Nicholas was selected along with his even better-known brother James Garden, former Professor of Divinity at King's College, Old Aberdeen. Introduced by the Earl of Mar, they were received most graciously and poured into the royal ear long tales of Presbyterian persecution. Both brothers were later in the delegation which presented to the Pretender in 1716 at the Earl Marischal's house at Fetteresso, Kincardineshire an address from the episcopal clergy of Aberdeen expressing solid support and loyalty to his cause.[33] Neither of the Gardens had the outward appearance of a political firebrand. Both were extremely interested in the mystical pietism connected with Madame Bourignon and Madame Guyon, a pietism eventually denounced by both the Church of Scotland and the Church of Rome, but none the less surprisingly influential in the North-East of Scotland in episcopal circles in the late seventeenth and early eighteenth centuries.[34]

James Garden has left correspondence from which it is possible to recreate at least part of his mental world. The intriguing point which emerges is that it was a mental world very like that of the Reverend Robert Kirk of Aberfoyle and Balquidder. Through a mutual acquaintance, Sir Robert Moray, a prominent Scottish politician of the Restoration period who died before the Revolution, James Garden had established contact by letter with the noted English antiquary John Aubrey. Aubrey and Garden corresponded at first on the 'Temples of the Druids' or the great standing-stone circles of the prehistoric North-East, but the correspondence rapidly widened its scope. Garden penned a fascinating account of the bards of the seventeenth-century Highlands. He plunged, for Aubrey's benefit, into a complex and sophisticated account of the phenomenon of the second sight in Gaelic Scotland — that strange gift of foreseeing the (usually horrific) future which seems to be hereditary in certain Highland families.[35] After the failure of the '15 some thirty episcopal clergymen were evicted from their charges in Aberdeenshire on grounds of rampant Jacobitism. Their Presbyterian opponents remarked bitterly that these often gentle, scholarly, and indeed saintly, men had mostly accepted the benefits of the Toleration Act, if necessary by swearing an Oath of Abjuration of the Pretender, and had then without exception prayed for him during the rebellion.[36]

It happens that we have a record of a rebellion sermon composed by James Garden for delivery in Aberdeen. It goes far to explain why those thirty men were evicted, for it is rampant chiliastic Jacobitism, lambasting the peoples of Britain for breaching God's law of indefeasible hereditary right; holding up the disasters of famine and war as God's scourge against the unrighteous; adding a heady dash of Scottish nationalism with the assertion that the acceptance of the Act of Union was yet another act incurring the wrath of God; and crowning it all with the triumphant assertion that only the restoration of the legitimate sovereign could bring peace, prosperity, and happiness to the three distracted realms.[37]

It was strong stuff, and it made a great deal of difference to the willingness of the all-important ruling classes to hazard their lives for the exiled Stewarts. It survived the débâcle of 1716, and the even worse débâcle of the rising in 1719 which was crushed almost before it began. Many evicted episcopalian clergymen became schoolmasters or chaplains in noble households. In both capacities they were to teach the young gentlemen who officered the Jacobite army in the last desperate venture of 1745-6. Cumberland's troops burned episcopalian chapels, as British troops in the American War of Independence were to burn Presbyterian meeting houses, as nests of sedition. Of course there were more 'qualified' episcopalians by 1745, legally tolerated because willing to pray for King George, but it would be quite wrong to suggest that the bigotry of the Hanoverian soldiery was misguided. It was in fact very clear-eyed. A Scots episcopalian was, in some cases until Prince Charles died in 1788, more often than not a Jacobite at heart.

In the last analysis episcopal spirituality provided the steel in the Jacobite soul. It was only one of a number of factors which explain the risings, but it was an important component of an explosive mixture. Although, like English Non-Jurors, Scottish episcopalians had their liturgical and theological preoccupations, they seem unlike their English counterparts to have accepted until at least the battle of Culloden the primacy of politics. Their political militancy was rooted in a struggle for a sacramental view of life. On the stricken field of Culloden, with its brutal butchery, an episcopal clergyman gave the last rites to a dying Jacobite officer, using for the elements all that was available — oatmeal and whisky. Even more revealing, perhaps is an episode from the earlier days of the '45. It concerns the elderly Lord Pitsligo, an episcopalian mystic of such sanctity that his fellow Jacobites felt that Religion and Virtue had joined their cause when he rode into their camp. Pitsligo led a troop of cavalry reinforcements south from Aberdeen to join the main Jacobite army. He knew perfectly well that the rebellion was a desperate venture doomed in terms of mere earthly calculation to catastrophic failure. His words of command as he set out on what he deemed his duty form a fitting conclusion to this paper. Before his men he raised his hat, lifted his eyes, and said: 'Oh Lord, Thou knowest our cause is just. Gentlemen, march.'[38]

NOTES

1. In her essay on 'The Tories' in R. Sedgwick (ed), *The House of Commons 1715-1754* (London, H.M.S.O., 1970), pp. 62-78.

2. E. Cruickshanks, *Political Untouchables: The Tories and the '45* (London, 1979).

3. 'Relation du voyage du Sieur Fleming en Ecosse et de l'etat present de ce royaume', Archives de Guerre A1/2089, No 183. I am extremely grateful to Dr E. Cruickshanks for making a photocopy of this document available to me.

4. The best introduction to this topic is P. F. Anson, *Underground Catholicism In Scotland 1622-1878* (Montrose, 1970), pp. 92-150.

5. Sir Bruce Seton and Jean Arnot, *The Prisoners of the '45,* Vol 1, Scottish History Society, 3rd Series, Vol 13 (Edinburgh, 1928), p. 224.

6. The controversy between Mr John Prebble and Dr W. Ferguson may be pursued to its indeterminate conclusion in the pages of *The Scottish Historical Review,* Vols 46 (1967), pp. 82-87, and 185-188, and Vol 47 (1968), pp. 203-209.

7. J. Gray (ed), *Scottish Population Statistics* (Edinburgh, 1975), p. 77.

8. G. Donaldson, *Scotland: James V to James VII* (Edinburgh, 1971), p. 358.

9. Some idea of Sharp's life-style may be gathered from an incomplete account book belonging to him and covering the years 1663-1666. It is preserved in the Archives of the University of St Andrews as MS BX 5395.S4M2.

10. Archbishop Sharp to Duke of Lauderdale, Oct 22, 1660, National Library of Scotland, MS 2512, f4.

11. Archbishop Sharp to David, Earl of Wemyss, December 6, 1665, printed in Sir W. Fraser, *Memorials Of The Family of Wemyss* (Edinburgh, 1888). pp. 131-2.

12. Same to same, May 14, 1667; Jan 22, 1678; and May 3, 1678, printed in *ibid.,* pp. 134-5, 137 and 140 resp.

13. J. D. Mackie, *The University of Glasgow 1451-1951* (Glasgow, 1954), p. 121.

14. This point is well brought out by W. R. Foster in *Bishop and Presbytery* (London, S.P.C.K., 1958) and *The Church before the Covenants* (Edinburgh and London, 1975).

15. A. I. Dunlop, *William Carstares and the Kirk by Law Established* (Edinburgh, 1964).

16. *Vide* T. Maxwell, 'Presbyterian and Episcopalian in 1688', in *Records of the Scottish Church History Society*, Vol XIII, pp. 25-37.

17. *The Register of the Privy Council of Scotland*, 3rd Series, Vol XV, A.D.1690, ed. E. W. M. Balfour-Melville (Edinburgh, H.M.S.O., 1967), pp. 335-336.

18. *Ibid.*, 3rd Series, Vol XVI, A.D.1691, (Edinburgh, H.M.S.O., 1970), pp. 134-6.

19. R. G. Cant, *The University of St Andrews: A Short History* (2nd ed., Edinburgh and London, 1970), pp. 78-9.

20. The volume is preserved in St Andrews University Archives as MS 36225.

21. *Ibid.*, pp. 45-7.

22. *Ibid.*, pp. 148-9.

23. *Ibid.*, p. 119.

24. Rev. Professor D. Maclean, 'The Life and Literary Labours of the Rev. Robert Kirk, of Aberfoyle', in *Transactions of the Gaelic Society of Inverness*, Vol XXXI (1922-24), pp. 328-366.

25. The best modern edition is that by Stewart Sanderson, published for the Folklore Society in 1976.

26. St Andrews University Archives, MS 36225, pp. 108-11.

27. D. B. Smith, 'Mr Robert Kirk's Note-book', in *The Scottish Historical Review*, Vol 18, no.72, July 1921, pp. 237-48.

28. *The Secret Commonwealth* (ed.cit.), p. 67.

29. A. C. F. Beales, *Education Under Penalty* (London, 1963), p. 257.

30. For the social and economic bases of the Jacobite risings see B. Lenman, *The Jacobite Risings in Britain* (London, 1980).

31. B. Lenman, *An Economic History of Modern Scotland* (London, 1977), p. 46.

32. Biographical material on specific ministers, when otherwise unacknowledged, is drawn from *Fasti Ecclesiae Scoticanae: The Succession of Ministers in the Church of Scotland from the Reformation* by Hew Scott, New Ed, 7 vols (Edinburgh, 1915-1928). For Robert Edward's commonplace book see H. M. Shire, 'Robert Edward's Commonplace Book And Scots Literary Tradition' and K. Elliott, 'Robert Edward's Commonplace Book And Scots Musical History', in *Scottish Studies*, Vol 5, 1961, pp. 43-56.

33. There is a good account of George Garden in *The Dictionary of National Biography*, Vol. 20, pp. 409-10.

34. G. D. Henderson, *Mystics of the North East* (Aberdeen, Third Spalding Club, 1934).

35. The correspondence, which dates from 1692-1695 is reprinted in the *Miscellany of the Third Spalding Club*, Volume III (Aberdeen, Third Spalding Club, 1960) pp. 1-56, edited by C. A. Gordon.

36. 'An Apology for the Aberdeen Evictions', edited by M. K. and C. Ritchie in *ibid.*, pp. 57-96.

37. 'Reasons for appointing and Observing a day of Solemn Fasting and Humiliation, to be read from the pulpit after the end of Divine Service', National Library of Scotland, MS 1012.

38. A. and H. Tayler (eds), *Jacobite Letters To Lord Pitsligo 1745-1746* (Aberdeen, 1930), p. 2.

3

*Literature and the Jacobite Cause: was there a Rhetoric of Jacobitism?**

Howard Erskine-Hill

I

TO revive in research the faded 'Royal Rose' and 'antique drum'[1] of Jacobitism is to challenge 'the enormous condescension of posterity'.[2] That confident retrospect, which presents the cause finally lost as never more than a forlorn or foolish hope, falsifies the historical experience and distorts the context in which we must read the later Dryden and the earlier, perhaps also the later, Pope.[3] I shall try to characterise some features of the historical experience and their literary consequences.

Since the Civil War, England had taught itself renewed lessons of loyalty to the throne. Perhaps a majority of Anglican clergy, between 1660 and 1688, considered Passive Obedience 'the distinguishing Character of the Church of England':[4] a church true to 'the Doctrine of the Cross'.[5] When William of Orange invaded England with his small army, and James II, deserted by many of his family and supporters, fled to France, the chief reaction of the political public was bewilderment and alarm.[6] Few were sure how to characterise what had happened or rationalise their real hopes. The view endorsed by James, and shared by many Anglican Non-Jurors, was that William owed his new position to conquest.[7] This was the distinguishing charge of the Jacobites against the Williamites, many of whom were zealous to repudiate it.[8] It found early expression in the polemical and sensational image of rape, in both senses,[9] which was however also turned by Williamites to accuse James of Violating the laws.[10] The extreme sensitivity to this charge, and this image, may be gauged by the reaction of the House of Commons to the publication, in 1693, of Charles Blount's *King William and Queen Mary Conquerors,* which argued on behalf of these rulers that they owed their throne to conquest over James, though in the interest of the people.[11] This 'Licentious Pamphlet' was condemned to be burnt by the common hangman; and the reply which was soon published averred in tones of unctuous horror that:

* This essay is a revised and considerably extended version of a paper entitled 'Jacobitism' originally delivered for the Eighteenth-Century Panel of the Modern Languages Association of America, at its annual conference, Dec. 1977-Jan. 1978, in Chicago. In that form, but under the title: 'Literature and the Jacobite Cause', it is published in Vol. IX, No. 3 of *Modern Language Studies* (Autumn 1979), a journal unlikely to be seen by historians. Since my concern is both historical and literary, I have not felt it improper to publish an extended version of the essay in the present volume. Besides other new materials, this version included a discussion, not previously printed, of Jacobite poetry written shortly before or during the '45.

in his [William's] proudest Tryumph (pardon the Barbarity of that Epithet) he would
have taken it very disdainfully to have been saluted with the Address of the Thief to
Alexander, viz. to be Entituled that Greatest of Robbers, however otherwise glorious
Name, a Conqueror. No; thanks to Heaven, a softer and gentler Coronation Glory,
Oblation and *Gift*, not *Rapine* and *Violence*, incircled that Brow.
                    Non Rapit Imperium Vis Tua, sed Recipit.[12]

The accusation of conquest and the image of rape reverberate through the political
pamphlets and poems of the next twenty years,[13] and certainly affect the poetry of
Pope.[14]

Other theories of the Revolution were that James had abdicated, deserted, or
'fallen from the crown';[15] that he had broken 'the Original Contract' with his
people; and that he had been overthrown and William enthroned by divine
Providence. Variations of the first (Abdication) were popular, but the theory was
vulnerable to objection that there had been no deed of formal renunciation, that
armies loyal to James had resisted William in Scotland and Ireland, and that a king
cannot abdicate on behalf of his heir.[16] The second (Violation of Contract) was
relatively insignificant at the time, save in so far as 'Contract' could be identified
with the laws and constitution of the hereditary kingdom, in which case it favoured
James, not William. The historical influence of Locke's *Two Treatises* (originally
projected to support Shaftesbury against Charles II in the Exclusion Crisis) was not
great in the early post-revolutionary period.[17] The third theory (Providentialism), as
propounded in Sherlock's *Case of Allegiance Due to the Sovereign Powers* (1691), was
potentially the most attractive of all; the *furore* of attack which it provoked is
witness to its powerful lure, as well as to its vulnerability to rigorous theological
thought.[18] In this situation, the broad political centre settled for a fourth 'theory',
that of possession: the uneasy distinction between *de facto* kingship (William) and *de
jure* (James): what J. P. Kenyon calls 'the triumph of *de facto* theory'.[19] A more
consistent position was not afforded by Lockian contract theory owing to the failure
of its exponents to address themselves to historical and constitutional precedent.

Jacobites and Non-Jurors, however, could be consistent in their loyal values if
they had the courage.[20] There is something epic in the situation of those who dared
to oppose by sword or pen the growing power of the Revolution.[21] Indeed Viscount
Dundee and his Highland army were the subject of a Latin epic, *The Grameid*
(1691), by his standard-bearer James Philip,[22] and the epic strain is plainly heard in
Pitcairne's elegy on the death of Dundee at Killiecrankie, and in Dryden's
translation.[23] In the learned, involved, but vigorous pamphlet writing of the
Jacobites and Non-Jurors the vein of courageous protest sometimes becomes overt.
Thus Jeremy Collier can charge Williamite legislation with resolving 'all Title into
Force and Success' and making 'the Devil, if he should prevail, the Lord's
Anointed'.[24] George Hickes, in a passage which Dryden certainly remembered when
he wrote his *Character of a Good Parson*, praised the Bishop of Carlisle's
denunciation of Henry IV's usurpation of the throne of Richard II:

. . . we must live *according to Laws* . . . *we have neither Power nor Policy either to depose King* Richard, *or to Elect Duke* Henry . . . King *Richard* still remaineth our Sovereign Prince . . . Thus, Sir, spoke that Heroick Prelate in the Court of Parliament . . . For *he chose not the safer but the juster side,* as all good Men ought to do.[25]

Hickes is equally eloquent against Sherlockian and *de facto* turncoats who, 'like to Summer Flies', 'make a great shew and buz for [their] King in fair Weather' but 'in the long Night-time, or Winter of Adversity . . . will say, *If he cannot defend himself, let him go . . .*'[26] The 'Whiggish' Jacobite Charlwood Lawton, in a pamphlet which I think it likely that Pope echoes in *Windsor Forest,* could contrast 'the *GLORIOUS TITLE* of *SUCCESSION*' with the 'mean, hated and precarious one of Conquest' and beg James to '*Come Home, Great Sir*' to 'preserve our Church, settle Liberty of *Conscience* in a *duly Elected* PARLIAMENT, and to Establish all the Liberties of the *English* Subject'.[27] For the publication of this and another pamphlet, William Anderton was executed for high treason in 1693.[28]

It will be noted that these extracts lay great stress on legality. This is the characteristic emphasis of almost all the Jacobite pamphlets I have read in this period. They stressed law and constitution because it was here they had the strongest case.[29] At its simplest, their argument was that the hereditary monarchy was established in the constitution. If James had legal right to the throne in 1685, he had it still. To deny this was to bring in notions of contract in the sense of conditional kingship, elective kingship, even the 'People's Right', ideas which, to the broad centre of the political nation, were not less alarming than that of the return of James and the Prince of Wales.[30] The Jacobites, unlike Locke, addressed themselves to those legal, historical and biblical precedents which were the touchstones of political validity in that age: Joash and Athaliah,[31] Alexander, Darius and Jaddus,[32] Edward II and Edward III,[33] Richard II and Henry IV,[34] Henry VII,[35] and of course Charles I and Cromwell.[36] These instances, Jacobites and Non-Jurors considered, proved the religious and political right of hereditary kings. If a divine and patriarchal origin for such monarchies was usually assumed, at least one Non-Juror, Collier, extended his notion of 'right' to different kinds of constitution.[37] But the British kingdoms, as Lawton asserted, were 'our Ancient, Legal, Limited, and Hereditary Monarchy'.[38]

It is, I suggest, the defining characteristic of Jacobite writing that it inherited the full authority of what had been only recently most central and orthodox doctrine, but, with the sudden revolution of power, could not express such doctrine with the old openness. Lawton and Anderton risked their lives by their explicitness; it was more common, particularly among the Non-Jurors, to be implicit. The relentless and common-sense logic of John Kettlewell's defence of legal right against Sherlock not only refuted the providential theory, but radically undermined the *de facto* position; yet since Sherlock never disputed James's *de jure* status, Kettlewell had no need to argue the point. He was saved from charges of treason by his austere academic precision.[39] In discussing the usurpation of Queen Athaliah, or King Henry IV, or whether the High Priest Jaddus in Josephus paid homage to Alexander before or after Darius's death, a cautious cryptic code might seem to have been evolved by the Non-Jurors for the discussion of William, James and the Church of England. This is, and is not, the case. These instances are not just disguises, but real and telling historical instances by which, far more than by hypothetical notions of 'Original Contract', political validity might be established in orthodox terms. Both in political outlook and literary idiom there is a world of difference between, for example, this assertion from a Whig pamphlet: 'That the late King *James* was induc'd by the *Emmisaries* of *Rome*, to trample upon the laws and Liberties of the Subjects of these Three Kingdoms, there is nobody who enjoys the use of their Reason, can deny'[40] and the argument of the relatively outspoken Hickes that Richard II's resignation, because exacted by force, had no validity.[41]

It is this literary idiom, apparently cryptic, yet openly evidence-bearing in historical context, which was deployed by the avowedly Jacobite Dryden[42] in his post-revolutionary phase, and inherited by Pope who, it may be thought, after intimate knowledge of the feeling of the Jacobite situation moves slowly away from any simple Jacobite position.

Scott, and in our time Alan Roper and William Myers, have taught us to notice the strong Jacobite implication of Dryden's late verse.[43] The deposed Edward and the 'Greater *Edward*' in *To Congreve*, pointing up the Jacobitism in the whole poem's exploration of writing and rule; *To Granville* with its references to 'Young Princes', 'Old Monarchs' and 'some Foreign Monster in a Bill'; the *Good Parson* in *The Fables*, with its clear endorsement of Non-Juror principle — all these are cast in the idiom I have described.[44] So is the satirical celebration of the conqueror in *Alexander's Feast*, which reflects, in the year of the Treaty of Ryswick, on the conquests of William.[45] Non-Juror pamphlets support this view: numerous references to the equivocal legal status of Alexander on his conquest of Darius point directly at William,[46] while Williamites made the comparison in straightforward praise. As the Jacobite Anderton put it, having criticised Alexander for ill care of his troops: 'since our Boobies will be thought to have made a wise Choice of their King, as they call him, and he must be a great Champion, let him be drest up with all the Imperfections of *Alexander*, with whom they are pleased so often to compare him.'[47] Dryden's *To the Dutchess of Ormond* has been recognised as a ceremonious reiteration of the poet's most loyal poetic gestures from *Astraea Redux* on; the Duke and Duchess ('O true *Plantagenet*') are bearers of legitimacy, and deputise for royalty in more than one sense.[48] Less often noted is the intimate connection with Dryden's elaborate letter to the Duke (*not* the Dedication to the Duke), with which it shares several leading *motifs*. This letter also avows the poet's Jacobitism, criticises William for enriching Holland with English wealth, refers to the usurpation of King John and reflects upon the political infidelity of England.[49] There is remarkable poetic independence in the way Dryden can seem to celebrate restoration without the prince; the two letters together leave us in no doubt of his identity.

The Doctrine of Passive Obedience, it has been argued, enabled Dryden to live contentedly enough under William's *de facto* monarchy, the extent of his resistance being his scruple to take the oaths.[50] While this describes the position of many Non-Jurors,[51] such an interpretation of the doctrine is not endorsed by its most rigorous exponent (Kettlewell),[52] and in the *Good Parson* Dryden is contemptuous of arguments which justify 'the next who comes in play', whatever his title.[53] The Dryden letters show that he undertook not to write against the new government, though he hoped for a Restoration.[54] However, *The Lady's Song* (written c. 1691, published 1704) is a deft and dancing incitement to arms,[55] and the published work, while refraining from direct attack, reiterates its radical opposition.

II

The position of the young Pope is harder to determine, but clearly his earlier poems are more political than used to be thought. Probably his first published verses, David Nokes has shown, are a scathing lampoon on the 'Dutch Prince' who conquered neither in love nor war.[56] Between 1705, when this was published, and the appearance of *Windsor Forest* which takes up the charge of conquest, occurred the Sacheverell Trial, which brought back all the terms of the post-revolutionary debate (and even a reference to Blount's pamphlet) to the very forefront of public news.[57] Whether written before or after the Trial, the passage of *Windsor Forest* which pursues the cryptic parallel of William III and William I as conquerors, associated with warfare, waste and rapine, would have had powerful topical interest.[58] We should note that the theme of rape, first used in this passage of the poem in relation to the countryside, is extended in the Ovidian myth of Lodona: escaping by metamorphosis from her would-be ravisher, she joins her purity to the Thames, the great river of English landscape, and English history, who proclaims, at the poem's end, not conquest, but a Golden Age of freedom and peace.[59] A further poem, *The First Book of Statius His Thebais,* may go back to roughly the same period as the lampoon against William and the origins of *Windsor Forest* and was published with the first version of *The Rape of the Lock*.[60] John M. Aden is certainly right to see in Pope's handling of Statius an exploration of Britain's situation, torn between rival royal claimants, one in possession, one poised in exile to take up his own right.[61] Yet this poem, though reflecting severely on William under the character of Etheocles, lacks Dryden's concern with legitimacy; it seems more concerned with exploring experience than asserting a right.[62]

This new flexibility in handling Jacobite issues is found in *The Rape of the Lock,* whose political dimension becomes apparent against the background of controversy over the Revolution,[63] the Sacheverell Trial,[64] and the tradition of *Poems on Affairs of State*.[65] (We may note the repudiation of the charge of political rape in the triumphal entry of William into The Hague after his Irish Campaigns;[66] and the poem of 1704, known to Pope, which exclaimed to Queen Anne: 'Why Madam, You're Ravisht, Your Queenshipp's Invaded'.[67]) In title and action *The Rape of the Lock* moves the charge of conquest and image of rape over into the realm of social discord, while still keeping real affairs of state in mind.[68] Thus the action culminates in a royal palace, Anne herself distantly presides, and the sylphs 'guard with Arms Divine the *British Throne*'.[69] Hence, after the rape, the political as well as epic tribute to 'The *conqu'ring Force* of *unresisted* Steel' (my italics).[70] The poem narrates the fate of both 'Foreign Tyrants' and 'Nymphs at home'.[71]

That Belinda's lock is pre-eminently a lock of shining hair; that it suggests honour, chastity and beauty, which Time, and Fate 'with th'abhorrèd shears'[72] will ravish away, I would never deny. That the poem is also, by allusion, an heroi-comical reworking of 1688, I am tempted to think. I have space for three more points on this subject. First, card-games, including Ombre, were an understood form of witty comment on international affairs.[73] Pope places his game just before the rape to put affairs of state into our minds at this moment, and to hint at political meanings relevant to 1688. Pope's game can, I believe, be politically interpreted, but it does not allegorise a particular historical sequence.[74] Secondly, while conquest is neither averted nor maintained in the poem, and the lock becomes a star, Pope must have felt uneasy at the implications, after George I, not James III, succeeded Anne. Hence, I suggest, he used *The Key to the Lock* (May 1715) to ridicule by exaggeration the idea of political meaning.[75] The relation of the pamphlet with the poem was remarked on in the Duke of Wharton's *True Briton*, No. 65 (13 Jan. 1723/24), in an essay ostensibly designed to ridicule the quest for political innuendo.[76] With typical *finesse* it instructed in the art of innuendo, and protested its innocence of the art, at one and the same time. It is a nice point as to whether this paper does not convict Pope's poem of the same art. Thirdly, in 1717, after the Jacobite Rising had failed, Pope added his imitation of the Episode of Sarpedon, thus making the poem something of a plea for submission to force, and aptly gave the speech to the lady (Clarissa) who proffered steel to the Baron in Canto III. As James Philip's *Grameid* shows, classical epic offered something to the poetic exploration of Jacobitism. Who knows what contemporary resonances the Episode of Sarpedon had for Jacobites, reminding perhaps of Dundee; Sarsfield; Derwentwater in the '15? Pope now adroitly turned an episode dramatising the heroism of (not necessarily Jacobite) resistance into an epic moral commending the heroism of submission.

III

If, in the foregoing discussion, there is a single answer to my subtitle: 'Was there a rhetoric of Jacobitism?' it is that there was; that it was shared (though with different emphasis) by the overlapping groups of Non-Jurors and Jacobites; and that it deployed the vocabulary and examples of legitimacy, and the powerfully opposing image of rape. That these arguments and images were to some extent also to be found in Whig polemic is hardly surprising. Rhetoric can persuade only in so far as it can appeal to something in common between persuader and those whom it would persuade. Early Jacobite rhetoric is not indistinguishable from that of its opponents — it does not, for example, resort to Sherlockian Providentialism, any more than later Jacobite rhetoric plays, as Whig rhetoric does, on the fear of Popery and Arbitrary Power.[77] Given the danger of prosecution for treason, however, the distinguishing features are not often the most conspicuous.

No. 74 of *The True Briton* (17 Feb. 1723/24) distinguishes between a sudden loss of liberty, as when the elective kingdom of Denmark became hereditary, and that gradual process by which liberty might be lost through a slow decline into corruption.[78] It is perhaps natural that, as time went on, Jacobite writing should have shifted its focus from what had happened in 1688 to what had happened since, and especially since the death of Anne. Jacobites naturally found themselves thinking about a process, rather than a few striking events. The crucial issue became (what *they* saw as) prolonged misgovernment. Seeking to extend its characteristic legal foundation toward common ground with some of its opponents, Jacobite journalism (as a young Cambridge scholar, Mr. Paul Chapman, has shown) seized on the idea of contract as a stick with which to beat the Hanoverian abuse of power.[79] *The True Briton* can speak of the abdication of James II without comment, and makes no special attack on William and Mary.[80] On the other hand, the charge of corruption, degeneracy, imminent slavery, is to be found in the pages of this journal, as it is in Lansdowne's significant *Letter from a Noble-Man Abroad . . .*, published in 1722 to encourage Tory efforts in the forthcoming election, and also, no doubt, to incite to an armed uprising.

To the reader of Pope, the opening of this inflammatory tract by the poet's friend and dedicatee of *Windsor Forest* comes with a shock of recognition:

> At this critical Conjuncture when the Rumour of a new Parliament sounds like the last Trumpet, to awaken the Genius of Old *England*, and raise departed Liberty to Life, it would be a Crime to be silent.[81]

Pope, denouncing the triumph of Vice sixteen years later, wrote:

> Lo! at the Wheels of her Triumphal Car,
> Old *England's* Genius, rough with many a Scar,
> Dragg'd in the Dust!

Pope, like Lansdowne, speaks of a bribed senate and the ennoblement of vice, and each adopts the stance of a Cato, or is it a Brutus?

> . . . wearied out with vainly wishing for better Times, I am yet ready to enter the Lists . . . to stand for Liberty and Old *England*, or fall an honourable Victim to God, my Country, and my Friends. (Lansdowne)[82]

> Yes, the last Pen for Freedom let me draw,
> When Truth stands trembling on the edge of Law:
> Here, Last of *Britons!* let your Names be read;
> Are none, none living? let me praise the Dead,
> And for that Cause which made your Fathers shine,
> Fall, by the Votes of their degen'rate Line! (Pope)[83]

I would not insist on direct influence, though that seems not improbable. The charge of corruption, and the urge to resist it or be lost, are of course characteristic of *The Craftsman* and Bolingbroke's campaign against Walpole, the strong influence of which upon Pope's political poetry of the 1730s it is now a commonplace to remark. More significant is the large overlap between

Lansdowne's *Letter, The True Briton,* and Jacobite journalism generally, on the one hand, and Bolingbroke's *Craftsman* on the other. Little of the more powerful rhetoric of *The Craftsman,* I suggest, cannot be found in fairly well-developed form in the pages of Lansdowne's *Letter* and of *The True Briton.*[84] And if we ask whether this charge of a pervasive corruption must not have been effective in persuading at least some crucial figures to take up arms for a new Restoration, we may find an answer in the letter Lord George Murray wrote to his son, on 9 Sept. 1745, in justifying his decision to join Prince Charles. Its remarks on corruption might have come *verbatim* from *The Craftsman,* and the whole letter from the Whiggish Jacobite journalism of the 1720s and 1730s.[85]

This raises a further question. It has always been accepted that Bolingbroke's campaign was a distinctively non-Jacobite Toryism. *The Letter to Sir William Wyndham* (1717), written before Bolingbroke's return from France but after he left the Pretender's service, repudiated Jacobitism in the clearest manner. No doubt this was in the first place quite genuine. But, largely owing to Eveline Cruickshanks's recent book, *Political Untouchables: The Tories and the '45* we now know of the Jacobite initiatives of Strafford, Bathurst, Gower and Cornbury in 1731,[86] following which Bolinbroke and Wyndham again dallied with the idea of a Stuart Restoration.[87] True, Bolingbroke's desire was to 'get hold of' the two princes and bring them up Protestant, but, as we now also know, much Jacobite journalism found no conflict between a contractual theory of government and resort to the hereditary line.[88] I would hypothesise (if only, perhaps, for the value of prompting a convincing refutation) that Bolingbroke's rhetoric depicting a prevailing social and political corruption and the need for a Patriot King was not only an appeal to a large political public including committed Jacobites, but also a weapon nicely judged to turn in either direction. If George II or Prince Frederick could indeed prove the patriot prince needed to save 'the Monarchy of Tories',[89] well and good. If a patriot prince appeared more likely to come from over the water, Bolingbroke's portrait (written in 1738 but printed only covertly by Pope) would serve very well. In that case gestures towards a patriot prince might in the meantime, though with a ludicrousness that only the idealising mode of panegyric could entirely overcome, be directed (for safety) at Prince Frederick.

This suggestion raises once again the vexed question of overt and covert intention and the character of the literary innuendo which mediates between the two. I shall give just one example. It may or may not be representative, but is telling because it concerns the only poet I know of who was executed for joining Prince Charles in England. His death is indeed his peculiar interest, as I shall show. A barrister from a good family in Monmouthsire, David Morgan was adviser to the third and fourth Dukes of Beaufort. His poem *The Country Bard* came out in two parts, the first, in 1739, dedicated to Sir John Morgan of Kinnersley, M.P., the second in 1741 to Sir Watkin Williams Wynne, M.P., the influential Welsh Jacobite. Each Part is 'Inscribed to . . . The Prince of Wales'.[90] The poem is generally modelled on Pope's *Epilogue to the Satires,* from which I have already quoted, and indeed both Bolingbroke and 'Seraphic POPE' are praised in the second Part.[91] It assails Walpole under the title of 'Marrall'[92] and, like Pope, plunges into a series of allusions to living political figures. It takes over from Pope's poem, and much extends, the idea of the pregnant footnote. It calls the reader to action to resist corruption and slavery, and one may think that the conclusion to the first Part, in which Morgan hails the outbreak of war with Spain, has a peculiar intensity. If one came on this poem in a collection of attacks on Walpole, one would probably classify it as standard Tory polemic. Only if one looks closely at the elaborate classical footnotes does the Jacobite innuendo appear. In the light of one or two of these,[93] and of Morgan's subsequent career, it seems probable that the Prince of Wales whom he actually addresses in Part I is Charles Edward, and that the martial spirit which he seeks to arouse is not only directed against Spain. Morgan wrote one other poem that we can identify, *The Christian Test. Or, The Coalition of Faith and Reason. A Sacred Poem* (1742), dedicated to Lord Noel Somerset, another committed Jacobite.[94] It shows in some detail that the poet was, as he declared in his dying statements, a firm Anglican.[95]

Morgan joined Prince Charles at Preston, accompanied him to Derby, was admitted into his confidence, urged a Jacobite march on London, but left the army on its retreat and was subsequently arrested. At his trial he tried to protest his innocence, then hoped for mercy, but, three days before he was hanged, after he had given up hope, he wrote a letter of striking personal candour, subsequently published as a broadside. Here he confesses that he had never 'been engag'd in that rash Undertaking, had my personal Affairs been more to my Liking'. Nevertheless he owns that 'my Notions of Government have ever led me to believe that the S[tuar]t's Family [was] unjustly deprived of the Crown of *Great-Britain*. I was never ashamed to assert the Doctrine of hereditary indefeasible Right, when ever I saw Occasion, and if ever I declin'd to avow my Principles, it was purely out of self-preservation, and a prudent regard to my own Interest and Comfort in Life'. He regrets his rashness, he says, but is not ashamed at what he has done.[96] The printed statement which he threw to the crowd a few minutes before he was hanged on Kennington Common is much more defiant. It is as good an example as one could find of free Jacobite propaganda, and while one hand may possibly have been engaged in the statements of many of those who suffered on Kennington Common, it also contains detail personal to himself, including an allusion to his poem *The Christian Test.*[97] This statement, I suggest, tells us what Morgan really believed when not restrained from free expression by the instinct for self-preservation. His approaching death and earlier confession of his worldly disappointment only make it the more authentic. He asserts his loyalty to King James III whose title to the throne is constitutional and parliamentary, and derives the subversion of British liberties from the Revolution. He sees Britain's true interests now betrayed in favour of those of Hanover. He repudiates the fear of Popery, subscribes to a notion of the patriot king similar to Bolingbroke's, praises the sagacity of James III, and the courage, fortitude and mercy of Prince Charles. 'I glory,' he says, 'in the honour I have had of seeing his royal highness, Charles, Prince Regent, and of being admitted into his confidence . . . His character exceeds anything I could have imagined or conceived.'[98]

Other examples of what I have called 'free Jacobitism' are to be found in the poems written to celebrate the victory at Gladsmuir (Prestonpans). In them we may pick up two themes conspicuous in the Opposition propaganda of the 1720s and 1730s. One, that of pervasive degeneracy, may, I would hypothesise, not be concerned solely with moral and political probity. May not such accusations, or confessions, betoken a situation in which it was widely recognised that most English and many Scots would not rise for a new Restoration without the support of foreign troops, just as the Hanoverians could hardly maintain themselves without the backing of foreign troops and a standing army?[99] The second theme, that of a stubborn and resentful nationalism, may be represented by that phrase 'Old *England*', which appears again and again in Jacobite and Tory polemic, and is (as one would expect) also to be found in Whig attacks on the Jacobites in 1745-6.[100] These two *motifs* may, I suggest, help to explain why the Tories changed from a Peace Party to something like a War Party in the 1730s, why so much Tory polemic celebrated the victories of Edward I and III and Elizabeth. Scottish nationalism was also present, from James Philip's *Grameid*, through the praise of Wallace and Bruce in *Fog's Weekly Journal*, 9 July 1737, to the poem *To His Royal Highness, Charles, Prince of Wales* (1745?), which praises Cameron of Lochiel for remaining 'unsullied' in a 'corrupt Age':

> Thou wast the first that lent thy friendly Aid,
> Of no *Usurper*'s bloody Laws afraid;
> Thou wast the first, and thy Example drew
> The honest, loyal, honourable Few,

and thus apostrophises the Highland army:

> See the bold CHIEFS their hardy Warriors lead,
> Eager in such a Cause, with such a Head,
> GLENGARRY, KEPOCH, APPIN, only weep,
> These thirty Years the Cause has been asleep;
> Nor good Glenbucket, Loyal thro' thy Life,
> Wast thou untimely in the Glorious Strife?
> Thy CHIEF degen'rate, Thou his Terror stood,
> To vindicate the Loyal GORDON's Blood,
> The Loyal Gordons own the gen'rous Call,
> With CHARLES and Thee resolv'd to live or fall.
>
> See how Hereditary Right prevails
> And see *Astraea* poise the Wayward Scales![101]

Unskilful as the heroic couplets of this anonymous poet are, to read the poem is to feel that Pope's *Epilogue to the Satires* has been granted the vision for which it despaired, in the sense that these heroic couplets can celebrate heroes as well as lament corruption.

In a different literary form, one which looks back to the poem on Atterbury in Wharton's *True Briton*[102] and forward to the odes of Gray, is William Hamilton of Bangour's *Ode on the Battle of Gladsmuir* (1745); but it has the same theme:

Loud as the trumpet rolls its sound,
  Her voice the power celestial rais'd;
Whilst her victorious sons around
  In silent joy and wonder gaz'd:
The sacred Muses heard the immortal lay,
And thus to earth the notes of Fame convey:—

"'Tis done! my sons! 'tis nobly done!
  Victorious over tyrant pow'r;
How quick the race of fame was run!
  The work of ages in one hour:
Slow creeps th'oppressive weight of slavish reigns;
One glorious moment rose and burst your chains.[103]

Thus 'Scotia, imperial goddess' hails the Jacobite victory. The same stance is adopted in some of the tracts issued with the Jacobite proclamations. *An Address to the People of England* (nd. ?1745) repeats the charge that under the 'Family of Hanover alone' corruption has been systematised and extended to all ranks of people, and declares, quoting from Pope's *Epilogue to the Satires,* that 'It could never be said justly, till of late Years, that *not to be corrupted is the Shame*'.[104]

No doubt it is as hard to distinguish Jacobite from Tory rhetoric as it is to tell a Jacobite from a Tory. All its most potent rhetorical gestures are shared, as are its positive values: its nationalism, its ideal of monarchy, its cult of moral integrity and independence. The example of David Morgan shows what may underly the expression of a prudent if indignant opposition to Walpole, but not until we come upon the inevitably rare examples of 'free Jacobite' writing can we distinguish it in any other way than by a scrutiny of the small print. The slippery art of innuendo is as unavoidable a problem for the modern scholar as it was, for its authors, a vital means of expression.

IV

The '45 did not put an end to Jacobite journalism. The five volumes of *The True Briton* (1751-3) are if anything more evidently Jacobite than the journals of the 1720s and 1730s.[105] A rarely explored body of poetry, couched in the polite English idiom, explores the experience of defeat after the '45.[106] The finest literary expression of Jacobitism is no doubt in the Gaelic,[107] but if there is an epic moment in eighteenth-century British history it is surely the hopeless charge of Charles Edward's exhausted and starving Highland army into the Hanoverian artillery at Culloden. There, in that century of neo-classical epic, was the real thing.

The best-known literary response to the event is popular and lyrical: neither Gaelic, nor polite English, but the language of Robert Burns —

Their waefu' fate what need I tell,
  Right to the wrang did yield;
My Donald and his Country fell
  Upon Culloden field.[108]

— touching an epic vein only in so far as the ballad sometimes carried the note. As Jacobitism ceased to be very serious politics, it attracted men like Burns, in whose 'abundantly motley' principles we may see the tentative flexibility of Pope's Statius carried to an extreme. Burns was receptive to (in his words) 'the Cause of Heroic Loyalty'[109] and to the pathos of defeat. In his Jacobite songs the theme of 'right', so prominent in the writings of the 1690s, is still stressed but has perhaps become sentimental. I do not find it less moving for that:

> It was a' for our rightfu' king
>   We left fair Scotland's strand;
> It was a' for our rightfu' king,
>   We e'er saw Irish land, my dear,
>   We e'er saw Irish land.
>
> Now a' is done that men can do,
>   And a' is done in vain:
> My Love and Native Land fareweel,
>   For I maun cross the main, my dear,
>   For I maun cross the main.
>
> He turn'd him right and round about,
>   Upon the Irish shore,
> And gae his bridle-reins a shake,
>   With, Adieu for evermore, my dear,
>   And adieu for evermore.

I do not want, however, to end this paper on a merely cathartic note[110]. The history of Jacobitism has a more active significance for us: one which concerns a critical or uncritical acceptance of the powers that be, or the powers that were, well conveyed in lines from a late poem of W. B. Yeats:

> Those banners come to bribe or threaten,
> Or whisper that a man's a fool
> Who, when his own right king's forgotten,
> Cares what king sets up his rule.[111]

What the history of Jacobitism peculiarly teaches us is the value of judging the *status quo* rigorously by its own proclaimed standards.[112]

NOTES

(The place of publication is London except where stated to the contrary)
   1. T. S. Eliot, *Four Quartets* (1944), The Dry Salvages, iii; Little Gidding, iii.
   2. E. P. Thompson, *The Making of the English Working Class* (1963) rev. edn. (1968), p. 13.

3. In writing of Jacobitism, I wish to acknowledge substantial debts to Dr. Eveline Cruickshanks of the History of Parliament Trust, and Dr. Mark Goldie of Gonville and Caius College, Cambridge, though neither bears responsibility for the views advanced in this essay. Scholars of eighteenth-century literature will wish to consult Dr. Cruickshanks's recent book, *Political Untouchables: The Tories and the '45* (1979). I wish to add a general acknowledgement to J. P. Kenyon, *Revolution Principles: The Politics of Party, 1689-1720* (Cambridge, 1977), which I take to be essential reading for all working on Dryden, Swift, Pope and Defoe.

4. Some of the last words of John Lake, Bishop of Chichester (1624-89), reported in Robert Jenkin, *A Defence of the Profession which . . . the Late Lord Bishop of Chichester Made . . .* (1690), p. 11.

5. John Kettlewell, *Christianity, A Doctrine of the Cross . . .* (1691; owned 1695). He here states Passive Obedience to be 'an unquestionable Gospel Truth, and primitive Doctrine' requiring '*Faith* and *Patience*' (To the Reader).

6. Kenyon, op. cit., Preface and Chs. 1-3.

7. Ibid., pp. 5, 38. Both Williamites and Jacobites wrote of William as a new conqueror, eg. *A Late Voyage to Holland . . .* (1691), *Harleian Miscellany* (1744 edn.),ii, 571-2; Nathaniel Johnston, *The Dear Bargain* (1690), p. 23; [Charlwood Lawton?], *The Vindication of the Dead* (1691), p. 7; Charlwood Lawton, *A French Conquest neither Desirable Nor Practicable . . .* (1693), p. 16. On each side the polemical usage was buttressed by the serious doctrine of rightful or wrongful conquest.

8. For Williamite use of conquest theory, see Mark Goldie, 'Edmund Bohun and *Jus Gentium* in the Revolution Debate, 1689-93', *Historical Journal*, xx, no. 3 (1977), 569-86; and Kenyon, op. cit. pp. 30-34. For Williamite repudiation of conquest theory as applied to 1688, see the anonymous pamphlet, *Political Remarks on the Life and Reign of King William III (Harleian Miscellany*, ed. cit., iii, 345).

9. Eg. 'Yet the ravishers' honesty she unjustly accused; She's made a mere whore, by a vote of our state/'Cause she freely her maidenhead did abdicate', a poem alluded to in G. de F. Lord, general ed., *Poems on Affairs of State*, v, ed. W. J. Cameron (1971), 59, and (in a slightly different version) Kenyon, op. cit. p. 38; also: 'If a silly Dutch Boor for a rape on a Girle/Was hanged by ye Laws approbation/Then What does he Merityt Buggers an Earl/And ravish's ye whole nation' (British Library, Sloane MSS. 2717, f. 98r., quoted in *Poems on Affairs of State*, v, 153-4, with 'silly' misquoted as 'wily'. The image of rape is the polemical extreme of the presentation of William as a warrior king associated with 'Insults, Ravages and Plunderings', as in, eg. [William Anderton], *Remarks upon the Present Confederacy . . .* (1693), p. 12, and throughout. See too Lawton, *A French Conquest . . .*: 'We lament the *Taxes*, the *Imprisonments*, the *Plunderings*, and the Pillaging of *England;* the *Torturing* against Law, and the Glenco-Massacre in *Scotland*, together with all the other Miseries that infest this *Island*: We would not bring more upon it; we would not depopulate it; we would not make it a *Golgotha* . . .', p. 1.

10. Eg. John Tutchin, *An Heroick Poem Upon the Late Expedition of His Majesty, To Rescue England from Popery, Tyranny and Arbitrary Government* (1689), where James is the ravisher and Britain a 'yielding Maid' tricked into a rape (p. 9). A related Williamite use of this *motif* is found in the triumphal entry into The Hague devised for William after victory over James in Ireland: 'On each side of the Arch are two Pictures, one representing *Europe* Distressed, and the other, *Neptune* Ravishing, with this Motto: *Eripe raptori miseram;* Snatch the Wretched from the Ravisher. The other, *Mea jura tuere*, Defend my Right' (*A Description . . . of the Arches erected at The Hague, for the Reception of* William the Third, *King of* Great-Britain (1691), *Harleian Miscellany*, ed. cit. v, 368-9. For further use of the

motif in a political context, see Nicholas Brady's play, *The Rape: Or, The Innocent Imposters* (1692), especially p. 5. The drama is full of references to Britain in the 1680s and 1690s.

11. Goldie, art. cit., pp. 573-4.

12. *An Account of Mr. Blunts late Book, Entitled, King William and Queen Mary, Conquerors, Ordered by the House of Commons to be Burnt by the hand of the common Hangman . . .*, The Second Edition (1693), B.L. pressmark: 8122.e.9; pp. 5-6. The writer goes on to repudiate the very words which seem so often to have been repeated, and denies that William is '*Third William, the Second Conqueror*' (p. 7). This pamphlet exchange may possibly be the origin of the repartee attributed by Coleridge to Swift: 'Yet Swift was rare. Can anything beat his remark on King William's motto, *Recepit, non rapuit,* "That the receiver was as bad as the thief"?' (*The Table Talk and Omniana of Samuel Taylor Coleridge* (Oxford, 1917), p. 116). The author of *King William and Queen Mary Conquerors* was the heterodox religious writer. His further views on the rival claims of James and William had been nicely set forth in his poem, *A Dialogue Between King William and the Late King James* (1690), reprinted in *Poems on Affairs of State,* vi, 235-7.

13. See especially the controversies arising from the Sacheverell Trial as described in Kenyon, op. cit., Ch. 8, and in Geoffrey Holmes, *The Trial of Dr. Sacheverell* (1973). For a late example of the image of rape used in political commentary, see *An Address to Our Sovereign Lady* (1704), *Poems on Affairs of State,* vi. 619-21.

14. See *Windsor Forest,* 11. 43-92, and 1. 91n., in John Butt, general ed., *The Twickenham Edition of the Poems of Alexander Pope,* i (ed. Emile Audra and Aubrey Williams, 1961), 159. I argue for a further influence on Pope later in this essay.

15. Kenyon, op. cit., pp. 9-10.

16. Ibid., pp. 21, 43. On the position of the heir of an abdicated king, see Sir James Montgomery, *Great Britain's Just Complaint . . .* (1692), p. 22; Dryden was to make the same point in 'The Character of a Good Parson', 11. 113-4, in the *Fables:* 'A King can give no more than is his own:/The title stood entail'd . . .' (James Kinsley, ed., *The Poems of John Dryden* (Oxford, 1958), iv, 1739. Of course the chief stress of Non-Jurors and Jacobites was that James had been 'forced away', as Montgomery put it (op. cit., p. 6). This phrase describes what happened in 1688 better than the word 'conquest', and since James in person attempted to assert his right by force of arms in Ireland soon after, the political significance was the same. All this amounted to a strong Jacobite argument that James had not abdicated but been deposed by force, and that the young Prince of Wales had been equally forcibly deprived of his right.

17. On the original composition of Locke's *Two Treatises of Government* (1690), see Peter Laslett's edition (1959), Introduction, Section iii (rev. edn. 1963; paperback reprint 1965), pp. 58-79. The reason for the relative insignificance of Locke's famous work in the controversies of the late seventeenth and early eighteenth century is no doubt the unhistorical nature of its discussion. As Laslett says (p. 91), 'Nothing in this book could be disproved by new evidence about what had happened . . .'. It was an ideological affirmation of the idea of contract, but failed to show that contract was recognised in the laws of England. See J. G. A. Pocock, *The Ancient Constitution and the Feudal Law* (Cambridge, 1957), pp. 229-31; Kenyon, op. cit., pp. 12, 17-20; Gerald Straka, 'The Final Phase of Divine Right Theory in England, 1688-1702', *English Historical Review,* lxxvii (1962), p. 639; and G. L. Cherry, 'The Legal and Philosophical Position of the Jacobites, 1688-89', *Journal of Modern History,* xxii (Dec. 1950), p. 315, each of whom lays a slightly different emphasis on the treatment of contract theory.

18. Straka is doubtless right to consider Sherlock's providentialism as a phase of 'Divine Right Theory' in a loose sense of this term. But what is striking about Sherlock's case is the

way it ignores legality; divine right and law had not previously been so much at odds. See Jeremy Collier, *Dr. Sherlock's Case of Allegiance Consider'd* (1691), p. 2. It is to Non-Jurors such as Collier, and above all John Kettlewell, that the honour of demolishing Sherlock's position must be accorded, though from his different standpoint Locke was almost equally hostile. A plain summary of Kettlewell's case is found on p. 5 of his *Duty of Allegiance Settled upon its True Grounds* ... (1691). For recent comment on the Sherlock controversy, see Kenyon, op. cit., pp. 24-9.

19. Kenyon, op. cit., pp. 32-4.

20. Cherry, art. cit., p. 321, notes: 'Clarendon stated that it was the general belief among fair-minded men that the Jacobites had the most logical arguments' in the Convention debates. Pocock's remark (op. cit., pp. 54-5) is relevant: 'The case for the crown was not that the king ruled as a sovereign and that there was no fundamental law, but that there was a fundamental law and that the king's prerogative formed part of it.'

21. Cf. the lines, 63-70, which the author of 'Tom May's Death' (probably Andrew Marvell) put into the mouth of the shade of Ben Jonson, passing judgment on the Civil War, *The Complete Poems of Andrew Marvell,* ed. E. S. Donno (Harmondsworth, 1972), pp. 59-60.

22. James Philip of Almerieclose was standard-bearer to Dundee in his 1689 campaign. His epic, *The Grameid, An Heroic Poem Descriptive of the Campaign of Dundee in 1689,* was published by the Scottish History Society, 1887-8.

23. Archibald Pitcairne (1652-1713), *Epitaphium in Vice-Comitem Dundee, English'd by Mr. Dryden.* Dryden may have done his version soon after Dundee's death in July 1689, but it was not published in the poet's lifetime for obvious reasons, and first appeared in *Poems on Affairs of State* (1704) and *Poetical Miscellanies: The Fifth Part* in the same year. See H. T. Swedenberg, general ed., *The Works of John Dryden,* iii, (ed. Earl Miner, Berkeley and Los Angeles, 1969), p. 222; and James Kinsley, ed., *Scottish Poetry: A Critical Survey* (1955), pp. 97-8.

24. Jeremy Collier, *Animadversions on 11 Henry 7 Cap. 1 Or, a King De Facto* (nd.), p. 8.

25. George Hickes, *A Vindication of Some among Our Selves Against the Principles of Dr. Sherlock* (1692), p. 19. Alan Roper, *Dryden's Poetic Kingdoms* (1965), pp. 171-3, draws on Scott's edition of *Somers Tracts* to re-assert the connection between the speech of Bishop Merks of Carlisle and Dryden's 'Character of a Good Parson'. But since he speaks only of a 'Tory pamphleteer of 1679' it is not clear whether he can be referring to Hickes's *Vindication.* The importance of this work for Dryden's poem is doubly clear when it is recalled that in the post-revolutionary period Hickes was an intimate of Samuel Pepys, who suggested the subject of the poem to Dryden. See James Kinsley, 'Dryden's *Character of a Good Parson* and Bishop Ken', *Review of English Studies,* N.S. iii (1952), pp. 155-8.

26. Hickes, *A Vindication,* p. 10.

27. Charlwood Lawton, *A French Conquest Neither Desirable Nor Practicable. Dedicated to the King of England.*[ie. James] (1693), Dedication. Compare Lawton's presentation of William III as a tyrant and warrior king (pp. 1, 5-6, 17), his reference to the '*Charta de Forresta*' (p. 2) and his affirmation that James does not wish to be 'King of *Trees,* of *Beasts,* and a *desolated Land,* or to leave such ruin'd Kingdom to his Son' (p. 7) with *Windsor Forest,* 11. 41-92. Lawton (1660-1721) was an active Jacobite pamphleteer, and a Protestant who defended both Roman Catholics (op. cit., pp. 2-3) and James's plan for 'a Civil Comprehension' in religion. He was in touch with Middleton, one of James's moderate Secretaries of State at St. Germain (G. H. Jones, *Charles Middleton: The Life and Times of a Restoration Politician* (1967), pp. 252-3), was a friend of William Penn, and for some time before and after 1688 lived in Windsor Forest (D.N.B. xxxii, 298-9).

28. I am indebted to Dr. Mark Goldie for this information.

29. For contract and the constitutionalist emphasis in early Jacobitism, see Cherry, art. cit. Sometimes Jacobites and Non-Jurors used the idea of contract against William rather than for James (see, eg. Howard Erskine-Hill, *The Social Milieu of Alexander Pope* (1975), pp. 142-4. Of course Jacobite pamphlets which did *not* stress law and constitution would hardly have been persuasive. Again, the whole basis of the stand made by the Non-Jurors was law, constitution and oaths, and their writings against the new regime naturally highlight these issues. The Jacobite court, however, and indeed James himself, were divided between moderates, or Compounders, led by Middleton and Caryll, and high-flyers, or Non-Compounders, led by Melfort (G. H. Jones, op. cit., pp. 24-52). While we cannot therefore assess Jacobitism entirely on the basis of writings and speeches within Britain, its legal and constitutional appeal was no doubt its strongest claim upon the British subject.

30. Pocock, op. cit., pp. 51-2, 229-31; Kenyon, op. cit., pp. 7-10. The problem for all but Non-Jurors and Jacobites was bluntly expressed in a letter by a Non-Juror on the position of Queen Mary, printed in the Life of Kettlewell: 'She has partaken with Thieves and Lyers against her own *Father:* she is a *Receiver* of what has been by them, and from him wrongfully taken away, unless it can be proved that the Crown of ENGLAND is *Elective*, the Kings of it *Punishable* and *Deposable*. If this is right you know *Sir,* all our Law-Books are in the wrong . . .' (*A Compleat Collection of the Works of John Kettlewell* (1719), i, 99.

31. Kettlewell's *Duty of Allegiance*, pp. 48-50; Collier's *Case of Allegiance Consider'd*, pp. 17, 43, 59, 89, 125; Hickes's *Vindication*, pp. 5, 25; *An Answer to a late Pamphlet Entituled Obedience & Submission to the Present Government, Demonstrated* (Cambridge University Library pressmark: Acton d. 25 989), pp. 3-4, 28. The biblical history of Athaliah, cited in Overall's *Convocation Book* and in Sherlock is so crucial in the English political debate that it may be thought to strengthen the case of Jean Orcibal, *La Genèse d'Esther et d'Athalie* (Paris, 1950), pp. 48-57, especially 55, on the contemporary political meaning of Racine's *Athalie.*

32. Collier's *Case of Allegiance Consider'd*, pp. 26, 154; Hickes's *Vindication*, p. 37; Kettlewell's *Duty of Allegiance*, p. 68; Anderton's *Remarks Upon the Present Confederacy . . .* (1693), p. 25; *An Answer to a Late Pamphlet . . .*, pp. 4-6, 10-12.

33. Hickes's *Vindication*, p. 17; Sir James Montgomery, *Great Britain's Just Complaint . . .* (1692), p. 23.

34. Hickes's *Vindication*, pp. 17-19. *The Jacobite Principles Vindicated*, p. 3; *The Price of the Abdication* (1693) (St. John's College, Cambridge pressmark: Gg.6.14), p. 18. Montgomery's *Great Britain's Just Complaint*, pp. 22-3.

35. Collier, *Animadversions; Great Britain's Just Complaint*, p. 23.

36. Hickes's *Vindication*, p. 26; Kettlewell's *Duty of Allegiance*, p. 61; *The Price of the Abdication*, p. 18. See Pocock, op. cit., pp. 46 and 237 on the general importance of precedent.

37. Collier, *The Case of Allegiance Consider'd*, p. 145.

38. Lawton, *A French Conquest*, p. 24.

39. Kettlewell, *Duty of Allegiance*, pp. 5, 71.

40. *An Address Given in to the Late King James . . .* (1690) (C.U.L. pressmark: Dd.2.23), p. 1.

41. Hickes's *Vindication*, p. 18.

42. C. E. Ward, ed., *The Letters of John Dryden* (Duke University Press, 1942), pp. 107-8.

43. Roper, op. cit.; William Myers, *Dryden* (1973), Chs. 8-10.

44. *To Congreve*, 11. 45-8; *To Granville*, 11. 11-22; 'The Character of a Good Parson', 11. 106-40, especially 108-26; *Poems*, ed. James Kinsley, ii. 853, iii. 1434, iv. 1739-40. Cf. Roper, op. cit., pp. 138-9, 165-84, 171-4, 196-8; and Myers, op. cit., pp. 143-5, 170-91.

45. Bessie Proffitt, 'Political Satire in *Alexander's Feast'*, *Texas Studies in Literature and Language,* xi (Winter, 1970), 1037-1315; Howard Erskine-Hill, 'John Dryden: The Poet and Critic', Roger Lonsdale, ed., *Dryden to Johnson* (1971), pp. 50-51.

46. See n. 32 above.

47. William Anderton, *Remarks on the Present Confederacy,* p. 25. Cf. Dryden's 'The Cock and the Fox', 11. 659-62, in *The Fables; Poems,* ed. cit., iv. 1621. *Alexander's Feast* was of course included in *The Fables.*

48. Roper, op. cit., pp. 113-124; Myers, op. cit., pp. 174-5.

49. See n. 42 above.

50. W. J. Cameron, 'John Dryden's Jacobitism', in Harold Love, ed., *Restoration Literature; Critical Approaches* (1972), pp. 277-8.

51. See Sir James Tyrrell's important and neglected *Biblioteca Politica* (1694), where the author with a measure of quiet satire causes Meanwell, the Jacobite, to adopt just this position (Dialogue 13, p. 968). Cf. Straka, art. cit., p. 656 (the citation of Sir John Bramston's *Autobiography).*

52. Kettlewell, *Duty of Allegiance,* p. 71.

53. 'The Character of a Good Parson', 11. 117-20; *Poems,* ed. cit., iv. 1739.

54. *Letters,* ed. cit., pp. 49, 59, 73, 85-6, 93-4 and, most important, 123. Cardinal Howard's letter, cited at p. 165, underlines what we gather from the poet: that he and his sons hoped for an early Restoration.

55. *Poems,* ed. cit., iv. 1774; cf. Myers, op. cit., p. 139.

56. David Nokes, 'Lisping in Political Numbers', *Notes and Queries,* N.S. xxiv, No. 3 (June 1977), pp. 228-9. The lines run: 'Behold, Dutch Prince, here lye th'unconquer'd Pair,/Who knew your Strength in Love, your Strength in War!/Unequal Match, to both no Conquest gains,/No trophy of your Love or War remains.' and purport to be an epitaph on Queen Mary and Marshal Luxemburg.

57. Kenyon, op. cit., Ch. 8, and especially his citation (p. 129) of Sacheverell's *The Perils of False Brethren.*

58. See nn. 7-10 above in the light of Kenyon's discussion of the Trial.

59. *Windsor Forest,* 11. 171-218, 329-422, especially 408; Twickenham Edition i, 165-9, 181-93.

60. For the dates see T.E. i. 406 and ii. 126. Also i. 125-6, 346-7. See too n. 56 above.

61. John M. Aden, ' "The Change of Sceptres and Impending Woe": Political Allusion in Pope's Statius', *Philological Quarterly,* 52 (1973), No. 4, pp. 728-38.

62. Like other politically allusive texts of the late seventeenth and early eighteenth centuries (with the notable exception of *Absalom and Achitophel*), this poem does not seem to offer a system of simple political correspondences. Aden appears uncertain over whether the Electoral Prince is in the poem or not, but it is fair to see the situation of Polynices as expressing that of James, 'the Old Pretender'.

63. See nn. 7-10 above.

64. See *The Managers Pro and Con* (1710), Sir Walter Scott, ed., *Somers Tracts* (1965 reprint), xii, 630. Kenyon, op.cit., pp.129-30; Holmes, *The Trial of Dr. Sacheverell* (1973), pp. 33. 'Two sermons preached as late as 1708, Blackal's before the Queen and Atterbury's before the Corporation of London, alarmed the Whigs. After that, the Highflying preachers seemed increasingly bent on convincing the Whigs that they were out to play the Pretender's game by casting doubt on the validity of the whole post-1688 Establishment'.

65. Eg. Arthur Mainwaring's *Tarquin and Tullia* (1689), *Poems on Affairs of State,* v. 46-54, and later poems by the same author. And see n. 74 below.

66. See n. 10 above.

67. *Poems on Affairs of State,* vi. 620.

68. I do not mean to deny the allusion in Pope's title to Tassoni's *La Secchia Rapita* (1611; publ. 1622; tr. by Perault 1678). The title is the kind of double allusion Pope loved. It is notable that Tassoni's subject is political and historical in a way that neither the subjects of *Le Lutrin* nor *The Dispensary* are.

69. *The Rape of the Lock,* ii. 90.

70. Ibid., iii. 178.

71. Ibid., iii. 6.

72. 8ee Milton, Sonnet vii ('How soon hath Time, the subtle thief of Youth . . .' and *Lycidas,* 11. 75-6: *Poetical Works,* ed. Douglas Bush (Oxford, 1966), pp. 105, 144.

73. The Twickenham Edition is inadequate on this aspect of Pope's poem. For an apposite example of the card game as political comment, see *The Royal Gamesters: Or, the old Cards new shuffled, for a Conquering Game* (nd.), *Harleian Miscellany,* ed. cit. i. 173-6. This poem deals with the politics of Europe between 1702 and 1706, a prefatory note declaring its relevance to more recent events arising from the treachery of France and Spain. It is apparently a game of Trump (ie. the same or similar to Ombre). This is not an isolated example. See *Harleian Miscellany,* ed. cit., vii. 211 for a mid-seventeenth-century game of the same kind. See also Edmund Goldsmid, ed., *Explanatory Notes of a Pack of Cavalier Playing Cards, Temp. Charles II, Forming a Complete Political Satire of the Commonwealth* (Edinburgh, 1886). In a more general connection, see the 'translation' from Boccalini, *The New-found Politicke* (1626), pp. 13, 207; and *Ombre Parlanti,* an Italian work of political commentary of 1669 (B.L. pressmark: 1071.a.25). A more pointed analogue is in B.L. Lansdowne MSS 927, f. 86: Basil Kennet's 'Le nouveau jeu de l'ombre' in which Queen Anne, Louis XIV and Marlborough figure in a card-war of the Spanish Succession. (I am grateful to Dr. Ian MacKillop of Sheffield University for this reference.)

74. Two unmistakable political allusions in Pope's game are: (i) 'the fights of *Lu*' (1. 62) and (ii) 'the *Queen* of *Hearts*' (1. 88). (i) refers not only to the card-game of Loo (see T.E. ii, 389-90) but to William's Dutch palace, as witness Bevil Higgons, *The Mourners* (so ascribed by Pope in his copy of *Poems Relating to State Affairs* (1705), B.L. pressmark: c.28.e.15): 'From *Windsor,* gutted to aggrandise *Loo*' (1. 8), *Poems on Affairs of State,* vi, 362. See too B.L. Sloane MSS. 2717, f. 94: 'Since I myself am fain to sue,/To them [Parliament] for leave to go to Loo' and f. 96: 'Do it Great Prince, for you are Rich enough/Witness your Loo; with all our household Stuff'. 'Mighty *Pam*' (1. 61) is thus one who has overthrown kings and queens, and mown down armies, in the interests of William and the campaigns against France in which William engaged Britain after 1688. Marlborough seems a likely candidate. (ii) seems to refer to Queen Anne as well as to the card, as witness: 'Hail Queen of Hearts! to whose true English praise/The faithful Commons vote new holy-days', On *8 March 1703/4,* 11. 1-2, *Poems on Affairs of State,* vi, 614. The immediate reference of this poem is probably to Anne's speech from the throne, 11 March 1700/01: 'And as I know my own Heart to be intirely *English* . . . There is not any thing you can expect or desire from me, which I shall not be ready to do, for the Happiness and Prosperity of *England*', A Collection of All Her *Majesty's Speeches* . . . (1712), p. 4. The terms 'Queen of Hearts' and 'King of Hearts' may possibly have implied a monarch by popular choice rather than by right; the extreme Whig Lord Delamer, who very early declared for William, was insultingly called 'King of Hearts' in a poem of that title by Arthur Mainwaring, *Poems on Affairs of State,* v. 83-94, especially 84. The political interpretation of Pope's game of ombre requires fuller exposition than space here permits. I would hypothesise that it may be interpreted, not as presenting a real chronological and historical sequence of events, but as alluding to real persons, aspects of

real persons, and real forces, arranged in a fictional play which bears upon William's 'rape' of James's throne.

75. [Alexander Pope], *A Key to the Lock* (1715), where 'mighty *Pam*' is stated, by Esdras Barnivelt, to be Marlborough (Norman Ault, ed., *Prose Works of Alexander Pope* (Oxford, 1930) p. 193). It seems likely that *Pam*' *is* Marlborough, and that the *Key* is, as was soon after contended, a blind, or 'ward', designed to pre-empt embarrassing political interpretation (G. V. Guerinot, *Pamphlet Attacks on Alexander Pope, 1711-55* (1969), pp. 33, 35).

76. This evidence is finely poised. Clearly the *True Briton* seeks guard himself by likening himself to 'so innocent' a poet, who has been ridiculously charged with propagating 'Popery, Tyranny, Arbitrary Power'. But since the political innuendo of which the *True Briton* protests innocence is undeniably present in his pages, the comparison reflects upon *The Rape of the Lock* too. Neither work, we may conclude, sought to introduce Popery, Tyranny and Arbitrary Power, but each had political implications which it was prudent to deny. *True Briton*, No. 65 was reprinted with the rest of the journal in *The Life and Writings of Philip Late Duke of Wharton* (London, 1732), ii. 553-5.

77. See, for example, *A Serious Address to the People of Great Britain* (1745), and other such tracts in Trinity College, Cambridge, Wren Library, pressmark: K 11 37.

78. It is the final paper of Wharton's *True Briton*.

79. Paul Chapman, 'Nostalgia or Radicalism?: Jacobite Argument under Walpole' (unpublished B.A. dissertation, 1979). This is the first examination of *The Freeholder's Journal, Mist's Weekly Journal*, and *Fog's Weekly Journal*, and brings forward much strikingly interesting evidence.

80. See, for example, No. 42 (25 Oct. 1723).

81. [George Granville, Lord Lansdowne,] *A Letter From A Noble-Man Abroad, To His Friend in England* (London, 1722), p. 3.

82. Ibid., pp. 4-5, 7-8.

83. Each extract from Pope is taken from his *Epilogue to the Satires;* the first from Dialogue I, 11. 151-3; the second from Dialogue II, 11, 248-253 (T.E. iv, 309, 327). Both parts of the Epilogue appeared in 1738.

84. Virtually the whole of Lansdowne's short *Letter* could be cited; and of *The True Briton* see especially Nos. 3, 7, 25, 35, 38 (with its Character of The Patriot), 41 and 58. Bolingbroke's debt to *The True Briton* has been noted by Maynard Mack, *The Garden and the City: Retirement and Politics in the later Poetry of Pope. 1731-1743* (1969), p. 117, n. 4.

85. See Katherine Thomasson, *The Jacobite General* (Edinburgh and London, 1958), pp. 39-40.

86. Eveline Cruickshanks, *Political Untouchables: The Tories and the '45* (1979), pp. 12-13.

87. H. T. Dickinson, *Bolingbroke* (1970), p. 232.

88. See n. 79 above.

89. Pope, *The Dunciad* (1743), i, 1. 212.

90. *The Country Bard: Or, The Modern Courtiers. A Poem, Inscribed to the Prince.* (1739); *The Country Bard: Or, The Modern Courtiers. A Poem. Inscribed to his Royal Highness The Prince of Wales.* (1741). Authorship is established by the reprinting of the second part in 1746, when a new title-page announced: 'By David Morgan, Esq; Counsellor at Law, Who was executed (as a *Rebel* against his KING and Country) on *Kennington-Common, Wednesday, July 30, 1746*'. The attribution is accepted in David Foxon, *English Verse 1701-50* (Cambridge, 1975), M440-42.

91. *The Country Bard*, part 2 (1746 printing), 1. 269, and 11. 266-93.

92. The identification of Walpole with 'Marrall' is clinched by the reference to the Excise Scheme in the footnote on p. 5 of part 1, and see 11. 69-88 (the debt to Pope's *Epilogue to the Satires* is clear, in both phrase and content).

93. See Morgan's footnotes '1' and 'n' on pp. 8 and 9 of part 1 (the latter notes how Brutus, 'animated with a Spirit of Patriotism', expelled Tarquin).

94. What appears to be the only surviving copy of this poem is in the Bodleian Library (pressmark: Vet. A. 4. c. 330). It is not attributed to Morgan in Foxon, but the authorship is established by Morgan's own claim to its authorship in his dying statement (see n. 97 below), where he refers to it by both title and subtitle (Robert Forbes, A.M., *The Lyon in Mourning*, ed. Henry Paton (Edinburgh, 1975), i. 47). For Lord Noel Somerset, see Eveline Cruickshanks, op. cit., pp. 73-5.

95. See his lines against Rome on pp. 6-7 of *The Christian Test*.

96. See Trinity College, Cambridge, Wren Library, pressmark: RW 8 2, f. 32: *Letters deliver'd at the Execution of F. Townley and D. Morgan . . . Delivered by Councellor Thomas David Morgan of Derby*, Southwark, July 27th 1746. For Morgan's advice to Prince Charles, see Cruickshanks, op. cit., pp. 99-101. In retrospect, Morgan seems right to have advised the Prince to press on to London.

97. Morgan's statement is most accessible in Paton's edition of Robert Forbes's *The Lyon in Mourning* (see n. 94 above), i. 43-7, where it appears with some other last statements and speeches of English Jacobites. I have compared Forbes's version with three 1746 editions; they are the same save for accidentals. *True Copies of the Papers of the Papers Wrote By Arthur Lord Balmerino, Thomas Syddall, David Morgan* [and others] *And delivered by them to the Sheriff at the Places of their Execution* (1746) (Cambridge University Library pressmark: Ddd. 25. 114) states in its Preface that the purpose of publication was to 'vindicate his *Majesty's Justice'* by demonstrating that '*they were fixed in their Principles,* and *irreclaimable'*. Another copy, C.U.L. pressmark: X. 28. 17, annotates the head of the statement as follows: 'Barrister of a Good Family in Monmouthshire, — called the P——ders Counsellor'. An eighteenth-century broadside dated 'London, July 31' (Trinity College, Cambridge, Wren Library, pressmark: RW. 8. 2, f. 33) gives an account of the death of those executed on Kenington Common on 30 July 1746, and of how they prayed, then consulted together, and finally scattered their hats, prayer-books and 'speeches' among the crowd, these statements affirming that they died bravely in the cause since it could not now be otherwise, and that they would do so again.

98. Robert Forbes, op. cit., i, 46.

99. See Atterbury's impression in June 1718; G. V. Bennett, *The Tory Crisis in Church and State, 1688-1730* (Oxford, 1975), pp. 218-19.

100. For example, at the beginning and end of Lansdowne's *Letter*, pp. 3, 8; *The True Briton*, No. 58; *Fog's Weekly Journal*, 19 Oct. 1728; *An Address to the People of England* (nd. ?1745), p. 42 of *A Full Collection of All the Proclamations and Orders, published by the Authority of Charles, Prince of Wales . . .* (C.U.L. pressmark: Ddd. 25. 114); *The True Briton* (1751-3), i. 134. For an example of the use of the phrase in an anti-Jacobite tract, see *A Serious Address to the People of Great Britain* (1745), p. 45 (Trinity College, Cambridge, Wren Library, pressmark: K. 11 37).

101. *A Full Collection of All Poems Upon Charles, Prince of Wales . . . Published since his Arrival in Edinburgh the 17th Day of September, till the 1st of November, 1745* (nd. ?1745), pp. 5-8 (C.U.L. pressmark: Ddd. 25. 114).

102. *The True Briton*, No. 43 (28 Oct. 1723).

103. William Hamilton of Bangour, *Poems and Songs*, ed. James Patterson (edinburgh, 1850), pp. 62-3. Hamilton of Bangour was a Jacobite fugitive and exile after the '45. The *Ode*, printed and distributed just after Gladsmuir, was not republished until 1773.

104. *An Address to the People of England,* p. 44 of *A Full Collection* . . . (see n. 100 above). In the context of Bolingbroke's writings, and Tory and Jacobite argument, 'Corruption' does of course refer to more than individual dishonesty and profiteering. It is a version of the Machiavellian concept of that historical process by which states decline and civilisations decay. Its poetic aspect is to be found in Pope's *Dunciad,* to which J. G. A. Pocock's phrase 'apocalypse by corruption' is especially apt (see *The Machiavellian Moment: Florentine Political Thought and the Atlantic Republican Tradition* (Princeton, 1975), p. 493. Chapters 13 and 14 of Pocock's book are of particular relevance to this subject. While statements about characteristic arguments and rhetoric must remain provisional until we have a comprehensive study of eighteenth-century political journalism, the accusation of corruption as an initiating charge does seem to distinguish the Opposition writers. The government press uses it too, but almost always as a *counter*-charge (see, eg. *The Gazetteer,* 25 Aug. 1737). As for Tory and Jacobite, it may be fair to say that they shared a diagnosis, but that the Hanoverian Tory differed from the committed Jacobite as to the right cure. Many Tories, including, it seems, Bolingbroke, wavered between the different solutions.

105. This *True Briton* was contributed to by John Baptist Caryll (Baron Caryll of Durford in the Jacobite Peerage), who had accompanied Prince Charles on the abortive naval expedition to England in 1744 (see Cruickshanks, op. cit., pp. 56-7), and who was to become his Secretary of State after 1767 (see Howard Erskine-Hill, *The Social Milieu of Alexander Pope* (1975), pp. 101-2). Drafts of Caryll's contributions to *The True Briton* survive in the Caryll Papers in the British Library: one such paper is to be found in vol. i. 506, in the bound set in the Bodleian Library (pressmark: Hope Adds. 311): it is B.L. Add. MSS. 28252, p. 106.

106. Some is to be found in the *Poems and Songs* of Hamilton of Bangour; some was collected by Robert Forbes in *The Lyon in Mourning.*

107. Douglas Young, 'A Note on Scottish Gaelic Poetry', in James Kinsley, ed., *Scottish Poetry, A Critical Survey,* pp. 284-5.

108. 'The Highland Widow's Lament' (publ. 1796), 11. 25-8; *The Poems and Songs of Robert Burns,* ed. James Kinsley (Oxford, 1968), ii. 878; iii. 1515.

109. Ed. cit., iii. 1221 (54-6n.), 1233. Burns 'publicly — if anonymously — declared his gratitude for 'the Glorious Revolution' . . . but also resented ridicule of the Stewarts . . .' (p. 1233).

110. 'It was a' for our rightfu' king', 11. 1-15; ed. cit., ii, 876. It is perhaps typical of the way Jacobite songs came into being that this, which James Hogg ascribed to a Captain Ogilvie who fought for James II and VII in Ireland (*Jacobite Relics of Scotland* (1819) No. XV) is in fact a refashioning by Burns of the chapbook ballad Mally Stewart (c. 1746); ed. cit., iii. 1515.

111. W. B. Yeats, 'The Black Tower', 11. 11-14; *Collected Poems* (2nd. edn. 1950; 1955 reprint), p. 396.

112. Cf. Edward Thompson, *Whigs and Hunters* (Harmondsworth, 1975), pp. 264-7, on the rôle of law. Whatever we may think of the Revolution Settlement, a study of Jacobitism points up the equivocal legal basis of the Williamite, Queen Anne, and Hanoverian establishment, upon which the Whigs set so much store.

4

Riot and Popular Jacobitism in Early Hanoverian England

Nicholas Rogers

DURING the opening years of the Hanoverian accession England resounded with riot and sedition. Although the proclamation of the new reign and the king's progress to London passed without serious incident, disturbances were reported in approximately thirty towns and villages on coronation day; and by the summer of 1715 the country was beset by demonstrations reminiscent of the High Church fury of 1710. In two months of almost continuous rioting, over forty Dissenting meeting-houses were pulled down — in the West Midlands hardly a chapel remained unscathed — and troops hurriedly occupied many leading towns. Even after the suppression of the Northern Rising and the almost total demoralisation of the Tory party, unrest continued. And indeed it was not until 1723, when the press had been effectively silenced and the last figurehead of Tory resistance, Bishop Atterbury, had been harried into exile, that the new regime seemed secure from internal rebellion. By that time the Whigs had taken new steps to contain popular discontent: redefining the laws against riot, avoiding an electoral contest in 1718, and circumscribing plebeian participation at the hustings.

In view of these developments it is surprising that historians have paid so little attention to the popular ferment of the accession years. Those interested in the Whig ascendancy have by and large concentrated upon the dynastic struggle in high politics and the growth of oligarchy. Within this context popular unrest appears simply as one of the problems the Whigs had to handle. Jacobite scholars have scarcely advanced beyond this; their abiding interest has been espionage, high conspiracy and Stuart memorabilia. In the few instances where disaffection has caught the limelight it has been imbued with an ultra-Tory sentimentality which clouds rather than clarifies its meaning. Early Hanoverian protest, in short, remains virtually uncharted territory, still part of the pre-history of the crowd. There has been no comprehensive appraisal of its regional dimensions, its insurrectionary implications, or its social character. Yet no assessment of early Hanoverian politics can be complete without it.

One of the major difficulties in undertaking a study of this sort is that Jacobitism covered a multitude of sins in the eighteenth century. It could, of course, signify a genuine commitment to a Stuart restoration. It was also a cause to be exploited for personal advantage. At least a handful of the cases that came before the Secretary of State during the accession crisis were malicious prosecutions. We find a Kentish yeoman using Jacobitism to recover tithes from a recalcitrant debtor and a soldier at

Kingston-upon-Thames nailing a quarrelsome drinking companion with a charge of disaffection.[1] The attribution of Jacobitism, in fact, became the classic frame-up of the early eighteenth century. It was used to embarrass opponents, to topple office-holders and to strengthen one's credentials with the ministry. More than one trading justice in Middlesex carved a career through Jacobite-hunting.

More pertinent to this essay, Jacobitism was also employed rhetorically, as an act of defiance or provocation. Jacobite toasts were drunk by smugglers and debtors at odds with the law and also by disappointed men. In 1714 a Customs collector at Whitehaven (presumably a Tory) ordered an alehouse fiddler to strike up a Jacobite tune, bidding a local doctor to 'goe and informe and get the Collection for himself if he would'.[2] Three years later a Somerset squire, described as 'a very rash young married man about 22, being very rich in money and lands' and said to be heavily influenced by Earl Poulett, was reported drinking disloyal toasts with his cronies.[3] Revels of this sort became quite commonplace among Tory landowners, prominent in their own counties but excluded from office on political grounds. In Wales in particular, toasting the 'king across the water' became a favourite pastime, nurtured by clubs like the Cycle of the White Rose and the Sea Serjeants of Pembrokeshire.

At a more popular level Jacobitism fitted easily into a tradition of street politics which placed great emphasis upon pomp and ceremony. It was entirely predictable, in the highly-charged atmosphere of the accession, that the Whigs' willingness to arrogate loyalism to their party should have prompted seditious outbursts. This was very apparent on coronation day, when the triumphant celebrations of the Whigs were disrupted by Tory mobs whose slogans sometimes escalated to seemingly treasonable proportions. In cases where the Whigs were overly zealous, the response could be extremely flamboyant. At Chichester, for example, where the loyalists rounded off their day with a pope-burning spectacle, demonstrators derided George I's cuckoldry by hanging an effigy of Old Noll with 'Horns on his Head' at High Cross. At Axminster in Devon, the country folk from surrounding villages not only stole the effigies of the pope and pretender, but actually proclaimed the Chevalier in mock triumph.[4] Even where Whig celebrations were not especially provocative, their solemn festivities could be devastatingly deflated by a little Jacobitical revelry. Thus at Frome a crowd mocked the clothiers' procession by parading a fool, whose turnip-topped wand mimicked the loyal emblems of their superiors, crying out all the while 'here's our George, where's yours?'[5] These counter-processionals, droll as well as seditious, where replaced on other anniversaries by other forms of revelry; Jacobite airs and roses; rue and thyme on Hanoverian birthdays; toasts for the impeached Ormonde. In Stafford in 1716 it was reported that the festivities on the king's birthday were ominously modest, while on the following day, the anniversary of the Restoration, they were observed 'with all the strictness possible'. Just over a week later, on 7 June, the day assigned to commemorate the suppression of the rebellion, only one peal was heard, and a 'little after midnight a Tory constable went about with a Gang and Fiddlers &c. playing a Tune called the King shall enjoy his own again'.[6] No doubt the glorious tenth, the Pretender's birthday, was celebrated with white roses.

I am not suggesting that popular Jacobitism was simply a frolic, although it was obviously an admirable idiom for the carnivalesque freedoms of the Tory crowd. Rather it was a singularly appropriate script in a world where royal anniversaries were solemnly observed to sanctify and legitimise the political order and where ceremonialism with its attendant festivities and folklore were still of decisive importance in fostering political allegiances. Jacobite symbolism could be deployed to deflate Whig pomposity, to tarnish the Whig supremacy, to reinforce territorial loyalties that did not square with Whig orthodoxy. It could be provocative, defiant, derisory, even consolatory in tone, for there is something to the nostalgic Jacobitism of the balladeers and literati. Unfortunately much of this has been missed by orthodox political historians. They have either trivialised Jacobitism to a point where it becomes virtually insignificant, or they have interpreted it in a strictly literal manner.

Where historians have followed the second course they have more or less bought the Whig line. Since the reversal of their fortunes in 1710, the Whigs had persistently asserted that the Tory party was prey to Jacobite proclivities and that their own return to power was absolutely essential to secure the Protestant succession and Revolution settlement. In their eyes the popular ferment simply confirmed this argument. Behind every demonstration Whig spokesmen saw the hidden hand of Jacobitism. Occasionally they alluded to the Pretender's emissaries who 'animated the mob' to riot. But more frequently they reserved their denunciations for the High Church clergy, by reputation the progenitors of mob violence, and their fellow-travellers among the gentry and leading townsmen. The pulpit, claimed Defoe, had become 'a Trumpet of Sedition', while the Tory Corporations raked the fires of sectarian strife and openly incited rebellion.[7] Although ministerial spokesmen doubted that the crowd was genuinely Jacobite, at least in any reflective sense, they argued that popular discontent was a prelude to insurrection. As the Secretary of State told the Lord Mayor of London in July 1715, a Jacobite invasion was 'abetted and encouraged by the fomenters of the rebellious insurrections which are carried on here'.[8]

But the more extravagant features of this view will not withstand close scrutiny. In the first place there is a noticeable lack of correspondence between riot and armed insurrection. The initial wave of protest was over before Mar's rebellion, breaking in Lancashire, London and the Midlands in June and July. Even in the West Country, where rioting was especially prominent in the early months of the reign, there is a decline in violence prior to the projected uprising there. Secondly, there is little evidence that popular unrest featured prominently in Jacobite strategy. The Stuart papers and the testimony of government spies like Thomas Wells reveal the poor state of Jacobite organisation, little if any co-ordination between the capital and the provinces, and a minimum of grass-roots activity.[9] Most Jacobites presumed they could muster a popular following by traditional methods, through the mediation of the client economy and the leadership of generals like Ormonde. Basically they distrusted the political sympathies of the common people and, taken aback by the strength of anti-Hanoverian sentiment, only alerted their followers to the possibilities of harnessing popular unrest late in the day. Even in London little attempt was made to mobilise popular support beyond distributing copies of the

Pretender's manifesto and other broadsheets. More energy was devoted to winning over the army.

Evidence of a co-ordinated Jacobite campaign at the grass roots, then, is hard to come by. Yet if Whig contemporaries exaggerated the conspiratorial dimensions of protest, they with reason highlighted the role of the extreme wing of the Tory party in fomenting discontent. In the opening years of the accession the high-flying clergy strove desperately to revive the flagging fortunes of their party, mobilising their congregations in defence of the Anglican inheritance and warning them of the dangers of Whig rule. Piqued by Hanover's clear preference for the Whigs, there is little doubt that their sermons bordered on sedition. Few were perhaps as audacious as the Reverend Edward Bisse, the rector of Portbury in Somerset, who had to be silenced by King's Bench for repeatedly denouncing the Revolution settlement, or the curate of Woodbury in Devon who declared he would 'rather live under a Popish Government than a Presbyterian Ministry',[10] but seldom did they miss an opportunity to snub the new regime. Defoe devoted four pamphlets to their provocations, singling out a handful of London preachers for their inflammatory anniversary sermons. He might well have extended his list, for the *Dublin Post Man* noted a Restoration-day sermon in London which featured some 'seditious digressions' on a text which concluded with the words 'so that they sent this word unto the King, Return thou and all thy servants'.[11] Nor was clerical hostility simply confined to the pulpit. In Liverpool the rector of St. Nicholas refused to commemorate the king's safe arrival at Greenwich and was chaired by the mob for his defiance. At Trowbridge, a local parson denounced the local celebrants of the coronation; at Newton Abbot the incumbent removed the clappers from the bells. More audaciously, a Cirencester parson observed the thanksgiving for the suppression of the rebellion by decking 'his House with Greens but instead of Gilding them put them in deep mourning with Lamblack'.[12] Not surprisingly, the accession years saw several clergymen in the dock for inciting disorder.

If the Tory clergy justly earned their reputation as 'gown-Incendiaries', their counterparts on the bench were scarcely less indiscreet. The mayor of Shaftesbury was fined £100 for encouraging a mob to intimidate crown witnesses. Several other dignitaries, including two mayors, two aldermen, and the former M.P. for Newcastle-under-Lyme, were indicted for riot. And one justice was turned off the bench 'for endeavouring at Shipton upon Stour upon the demise of Queen Anne to have the Pretender proclamd'.[13] These, of course, were outstanding cases. More typical was the case of Sir Henry Gough, who was reprimanded for neglecting his duty during the West Bromwich riots 'both by your taking trifling security for those who were bound over and by your not discouraging even your own servants from joyning with the Mobb in disorderly and seditious crys'.[14] Trifling securities and loosely phrased informations were also levelled against the mayor of Bath, who was told late in 1715 that his town was 'pretty famous for riots' and that his remission of duty had encouraged disorder.[15] Not that this reprimand proved very effectual, for in April 1718 it was reported that the mayor and his fellow aldermen sported white roses and blue ribbons on the Duke of Ormonde's birthday.

Instances of magisterial incitement or inactivity crop up fairly frequently in the state papers domestic. They lend weight to the reflections of George Lucy, a Staffordshire justice of the peace, that disaffection was rife among the gentry, particularly in Tory counties like his own.[16] At the same time, one should not infer from this evidence that the accession disorders, even in prime Tory country, were necessarily generated from above or indeed received the tacit approval of leading townsmen and landowners. In some instances magistrates connived at disorders because they feared the consequences of not doing so. At Stamford, for example, the mayor was 'terrified by the Rabble' to release several rioters from prison, and refused to intervene when they demonstrated in the streets several days later.[17] On other occasions magistrates countenanced a few seditious revels rather than lose local goodwill. This was the case at Nuneaton, where the local justices disregarded the complaints of one Whig partisan and bound him over for disturbing the peace on coronation day.

But however conniving Tory justices may have been, it is clear that many disturbances were spontaneous rather than planned, popular rather than gentry-instigated. In London, for example, where the main sources of Tory leadership were under close surveillance, Jacobite demonstrations were distinctly plebeian, emanating from the industrial suburbs and riverside parishes and drawing upon a tradition of independent street politics for their momentum.[18] Similarly in Manchester, where it was reported in July 1715 that the mob had 'been up (more or less) about three weeks', breaking illuminated windows on the king's birthday, parading oak branches on the morrow (Restoration day) and sacking the local meeting house during the first eleven days of June, one finds no evidence of direction from above. Even in Oxford, where one informant reported that the inhabitants were 'generally debauched with Jacobitism' and every night had 'a parcel of Rioters going along the Streets crying Down with the Rump, Down with the Roundheads, an Ormond forever and other expressions not fit to be mentioned', one uncovers a rambunctious crowd operating alongside the collegiate centres of disaffection, an alliance between town and gown.[19] Elsewhere too, one can detect a genuinely indigenous brand of Jacobitism, for it is significant that the most troublesome areas of the country were the industrial communities of the West Midlands and towns with a strong tradition of civic politics, places where gentry leadership was neither habitual nor automatic. In fact the principal rioters from these regions included groups who were to feature prominently in public disturbances later in the century: nailers and bucklemakers from the industrial hamlets of the upper Stour, for instance, by reputation masterless men; the colliers of Kingswood Forest near Bristol, whose rough manners and recalcitrance marked them out as an 'ungovernable people'.[20] All this suggests a more complex pattern of activity than the orthodox interpretation permits; a view interestingly held by Defoe who, pressed into government service to expose incitement from above, revealingly admitted in 1717 that disaffection was general and 'not at all well managed'.[21]

Management from above is most evident, in fact, during the coronation-day riots. These occurred principally in open constituencies where there were fierce party rivalries and where the Hanoverian succession was likely to tip the balance in favour of the Whigs. Canterbury, Chichester, Cirencester, Gloucester, Hereford and

Salisbury, for example, all experienced disorders during the coronation-day festivities and all had a record of disputed elections during the eighteenth century, leading sometimes to counter-petitions in the Commons. So too did Worcester, where the Pakington faction was matched by the mitre and dissent, and Norwich, where the bench, clergy and principal civic leaders were evenly distributed between the two parties in the years 1710-1715.[22] In towns like these the riots sometimes resembled pre-electoral showdowns, orchestrated by Tory élites who resented the Whigs' readiness to transform loyalist celebrations into party fanfares. Such was the case in Norwich, where the High Church party incited rioters to disrupt the celebrations at the market-place to the cry 'Bene and Berney', the standing members.[23] The same was true of Salisbury and Canterbury, where several esquires and gentlemen were indicted for riot. And of Taunton and Shrewsbury.[24] At the Shropshire town, where the country gentry jostled for power with a predominantly non-conformist group in alliance with Lord Bradford, his lordship's celebration was interrupted by a crowd 'crying High Church and Dr. Sacheverell for ever'. At Taunton, a clothing town deep in Tory country, noted for its dissenting academy and imposing meeting-house, the mayor's son played a leading role in the disruption of the coronation festivities while his father and the town recorder looked on. On occasions like these one sees a licensed crowd in action, encouraged to steal the Whig show, and inflamed, if one can believe the depositions presented to the government and the charges in the press, by rumours that the Whigs planned to burn Sacheverell in effigy.

At the same time one should not conclude that all the coronation-day riots were similarly organised. Some of the demonstrations had a distinctly popular flavour. At Bedford, for instance, it was the common people who disrupted the festivities and dressed the town maypole in mourning.[25] Incidents like this recalled a tradition of Tory conviviality which proved remarkably resilient in the eighteenth century. It was especially vigorous in Lancashire and the West Midlands, where the gentry's theatre of hospitality and tolerance of popular recreations contrasted markedly with dissenting piety.[26] It was also an important source of popular Toryism in the clothing towns of the West Country, where the Dissenting bourgeoisie were especially prominent, and in commercial centres like Bristol, all of which were trouble spots during the accession years. Indeed in Bristol, where the powerful non-conformist interest pioneered the campaign for the reformation of manners and where Tories rallied to the Loyal Society, whose members, one Whig claimed, 'make more Noise, drink more Beer and swear more oaths than half the rest of their Fellow Citizens',[27] the contrast in sociability could not have been more striking.

The Tories could, therefore, attract a substantial popular following in their own right. And it is possible to see genuinely self-activated crowds operating alongside patrician-directed mobs in the early stages of the accession crisis. But if the initiative rested principally with the Tory gentry and townsmen during these opening months, the same was not true six months later. The Tories had calculated that their electoral showing and grass-roots popularity would deter the Whigs from embarking upon a policy of retribution. As Swift reflected a month before the coronation, 'If anything withholds the Whigs from the utmost violence, it will be only fear of provoking the Rabble, by remembering what past in the Business of Sacheverell'.[28] But Tory strategy backfired. The Whigs ran a successful campaign on the threat to the succession and began their attack upon the Tory ex-ministry. The defection of Bolingbroke and Ormonde completed the demoralisation of the Tory party and forced its remaining leaders on the defensive. In the summer of 1715 some of the ultras may well have contemplated insurrection. But outside the inner circle they were already bickering among themselves and, unnerved by the Whigs' iron will and the dilatory response of St. Germains, retired to their cups and kennels.

What is clear is that the ferment of 1715 was essentially generated from below. It is true, of course, that the Tory clergy fired hostility with the occasional sermon, although their audacity waned dramatically in the face of episcopal vigilance. It is also apparent that the universities buoyed up disaffection in their respective towns, snubbing the government by honouring well-known supporters of the former Tory ministry and celebrating Jacobite festivals behind closed doors.[29] Cases can also be found where the well-to-do aided and abetted disorder. At Worcester one alderman bailed out the leader of the meeting-house riot on the grounds that he was an 'honest fellow' and that the witnesses against him would 'swear anything'.[30] In Denbighshire miners and labourers were encouraged by their employers to destroy the Wrexham chapels; while at Newcastle-under-Lyme the leading townsmen actually conspired with Keele Hall to pull down the meeting-house of their opponents, raising a mob by advertising a 'duel' at the Monday market with drums and violins playing that familiar tune 'The King shall enjoy his own again'.[31] But such incidents were exceptional. The Tory gentry might wink at disorder; their counterparts in the towns might stiffen resistance by exploiting the civic calendar. But the patrician role in the 1715 disturbances was less conspicuous and significant than it had been earlier.

The first signs of an upswing in popular violence occurred in London. In a sense this was unexpected. Although there had been a few minor incidents in the opening months of the reign which revealed the continuing intensity of party strife, the Whigs were understandably elated by the king's reception in the capital and their landslide victories at the hustings. But by May 1715 they were lamenting that the metropolis had become 'the scene of the most scandalous mobs ever known in a civilized nation'.[32] The trouble began with the impeachment trials. In April the Duke of Ormonde's birthday was riotously celebrated in Drury Lane and the western out-parishes of the City. In May there were large-scale demonstrations in Smithfield, Cheapside and Highgate, where a Dissenting chapel was attacked on the king's birthday. And in June the London populace served notice of a second Sacheverell uprising.[33] Much to the consternation of the Commons, bells were rung on the Pretender's birthday in Clerkenwell and St. Dunstan-in-the-West; the Blackfriars meeting-house was gutted; and the Pretender's declaration was stuck to the door of the former chapel in Lincoln's Inn Fields, ransacked five years earlier by Sacheverell's supporters.

Similar demonstrations were reported elsewhere. The Pretender's birthday was celebrated at Cambridge, Leeds and in several Somersetshire villages.[34] At Norton

St. Philip, between Bath and Frome, the Pretender was again proclaimed. And at Oxford riots on the king's birthday culminated in the destruction of both the Presbyterian and Quaker meeting-houses.[35] But the most important centres of protest outside the capital were Lancashire and the West Midlands. In Manchester, where the Cross Street chapel was ransacked, there was a spate of rioting from 28 May until 23 June, when three companies of Lord Cobham's dragoons eventually restored order.[36] By that time the contagion of riot had spread to the outlying districts. The chapels at Monton and Houghton were attacked on 13 June; those of Blackley, Greenacres, Failworth and Standing a week later, reaching Platt, Pilkington and Wigan by the twenty-fifth. Quite independently, and no doubt triggered by the news of Ormonde's impeachment, meeting-house riots swept through the Midlands in late June and July, beginning at Wolverhampton during St. Peter's fair and ending at Kingswinford in Worcestershire on the first day of August.[37] The ministerial press attributed these disorders to the work of roving mobs operating on behalf of a disaffected gentry. At Whitchurch it was said that the mob had been encouraged by gentlemen 'of no small quality'.[38] But such allegations were rarely substantiated. Only at Newcastle-under-Lyme and Wrexham is there conclusive evidence of incitement from above.[39] Admittedly eight gentlemen from other towns are listed among the five hundred rioters in the process book of the Oxford circuit, but only one was found guilty, and one presumes, as Lord Bradford reported on the Shrewsbury allegations, that the charges against them were based on hearsay.[40] As for the roving mobs, there is little evidence that rioters operated outside a ten-mile radius. What the indictments do show is that the great majority of demonstrators came from the towns and hamlets where the meeting-houses were located, headed by local men: in Manchester by a blacksmith; in Worcester by a butcher; and in Shrewsbury by a skinner, one Henry Webb, alias Captain Rag.[41]

What prompted such popular fury, and how can one account for the persistent undercurrent of disaffection which transformed the annual round of anniversaries into a calendar of riot and sedition for the next few years? Undoubtedly local tensions played their part, for the principal centres of disorder were those Tory strongholds where the power of Dissenting minorities was substantial enough to be seen as a threat to local interests. In Lancashire, for example, the electoral presence of non-conformity was growing; by 1722 the leaders of Dissent were confident enough to challenge the county leadership of local magnates.[42] In the West Midlands some of the most riotous towns inherited a legacy of religious rivalry from the seventeenth century and included in their midst a very visible and prestigious non-conformist community. Birmingham, for instance, had been a haven for religious dissent since the Five Mile Act and, despite persistent prosecution from Aston Hall, continued to attract members to its two Presbyterian congregations, principally ironmasters. Comparable conditions existed in nearby Walsall, where a resilient Presbyterian meeting survived the Clarendon code to dominate the corporation and double its membership between 1676 and 1717. In towns like these it would be possible to reconstruct the sectarian strife which fuelled the meeting-house riots of 1715, as J. H. Y. Briggs has done for Newcastle-under-Lyme.[43] Not that the visibility of Dissent was a sufficient cause for riot. The areas where rioting was most frequent were not necessarily those where the number of Dissenters was above the national average. Rather Dissent aggravated discontent where it was socially isolated from county society and where its social attitudes contrasted with the more permissive, convivial stance of the local gentry. This was especially the case in Manchester, where the gentry's tolerance of popular recreations was deplored by local non-conformists and where one beleaguered Whig diarist, Edmund Harrold, a wigmaker, resolved to 'avoid all ye dissolute Revellers that spend their lives in Riot and Debauchery, turning the day into night and the night into day'.[44] Significantly the Cross Street chapel sermon of 1717 commemorating the battle of Preston and alluding to the late troubles in Manchester had annexed to it a copy of the *Book of Sports*.

But if the 1715 disturbances can in some sense be seen as a continuation of local rivalries, it is important to attend to the conjunctural aspects of protest. For the purge of Dissenting chapels was not simply an attack upon non-conformity. It was also a symbolic protest against the Whig government, orchestrated in some instances by Jacobite slogans and ritual. The reasons for the unpopularity of the Whigs and their Hanoverian allies were diverse, but foremost among them was the fear of war. The strain of the war years had been considerable, aggravated by a series of poor harvests that pushed some areas of the country to the brink of a subsistence crisis. The price of bread in 1709-10 had reached famine proportions and credit had been extremely tight. The parson of Wellesbourne in Warwickshire reported in 1710 that 'Everything is very dear & money very scarce in ye Country & ye poor now in great streights & the Rich scarce able to supply them'.[45] Consequently the drive for peace brought the Tories great popularity. Outside merchant and high political circles the treaty of Utrecht was widely acclaimed. Thanksgiving celebrations were enthusiastically staged throughout the country with maypoles and garlands. At Lichfield the populace wore laurel leaves with the motto 'Peace and Plenty' inscribed upon them, while in Bristol, Birmingham, Norwich and Warwick the festivities took on the air of a Tory triumph, with mobs demanding illuminations or some other token of appreciation.[46]

The Hanoverian succession, however, raised fears that this policy would be abandoned. The new monarch was known to be hostile to Utrecht, and it was widely believed that his Whig ministry would involve Britain in further continental campaigns to their own and Hanover's benefit. Such sentiments were widely circulated during the 1715 elections and again the following year during the thanksgiving celebrations for the suppression of the Northern Uprising, when one poem warned of 'the dire Prospect of approaching war'.[47] But they surfaced most visibly during the impeachment trials. At the outset of the meeting-house riots, a letter from Staffordshire recorded the anxieties of the populace and the anger that the Tory peacemakers had been tried for high treason. 'If the Ministry and Secret Committee and their Friends will not let the country have Peace and Trade,' it threatened, 'the Dissenters shall not have a quiet Toleration.'[48] In Stafford itself the attack upon the Presbyterian chapel began on 7 July, the day traditionally observed to commemorate Utrecht. At Leek, Stone, Dudley and Walsall the riots began on the day following. Likewise in London one finds an equation between disaffection and fear of war.[49] The Duke of Marlborough was regularly cursed in the streets of the capital, partly because of his reputation as a wartime profiteer, but also because he symbolised the war effort. By contrast, the Duke of Ormonde, the general responsible for the withdrawal from Europe, was continually championed. If one looks, too, at the social composition of those indicted for disaffection in London, one finds a clear correlation between protest and those trades which faced privation during the war and its aftermath. Tailors, weavers, shoemakers, watermen and riverside porters in a market glutted by demobilisation, all feature prominently among the accused. Similarly in the West Riding, riots were said to be rife in areas that had 'sadly suffered in their Business',[50] while their absence in towns like Sheffield was attributed to cheap provisions and prosperity.

Anti-war feeling was also associated with the political venality and financial legerdemain which prompted the debate on the monied interest and achieved new literary expression in the 1720s and 1730s. The Whigs were quite frequently portrayed as a mercenary crew, grown rich on Marlborough's wars, in league with a petty monarch whose abiding interest was the safety and prosperity of his German electorate. As John Withers explained in one of the few pamphlets that made any attempt to capture popular hostility to the government, it was widely believed that the Whigs had 'cheated the nation, and put immense sums of the public money into their pockets'.[51] In *Britannia's Memorial*, a 1715 broadsheet, 'Interest and Rule' had warped the Whigs' principles. As for the king, when he was not satirised as a cuckold he was pictured as a turnip-hoer, ignorant of British customs and ill-fitted to assume the throne.[52] Underlying these notions was a rudimentary nationalism, a feeling that the country had been farmed out to political speculators and parasites. 'Down with Foreigners', 'Down with the Rump and the German', 'No Foreign Government' were among the slogans voiced during the disturbances of 1714 and 1715.

What made matters worse was the sight of petty functionaries exploiting the accession crisis to personal advantage. In London, for example, it was decided in October 1716 to review victualling licences in an effort to stamp out disaffection. This opened up opportunities for extortion which were quickly seized upon by the minions of the courts, for just over a year later the beer retailers of Holborn complained that 'they had great sums of money demanded from them by the justices' clerks and the beadles of the several parishes where they dwelt, which they were forced to pay before obtaining the licences'.[53]

Even when Jacobite-hunting was less opportunist, it could collide with custom. An example of how Whig vigilance could intrude upon local rights occurred in Bridgwater, where the journalist John Oldmixon was planted to observe the populace. As the commissioner of the Customs he soon interfered with the local practice of wrecking, and by 1720 he was writing to Sunderland to tell him that the town's old charter had never been surrendered and that the new one was technically void, a plausible loophole for a Whig purge. Without doubt his actions did not endear Bridgwater to the new regime, and one suspects that his officiousness greatly fuelled discontent. He certainly believed that a Tory victory in the constituency at the next election would make him 'the first Victim of their Triumph'.[54]

But the hostility towards Hanover was also fed by the fear that the government would subvert plebeian birthrights. It was reported from Worcester during the disturbances there that 'the whole cry of the Mobb was they would fire (viz. burn) the king if he molested them'. Such a fear, heightened by the suspicion that a new war would bring widespread impressments, was not without foundation. The Whigs were quite prepared to use judicial terror to stamp out disaffection, and where local juries appeared unlikely to take a tough line, they smartly removed cases to King's Bench. In response to the Bristol coronation-day riots they even created a special commission of oyer and terminer, whose members were welcomed to the West Country to the cry of 'No Jefferies, No Western Assizes'.[55] When this strategy failed to intimidate rioters, the Whigs forced through a new act which supplemented the common law definition of riot in ways that struck hard at customary practices, facilitating the suppression of popular assembly by ignoring the causes of riot and strengthening magisterial authority. Provided the correct procedures were observed, justices could disperse demonstrations without fear of prosecution. Rioters were hanged under the act on the first day of its implementation for pulling down the meeting-house at Kingsnorton, and a further five were gibbeted in London within the year, even though there were mitigating circumstances.[56]

These trials caused great Whig unpopularity and the Riot Act itself became known as 'the Hanoverian proclamation'. In its train came a crack-down on political licence which contrasted dramatically with the Augustan era and which, together with the Septennial Act, sullied the Whigs' reputation as libertarians. The plebs resented the fact that the wearing of oak sprigs on Restoration day was suddenly regarded as disaffection, and, in the words of one Bristolian, that judgments were 'passed upon their Thoughts, Innuendo's drawn from Gestures of the Body and Motions of the Fingers'.[57] Especially so, when it appeared that there was one law for the Tories and another for the Whigs. In London, for instance, the Duke of Newcastle's mughouse squads were allowed to cudgel demonstrators and harass Tory clubmen with impunity. At Oxford the provocative rallies of the Constitution Club and the riotous activities of the troops were openly tolerated, but the government sent rattling letters to the mayor and vice-chancellor every time the Tory crowd indulged in seditious revelry. General Pepper even told the college heads in October 1715 that if he had any trouble from the inhabitants he would enforce the Riot Act and 'mow them down'.[58] Not surprisingly, such overbearing attitudes, even where they might have been merited, did not improve relations between townsmen and troops. At Oxford these relations reached breaking point on the Prince of Wales' birthday in 1716 when Major D'Offranville's soldiers roughly handled the mayor when he arrived to mediate between the troops and the crowd, and even opened fire on the mace-bearer. Further affrays between soldiers and citizens were reported at Ashbourne in Derbyshire, at Leicester, Manchester, Uttoxeter, and at Bridgwater. Here tensions reached such a pitch that when the company commander pressured the town council to ban celebrations on the pretender's birthday, his patrols were confronted with a sea of white roses, and, as the ultimate act of defiance, by a garland of 'Roses, Hornes & Turnipps' over the officers' quarters.[59] Understandably the eventual departure of troops was sometimes greeted with Jacobite irreverence. On the evening of their departure from Newcastle-upon-Tyne, for instance, William Cotesworth recalled that 'a parcel of fellows went about the streets singing songs reflecting on the govt. and calling out James Stewart'.[60]

Only a close attention to the accession crisis, then, can fully capture the complexity of popular disaffection during these early years. For if the riots can partly be read as an extension of the party strife of the previous reign, their full character can only be grasped within the context of subsequent Whig policy. The steps that the Whigs took to consolidate their return to power genuinely challenged plebeian norms and expectations, curbing political licence and libertarian traditions, and intruding, on occasion, upon customary rights and perquisites. And while some popular anxieties might be written off as insular, xenophobic, sectarian and unduly alarmist, there remains, at the core, a deep-rooted hostility to Whig authoritarianism and to the systematic pursuit of spoils that characterised the Walpolean era.

We must confront, finally, the issue of popular Jacobitism; how literally should we interpret it? The question cannot be answered with any certainty. There was always a strain of Jacobitism that was simply braggart, the product of high spirits and impudence. In the case of Joseph Merryweather, for instance, a Bristol house carpenter indicted for toasting the Pretender, the grand jury acquainted 'ye Court that the Defdt was very drunk att ye time . . . and appearing to ye Court to be sorry for his offence is fined two nobles'.[61] There was another that might more aptly be described as a form of political misrule, irreverent but critical of Whig loyalism, reaffirming perhaps the right to huzza and insult the great as the plebeians pleased. The coronation-day riot at Tewkesbury could be interpreted this way.[62] Here bargemen and watermen demanded money to drink the health of Dr. Sacheverell and the king, and 'being reprimanded for putting Sacheverell before the king, they replyd it should be the king if they would have it so, and being refused money for that', damned the assembly to the cry of 'Sacheverell for ever, Down with the Roundheads'.

But popular Jacobitism went beyond these essentially sub-political responses. In the early years of the accession it denoted an enraged Toryism and at times a genuine sympathy for the rebel cause. The judicial records for London and the Oxford circuit disclose that in the summer of 1715 there were men and women who openly countenanced a Jacobite coup. We find Staffordshire shoemakers 'drinking King James's health and saying we hope in a short time we shall have him among us' and a Bilston bucklemaker rallying fellow rioters to the cry of 'Now boys goe on, we will have no king but James the third & he will be here in a month and we will drive the old Rogue into his country again to sow Turnipps'.[63] Similar hopes were echoed in London and in Gloucestershire, where a yeoman was arraigned for countering the king's health with Ormonde's, and 'success to the king's forces' with 'up with Mar'. But such Jacobite euphoria was short-lived, and what insurrectionary impulses there were proved only momentary. To be sure, there was considerable sympathy for the captured rebels, both in the capital and in the provinces. At Manchester, Townley and Tildesley's acquittal was openly celebrated, while at a bull-baiting near Shaftesbury several dragoons in General Carpenter's company were assaulted by a crowd to shouts of 'Murder the Rogues, they are the Villains that beat the King's army at Preston'.[64] Five months later Stephen Poyntz reported to Walpole that although Jacobitism was on the wane in the home counties, it was 'as violent as ever' in the Midlands, Wales and the West.[65] But the judicial evidence suggests that the fury generated by the trials was beginning to evaporate. To be sure, there was a persistent undercurrent of Jacobitism until Atterbury's trial, especially in London where the spectre of further executions inflamed the disaffected.[66] Yet despite the continuing unpopularity of the new regime, an English insurrection in favour of the Stuarts was never a serious possibility. Outside Catholic and non-juring circles, Jacobite militancy relapsed into nostalgia. As a Hereford lawyer put it as early as 1717, 'There will be no good times till King James the third comes again'.[67]

Jacobite symbolism continued to be used, however, to plague the Whigs. In towns where a vigorous Toryism survived the succession, royal anniversaries were marked by seditious revelry and calculated insults. For a decade and in some areas a good deal longer, oak garlands and white roses were displayed on Stuart holidays, bells rung, and Jacobite airs whistled long into the night. Contrariwise, Hanoverian anniversaries were punctuated by muffled bells, evanescent demonstrations at Whig bonfires, and very occasionally by flamboyant counter-professionals mocking George's cuckoldry. We cannot dismiss these confrontations as a joke, but we should not interpret them too literally either. Rather we should see them as attempts to reassert the traditions of the plebeian crowd in the face of official disapprobation, to debunk Whig homilies, and to strip Whig power of its symbolic supports — for there is no doubt that the Whigs went to great lengths to contain and reorient the political calendar. In London, for example, where great efforts were made to promote Restoration day as a loyalist event, one discovers regular encounters between the authorities and revellers sporting 'oak leaves and green knots' and bantering, 'make room for the Cuckoldy King and Send him to Hanover'.[68] As late as 1726 the Westminster bench directed that the precepts against seditious balladry be read in open court on the first day of every session, while the following year the Lord Mayor warned inhabitants against wearing mourning dress on Hanoverian holidays. In Bristol, too, one finds similar confrontations. Here the Whig caucus was initially teased by the sight of bonfires blazing from Brandon Hill on the Pretender's birthday and ambiguously royal Restoration garlands. Then, following a Tory victory at the 1734 election the plebeians moved in on a Hanoverian anniversary. 'As the magistrates and other gentlemen were met at the Council House to celebrate the evening,' one newspaper reported, 'and had made a fine illumination representing his Majesty's name in cypher and under it an Orange, from which issued a spear wounding a dragon, the mob rose and pelted out the lights with dirt and stones.'[69] Clearly the Tory boys were not going to allow the Whig corporation to steal their thunder.

If the examples of Bristol and London force us to look at Jacobitism within the context of a symbolic contest of authority, the West Midland counties take us on a slightly different path. In these solidly Tory strongholds noted for their cock-fighting, bull-baiting and village wakes, one encounters a more resilient tradition of Jacobite festival. In Shropshire and Staffordshire in particular, it became customary to vilify the Whigs on Stuart anniversaries. As late as 1750, five years after the final humiliation of the Jacobite rebels, the Hill Top boys of Walsall paraded George II's effigy on Restoration day, setting up a 'Barber's Block dressed with a Wigg and Hat, with a pair of Rams Horns on the Forehead' and using it as a cock-shy.[70] Forty miles away at Shrewsbury it was reported that 'for some Years past the town maypole had been decked with garlands of roses on the Pretender's birthday, & that last year a White Flag was carried about some part of the Town with Long Live Prince Charles wrote on it'.[71] Throughout the region, moreover, it was common practice to sport Jacobite emblems at the hustings. At the Lichfield by-election of 1718, for instance, the supporters of the Whig candidate William Chetwynd were confronted by 'a very great mob with papers in their hats ressembling white roses'. Jacobite colours were also paraded at the Coventry election of 1722 and at the Cheshire contest twelve years later.[72] The custom was still going strong in 1747, for plaid waistcoats were spotted at several Midland hustings. In Staffordshire in particular, where the Tories were incensed by the defection of Lord Gower, Jacobite favours flourished. Nor did matters end there. At the Lichfield hunt two months after the general election, one spectator recalled the town entry of the Burton contingent, 'most of 'em in Plaid waistcoats, Plaid ribbon round their hats and some with white cockades', and their Birmingham allies, 'most of 'em in the same dress', who 'drank the Pretender's health publicly in the streets, singing treasonable tunes'.[73] Indeed, the plaid seemed so engaging that the Lancashire Tories sported it at the Newton races the following year, and it may even have made its appearance at Tothill Fields, Westminster, within a ten-minute walk of Whitehall.

It is difficult to regard these revels as genuine Jacobitism. They were designed to draw Whig anger, to tease and unsettle the Court. To wear tartan in the wake of the Disarming Act, which specifically banned Highland dress in Scotland, was to snub the ministry in a most pointed way; just as the display of white roses in the face of official proscription had been earlier in the century. But parading the plaid can also be seen as a defiant vindication of freedom of expression against a background of Jacobite scares and staged trials, the last of which was concluded only a few months before the general election of 1747.[74] Tartan hunts were in addition a telling reminder of Cumberland's retributive campaign north of the border, especially when the quarry was rumoured to be a red-coated fox! Jacobite theatre, in other words, combined carnival with political commentary, licence with liberty. For the Tory gentry of the Midland shires Jacobite symbolism also expressed a sense of place, a defence of local traditions, a heritage of anti-Whiggery, while the irreverent processions of the Walsall lands demarcated *their* territory and warned their respectable town leaders that they were not to be meddled with.[75] The Hill Top rules, ok.

A similar, although again squirearchal, territorialism can also be found in Wales. Here the hard-drinking gentry congregated in their regional Jacobite clubs and regaled the populace on royal anniversaries. In Pembrokeshire it was said that the Philipps clan used 'all the means that they could to make the common sorte of the people to turn to the Pretender's side', including some flamboyant interventions at Hanoverian celebrations.[76] In Anglesey, too, Lord Bulkley appears to have encouraged Jacobite festival to reassert his influence. On the christening of his youngest son in 1717 he treated the inhabitants of Beaumaris at the cross of the town. One deponent swore that 'the sd Lords Head Gardener, William Jones & Marris Roberts likewise his servt. cry'd down with the Rump', threw stones at the house of the constable of the castle, and drank Jemmy's health at a local tavern. Such revelry proved of long standing in Anglesey. As late as 1747 objections were raised against the readmission of William Lewis of Llanddyfnan to the bench because he encouraged the locals to drink 'Right to him that suffers wrong' on the anniversary of Culloden, and on Oak Apple day organised a cock-fight 'when unfit toasts were named, and a fiddler playing the tune "When the King shall enjoy his own again" '.[77] Such a tradition of Jacobite conviviality, drawing some of its strength from the anglicanisation of the Church, did not long survive the death of its leading patrons. But it did represent, in its heyday, the local supremacy of the Tory squires in an age when political power was increasingly centralised and dependent upon Court favour.

But Jacobitism was not only used to define one's territory. It also entered the language of social protest. We discover the Southwark minters, driven to find a new sanctuary in Wapping, bidding defiance to king, justices and bailiffs in a rollicking Jacobite song. We find evocations of Jacobitism in Hampshire Black country, among Devonshire weavers, Newcastle keelmen, and Staffordshire poachers locked in a struggle with Beaudesert Hall.[78] During the 1756 bread riots, Midland miners warned that 'the Pretender would soon come and head them', while six years earlier the dragoons quartered at a hostile Shrewsbury were taunted with the following ditty:[79]

> Charley's Red & Charley's White
> And Charley he is Bonny O
> He is the son of a Royal King
> And I love him the best of any O
>
> When he came to Derby Town
> Oh but he was Bonny O
> The Bells did ring & the bagpipes Play
> And all for the Love of Charley O

We may regard this evidence as trivial. We may regard it with suspicion. For the depositions on these incidents may have been malevolent, designed to force the government's hand in sending troops, or simply to prejudice the case against rioters. But if we are not transfixed by literal interpretations of Jacobitism, then these incidents begin to make sense. For they all occurred in or near areas where there had been riots or demonstrations during the early accession years, in areas where Jacobitism was a familiar idiom of defiance. And it was quite understandable that the language of political blasphemy should be transferred to other contexts. By the mid-fifties, of course, very few regarded Jacobitism as a serious political force and the script lost favour. Allegations of Jacobitism still continued. The failure of some Tories to associate during the Forty-Five was raised on the Bristol hustings as late as 1781, and Wilkes exploited the Jacobite bogey in his attack upon Bute.[80] But as a creed Jacobitism was increasingly seen as quaint and quixotic, recalling at best a declining tradition of Tory paternalism. In a 1774 pamphlet 'an honest sociable cobbler' was suspected of harbouring a strong attachment to the Stuart family, 'though this attachment', the author added,

> seemed to have no other foundation than a compassion for the distressed, and never showed itself but in a harmless pun once a year; in wearing a sprig of rue and thyme on the eleventh of June (the accession of his late Majesty) as the tenth was honoured with a white rose.[81]

NOTES

1. P.R.O., SP 44/79A/152-6, 189-91.

2. B.L., Add. Ms. 38,507 fo. 128.

3. SP 35/11/125.

4. Abel Boyer, *The Political State of Great Britain*, 60 vols. (London, 1711-40), VIII, 438; *Flying Post*, 16/18 Nov. 1714.

5. *Flying Post*, 30 Oct./ 2Nov. 1714.

6. *Flying Post*, 14/16 June 1716.

7. Daniel Defoe, *Bold Advice: or Proposals For the Entire Rooting out of Jacobitism in Great Britain* (London, 1715), p. 29 and *Faction in Power: or the Mischiefs and Danger of a High-Church Magistracy* (London, 1717) *passim*. See also the *Freeholder*, 11 June 1716.

8. SP 35/3/77a. See also Abel Boyer, *A Compleat and Impartial History of the Impeachments of the Last Ministry* (London, 2nd edn., 1716), p. lxi.

9. B.L., Landsdowne MS. 817 fos. 27-44; *H.M.C. Stuart MSS.*, I, *passim*.

10. *St. James's Evening Post*, 23/25 Aug. 1715; Boyer, *Political State*, XVI, 499-501.

11. Daniel Defoe, *A Letter from a Gentleman of the Church of England to all the High-Flyers in Great Britain* (1715, reprinted Dublin 1716); *The Justice and Necessity of Restraining the Clergy in their Preaching* (London, 1715); *The Immorality of the Priesthood* (London, 1715); *The Pernicious Consequences of the Clergy's Intermeddling with Affairs of State* (London, 1715). The *Dublin Post-Man*, 6 June 1715.

12. *Flying Post*, 28/30 Sept. 1714, 30 Oct/2 Nov. 1714, 14/16 June 1716.

13. Add. MS. 35,600 fo. 290; SP 44/117/227; SP 44/79A/82; SP 35/74/6, 7, 12, 20; *St. James's Evening Post*, 23/25 August 1715; *Flying Post*, 21/23 June 1716.

14. SP 44/117/227-8.

15. SP 44/118, 15 Dec. 1715; *Pue's Occurrences* (Dublin), 10/12 May 1718.

16. Warwickshire Rec. Off., L 6/1638.

17. SP 44/118/16; Anon, *An Account of the Riots, Tumults and other Treasonable Practices since his Majesty's Accession to the Throne* (London, 1715), pp. 9-11.

18. See my 'Popular Protest in Early Hanoverian London', *Past and Present*, LXXIX (1978), pp. 70-100.

G

19. *An Account of a Dreadful Mob at Manchester and other places in England* (Edinburgh, 1715), pp. 3-4; SP 35/2/252-3.

20. On the Kingswood colliers see Robert Malcolmson, "A Set of Ungovernable People': The Kingswood Colliers in the Eighteenth Century', in John Brewer and John Styles, eds., *Ungovernable People? The English and their Law in the Seventeenth and Eighteenth Centuries* (Hutchinson: London, 1980).

21. Daniel Defoe, *A General Pardon Considered in its Circumstances and Consequences* (London, 1717), pp. 11-12.

22. Add. MS. 38,507 fo. 147; Joseph Grego, *A History of Parliamentary Elections* (London, 1892), p. 72; Alec Macdonald, *Worcestershire in English History* (London, 1943), pp. 125-6. For information on contested elections, see W. A. Speck, *Tory and Whig. The Struggle in the Constituencies* (London, 1970), pp. 126-31.

23. Anon, *An Account of the Riots, Tumults and other Treasonable Practices*, p. 8.

24. SP 35/11/141; SP 35/74/6-7.

25. *Flying Post*, 18/20 Nov. 1714.

26. Useful suggestions on this theme can be found in Robert Malcolmson, *Popular Recreations in English Society 1700-1850* (Cambridge, 1973), p. 158 and Michael Watts, *The Dissenters* (Oxford, 1978), pp. 313-14. On the resilience of popular sports in the West Midlands and Lancashire, see the *Victoria County Histories* for Staffordshire and Warwickshire, and tracts like *A Serious Disswasive from an Intended Subscription for Continuing the Races upon Kersal Moore* (Manchester, 1733).

27. [John Oldmixon], *The Bristol Riot* (London, 1714), p. 4.

28. *The Correspondence of Jonathan Swift 1714-23*, ed. Harold Williams, 5 vols. (Oxford, 1963), III, 131.

29. *The Weekly Journal or British Gazetteer*, 9 June 1716; Charles H. Cooper, *Annals of Cambridge*, 5 vols. (Cambridge, 1852), IV, 142-3; W. R. Ward, *Georgian Oxford. University Politics in the Eighteenth Century* (Oxford, 1958), 59.

30. *H. M. C. Townshend MSS.* p. 158.

31. J. H. Y. Briggs, 'The Burning of the Meeting House, July 1715: Dissent and Faction in late Stuart Newcastle', *North Staffs. Jor. of Field Studies*, XIV (1974), pp. 70-3; on the Wrexham disturbances, see E. D. Evans, *A History of Wales 1660-1815* (Cardiff, 1976), p. 57 and Nat. Lib. of Wales, Wales 4/41/4.

32. *Flying Post*, 26 April 1715.

33. Rogers, 'Popular Protest', *Past and Present* (1978), 71-3; *Dublin Post-Man*, 4 July 1715; P.R.O., WO 4/17/144.

34. *Flying Post*, 14/16 June 1715.

35. W. R. Ward, *Georgian Oxford*, p. 55.

36. *An Account of a Dreadful Mob at Manchester*, pp. 3-4.

37. *Flying Post*, 12/14 July 1715 and subsequent issues. See also P.R.O., Assi 4/18.

38. *The Weekly Journal or British Gazetteer*, 9 July 1715. See also *Flying Post*, 13/15 Sept. 1715.

39. See 31n.

40. Add. MS. 38, 507 fo. 136.

41. Samuel H. Ware, *Lancashire during the Rebellion of 1715* (Chetham Soc., V, 1845), pp. 16-19; *Flying Post* 16/19 July 1715; Assi 4/18/315.

42. Romney Sedgwick (ed.) *The History of Parliament: The House of Commons 1715-54*, 2 vols. (London, 1970), I, 271-2. The John Evans MSS. in Dr. Williams' Library, London, reveal that over a third of the Lancashire electorate was non-conformist.

43. See 31n.

44. Chetham Lib., Manchester, MS. diary of Edmund Harrold, 18 May 1716; Charles Olwen, *The Jure Divino Woe* (London, 1717).

45. Elizabeth Hamilton, *The Mordaunts* (London, 1965), p. 103.

46. *Post Boy*, 12/14, 21/23 May, 11/14, 18/21 July 1713 and the *Flying Post*, 19/21 July 1713.

47. Anon, *On Thanksgiving Day* (20 Jan. 1715). A copy of this poem can be found in the Houghton Library, Harvard.

48. Chetham Lib., Manchester, Halliwell-Phillipps Collection, no. 1187.

49. Rogers, 'Popular Protest', *Past and Present* (1978), 92-4.

50. *Flying Post*, 16/19 July 1715.

51. John Withers, *The Whigs Vindicated* (London, 8th edn., 1715), p. 31.

52. W. R. Ward, *Georgian Oxford*, pp. 90-1. *Britannia's Memorial* is in the Houghton Library, Harvard.

53. Greater London Rec. Off., MJ/OC/1/21-23.

54. B.L., Blenheim Papers D I, doc. 57; *H.M.C. 3rd Report*, pp. 319-20; J. P. W. Rogers, 'John Oldmixon in Bridgwater 1716-30', *Proc. Somerset Arch. & Nat. History Society*, CXIII (1969), pp. 86-98.

55. [John Oldmixon], *The Bristol Riot*, p. 7.

56. Rogers, 'Popular Protest', *Past and Present* (1978), 73-5, 81-3.

57. *A Letter to a Member of Parliament from a Gentleman of Bristol Containing a Particular and True Account of the Extraordinary Proceedings relating to the late Election of Members of Parliament for that City* (London, 1715), p. 6. A copy can be found in the Central Reference Library at Bristol.

58. *Whalley's Dublin Post-Man*, 20 Oct. 1715; W. R. Ward, *Georgian Oxford*, pp. 60-4.

59. SP 35/27/39-42, 67, 246-89.

60. Edward Hughes, *North Country Life in the Eighteenth Century. The North East 1700-50* (Oxford, 1952), p. 22.

61. Bristol Rec. Off., QS. indictments, 13 March 1716.

62. SP 35/74/16-17.

63. Assi 4/18/232, 248.

64. *Flying Post*, 31 May/2 June 1716.

65. William Coxe, *Memoirs of the Life and Administration of Sir Robert Walpole*, 2 vols. (London, 1798), II, 97.

66. SP 35/40/50, 35/11/260, 44/79A/146-8. See also John Doran, *London in the Jacobite Times*, 2 vols. (London, 1877). In his charge to the Grand Jury of Dorset in April 1720, James Montagu complained of 'the most daring and insulting behaviour, both in Words and Actions, perhaps that ever was heard of, towards our Great and Good King' (*Weekly Journal or British Gazetteer*, 18 June 1720).

67. Assi 4/18/402.

68. SP 44/79A/235; Greater London Rec. Off., WJ/OC/II/32; *Historical Register*, 23 vols. (London, 1717-38), XII, 260. For some illuminating remarks on Jacobitism as counter-theatre, see E. P. Thompson, 'Patrician Society, Plebeian Culture', *Journal of Social History* (Summer, 1974), pp. 400-02 and 'Eighteenth-century English society: class struggle without class?', *Social History* III, no. 2. (1978), pp. 158-60.

69. John Latimer, *The Annals of Bristol in the Eighteenth Century* (Bristol, 1893), pp. 20, 110-11, 113, 164, 193. For another demonstration in the Bristol suburbs see P.R.O., KB 35/5/3.

70. SP 36/113/88-101, 161-6.

71. SP 36/113/183-5.

72. Sedgwick (ed.), *House of Commons 1715-54*, I, 319, 340; *V. C. H. Cheshire*, II, 122; *Northampton Mercury*, 13/20 Nov. 1722.

73. Lichfield Papers, Mr. Hinton to Lord Anson, 26 Sept, 1747. I am indebted to Dr. Eveline Cruickshanks for this reference. For Jacobite festival 1747-48, see Eveline Cruickshanks, *Political Untouchables. The Tories and the '45* (London, 1979), pp. 106-8; Henry Fielding, *The Jacobite Journal and Related Writings*, ed. W. B. Coley (Oxford, 1974), pp. lxx, 93n., 126, 368-70; and F. G. Stephens (ed.), *Catalogue of Prints and Drawings in the British Museum*, III, pt. 1 (London, 1877), nos. 2863-5.

74. On the pre-electoral theatre of the Whigs, see my 'Aristocratic Clientage, Trade and Independency: Popular Politics in Pre-Radical Westminster', *Past and Present*, LXI (1973), pp. 75-6.

75. My views on plebeian Jacobitism in Staffordshire owe much to Doug Hay's paper on the subject, presented to the Conference on Sedition and Crime in Eighteenth-Century England at the University of Toronto, Canada, March 1978. See also Ernest J. Homeshaw, *The Corporation of the Borough and Foreign of Walsall* (Walsall, 1960), pp. 91-5.

76. Add. MS. 36,686 fo. 106.

77. Add. MS. 35,602 fo. 298; SP 44/79A/105-110. See also P. D. G. Thomas, 'Jacobitism in Wales', *Welsh Historical Review*, I (1960), pp. 279-80, and Donald Nicholas, 'The Welsh Jacobites', *Trans. Hon. Soc. Cymmrodorion* (1948), pp. 467-74.

78. R. L. Brown, 'The Minters of Wapping: The History of a Debtors' Sanctuary in Eighteenth Century East London', *East London Papers*, XIV (1972), pp. 77-86; John Oldmixon, *The History of England During the Reigns of King William . . . George I*, pp. 751-2; P. D. G. Isaacs, 'A Study of Popular Disturbances in Britain 1714-1754' (Univ. of Edinburgh Ph.D. thesis, 1953), p. 182; Douglas Hay, 'Poaching and the Game Laws on Cannock Chase', in Douglas Hay, Peter Linebaugh and E. P. Thompson (eds.), *Albion's Fatal Tree* (London, 1975), p. 225; E. P. Thompson, *Whigs and Hunters. The Origins of the Black Act* (London, 1975), pp. 164-6.

79. Add. MS. 32,867 fo. 3; P.R.O., TS 11/929/3268.

80. *North Briton*, 6 Nov. 1762, 15 Jan., 19 Feb. 1763; Latimer, *Annals of Bristol*, p. 446.

81. Anon, *The Spiritual Quixote, or the Summer's Ramble of Mr. Geoffrey Wildgoose* (London, 1774). I am indebted to Johanna Innes of the University of Cambridge for this reference.

5

Sham Plots and Real Plots in the 1690s

Paul Hopkins

A MAJOR difficulty in studying the Jacobitism of the 1690s is the mass of allegations about supposed plots which fills the state papers and newsletters of the period. Wild rumours are of course common in times of upheaval. In every reign informers invented assassination plots which have been rightly ignored by historians, but their sheer number and the serious attention given to them under William is unusual.

Historians generally discount the Jacobite explanation that the King and his ministers — 'insolent Dutch and sneaking, mercenary Englishmen', Princess Anne called them — cynically encouraged false accusations to alarm the country into blind support and destroy men for their estates.[1] Yet they are sometimes uneasy in dealing with specific instances; could the William of their usual picture, so well-informed that he could be confident the intrigues of Compounders such as Marlborough were merely for reinsurance, really be taken in by such stories?

The genuine Jacobite history of the reign has never been written in detail, largely because the loss of so much evidence, particularly the main Stuart archives for the period, makes it uncertain which of the more plausible reports and allegations are true. Some writers deduce from the partial unreliability of this one class of evidence that all Jacobite material can safely be ignored. This essay attempts to set some of the unsifted allegations, false witnesses and legends in context.

A salient fact about the 1690s is that the whole period lay in the shadow of the Popish Plot. A large proportion of the political nation — including, probably, several of William's ministers — interpreted contemporary politics in the light of what they imagined it had revealed. After subsiding in the 1680s, belief in the reality of the Plot re-awakened at the Revolution when Titus Oates was rehabilitated. His previous successes inspired new hordes of would-be perjurers, who made their own secret deductions from the events of the Plot. The most significant of these was that the more important the person accused, the more enemies would be ready to support the charge, and the greater the possible reward. The Whigs had protected Oates because he accused the Queen and the Duke of York. Had he continued to look no higher than the Catholic peers, he would have been considerably less safe.

Ironically, this principle partly protected the Catholics after the Revolution had destroyed their power at Court. They were, of course, all supposed to be plotting:

several defendants charged with treason produced evidence of their Anglicanism as a partial refutation.[2] Yet, although alleged assassination plots were generally blamed on Papists, the most dangerous false witnesses looked higher. The Popish Plot and Catholic counter-plots, the exposure of Danby's French intrigues and the false Court-backed charges of treason against Shaftesbury in 1681 had created a belief that any accusation against Opposition Whigs, however plausible, would ultimately be proved false, whereas any charge of treason against their Court opponents — Tories replacing Catholics after 1688 — would ultimately be confirmed, however often it was 'stifled'.[3] Fear of arousing this irrational conviction prevented William's government from punishing effectively the most absurd accusations against ministers. As late as 1696, Danby, now Duke of Leeds, was alarmed by an attempt to link the Assassination Plot with Oates's old accusation that he was behind the Popish Plot.[4] It had always been obvious that false accusations of treason could succeed with the Court's support; the Popish Plot established that such accusations could also succeed despite the Court's hostility.

Deprived of the automatic credulity of anti-Catholicism, which had led one judge to lay down as a principle for trying Papists, 'when there are two men that positively tell you a thing that is within their knowledge, and swear it is true; it is scarcely any improbability that should weigh against such an evidence', would-be plot-makers had to produce stories more credible than Oates's allegations and forgeries.[5] Almost all the Popish Plot witnesses, discredited by changing sides in the 1680s, had vanished.[6] Significantly, the major perjurers now usually worked in pairs, a youth who actually laid the information, and an older, experienced man who prepared it and advised him, sometimes a skilled forger, often too notorious to testify himself: Fuller and Titus Oates, John Lunt and John Taaffe, Aubrey Price and William Chaloner, Stephen Blackhead and Robert Young.[7] All were swindlers, claiming to be gentlemen or clergymen, but of lower social status than the Popish Plot witnesses. Two of the youths, Fuller and Lunt, the offspring of mixed Catholic-Anglican marriages, were unbalanced fantasists. They had gained genuine knowledge of Jacobitism, but both were babblers and had need of a cool prompter.[8] They found it easy to gain some credentials from credulous Jacobites, who, despite frequent warnings, believed anybody claiming to be a messenger from the exiled Court at St. Germain.[9] On a higher level, much Jacobitism was sufficiently barefaced to provide them with background information (even on so delicate a matter as Whig negotiations with James), and rumour filled the gaps. Fortunately for the historian, though the accessories were plausible, the main stories were usually crude and stereotyped; the same elements recur, and the tone is consistently theatrical. Dramatic gestures, it is true, were not confined to sentimental or alcoholic Jacobites: Halifax bared his breast to one agent and wept over James' misfortunes before another.[10] Most characters in sham plots, however, were always at this hysterical pitch, reading treasonable letters aloud, waving swords, receiving Jacobite commissions on their knees[11] and trampling on Williamite ones; every act was underlined for the benefit of a jury.

The perjurers' real skill was to adapt their stories for the patrons or groups they approached, implicating their enemies and playing on their prejudices. It was common knowledge that Thomas Wharton wished to destroy Nottingham, and Carmarthen to ruin Halifax. Even when deliberate subornation took place, it probably seldom needed more than veiled hints. Most of those approached, unaware that a careful study had been made of their prejudices, accepted without question 'accidental' confirmation of them. Great men, said an agent who later duped Harley, were far easier to deceive than commoners.[12] Fuller pushed this law of supply and demand to the point of parody; telling his story of the True Mother of the Prince of Wales when the Court was anxious to refute proof of the Prince's legitimacy; providing the Parliament of 1691-2 with the gigantic plots it was hunting for, and Carmarthen with charges against Halifax which Fuller altered, when fashion changed the next year, to implicate Marlborough instead; claiming in 1696 to have evidence against Sir John Fenwick, and finally alleging treason and French bribery of the Tories in William's last Parliament.[13]

Impudence was the perjurers' most alarming trait. Oates had been freed and pensioned after years of punishment. By being equally brazen other convicted perjurers might profit from a change in political circumstances, however often they had been exposed. The weakness in the legal system against perjury made them almost indestructible. It was rare for one to confess when his story broke down. Those accused by perjurers and subsequently cleared could never be certain, under the old treason trial laws, that even a discredited witness, choosing his time and political backing, might not succeed by surprise — the judicial murder of Alderman Cornish in 1685 was a recent example. The best safeguard, apparently invented by Pepys, was to prepare an attested account of the accuser's previous crimes to undermine his general credibility. Bishop Sprat published his life of Robert Young with unique success: Young was the one plot-forger who made no comeback.[14]

The danger from perjurers was greatest if the Government supported them. Many, besides Jacobites, suspected that it did. William clung to the legal advantages in treason cases which his predecessors had so abused, and this has led some 'Country' historians to suspect his motives.[15] Most perjurers, however, were not sponsored by the Government, whose behaviour was determined largely by the intelligence available and by the practical difficulties of state prosecutions.

Contrary to general belief, William and his most trusted ministers had only fragmentary intelligence of significant Jacobite activity, gathered by scattered agents and not analysed to form a coherent picture. Although security at St. Germain was lax, and in the quarrels between Compounders and Non-Compounders (as the constitutionalist and absolutist parties were called) each side accused the other of being in William's pay, the English Government gave priority to obtaining intelligence of French military and naval activity, so that there were probably few real spies at St. Germain.[16] The system was so rudimentary that the most professional agent, John Macky who later served Walpole, lacked all means of communication and had to return himself to make his report.[17] One instance indicates the Government's ignorance. When the worthless spy Matthew Smith was claiming that Shrewsbury, by neglecting his reports, had allowed the Assassination Plot to proceed, he said that his chief Jacobite contact received regular instructions from James's minister Lord Melfort. None of those anxious to discredit Smith, not even William or his favourite Portland, apparently realised that since his dismissal in 1694 Melfort had been exiled from St. Germain.[18]

William himself was probably seldom better informed. It has sometimes been assumed that Portland ran an anti-Jacobite intelligence network after 1688 as reliable as his pre-Revolution English correspondence had been. In fact, Portland seems to have been unlucky in his choice of agents. His surviving papers indicate that his main source at St. Germain was a French Catholic, a former Court hanger-on who had access to James but used the real information he obtained to build great fantasies of English peers crossing to and from France.[19] In England, Portland chose the best agent the Government ever had, Richard Kingston, but also the Jacobite Simpson, who completely deceived him, and the professional perjurer Taaffe.[20]

When the Duke of Devonshire told Fenwick in 1696 that William had already heard most of his allegations about his ministers' intrigues, he was probably nearer the truth than Shrewsbury, who assumed that nothing was known against him. Yet the King's letter to Portland about the Earl of Middleton's mission to France in 1693 indicates a lack of knowledge of the Compounders' negotiations and a wish to know more.[21] In 1691, contrary to general belief, it was William, not Carmarthen, who tried to make the captured Lord Preston tell more of his negotiations with Whig nobles.[22] When Sir James Montgomerie was captured in 1694, the King intended to use torture to make him confess his intrigues with the Whig ministers just appointed to office.[23] There were two occasions when he applied political pressure by showing the men concerned knowledge of their intrigues: in 1694, by telling Shrewsbury of a fairly innocuous conversation with Montgomerie, and by frightening the Duke of Hamilton in 1700 with recently gained knowledge.[24] The degree of credence he gave to allegations (mostly from unreliable sources) against prominent men depended on his personal likes and dislikes. For instance, he believed that his *bête-noire* the Earl of Monmouth would not only negotiate with James but also start corn riots.[25] Ministers were equally prejudiced: Nottingham, on hearing of Admiral Russell's Jacobite negotiations, wrongly assumed that he had wrecked the 1692 naval campaign deliberately, and Secretary Trumbull convinced himself that his overbearing colleague Shrewsbury was an active Jacobite.[26] Halifax, hovering on the edge of Jacobite intrigues, probably knew more about them than did William.[27]

The Government, however, was well-informed about the activities of committed Jacobites. To keep them in check and deter others, it must ensure that the choice between mercy and severity lay in William's hands; and for this successful prosecutions were essential. It has sometimes been assumed that the old procedure in treason trials made success easy, but to ministers this was the one advantage in a process full of irrational legal obstacles.

Parliament failed to pass a Treason Trials Act until 1696, but it also refused to strengthen the law significantly. For instance, correspondence with James or his adherents did not become treason until 1697. After repeated suspensions of the Habeas Corpus Act in 1689, MPs, alarmed at the precedent, forced the Government in the crises of 1690 and 1692 to use arrest 'on suspicion of treason' against men it wished only to detain and to lessen its power and credit by failing to prosecute them afterwards.[28]

One particular problem facing William's Government was treachery in its executive branch. Not only did Marlborough, a member of the cabinet, warn endangered Jacobites during 1691,[29] but they also received constant information from the Secretaries' clerks on warrants and charges against them. Shrewsbury and Trenchard during the Lancashire Plot, and Trumbull at the time of the Assassination Plot, bypassed the offices and filled in warrants themselves.[30] The messengers who made arrests and detained prisoners in their own homes were often unreliable. Prisons were not secure, as the officers bought their places and were difficult to remove. This applied even in the Tower, where the judges declared that only the Governor was legally responsible so that, not surprisingly, three important prisoners escaped in one year. The keeper of Newgate, who connived at the escape of an important suspect in 1696, retained his place on a technicality. Finally, Jacobites who reached trial in Middlesex might be informed of the indictments and of the witnesses' names beforehand by the Clerk of the Peace, Simon Harcourt.[31]

Little could be done about such freehold posts. In the Secretaries' offices, as in other departments, it was at least debatable whether the professional skill of experienced officials compensated for potential, or even actual, disloyalty. William and his ministers, even Whig ones, usually preferred the old officials, but they neglected the corollary that close control was essential. As the treason of Harley's clerk Greg showed in Anne's reign, the offices were always security risks. Yet refusal to mount witch-hunts, admirable in itself, could deteriorate into careless indifference. Shrewsbury in 1694 re-employed a clerk of Nottingham's even though agents in France twice warned that he was writing regularly to James. Nottingham, though more conscientious, was no better at security. Both Secretaries were often accused of treason, and if the treachery of their subordinates had been proved in 1691 and 1697, their enemies' wilder charges might have been believed.[32]

Most prosecutions failed where there was no treachery. Evidence had usually to be collected far too quickly. Even when the accused was not bailed under the Habeas Corpus Act, witnesses got bail and vanished.[33] Money was so short that Treasury Solicitor Aaron Smith sometimes forced prisoners by his extortions to pay for their own prosecutions.[34] Mistakes in procedure and failure to construct adequate cases[35] had a disastrous effect on government attempts to quash major conspiracies. After Preston's plot, the Jacobites were able to lure a vital witness to France, a trick they repeated in 1696 with Goodman, one of the witnesses against Fenwick (whom the Government desperately wanted to silence).[36]

The failure of prosecutions encouraged the Jacobites to attribute William's genuine forbearance to weakness and constantly tempted the Government to bend or strain the law. In the courts, the advantage given to the Crown by the old treason trial procedure and the judges' natural bias as the King's servants was reinforced by devices such as whittling away the time conventionally allowed to prepare a defence, and packing panels for juries.[37] The trial of Walter Crosby in 1695 explains why such management was thought necessary. A Jacobite messenger for five years, he was one of a large number captured in 1694, but all the rest escaped or were bailed. His lodgings were full of treasonable papers and invasion plans; the most notorious men on the run had visited him; yet, because the Government case relied entirely on the papers, Lord Chief Justice Holt acted for once in the judge's theoretical role as 'prisoner's counsel', and threw it out.[38]

The comparison Ferguson drew in his *Letter to Trenchard* with Government conduct in the 1680s had some validity, however untrue his individual charges were. Both regimes strained the law to secure the conviction of real or supposed traitors, although it was now Whig lawyers who tried to extend Crown power and Tories who defended the liberty of the subject.[39] Yet William, unlike Charles II, has comparatively seldom been criticised for his infringements of the law. One obvious reason was that the Jacobites were defeated and their complaints, unlike those of the first Whigs, were forgotten. Besides, it was not the King's courts but Parliament which enacted the two most dubious legal measures of the reign, the attainder of Fenwick and the detention — for life, it proved — of Assassination Plot suspects.[40] While even Jeffreys' most understandable judgements had been incorporated in a systematic campaign against liberty, the ingrained lack of system which characterised all William's government reduced the need for alarm. He retained, for example, the right of judicial torture in Scotland, and attempted to exploit a pre-Revolutionary practice, now illegal, of shipping Scots home to interrogate them on English plots. However, in his general neglect of Scottish business, the right of torture itself lapsed.[41] In fact, William's reputation for leniency was largely deserved. The hope that the Jacobites would accept defeat which induced him not to press charges after the 1690 crisis did not, however, survive Preston's plot. Although no major conspiracy was successfully prosecuted until 1696, it was legal failures, not Government policy, which prevented convictions in 1691, 1692 and 1694. The 1695 General Pardon gave the Jacobites a final chance to submit, and 'after soe publick a warning' they could not be surprised by the ruthlessness shown following the Assassination Plot.[42] William's previous clemency is more striking since he believed in many false plots as well as real ones.

It was more profitable to be a witness than a spy. Witnesses after the Popish, Rye House and Assassination Plots received pensions for years, while the best spies were forgotten — Kingston was left to scrape a living by pamphleteering.[43] False witnesses found the ministers 'the easiest to be cheated of any men in the world'. Ministers, on their side, could not be overscrupulous. 'The Generality of Informers are scoundrels,' wrote Vernon, 'and yet their oaths must pass until they are disproved.'[44] Yet Kingston, the Government's best spy, was in these terms also a 'scoundrel' — but not, apparently, a liar. The evidence indicates that ministers did not, in their official capacities, deliberately suborn witnesses, although a few — such as Carmarthen and the Scottish Secretary Johnston — who did so for party political ends, inevitably damaged their colleagues' credit.[45] Lacking a coherent picture of Jacobite activity, William and his ministers could not evaluate informers' stories or see when alleged plots were out of character. Their frequent willingness to leave doubtful matters to the law — shared even by Shrewsbury, whose support for the Treason Trials Act was astonishing in a Secretary of State[46] — and the clumsiness of their examination technique gave false witnesses their chance.

Nearly all the Assassination Plot witnesses were untrustworthy, yet confessions confirmed their stories. A Jacobite complaint that Captain Porter, the ringleader who turned King's Evidence, was an *agent provocateur* employed by Portland can be disproved.[47] One vital witness, however, did commit perjury. On 14 March 1695/6, Porter described two meetings of Non-Compounding leaders to urge James to invade. Jacobite documents largely confirm his account.[48] He was not yet pardoned, and, if the Assassins only were tried, his bad character might make the Government discard him as a witness, leaving him, at best, to a debtors' prison.[49] To make this prosecution possible, Porter named another conspirator, Goodman, who had arrived after one meeting, as present throughout. Goodman was called in. The ministers' notes show that at first he showed himself ignorant of the invasion project: 'Hee knew that Charnock went over with a message 5 or 6 months ago . . . but hee does not know his arrant.' Then, urged to 'show his sincerity', and taking his cue from leading questions, he blundered on until he had confirmed Porter and ensured both their safeties.[50] Yet the ministers' interpretation was apparently that Goodman had prevaricated before telling the truth. When Peter Cook, condemned on this evidence, claimed that he was almost sure Goodman was not present, and would declare so if executed, Vernon, who had attended Goodman's examination, felt no doubt that this was a lie by Cook to make himself indispensable as a second witness.[51] It was a little-noticed assumption under the late Stuarts that such a use of perjurers, even to support a true charge, entitled the accused to consider himself innocent. Therefore, Ailesbury, who had attended the meetings, gave, even in his memoirs thirty years later, not the truth but the alibis he had prepared.[52]

Any such Government involvement with false witnesses alarmed not only the Jacobites but the Opposition Whigs, whose traumatic fears dated back to 1681. In 1689, a Jacobite agent playing on them stampeded Sir James Montgomerie and other Scottish Whigs into actual Jacobite intrigues.[53] In practice, however, an unsuccessful sham plot against an opponent of the Government might make him immune from justified prosecution. When Marlborough was arrested for treason in 1692, a professional swindler, Robert Young, forged a Jacobite 'Association' with his signature. Another intended victim, Bishop Sprat of Rochester, exposed Young's plot, which was automatically blamed by the Opposition for Marlborough's arrest.[54] False accusers knew better than the Whig alarmists which side their bread was buttered on. Marlborough, whom William hated, was accused only once; Nottingham and Shrewsbury, whom he favoured, constantly. The main barrier against miscarriages of justice was the sifting of allegations by the ministers, who accumulated a working knowledge of regular perjurers and typical stories. Prosecutions in which ministers were not involved seem more often to have resulted in convictions based on false accusations.

The Lancashire Plot shows how dangerous the treason laws were without this preliminary sifting, and how completely the Government could convince itself that false accusations were true, while seeming to outsiders to be attempting judicial murder. Many Lancashire Catholic gentry were planning a rising from 1689 to 1694. From 1692, they were led by Colonel Parker, an agent from St. Germain. Early in 1694, John Lunt, a youthful fantasist who had been slightly involved with them four years earlier, was in London. His brother-in-law John Taaffe was the leading perjurer in a group which since the Revolution had been swearing, for a share of the forfeitures, that the Catholics in various counties had illegally given lands to their Church — a last flicker of the Popish Plot in the civil courts. Lunt was recruited to provide local colour in an Exchequer suit.[55] When the Lancashire victims began to prove alibis and to threaten a prosecution for perjury, he prepared, perhaps under Taaffe's direction, a sham plot involving them and other gentlemen, Protestant as well as Catholic, interwove earlier stories in his narrative and presented the result to the Whig ministers, Shrewsbury, Somers and Trenchard.[56]

Some historians have supposed that Lunt had knowledge of the real plot, since he claimed that a messenger from France called a meeting of conspirators in February 1691/2, as Parker did that April, and that the Catholics sent James in July 1693 an assurance of support similar to one really sent in November. This was mere coincidence. His story of an assurance sent to James was adapted from one about a meeting of Catholic trustees to which he had sworn in the Exchequer. The passage about Walmesley was added later. He was the richest Catholic in Lancashire, but Carmarthen, his relation, had protected him from the 'superstitious lands' prosecution, and a particularly strong charge would be needed to convict him. Parker, whose role Lunt did not know, was then in the Tower, but a warrant was issued for him under his Lancashire *alias*.[57]

The ministers, who acted in this case without consulting William, are sometimes accused of having accepted an implausible story in the hope of confiscating rich estates; and, as this could not be believed of Shrewsbury, who managed the affair, the Jacobite Ferguson blamed his colleague Trenchard.[58] In fact, Lunt's story was plausible, as the parallels with the real plot show. It resembled the vague reports of conspiracy which had been received from Lancashire for years and confirmed by recently captured documents. One of Lunt's supporting witnesses had actually carried arms to Lancashire, and, when the arrests were made, considerable evidence of a planned rising was found.[59]

The Jacobites, however, had advance warning, so that only two of the ten gentlemen arrested and tried were actual conspirators. Even they, being ignorant of the accusations, were in more danger than if tried for their real crimes.[60] Attempts to expose witnesses, the only means of defence possible, were blocked by the Government as typical Jacobite tricks, so that Ferguson, who had praised Chief Justice Holt as a bulwark against tyranny in the summer, was complaining in the autumn of his refusal to hear the plainest evidence.[61] It was mere accident that Taaffe, resentful at being ill-rewarded, changed sides and helped discredit Lunt, with the result that, even before a strongly biased Whig judge, all the defendants were acquitted.

In an attempt to strike a decisive secret blow at Jacobitism, the ministers had employed Lunt's private backers rather than undersecretaries or local JPs — and had merely laid themselves open to deception. The lesson that the innocent were more in danger from existing treason trial procedure than the guilty was lost in party struggles that winter.[62] When a parliamentary inquiry produced evidence that there had been a plot, the Government accepted Lunt's account as gospel and felt such resentment about being tricked that it became, if anything, less alert to the dangers from false witnesses.

Parliament had been the driving force behind the Popish Plot. It had accepted the charges against James, the Queen and Danby, had deciphered the treasonable letters of James's secretary Coleman, and had forced the Privy Council and ministers to show more vigour to avoid charges of 'stifling the Plot'. In the eyes of most MPs Parliament had uncovered a monstrous conspiracy, gaining for a while considerable control over the executive. This explains why William's government, while exploiting the discovery of Jacobite plots for parliamentary advantage, was careful not to produce before either House intercepted documents which might lead to independent inquiries.[63]

Plot-forgers and witnesses were able to play the Government and Parliament against one another, and looked to the Commons as their patrons. 'You shall find it to your sorrow all is not confessed yet,' snarled Robert Young after his exposure, 'a parliament shall come, and then you shall hear from me.' All sections of the Opposition were ready to act on unjustified complaints against departments of state. 'Very many think themselves little concerned what right is done to particular persons under false accusations,' wrote Vernon.[64] However useful the use of perjury had been to unite opposition against Charles II, it did lasting harm: the Whig party was born tainted. One section, like the notorious MP John Arnold, who had been driven to use perjury in the Popish Plot to achieve populist aims, regularly exploited it after 1689 for personal ends. Their Parliamentary experience made them formidable.[65]

Rather than face constant Parliamentary criticism, ministers had to treat seriously allegations they disbelieved. They were often blamed for paying attention to the evidence of men they would have discarded if they dared. Nottingham told the Queen 'he could not avoid the hearing Fuller because if he refused it he would be fallen upon'. Yet Halifax, whom Fuller accused, suspected Government complicity.[66]

The best-organised single attempt to use Jacobitism in attacking the Government was in the 1691-2 session. That spring, Carmarthen had expected Preston's confession to 'breake the teeth' of opponents like Sir Edward Seymour, who was named in it, but failure to prosecute gave the Opposition the initiative. One correspondent suggested to Robert Harley that Preston should be forced 'to testify by an Act of Parliament . . . seemingly . . . carried on to Cutt off his Estate for ever,' adding queries which would tell him plainly whom to implicate, Privy Councillors, Secretaries, Lords of the Treasury.[67] This course was not followed. Instead the chief victim, Nottingham, was attacked in both Houses on his weakest point, his own department. John Arnold pointed to passes allegedly given to smugglers, and the Duke of Bolton supported allegations that secret orders had been leaked to the French. This led the Commons to send for Preston's confession. William Fuller, apparently primed by Arnold, now told detailed stories of Jacobite intrigues.[68] The plan miscarried because Preston's confession implicated the Opposition not the ministers, and the charge against Nottingham was dismissed. Everything now depended on Fuller. The House committed itself by asking William for a blank pass to bring over his two Jacobite witnesses from France, but when there was no sign of them at the end of the session, Fuller was voted an impostor. After this, the Commons never fully regained the initiative.[69]

In 1693, Wharton prepared an attack on Nottingham, using perjurers, but was forestalled by the Secretary's dismissal.[70] However, the enquiry into the loss of the Smyrna convoy encouraged subornation on party lines. A captain of a merchant ship with a private grudge claimed that the three admirals of the fleet — two of them Tories — had ignored his warning that the French fleet was out. Only Tory solidarity preserved the admirals in the Commons, but the Lords discovered that he was lying. The good official posts he received afterwards in Whig-controlled departments show who his prompters were. They had been prepared to sacrifice the innocent Admiral Shovell, but had been correct in guessing that the two Tories had been in contact with James.[71]

Fenwick's charges of Jacobitism against ministers in 1696, therefore, crystallised MPs' suspicions of treason in high places. They cut across a campaign against Shrewsbury already started by the eccentric Earl of Monmouth, a fellow-Whig who had an irrational hatred of him. Monmouth's main allies were John Arnold and his cousins Sir Harry and John Colt, place-hunting MPs and, like Monmouth, political protégés of Sunderland. After the Assassination Plot, they attended as J.P.s on a witness, Fisher. Presumably at their bidding, he falsely informed the King that the organiser of the Plot, Sir George Barclay, had said that Shrewsbury and many others, mostly Tories, were Jacobites. Being a Crown witness, Fisher must not be exposed, and by September his prompters were encouraging him to petition Parliament.[72] Shrewsbury had neglected warnings about the Assassination Plot from an unreliable spy, Matthew Smith, whom Monmouth subsequently directed in appeals to William and Parliament.[73] Once rumours of Fenwick's confession spread, Monmouth backed the demand that Parliament should intervene.[74] However, since Fenwick's papers had strong accidental similarities to past false accusations, and seemed to imply that the Whigs had not only intrigued with James but were involved in the Assassination Plot, his refusal to give further evidence suggested a trick to gain a pardon, after which he would refuse to testify.[75]

For once, the Government, treading carefully, kept the advantage. Crucial was Sunderland's success in persuading the Junto Whigs that the charges against the Tories must also be condemned, since Monmouth and his henchmen depended for their attack on Shrewsbury on confirmation of Fenwick's accusations against Marlborough and Godolphin.[76] The presentation of Fenwick's confessions to the Commons was well managed. On his first appearance, not knowing that William had allowed the Commons' examination, Fenwick assumed that this was an unauthorised parliamentary inquiry by which he could never gain a pardon. Nor did he realise that his second confession, implicating the Non-Compounders, had been read.[77] The Whigs then introduced a bill of attainder to silence him for good, but, until it passed, the Government was on very thin ice. Although in the debates only Sir Edward Seymour defied the convention that Fenwick must be lying, many Members knew otherwise; Tories secretly pledged support if he would substantiate his charges, while Whig malcontents had 'unintelligible notions of advantages to be made' through them. However, some leading opponents of the bill such as Harley disbelieved Fenwick, and, by demanding impossible safeguards and 'neither owning nor denying' his papers, he gave the appearance of a perjurer who had lost his nerve.[78] Fenwick was pessimistic from the start, and his defence was further hampered by his fellow prisoner Ailesbury making an informal bargain with the accused ministers to keep silent.[79] Monmouth, whose help to prove his charges Fenwick declined, supported the bill in the Lords out of revenge. Fenwick's kinsmen retaliated by exposing Monmouth's machinations. He was only briefly imprisoned, but his evidence was discredited.[80] Fenwick was executed — less owing to William's longstanding enmity or Whig anger at his revelations than to the danger that, unless he was silenced for good, he might sooner or later justify his allegations.

Fenwick's fate did not, as was hoped, deter further false witnesses, whose charges caused Shrewsbury more trouble than the truth had done. Vernon, Somers and Portland spent the next three years protecting their colleague, whose illness in the country made him particularly vulnerable. The revengeful Monmouth (now Earl of Peterborough), and Arnold and the Colts, whose preferment Shrewsbury was blocking,[81] employed Fisher, Smith and several other false witnesses to hint at charges and press for rewards, which might then be represented as 'hush money' to Parliament. They still had many allies there frustrated by the failure to make Fenwick talk, and Arnold's ability to manipulate Commons committees created a real danger.[82] Sunderland tried to restrain them, but without success. Their activities helped to ruin his credit with the Junto — apart from Shrewsbury, whose gratitude to him for his help over Fenwick's charges damaged his own relations with them.[83] The worst year was 1697, with three separate accusations being spread against Shrewsbury, but the attacks persisted until he left England in 1700. By then Arnold and the Colts, whose attempts to obtain office by this blackmail had failed in 1698 only because they were too greedy,[84] had exhausted Parliament's credulity — when Fisher finally told his story to the committee preparing the impeachment of the Junto Lords, he was ignored.[85] They had, however, played a major part in driving Shrewsbury from public life.

Only in Anne's reign was the precedent of the Popish Plot successfully applied, when the Lords, now a Whig preserve, twice took out of the Government's hands the examination of conspiracies: the 'Scotch Plot' of 1703 and the case of William Greg in 1708. Party feeling dictated the findings, and there were attempts in 1708 to suborn witnesses against Secretary Harley, in whose office Greg had been employed, but there was no general alarm. The events of the 1690s had probably, by degrees, educated the Commons and the public.[86] The genuine intrigues of some of William's ministers, and the willingness of the Commons to hear all accusations, gave Parliament after the Revolution the chance to set a precedent for partisan investigations. Had Fenwick's accusations been proved, the repercussions might permanently have altered the relations between legislature and executive. However, the ground lost in 1691-2 was never fully recovered, because most accusations were on party lines, and an Opposition which was recruited from both Whig-Tory and

Court-Country groups could not press the charges effectively without permanently splitting itself. Further, the corrupt Court Whigs like Arnold and the Colts who most often employed perjurers, inspired by envy of ministers, were increasingly distrusted by the 'Country' allies they used.[87] Yet, although they failed, there had several times been a real danger that they would endow the 'respectable' Glorious Revolution with one truly revolutionary characteristic — a Terror.

False plots became accepted not only as propaganda but in Government thinking largely because of very real, though baseless, fears of William's assassination. Perjurers would obviously invent plots which the ministers dared not ignore and which were hard to disprove, but it is harder to see why William's government should have been so credulous. On the face of it, Louis XIV had more reason to fear assassination in 1689, from Huguenot extremists, Catholic fanatics (who had killed two of the last three kings) or private aristocratic poisoners.[88] The Jacobites suggested that William was cynically exploiting lies, and certainly in Holland before 1688 he or his ministers had used supposed plots in difficult political times to remind the thankless Dutch of his worth. The perjurer whose accusations caused the murder of the de Witts was rewarded with a place and a pension, and William's tutor led the lynch mob.[89]

The explanation seems to lie in William's role as the main hope of the anti-French and Protestant cause in Europe. His ancestor, William the Silent, in a similar position, had been assassinated by the Spaniards. 'To see him go about with a footman or two when so much depends on his life has been called rather a tempting of providence than a trusting to it,' wrote Burnet in 1685.[90] Similar wild fears were felt in the next generation by the entourage of another young prince on whom a great cause depended — the Old Pretender.[91]

Rumours that James was planning William's murder were exploited for propaganda purposes at the Revolution, but William's best agent in England took them seriously. When William reached London, such reports continued. There was no lull to induce scepticism. The most convincing stories involved not only James but Louis XIV, whom Williamites, apparently unjustly, supposed capable of using the weapon of assassination.[92] Ministers might frequently detect rational perjury, but they overlooked the possibility of lunacy. In 1690, the agent Simpson alias Jones, a pathological liar, who was negotiating with James in Dublin on behalf of the Scottish Whigs, publicly declared that he was plotting William's death. Every reference in the papers captured after the Boyne to French approval of his real mission was therefore taken to refer to assassination.[93] In 1692, a conspiracy by soldiers of fortune to kill William in Flanders was uncovered. The only plotter executed, the Sieur de Grandval, made a full confession without any threat of torture, implicating the French ministers, James and the Jacobite Colonel Parker. Because it condemned him, his confession was believed. Yet two of the four conspirators were double agents, and Grandval was never properly cross-examined, to avoid allegations of prompting. Nottingham's best French agent commented that all those involved had the reputation of being partly mad, and that Louis would never support such a scheme. Parker, who had alibis for the period in question, protested that charges made by a man who believed the assassins could make themselves invisible by magic could not be taken seriously.[94]

There were genuine reasons for alarm. Attempts against Cromwell, to whom propagandists regularly compared William, had been endorsed by Charles II's ministers. The Simpson affair showed that Melfort's relations had discussed the possibility of assassination, and some London Jacobites knew of Grandval's conspiracy a month before the arrests. Proposals made to James from 1693 onwards to kidnap William, at first genuinely intended to take him alive, had degenerated into a euphemism for assassination by 1695.[95] Mary and men like Halifax, who had obsessive fears for the King's safety, might possibly have been the victims of insincere propaganda; but Portland genuinely believed that Louis was behind the Grandval and Assassination Plots, telling Dykveldt in 1697 to pass on to that king the warning that such conduct might recoil on his own head; and William drew on the charges as the central argument in a memorial intended for use at Ryswick.[96] Belief was strengthened by correspondents who viewed every ex-Jacobite begging his way home as an assassin and every Jacobite expression of optimism as proof of guilty knowledge.[97] The ministers looked for assassination plots, and saw sinister patterns in what was merely repetition by perjurers. In 1693, Whitney, a convicted highwayman, vainly tried to avert execution by claiming that his gang had been hired to kill William. The following year, Lunt adapted the story for use in his 'Lancashire Plot' narrative. Evidently, the ministers had dismissed Whitney's allegations too quickly.[98]

Every element in the real Assassination Plot had appeared in its sham predecessors, which may partly have inspired it. James, when preparing an invasion in early 1696, sent Brigadier-General Sir George Barclay from France to be second-in-command in a projected rising, with thirty officers to command the rebel regiments. He was nearly recalled lest Fenwick, his immediate superior, might resent his seniority, a proof that James intended to use him for the rising only. Finding the English hopelessly unprepared to rise, Barclay consulted the officers of Parker's regiment, an extremist group, several of whom had wanted to assassinate William in 1695.[99] They, in concert with Barclay's officers who were obeying orders only reluctantly, arranged to attack William's coach when he returned from hunting. The Plot was not timed to coincide with the invasion — on the first date set, James had not left St. Germain — and no arrangements were made for the Assassins to use the Jacobite escape routes afterwards, which may have been one factor in persuading some conspirators to betray the Plot.[100]

The Government's belief in so many false tales had, if anything, made detection of the real Assassination Plot more difficult. Shrewsbury would have investigated Matthew Smith's claims further had they not resembled so many already exploded stories. After the Peace, a proper spy system might finally have been established at St. Germain. Had destitute agents reported truthfully that there was almost no Jacobite activity, they would have been discharged, so they sent stories of assassins flocking towards England. Such tales, discredited only after weeks of suspense, did nothing to assuage general anxiety. The English ambassador's secretary, exposing the lies of one genial Irish rogue, who claimed he got information by making leading

H

Jacobites drunk (at the Embassy's expense), added that he would also report real plots, when they occurred.[101] Only with Anne's accession and the obvious quiescence of English Jacobitism did the number of allegations significantly decrease.[102] The belief had helped to preserve the Jacobite movement. Because the Assassination Plotters had crossed to England pretending that poverty had driven them from St. Germain, a clause in an Act of 1697 made guilty of High Treason those who returned from France without licence. As the Jacobite movement was then suffering financial and moral collapse, most of its inhabitants would have left St. Germain had William granted a general amnesty.[103] The sterner measures pursued cowed Jacobitism in William's reign, but ensured that the exiles would still be there when better days returned.

The Jacobites suffered far less from perjurers after 1702, when the new statutory rewards offered for coiners, highwaymen and other felons opened fresh fields. A generation of 'thief-takers' arose, organisers of crime who obtained blood-money by pinning charges on petty offenders. This sort of perjury had, of course, always existed, but it was the Popish Plot and its sequels of the 1690s, the decade when the rewards were set, which most conspicuously showed the weakness of the law. Weak ministers and unscrupulous MPs were partly responsible for the harm done to English justice in the next century.[104]

NOTES

1. Thomas, Earl of Ailesbury, *Memoirs,* ed. W. E. Buckley, 2 vols. (Roxburghe Club, 1890), i, 279; ii, 370-1, 441, 526; Sarah, Duchess of Marlborough, *An Account of the Conduct of the Dowager Duchess of Marlborough* (Sarah, *Conduct,* London, 1742), 68, Anne to Sarah, n.d.

2. Sir John Freind, when tried in 1696, revived the Whig argument, that Papists considered it meritorious to swear anything to destroy Protestants, as his main line of defence. *A Complete Collection of State Trials,* ed. T. B. Howell, 23 vols. (Hereafter *State Trials*) (London, 1809-26), xii, 292-4; xiii, 31-2, 41, 380-1.

3. Doctor Williams's Library, London, Morrice MS R, 187.

4. Nottingham University Library, Portland Collection (NUL, Portland), PwA 1004, Leeds to Portland, 22 July 1696.

5. *State Trials,* vii, 1041.

6. Oates himself was still legally incapable of testifying, and Crown witnesses were warned against associating with him. W. Fuller, *The Life of Mr. William Fuller* (London, 1703), 64.

7. There was a Jacobite equivalent, the partnership of the Whig Sir James Montgomerie and his agent John Simpson, both brilliant liars. NUL, Portland, PwA 2698, Langton to James II, 14 Aug. and 18 Aug. 1691.

8. Despite Oates's proclivities, the partnerships of youths and older men were, apparently, usually only professional. Although Fuller's enemies accused him of homosexual activity, he, like other false witnesses, had a confidence trickster's success with women. Lunt and Young were bigamists, like the Government spy Richard Kingston, who had all the characteristics of the older suborners. *Reports of the Historical Manuscripts Commission*

(HMCR) Downshire MSS, i, 536-7, Rev. J. Knighton to Tenison, 17 Aug. 1695; *HMCR Finch MSS,* iii, 342-5, M. Crone's confession, 20 June 1691; *HMCR Kenyon MSS,* 310, 316, Kenyon's account of Lunt; *State Trials,* xii, 1085; Fuller, *Life* (1703), 1, 18-56 (unreliable); [——] *Life of William Fuller alias Fullee* (London, 1701), 43, 60; NUL, Portland, PwA 446, Fuller's expense account.

9. *HMCR Kenyon MSS,* 310-11, Kenyon's account of Lunt; *Letters illustrative of the reign of William III,* ed. G. P. R. James, 3 vols. (London, 1841), i, 362-3, Vernon to Shrewsbury, 11 Sept. 1697.

10. *Life of James II,* ed. J. S. Clarke, 2 vols. (London, 1816), ii. 444-5; NUL, Portland, PwA 1457b p. 3, P. Cook's confession, 12 June 1696.

11. A difficult matter, it was pointed out during the Lancashire Plot, for Lord Molyneux, who was crippled by gout. *HMCR Kenyon MSS,* 312, Kenyon's account of Lunt.

12. *Journals of the House of Lords (LJ),* xviii, 527b, report on Valière alias Clarke, 18 Mar. 1707/8.

13. *Journals of the House of Commons (CJ),* xi, 584; Narcissus Luttrell, *Parliamentary Diary,* ed. H. Horwitz (Oxford, 1972), 67, 202-3; H. C. Foxcroft, *Life and Letters of Sir George Savile, bart., First Marquis of Halifax,* 2 vols. (London, 1898), ii, 148 & n.; N. Japikse, ed., *Correspondentie van Willem III en van Hans Willem Bentinck,* 5 vols. (The Hague, 1927-37), ii, 30-1, Fuller's paper, 23 Jan./1 Feb. 1690/1; Ailesbury, i, 282; W. Fuller, *Mr. Fuller's Appeal to both Houses of Parliament* (London, 1697), 16-19; Fuller *Original Letters of the late King's, . . .* (London, 1702).

14. Sir A. Bryant, *Samuel Pepys: the Years of Peril* (Cambridge, 1936), 203-9, 269-307; *State Trials,* xii, 1080-1164, Bishop Sprat's *Relation,* second part. There are similar biographies of Lunt and Chaloner, *HMCR Kenyon MSS,* 310-20, Kenyon's account of Lunt; Public Record Office (PRO), MINT 19/1, fols. 501-2, Chaloner's case. The two parts of *The Life of William Fuller alias Fullee . . .* (London, 1701: the first part largely a reprint of Abel Roper's *Life* of 1692) and Fuller's autobiographies of 1701 and 1702 were part of a pamphlet war, alternatively revealing his swindles and supposed services. Robert Ferguson's *A Letter to Sir John Holt . . .* and *A Letter to Mr. Secretary Trenchard* (both London, 1694) contain several brief portraits of witnesses and suborners.

15. D. A. Rubini, 'The Precarious Independence of the Judiciary 1688-1701', *Law Quarterly Review,* lxxxiii (1967), 343; S. Rezneck, 'The Statute of 1696; a pioneer measure in the reform of judicial procedure', *Journal of Modern History,* ii (1930), 5-27.

16. The complete or partial destruction of the papers of ministers, particularly Carmarthen, who, according to one Jacobite source, was the chief organiser of anti-Jacobite intelligence in France, must qualify this statement. NUL, Portland, PwA 2698b p. 2, Langton to James II, 18 Aug. 1691.

17. J. Macky, *Memoirs of the Secret Service of John Macky* (Roxburghe Club, 1895), 9-10; *State Papers and Letters addressed to William Carstares,* ed. J. McCormick (*Carstares S.P.;* Edinburgh, 1774), 148-52, [Macky] to Carstares for Sydney [1691]; Scottish Record Office (SRO), GD 26/viii/122/1, same to Melville, n.d.

18. *HMCR Lords MSS New Series (NS),* ii, 292; *Private and Original Correspondence of Charles Talbot, Duke of Shrewsbury,* ed. W. Coxe (*Shrewsbury Corr.*; London, 1821), 459, Somers to Shrewsbury, 12 Jan. 1696/7; M. Smith, *A Reply to an Unjust and Scandalous Libel* (London, 1700), 21; National Library of Scotland (NLS), MSS 14,266 (Sir David Nairne's journal), fol. 129 (entry 27 May 1697).

19. These reports probably inspired William's conviction that Ailesbury frequently crossed. Ailesbury, ii, 445; NUL, Portland, PwA 1419, Trenchard to Portland, 29 Aug. 1693; *ib.,* PwA 2840, Clairand to Portland, 12 Feb. 1694; *ib.,* PwA 2847, same to same, 12

Mar. 1694; *ib.*, PwA 2856, same to same, 9 Apr. 1694; *ib.*, PwA 2860, same to same, 19 Apr. 1694.

20. *HMCR Lords MSS (NS)*, i, 444; *HMCR Kenyon MSS*, 333-4, Commons examinations; *ib.*, 388, Taaffe's 'discovery'; G. Burnet, *A History of his own time*, ed. M. J. Routh, 6 vols. (Oxford, 1833), iv. 60-2; Ailesbury, ii, 405-6; NUL, Portland, PwA 2504, deposition of Mr K[ingston], 1/11 June 1692.

21. Japikse, i, 177, William to Portland, 28 Apr. 1693; ii, 68-9, Shrewsbury to same, 8 Sept. 1696; *Shrewsbury Corr.*, 147-8, same to William, 8 Sept. 1696; Vernon, i, 194, Vernon to Shrewsbury, 30 Jan. 1696/7; *State Trials*, xiii, 758, Fenwick's dying speech.

22. If the story Dalrymple popularised that William checked Carmarthen's questions is true, it must have occurred when Preston was brought drunk to Kensington Palace before his trial. William did not see him afterwards. Clarke, ii, 443-4; Sir J. Dalrymple, *Memoirs of Great Britain and Ireland*, 3 vols. (London, 1771-88), i, 467; *HMCR Finch MSS*, iii, 43, Preston to Devonshire, 2 May 1691; *ib.*, 46, Nottingham to Sydney, 5 May 1691; *ib.*, 310-11, Preston to William: *HMCR 8th Report Part 2*, 66, H. Willaston to Manchester, 17 Jan. 1690/1; Westminster Diocesan Archives, Westminster Cathedral, Henry Browne Manuscripts (WDA, Browne), 25, 'Parker' [Lord Castlemain] to [Mary of Modena], 20 Feb. 1690/1.

23. F. Ravaisson (ed.), *Archives de la Bastille*, 19 vols. (Paris, 1866-1904), 446, Renaudot to Croissy, 6 Feb. 1694; British Library, Additional Manuscripts (BL, Add. MSS) 51,511 fol. 62v.

24. Montgomerie himself presumably denounced Shrewsbury while trying to make his peace after his capture. Clarke, ii, 520-1; *HMCR Buccleuch MSS*, ii, 625, Peterborough — Vernon conference, 16 Aug, 1699; *HMCR Bath MSS*, iii, 412, Macky to Prior, 23 June 1700; *Original Papers containing the secret history of Great Britain*, ed. J. Macpherson, 2 vols. (London, 1775), i, 481, Lloyd's memorial, 1 May 1694.

25. *Shrewsbury Corr.*, 52-3, William to Shrewsbury, 15 July 1694; *ib.*, 54, Shrewsbury to William, 17 July 1694.

26. W. L. Aiken, *The Conduct of the Earl of Nottingham* (New Haven, 1941), 101; Berkshire Record Office, Downshire Manuscripts, Trumbull Additional Manuscripts (Berks. RO, Trumbull Add. MSS) 125, (diary of Sir W. Trumbull), entries 25 July 1696, 13 Aug. 1696, 12 Apr. 1697, 1 June 1697, 17 Oct. 1697, 2 Nov. 1697, 5 Nov. 1697.

27. See his 'Holland House Notebook', BL, Add. MSS 51, 511.

28. *Statutes of the Realm*, ed. T. E. Tomlins, 11 vols. (London, 1810-28), vi, 320; *ib.*, vii, 116-17, 295-6; *CJ*, x, 121; *HMCR Lords MSS 1689–90*, 96-8; A. Grey, *Debates of the House of Commons . . .*, 10 vols. (London, 1763), ix, 205-11, 233-4; *HMCR Downshire MSS*, i, 528, Kingston to Trumbull, 4 Aug. 1695; Foxcroft, *Halifax*, ii, 251-2; E. E. Crawford, 'The Suspension of the Habeas Corpus Act and the Revolution of 1688', *English Historical Review (EHR)*, xxx (1915), 613-30.

29. WDA, Old Brotherhood Manuscripts, iii, 232, 'Mr Davis's' [David Lloyd's] memorial [1691], p. 5.

30. *HMCR Downshire MSS*, i, 625-6, Trumbull's memoranda, 16-23 Feb. 1695/6; Ailesbury, i, 247, 258; *ib.*, ii, 394; Burnet, iv, 32-4; [R. Kingston], *A True History of the Several Designs and Conspiracies against his Majesties Sacred Person and Government* (London, 1698), 110; NUL, Portland, PwA 2486, Hunt's examination, 26 Mar. 1696.

31. *Calendar of State Papers Domestic (CSP Dom.) 1694-5*, 383, Fells' petition, 23 Jan. 1695; *ib. 1696*, 374-5, Lords Justices' proceedings, 4 Sept. 1696; *ib.*, 389, same, 15 Sept. 1696; *Calendar of Treasury Books (CTB)*, xv, 10-11, 13-14, 303; *HMCR Lords MSS* (NS), i, 8; *HMCR Buccleuch MSS*, ii, 321; *HMCR Downshire MSS*, i, 494, Kingston to Trumbull, 5

July 1695; *ib.*, 676, Trumbull to Blathwayt, 30 June 1696; *State Trials*, xii, 1334, Goodman's information, 24 Apr. 1696; Ailesbury, ii, 389, 397; Kingston, 64-6; *The English Reports* ed. A. Wood Renton, 176 vols. (London, 1900-30), lxxxvii, 738-9, R. v. Fells; BL, Add. MSS 37,662 fol. 173, Sir R. Bulstrode to H. Browne, 25 June 1691; Berks. RO, Trumbull Add. MSS 116, minute 4 May 1695.

32. *Shrewsbury Corr.*, 11-12, Shrewsbury to William, 1 Sept. 1689; Vernon, i, 385-6, Vernon to Shrewsbury, 18 Sept, 1697; *ib.*, ii, 319-20, same to same, 13 July 1699; *HMCR Denbigh MSS*, v, 89, [Blancard] to Dykveldt, 31 July/10 Aug. 1691; Luttrell, *Parliamentary Diary*, 17, 78; J. C. Sainty, *Officials of the Secretary of State 1660-1782* (London, 1977), 66; Northamptonshire Record Office, Buccleuch Manuscripts (Northants. RO, Buccleuch), Vol. 46, No. 151, Vernon to Shrewsbury, 12 Oct. 1697; *ib.*, No. 154, same to same, 19 Oct. 1697; *ib.*, No. 158, same to same, 2 Dec. 1697; *ib.* Vol. 77, Nos. 17, 102, anon. to same, [1694].

33. *Carstares S.P.*, 218-19, A. Johnston to Carstares, 4 Sept. 1694; *ib.*, 222, same to same, 7 Sept. 1694.

34. Smith's total receipts during seven years of war were under £20,000, in contrast to the £52,000 his predecessors spent between 1684 and 1688. *CTB*, ix-x, indices (for imprests to Smith); Ferguson, *Letter to Trenchard*, 26-7; S. B. Baxter, *The Development of the Treasury* (London, 1957), 240-6; PRO T1/28, fol. 171, Smith to Treasury, 21 June 1694; BL, Harleian MSS 1494 fols. 45, 115.

35. A rough estimate from the accounts of Smith's Deputy Solicitor (PRO, A03/1101, Part I No.1) would be that perhaps half the direct Government prosecutions for seditious libels or words were rejected by Grand Juries or dropped before reaching court.

36. *HMCR Downshire MSS*, i, 713, Somers to Trumbull, [Nov. 1696]; N. Luttrell, *A Brief Historical Relation of State Affairs . . .*, 6 vols. (Oxford, 1857), ii, 271; Ailesbury, i, 282; *ib.*, ii, 398-9; Bodleian Library (Bodl.) MS Carte 181, fol. 598, Caryll to Crone, 19 Apr. 1695; NUL, Portland, PwA 1445, Vernon to Portland, 8 May 1696.

37. In 1696, at least two-thirds of the jurors who tried Sir John Freind were put on the panel of Peter Cook, the next man tried on that evidence. *State Trials*, xii, 666-70, 1381, 1384, 1389; *ib.*, xiii, 70-1, 313-14; WDA, Browne, 21, Summary of Preston's trial, 17 Jan. 1690/1.

38. While on bail before his trial, Crosby organised an assassination plot, which made the Jacobites claim (untruly) that he was an *agent provocateur*. Clarke, ii, 545-6; *CSP Dom. 1696*, 344-5, Devonshire to William, 14 Aug. 1696; *State Trials*, xii, 1291-8; *ib.*, 1311, de la Rue's information, 26 Feb. 1695/6.

39. Ailesbury, ii, 427-8.

40. Some MPs feared that this was a covert attack on *habeas corpus*. Bodl., MS Carte 130, fol. 375, R. Price to Duke of Beaufort, 31 Dec. 1696.

41. *Acts of the Parliament of Scotland*, ed. T. Thomson etc., 12 vols. (Edinburgh, 1814-75), ix, 39, 102, 192; *LJ*, xvii, 411b, R. Ferguson's narrative; *HMCR Finch MSS*, iii, 368-71, Neville Payne's case; *Carstares S.P.*, 219-20, A. Johnston to Carstares, 4 Sept. 1694; Ravaisson, ix, 444, Renaudot to Croissy, 5 Feb. 1694; *ib.*, 446, same to same, 6 Feb. 1694.

42. *Statutes*, vi, 607-9.

43. Fuller and Lunt were so obsessed with pensions that they refused army and customs posts. *CTB*, xi, 226, 234, 286; *ib.*, xii, 28; *ib.*, xv, 39; *HMCR Lords (NS)*, vii, 358-9; Vernon, ii, 401-2, Vernon to Shrewsbury, 4 Jan. 1699/1700; Kingston's petition, 1699, *Notes & Queries*, 3rd series, iii (1876), 76; NUL, Portland, PwA 1334, Sydney to Portland, 4 Dec. 1690.

44. Vernon, i, 366, Vernon to Shrewsbury, 14 Sept. 1697; BL, Add. MSS 40,772, fol. 135, same to Mountstevens, 24 Sept, 1698.

45. *HMCR Downshire MSS,* i, 530, Kingston to Trumbull, 10 Aug. 1695; *HMCR Portland MSS,* iii, 485, E. Harley to Sir E. Harley, 10 Dec. 1691; Dalrymple, ii. Appendix, 200, Lord Keeper North's memorandum; *ib.,* 231, Barillon to Louis, 16 Mar. 1679; Berks. RO, Trumbull Add. MSS 125, entries 1 June 1697, 17 Oct. 1697.

46. *HMCR Hastings MSS,* iv, 318, notes of Lords debate, 23 Dec. 1695; Ailesbury, i, 286-7 (inaccurate); *ib.,* ii, 371.

47. A surviving note from William during the examinations authorised Portland to offer Porter his life if he confessed. The note signed 'P' from an informer which Japikse attributes to Porter must, then, be from Prendergrass, the original informer. Japikse, i, 178, William to Portland, Mar. 1696; *ib.,* ii, 669, 'P' to same, [22 Feb. 1695/6]; Ailesbury ii, 370.

48. Macpherson, i, 515-18, Charnock's paper, 17 June 1695; *State Trials,* xii, 1304-5, Porter's information, 14 Mar. 1695/6.

49. *CSP (Dom.) 1696,* 160, Porter's pardon, 1 May 1696; *ib. 1699-1700,* 366, Porter to Lord Jersey, Jan. 1700; Ailesbury, ii, 368-9.

50. Ailesbury claimed that Goodman testified because Archbishop Tenison falsely told him Peter Cook had sworn against him. Some such device may have been used to prevent him from retracting, but Cook was not arrested until after the 14th March examination. *State Trials,* xii, Goodman's information, 14 Mar. 1695/6; *ib.,* xiii, 362; Ailesbury, ii, 383; Lambeth Palace MSS 942, No.120, Goodman to Tenison, 16 Apr. 1696; *ib.,* 1029, No.34, Cook to same, n.d.; Berks. RO, Trumbull Add. MSS 116, minute 14 Mar. 1695/6; Northants. RO, Buccleuch, Vol. 63, No. 28, examinations, 14 Mar. 1695/6; NUL, Portland, PwA 2477, Goodman's examination, 14 Mar. 1695/6.

51. *Ib.,* PwA 1456, Vernon to Portland, 19 June 1696.

52. This assumption may partly explain Russell's and Sidney's legalistic dying declarations of innocence in 1683. Evidence exists that Ailesbury tried to cross to France to support the message. Ailesbury, i, 353-7; *ib.,* ii, 368-9, 371-2; *State Trials,* xii, 1338, J. Hunt's information, 5 Apr. 1696; PRO 30/53/8, fol. 157. 'W. Thompson' [Lord Montgomery] to [Mary of Modena], 31 July 1695.

53. Burnet, iv, 60-2.

54. *HMCR Finch MSS,* iv, 120-1, Nottingham to Russell, 5 May 1692; *ib.,* 127, same to same, 7 May 1692 (establishing the date of Young's charge); *ib.,* 136, same to Blathwayt, 10 May 1692; *ib.,* 505, same to Kingston, 16 Nov. 1692; *State Trials,* xii, 1053-79, 1157-60, 1165; Sarah, *Conduct,* 63; Foxcroft, *Halifax,* ii, 148, 154-5; PRO, PC 2/74, 387-8.

55. Lunt's biography by Roger Kenyon, *HMCR Keynon MSS,* 310-20, shows his constant fantasising, but minimises his real activity in 1690. P. A. Hopkins, 'The Commission for Superstitious Lands of the 1690s', *Recusant History* xv, (1979-80), 265-82.

56. *HMCR Lords MSS (NS),* i, 436, 444, 446; Northants. RO, Buccleuch, Vol. 63, Nos. 72-6, Lunt's original information [4 June 1694].

57. *Ib.,* 8-9, 16; *ib.,* No. 79, list of warrants; *HMCR Kenyon MSS,* 295-6, Lunt's information, 27 June 1694; *ib.,* 388, Taaffe's discovery; *The Jacobite Trials at Manchester in 1694,* ed. J. Beamont (Chetham Soc., 1853), 37, J. Wombwell's information, 28 June 1694; *ib.,* 107, E. Brown's information; A. Browning, *Thomas Osborne, Earl of Danby,* 3 vols. (Glasgow, 1944-51), i, 8; T. C. Porteus, 'New Light on the Lancashire Jacobite Plot, 1692-4', *Transactions of the Lancashire and Cheshire Antiquarian Society (TLCAS)* 1, (1934-5), 46-7, Declaration of loyalty to James II, 18 Nov. 1693; M. Briggs, 'The Walmesleys of Dunkenhalgh', *ib.,* lxxv-vi, (1965-6), 93-5, 101; PRO, E133/151/50, 8th interrogatory, fols. 18-19, Lunt's deposition, 6 Apr. 1694; BL, Add. MSS, 36, 913, fol. 177,

Taaffe's examination [4 May 1693]; *ib.*, fol. 188, R. Norcrosse's petition to the Queen in Council; WDA, Browne, 172, anon. to Browne, 10 Aug. 1694.

58. *HMCR Hope-Johnstone MSS*, 71-2, Johnston to Annandale, 19 Jan, 1695; R. Ferguson, *Letter to Trenchard, passim;* NUL, Portland, PwA 1179, Somers to Portland, 2 July 1695.

59. *HMCR Lords MSS (NS)*, i, 445-6; Kingston, 83-9; Porteus, 'New Light', *TLCAS* 1, 42, 'J. H.' to 'Mrs Duckett' [Parker], 11 Feb. 1692/3.

60. Clarke, ii, 524-5; Bodl., MS Carte 181, fol. 561, regimental lists of Lancashire Jacobites.

61. *HMCR Lords MSS (NS)*, i, 439-41; Ferguson, *Letter to Holt* (2nd. ed.), 3; Ferguson, *Letter to Trenchard*, 32.

62. 'It appeared that there was no just occasion, given by that trial, to alter the law,' claimed Burnet. Burnet, iv, 252.

63. After mid-1689, the only voluntary exception was a very revealing letter by Lord Melfort in 1701. Fenwick's confession was produced only to forestall an inevitable opposition demand. *CJ*, x, 101, 179, 187, 195-6; *ib.*, xiii, 333-4, Melfort to Perth, 18 Feb. 1701; *HMCR Lords MSS 1689-90*, 144-56, intercepted Jacobite correspondence.

64. Vernon, i, 349, Vernon to Shrewsbury, 9 Sept. 1697; *State Trials*, xii, 1041.

65. Sir R. L'Estrange, *Observator*, 3 vols. (London, 1684-7), i, Nos. 447-8; J. P. Kenyon, *The Popish Plot* (London, 1972), 94-5, 107-9, 208, 213-15; P. Jenkins, 'Anti-Popery on the Welsh Marches in the seventeenth century', *Historical Journal*, xxiii (1980), 287-8.

66. BL, Add. MSS 51, 511, fols. 57v, 65v.

67. BL, Loan MSS 29/206, fol. 124, queries for Preston; NUL, Portland, PwA Hy 367, R. Wilde to Harley, 7 Oct. 1691.

68. *CJ*, x, 584-5, 595, 614-15; *LJ*, xv, 649-50; Luttrell, *Parliamentary Diary*, 17, 22-3, 67-9, 78, 95-6; *HMCR Denbigh MSS*, v, 89, Blancard to Dykveldt, 31 July 1691; *HMCR Downshire MSS*, i, 390, R. Hill to Trumbull, 8 Dec. 1691; BL Harleian MSS 6846, fol. 386, trial of B. Clayton; W. Fuller, *The Sincere and Hearty Confession of Mr William Fuller* (London, 1704), 13-17.

69. *Ib.*, 17; *CJ*, x, 587, 610, 681-5; *LJ*, xv, 660-1, 685; Luttrell, *Parliamentary Diary*, 68, 79, 103, 110, 199, 201-5; *HMCR Portland MSS*, iii, 485, E. Harley to Sir E. Harley, 10 Dec. 1691; Bodl., MS Carte 130, fol. 338, R. Price to Beaufort, 23 Feb. 1691/2.

70. *HMCR Downshire MSS*, i, 530, Kingston to Trumbull, 10 Aug, 1695; Historical Manuscripts Commission, Quality House, Chancery Lane, transcripts for a fifth volume of *HMCR Finch MSS*, No. 411, R. Holland's depositions 8-16 Oct. 1693; *ib.*, no. 419, R. Holland's information, 20-22 Oct. 1693.

71. *CJ*, xi, 8, 14; *LJ*, xvi, 319, 330; *Calendar of Treasury Papers 1697-1702*, 9, Commissioners of Prizes to Treasury, 20 Feb. 1697; *CTB*, xi, 408; *ib.*, xiii, 333; *HMCR Lords MSS (NS)*, i, 93, 97-102, 104, 197-200; Grey, *Debates*, x, 312, 320, 333-8; Ailesbury, i, 313-15.

72. *HMCR Downshire MSS*, i, 693, J. Colt to Trumbull, 26 Sept. 1696; Clarke, ii, 549, Sir G. Barclay's declaration, 8 Aug. 1697; NUL, Portland, PwA 2501, Fisher's information, 20/30 Mar. 1696; *ib.*, PwA 2516, [Fisher's account]; Berks RO, Trumbull Add. MSS 116, minutes 29 Feb. 1695/6, 3 Mar. 1695/6.

73. *Ib.*, Trumbull Add. MSS 125, entries 13 May 1696, 21 [May 1696 — divided in present pagination], 10 Jan 1696/7; *HMCR Downshire MSS*, i, 694, Smith to Trumbull, 5 Oct. 1696; Vernon, i, 260-2, Vernon to Shrewsbury, 10 June 1697; *Shrewsbury Corr.*, 427-8, Somers to same, 7 Nov. 1696.

74. Monmouth's agents had earlier been spreading rumours that summer that Shrewsbury was treating Fenwick with suspicious kindness, and the delay before he changed to the tactic of approaching Fenwick may have been crucial. Berks. RO, Trumbull Add. MSS 125, entries 25 July 1696, 13 Aug. 1696, 26 Sept. 1696; Vernon, i, 12-13, Vernon to Shrewsbury, 1 Oct. 1696.

75. *Ib.*, 37, same to same, 31 Oct. 1696; *Shrewsbury Corr.*, 419, Somers to same, 31 Oct. 1696; *CJ*, xi, 577-8, Fenwick's information.

76. J. P. Kenyon, *Robert Spencer, Earl of Sunderland* (London, 1958), 282-6.

77. *State Trials*, xiii, 540; BL, Add. MSS 47,608, fols. 3, 35, Fenwick to Lady M. Fenwick, n.d.; *ib.*, fol. 125, 'Reasons Sir John gave me why he named the select number.'

78. *Ib.*, fol. 35v, Fenwick to Lady M. Fenwick, n.d.; *Shrewsbury Corr.*, 328-9, Villiers to Shrewsbury, 23 Nov. 1696; Vernon, i, 52-3, Vernon to same, 10 Nov. 1696.

79. *Ib.*, 154-5, same to same, 2 Jan. 1696/7; Ailesbury, ii, 392-3, 432; BL, Add. MSS 47,608, fols. 3, 40v, 56v, 58v, Fenwick to Lady M. Fenwick, n.d.

80. Vernon, i, 163-5, Vernon to Shrewsbury, 9 Jan, 1696/7.

81. *HMCR Downshire MSS*, i, 664-5, Trumbull to J. Colt, 19 May 1696; *Ib.*, 683, Colt to Trumbull, 10 Aug. 1696; Berks. RO, Trumbull Add. MSS 125, entries 9 Apr. 1697, 11 Apr. 1697.

82. *HMCR Lords MSS (NS)*, iii, 15-16; *HMCR Bath MSS*, iii, 108-9, Vernon to Prior, 9 Apr. 1697; Vernon, i, 453-4, same to Shrewsbury, 29 Dec. 1697; Northants. RO, Buccleuch, Vol. 46, No. 78, same to same, 11 Mar. 1697/8.

83. Earl of Hardwicke, *Miscellaneous State Papers from 1501 to 1726*, 2 vols. (London, 1778), ii, 436-7, C. Montagu to Somers, 2 May 1700; *ib.*, 437-9, Duke of Bolton to same, Sept. 1700.

84. *HMCR Downshire MSS*, i, 781, J. Colt to Trumbull, 12 July 1698; Northants. RO, Buccleuch, Vol. 46, No. 181, Vernon to Shrewsbury, 18 Jan, 1697/8; *ib.*, No. 195, same to same, 19 Feb. 1697/8.

85. Vernon, iii, 148, Vernon to Shrewsbury, 9 June 1701.

86. I owe this suggestion to the kindness of Professor H. Horwitz. *HMCR Portland MSS*, iv, 455, E. Lewis to Harley, 9 Oct. 1707; *ib.*, 503-4, same to same, 28 Aug. 1708; *ib.*, v, 647-8, Auditor Harley's memoirs; G. Holmes & W. A. Speck, 'The Fall of Harley in 1708 Reconsidered', *EHR* lxxx (1965), 673-4, 697.

87. Northants. RO, Buccleuch, Vol. 47, No. 122, Vernon to Shrewsbury, 20 Dec. 1698.

88. There were occasional alarmist rumours as the war started, but they did not, as in England, become an epidemic. Marquis de Sourches, *Mémoires*, ed. Comte de Cosnac & E. Pontal, 13 vols. (Paris, 1882-92), iii, 54, 111.

89. *HMC 7th Report*, 497, newsletters, 5 Dec. 1681, 12 Dec. 1681; Ravaisson, viii, 331-6, papers on the Comte de Morlot; H. H. Rowen, *John de Witt, Grand Pensionary of Holland* (Princeton, 1978), 841-2, 862-5, 873-6, 889, 891-2; G. Mongrédian, *Daily Life in the French Theatre at the Time of Molière* (London, 1969), 203-4.

90. H. C. Foxcroft, *A Supplement to Bishop Burnet's History of his own time* (Oxford, 1902), 191.

91. The alarms culminated in 1717 in the arrest of the notoriously eccentric Earl of Peterborough (the Monmouth of the 1690s) for suspicious conduct. *HMCR Stuart MSS*, v, 74-9, Peterborough's reflections on his arrest [1717]; *ib.*, 166-7, J. Menzies to L. Innes, 17/28 Oct. 1717.

92. Macpherson, i, 289, A. Norton to [T. Carte]; Mary II, *Memoirs 1689-93*, ed. R. Doebner (London, 1886), 6; S. B. Baxter, *William III* (London, 1966), 251; V. L. Tapié, 'Louis XIV's Methods of Foreign Policy', *Louis XIV and Europe*, ed. R. M. Hatton

(London, 1976), 6; NUL, Portland, PwA 2145, J. Johnston to [Portland], 21 Feb. 1688; *ib.*, PwA 2159, same to same, 4 Apr. 1688.

93. *HMCR Finch MSS*, ii, 345, Sir R. Southwell to Nottingham, 6 July 1690; Burnet, iv, 98-101; Lord Tyrconnell, 'Letter-Book of Richard Talbot, 1689-90', ed. L. Tate, *Analecta Hibernica*, iv, (Dublin, 1932), 130, Tyrconnell to Mary of Modena, 26 June 1690; *ib.*, 132, same to same, 4 July 1690; BL, Add. MSS 33,924, fol. 74, J. Trench's report; *ib.*, fols. 82-3, memorial to Carmarthen, 5 Mar. 1690/1.

94. *A True Account of the horrid Conspiracy against the Life of his Sacred Majesty William III* (London, 1692); Burnet, iv, 171-3; Foxcroft, *Supplement to Burnet*, 376; Porteus, 'New Light', *TLCAS* 1, 39, 'J. H.' to 'Mrs Duckett' [Parker], 15 Dec. 1692; BL, Add. MSS, 34,096, fol. 106v, Vernon to Sir W. Colt, 11/21 Aug. 1692; *ib.*, Add. MSS 37,513, fol. 163, Sir W. Colt to Blathwayt, 29 Apr. 1692; Northants. RO, Buccleuch, Vol. 77, No. 49, Parker to Shrewsbury, 7 Aug. [1694].

95. Clarke, ii, 536-8, 545-6; Macpherson, i, 388, Major Holmes' Paper, Oct. 1691; *ib.*, 467, Williamson's memorial, 28 Dec. 1693; *State Trials*, xii, 1332-3, Goodman's deposition, 24 Apr. 1696; D. E. Underdown, *Royalist Conspiracy in England 1649-1660* (Yale, 1960), 100-1, 172-4, 192-3. The commission for kidnapping William printed in F. A. J. Mazure, *Histoire de la Révolution d'Angleterre en 1688*, 3 vols. (Paris, 1825), iii, 443, is presumably a draft prepared by one of the proposers.

96. Japikse, Second Part, iii, 381, Portland to Vaudemont, 6/16 Mar. 1695/6; *HMC 8th Report Part I*, 559, same to Dykveldt, 26 Jan./5 Feb. 1697; Mary, *Memoirs*, 54-5; Sir John Reresby, *Memoirs*, ed. A. Browning (Glasgow, 1936), 561, 577; *A Memorial drawn by King William's special direction, intended to be given in at the Treaty of Ryswick, Somers Tracts*, ed. Sir Walter Scott, 13 vols. (London, 1809-15), x, 104-5, 111.

97. E.g. a harmless letter of James to the Electress Sophia. BL, Add. MSS 37,513, fol. 141v, Sir W. Colt to Portland, 26 Feb. 1692.

98. The Jacobites reported that Whig MPs, including John Colt, had inspired Whitney's accusations. Luttrell, iii, 1, 7, 23, 26-7; *HMCR Kenyon MSS*, 295, Lunt's information, 27 June 1694; *ib.*, 311, Kenyon's account of Lunt; S. Grascomb, *New Court Contrivances* (London, 1693), 4-7; Bodl., MS Carte 79, fol. 475, C. Godfrey to Wharton, 28 Jan. [1692/3].

99. The belief that assassination was the only solution was spreading. Charnock, who had been sent to James to prevent Crosby's plot the previous year, was now one of the chief proposers. *CSP Dom. 1696*, 344, Devonshire to William 14 Aug. 1696; Clarke, ii, 546-8; *State Trials*, xii, 1305, Porter's deposition, 3 Mar. 1695/6; *ib.*, 1323-5, Harris's deposition, 28 Mar. 1696; *ib.*, 1338-9, Hunt's deposition, 4 Apr. 1696; James, Duke of Berwick, *Memoirs*, 2 vols. (London, 1779), i, 130-2, 134-5; NLS, MS 14,266, fol. 103, (entries 31 Jan. 1696, 1 Feb. 1696, 3 Feb. 1696).

100. *State Trials*, xii, 1310, Porter's information, 3 Mar. 1695/6. For a good narrative account of the Assassination Plot see, J. Garrett, *The Triumphs of Providence* (Cambridge, 1980).

101. The one truly suspicious Jacobite action then was the publication of Charnock's *Letter to a Friend* justifying the Asassination Plot, in 1700 (four years after a copy reached St. Germain), when the death of the Duke of Gloucester again made William's death more advantageous. *HMCR Bath MSS*, iii, 360, Prior to Jersey, 24 June 1699; BL, Add. MSS 40,771, fol. 238, same to Vernon, 14/24 July 1698; C Cole, *Historical and Political Memoirs* (London, 1735), 206, Manchester to same, 8 Sept. 1700; Luttrell, iv, 681; NLS, MS 14,266, fol. 114 (entry 21 July 1696).

102. Anne herself, however, had strong fears of being assassinated by Papists. E. Gregg, *Queen Anne* (London, 1980), 149-50.

103. The great exodus inspired by the limited Scottish indemnity of 1703 shows what could have been achieved. *Statutes*, vii, 295-6; *LJ*, xvii, 405, Sir J. Maclean's narrative; *HMCR Bath MSS*, iii, 284, Prior to Portland, 7 Nov, 1698; *ib.*, 295, same to Vernon, 26 Nov. 1698; Ailesbury, ii, 445, 448, 469-70.

104. G. Howson, *Thief Taker General* (London, 1970), 34-40, 283-4; Sir James Stephen, *History of the Criminal Law of England*, 3 vols. (London, 1883), i, 400-2.

All references to and quotations from the Portland MSS are by the kind permission of Lady Anne Bentinck and the Keeper of Manuscripts, Nottingham University Library. All references to the Buccleuch MSS, on deposit in the Northamptonshire Record Office, are by the kind permission of the Duke of Buccleuch. All references to the Trumbull MSS, the property of the Marquess of Downshire, on deposit in the Berkshire Record Office, are by the kind permission of the County Archivist. The reference to the Morrice MSS in Dr Williams' Library is by permission of the Librarian.

6

Spymaster to Louis XIV: A Study of the Papers of the Abbé Eusèbe Renaudot[1]

Pierre Burger

THE Renaudot papers, comprising 45 volumes of manuscripts in the Bibliothèque Nationale in Paris, have been calendared,[2] and some extracts have been published,[3] but they have been little used by French or British historians, even though a sizeable proportion deal with English affairs. If complemented by other Renaudot papers in the archives of the French Foreign Office, the Navy, and the Police,[4] they add substantially to our knowledge of Jacobitism in the 1690s and help to bring to life relations between the courts of St. Germain and Versailles.

The Abbé Eusèbe Renaudot (1648-1720) was the grandson of Théophraste Renaudot, who founded, under the patronage of Richelieu, the *Gazette de France*, a weekly and the first paper in France to print political news, foreign news especially. Théophraste's son, Eusèbe, was physician to the Dauphin as well as editor of the *Gazette*, and when he died in 1679, Eusèbe the grandson took over and for the rest of his life remained in charge of what was a lucrative commercial operation. An able and versatile scholar, who made his mark as a theologian and orientalist, Renaudot was also a friend of Bossuet, Racine, La Bruyère and Boileau. He became a member of the French Academy in 1689 and of the *Académie des Inscriptions* two years later. The only interruption to a career of forty years as a journalist was a journey to Rome in 1700-1 to accompany the Cardinal de Noailles, Archbishop of Paris, to the conclave which elected Clement XI.[5]

Renaudot's gifts as a linguist — he knew several foreign languages and could compose in as well as translate from English — singled him out as a suitable intermediary between the French court and the exiled Stuarts. His connection with the Colbert family was another advantage: he served under Colbert's brother, Charles Colbert, Marquis de Croissy (1625-1696), the secretary of state for foreign affairs; under Colbert's son, Jean-Baptiste Colbert, Marquis de Seignelay (1651-1690), the minister for the navy, and then under his successor Louis Phélypeaux, Comte de Pontchartrain (1643-1727). His labours on English affairs over the twenty years which followed the Revolution of 1689 resulted in a mass of analytical memoranda, enough as he told the Cardinal de Noailles in 1705, to 'fill several volumes'.[6] In a document written in 1694 at the height of his quarrel with Lord Melfort, James's secretary of state, he explained the nature and scope of his duties.[7] From 1689 on he was responsible for keeping up correspondence with and sending agents into England, as well as drawing up instructions and memoranda on behalf of Seignelay who, he wrote, had been very satisfied with his conduct, as indeed had James's Queen. Soon after Seignelay's death in 1690, Melfort returned from Italy, whereupon correspondents were instructed not to write to Renaudot but to Melfort, who communicated to the abbé only extracts of the letters he received. Renaudot thought it better not to remonstrate, even when the most zealous servants of James II complained of this practice. Notwithstanding, the abbé was ordered by Pontchartrain to carry on the work he had undertaken for Seigneley, so that he continued to receive a large number of letters, packages and trunks full of papers, which gave him a good deal of trouble, not to mention the files dealing with English prisoners. All this, Renaudot went on, damaged the relations between Versailles and St. Germain, but he managed to remain on good terms with Melfort until 1692, when Melfort accused of treachery Simpson *alias* Jones (outwardly an agent of William III's Dutch minister Portland, but in fact a Jacobite double-agent) before James II and his Queen. As a result, Simpson was sent to the Bastille, where Pontchartrain ordered Renaudot to examine him. This alarmed Melfort, who first tried to find out what was going on and, when he failed, tried to discredit Renauddt at St. Germain. At the heart of the dispute between Melfort and the abbé was disagreement over the terms of the Declaration of James II of April 1692, which it was part of Renaudot's duties to distribute. Renaudot regarded this declaration as 'harmful' and believed it should have incorporated the proposals sent over to France by influential Presbyterians, some of them Members of Parliament, on religious toleration. In the winter of 1692-3 an organised attempt was made by the abbé in alliance with Simpson and Sir James Montgomerie, a prominent Scottish Jacobite,[8] to obtain a recantation from James II, confident that this would have a good effect.[9] Failing in this, Renaudot set up the 'escape' of Simpson with official connivance. In a letter to Croissy of 31 January 1693 the abbé made himself Simpson's spokesman against Melfort:

> it is regarded as impossible to make much headway so long as the man they all hate is in place . . . not only those who correspond but nearly all the others feel the same disapproval . . . Three months ago letters were handed over personally to the King of England [James] which gave him notice that this would be the first article in the proposals to be made to him for his restoration.[10]

This pressure led to the canonical consultation in which Bossuet was involved in February 1693, paving the way for new concessions. These were based on a paper produced at the trial of Lord Preston in 1691 headed 'The Result of a Conference between some Lords and Gentlemen, both Tories and Whigs, in which it was undertaken to prove the possibility and method of restoring by a French power, without endangering the Protestant Religion and Civil Administration, according to the laws of this kingdom'. Urging Louis XIV to assume the position of a 'friend and mediator' rather than that of a conqueror, the proposals argued:

> Since there is a great body of Protestants that never defected, and that many thousands are returning, and that they are the natural weight and power of these kingdoms, by having the heads, hands and wealth of their side, to the odds and advantage of at least two hundred Protestants to one Catholic; the King may think of nothing short of a Protestant administration, nor of nothing more for the Catholics than a legal liberty of conscience . . . He may reign a Catholic in devotion, but he must reign a Protestant in government.[11]

On a favourable reply from Bossuet and the doctors of the Sorbonne,[12] James II's declaration of April 1693 was issued, designed to reassure Protestants without looking like a climb-down on the part of James.[13] While he sought to give an impression of moderation and impartiality, Renaudot waged what has been rightly called 'a vigorous and often unscrupulous campaign' for Melfort's removal.[14] It is remarkable to see how far he was able to involve Croissy in his partisanship.[15] This war to the knife lasted until 1 June 1694 when there took place the meeting between James and Simpson which led to Melfort's dismissal.[16]

Renaudot was, therefore, a man at the very centre of great events. Memoranda written by him were read to Louis XIV himself on at least seven occasions between November 1692 and January 1695. For the most part, they were written for Frenchmen, and the Jacobites at St. Germain figure as pawns, never entirely trusted and of marginal importance, rather than partners to be consulted on measures to be taken in common. The abbé was faithful to his masters and to them alone. He was allowed a good deal of leeway in carrying out his duties. For instance, on the basis of a newsletter of 20 November/30 December 1691 from London, reporting a canonical consultation of the Universities of Louvain and Salamanca asserting that it was lawful to take the oaths to a King by right of conquest, he immediately indulged in speculation on the advantages to be obtained if Catholics and Jacobites could be allowed to take the oaths to the Prince of Orange as King by right of conquest.[17] His very single-mindedness gives his papers special value provided they are taken for what they are: the reports of spies reflecting not so much the actual relations between the English Jacobites on one hand and Versailles and St. Germain on the other as the view which Louis XIV, his ministers and the abbé himself took of them. From the Renaudot papers alone, without going to English sources, it would be impossible to disentangle 'sham plots' from real ones. They cannot provide the kind of evidence a man such as Macky looked for, the kind which led to the arrest of spies. They show what Renaudot knew and understood of conspiracies, or, rather, what he was allowed to know, believe and understand.

Reflecting the views of a rather narrow governing group wherein the question *quis custodies ipsos custodes?* was never asked, the Renaudot papers also show the ways of spies and of government policy at the time. The risks the spy ran should not be forgotten. One case of naval espionage ended in three executions.[18] The diary of one Hurel mentions over a dozen suspected spies imprisoned in Caen in 1689, one hanged in Paris in June and two more in September of that year.[19] There was also the possibility of judicial torture: at the time of Sir James Montgomerie's arrest in England 'the Prince of Orange, who was delighted, boasted publicly of being able to send him to Scotland to put him to the torture, which is well known to be dreadful in that country'.[20] As a proof of good faith, one Duval *alias* Nickson, a suspected double agent, pointed out that he would have to face the rack if caught.[21] Obviously, in his relations with St. Germain, Renaudot himself never ran these risks, but still he did not hesitate to take the obvious precautions: 'I am keeping Montgomerie's and Irving's letters as pledges of their engagements and which would provide means of holding them in check'.[22] He appears to have been wary of his own master, writing to Pontchartrain on 7 November 1692: 'I would beg you to let the King know that this negotiation was undertaken by your orders. The past has taught me to avoid misunderstandings and I rely on your kindness for the future.' [23] Similarly he asked for orders to be sent direct to him on 8 January 1694 'if only to avoid giving the impression in Calais or in England that I have done the least thing except on your specific instructions'. [24] A world of blackmail and reinsurance, the world of spies could also be a world of misleading reports, crossed trails and false appearances. Croissy wrote to Renaudot, 'the King has much approved of the contents of your last memorandum and I here enclose the King's order to Monsieur de Besmaux [the governor of the Bastille] to allow Simpson to escape in circumstances making for the greatest possible secrecy'. [25] Another case, also involving Besmaux, saw not only the gaoler ordered to turn a blind eye but the Duc d'Aumont, governor of Boulogne, told to help an escaping prisoner get out of the kingdom. [26] On the other hand, a man could be locked up for odd reasons: Kenmis, a Scottish gentleman and an Episcopalian, was accused of secret dealings because he fainted after reading the news of the death of the Prince of Orange in the *Gazette*. [27]

Renaudot's papers also confirm the involvement of eminent Quakers with St. Germain and their help to France in beating the English blockade. On the occasion of an acute grain shortage in France, Bromfield the Quaker offered his services to Renaudot, who immediately wrote a letter to Pontchartrain which leaves no doubt as to the truth of the charges levelled against William Penn in those years:

> Mr. Bromfield, Quaker or Shaker . . . has written to me . . . he claims to be able to bring over a fairly large quantity of wheat and other goods made scarce by the war in order to sell it to merchants at a reasonable price and one which will satisfy you . . . I have often heard him spoken of as an able man; as the Quakers are strongly attached to the King of England, he may through them have access to supplies by means not available to others. Mr. Penn their head has long had dealings with us, and will no doubt play his part in the success of a fellow member. [28]

Despite his own experience in such tricky matters, Renaudot had to admit that:

> his idea is an unusual one . . . he is very capable in affairs of this kind and all the English say that without him the army would have died of hunger in Ireland. He also found means to clothe it when everyone else had given up. He has asked me to write to Mr. Penn . . . who is a clever man and one much devoted to the King. [29]

In order to bring grain into France, Bromfield contemplated a tortuous device which may be worth explaining as a contribution to the history of commercial wars and blockades:

> those who are ready to send some [grain] to France can still declare it and go through the same procedure as if they were despatching it to neutral or allied territory, even to Holland, which would ensure the safety of transports from the enemies of France, so that once the grain ships have got through the Irish channel, they could make for the French ports they are bound for as soon as they are within reach. Furthermore, to fulfil the obligation they are under in Ireland to bring back a certificate of unloading from the

place their grain was bound for, one could go through the motions of a prosecution and judgment of seizure as if the vessels had been captured after anchoring near the French coast owing to bad weather. It could even be agreed in advance which port they were making for so as to take them before they entered it, the better to disguise their 'capture' and it could then be made out they had repurchased their own ships.[30]

Whether this method was ever used has not been ascertained, but it may have been, for on 23 January 1694 six blank passes were issued to Renaudot for English ships destined to bring wheat to France.[31] Bromfield the merchant was also involved in another of the main branches of trade of that time: 'Monsieur de Pontchartrain would be obliged if you could procure a good, steady English horse for him . . . Let me know if you have an opportunity to fetch another one over for a lady who is a friend of mine and a friend of the Master of the Horse'.[32] It took from May to October 1695 for Pontchartrain to get his English horse.[33] Similarly, Melfort tried to procure from England two good horses for James II, which shows that the embargo was neither systematic nor general.[34]

Bromfield, a secondary figure, is interesting not only in the history of commercial relations. For instance, Renaudot reported to Pontchartrain on 14 June 1696:

> Among those who went to la Trappe [the Carthusian monastery where James II went into retreat] Bromfield the Quaker, as you will know, distinguished himself. This enthusiast had wanted to make the trip and came back much impressed, declaring he had found genuine Quakers filled with the same spirit as himself. Had he but said the same thing of the Jansenists, it would have made no small impression!

Bromfield was then staying in St. Germain in the house of the Prince de Conty, a Prince of the Blood.[35] We cannot leave Bromfield without referring to the general report on English affairs written by Renaudot on 11 February 1698:

> The Quakers or Shakers were at first very much attached to the legitimate King and were of great use to him, especially Mr. Penn, their Patriarch: but some time ago they changed their ways and Mr. Penn betrayed him.[36]

Gradually, the Quakers changed sides and, like others in England, travelled the slow and doubtful road leading to acceptance of the ruler they still called 'the Prince of Orange'.

Renaudot's papers, however, deal mainly with espionage, and the difficulties in maintaining regular communications with England are explained in them. Seignelay, the abbé wrote,

> wishing to get reliable intelligence of enemy vessels going in and out of the Thames and the Downs, and to collect on the English coast letters sent by those corresponding with the King of England had an armed sloop in Calais ready to sail under Monsieur de Thosse, a lieutenant in the Navy and this boat has been employed in the service ever since.

Laubanie, the commander at Calais, complained that his authority was being ignored and that he should decide when the sloop should go into enemy territory, but he was over-ruled.[37] During the crossings, an English ship was sometimes sighted and moments of alarm ensued:

> I have just heard of the great danger which the sloop has run into on the coast of England, which caused the packet meant for Mr. South to be thrown into the sea. These are accidents which cannot be avoided and to which one must become resigned ... Would you please warn our correspondent of the loss of the packet.[38]

Rather than go on throwing compromising documents in the sea lest they be captured, it was sometimes preferable to give up a trip:

> So full of enemy privateers are the Straits of Dover, that the sloop has had to return without getting to the English coast. She had to turn back to pick up supplies and for repairs. Tomorrow morning I shall order her out without fail with instructions to risk everything in order to collect our friend. And if she cannot land tomorrow night, Mr. Holmes, the last person to go over, will be waiting in the place appointed on Friday, so that there will be three men to carry. I will try and arrange with the captain to do everything possible so that our friend will not be sighted ... I made it clear to the captain that we shall be very pleased with him if he can but bring over our friend.[39]

These sea communications were, however, kept up with niggardly financial resources and an insufficient number of men, or so it would seem from a letter written to Renaudot from Calais in February 1693 from Pigault, a merchant and one of Renaudot's French agents:

> the sloop left yesterday morning and I had some trouble in getting the master to set out, the more so as his crew was taken away and replaced by invalids or by people who do not know the drill and on whom the master cannot rely. Since they will have to go ashore and make their way to a particular house well armed and resolute, a good crew familiar with the roads and the vicinity of the house is absolutely essential, whereas invalids will not even land, and this will make it practically impossible to make a success of anything. For these reasons, be good enough, Sir, to make a full report to the minister so that he may give appropriate orders to the commissioner for naval recruitment, so that a crew of a dozen stout, resolute fellows, determined to carry out orders, may be got together ... be good enough to give immediate instructions about manning the sloop for, as I see it, the master will quit unless he gets a good crew. Or, rather, he'll put out to sea but will do nothing more than observe, and for my part I dare say he's right for there are great risks involved when they have to go ashore ...

To back up the discreet support he had given to the grievances of his subordinates, Pigault repeated them later in the month, recalling that this was the very time when the sloop could be of most service since the spring was approaching, when good weather made both war and navigation easier.[40]

This ship not only conveyed persons between London and St. Germain, but carried messages the deciphering of which appears to come out of some romance:

When I had the honour of writing to you the day before yesterday [wrote Renaudot to Croissy on 3 January 1694] I did not as yet know what these letters contained, so full were they of names very difficult to guess at. One for Mr. Francis Ireton was particularly recommended to me: and, since one of the codes for names is to take the first letter of the first name and the first syllable of the next, it eventually occurred to me that it meant fire and, in exposing it to the fire, there emerged a long letter written between a few lines of insignificant matters.[41]

Renaudot also had to decipher letters received, such as letters in code sent from Constantinople to London in 1691 concerning relations between the Prince of Orange and the Porte. He set to at once:

I have done my best to find someone who could decipher the letters . . . I have never been used to coding and decoding and cannot do it by myself and persons capable of cracking such a code are few and far between . . . I despair of being able to find anyone suitable, since I would not like to trust the first comer and yet in such a matter I may have no choice. This leaves me only two ways to propose: the first is to seek some reliable person at the court of St. Germain, taking all precautions possible in doing so, the other would be for the King's cipher clerks to try their hand at these letters and see if they could make out a few lines. And although I am not familiar with coding methods, I might be able to help them by applying their results to my knowledge of English. I know the handwriting of Mr. Trumbull, the English ambassador at Constantinople, and although it is difficult to be certain about anything in cipher, I don't think these are in his hand. Yet I am aware that while he was here he did not use a secretary to do his coding. I will, however, keep these letters handy in case I should discover what has eluded me until now.[42]

It should be added that the capture of enemy documents to be decoded at Versailles had been encouraged by an ordinance of 16 September 1692 granting naval captains on active service two thousand *livres* for each Spanish or English ship captured and a thousand *livres* for any other ship provided they handed over mail-trunks or letters found on these ships. Besides intercepting other people's letters, the task of the spy network was to post agents to gather intelligence in enemy territory. Even then, they had to know what they were after. For this reason, documents setting out 'lines of inquiry' were preserved in the archives for different periods. A typical one listed the following points:

It is necessary to draw up a list of all ships . . . remaining at sea this winter and if possible Dutch ones too.
It should also be ascertained where these ships are bound for . . . how many of them will sail in the Channel in how many squadrons and what number in each fleet will serve as convoys.
Plot out the course of each squadron so as to discover the time of departure of each fleet and their ultimate destination.
Find out too which warships and other ships are bound for English colonies in America, the strength of each warship, the number of other ships and the exact moment of their departure.
Try and compile an exact list of English warships port by port. That is to say those in Chatham, those in Portsmouth and so on . . . make a note in the margin of those which

are in dock in winter. This list must contain the ships actually being built, remembering to note by their name the approximate date when they will be ready for service.

Find out whether guns are being made for the new ships of if old vessels will be disarmed in order to use their artillery.

Discover whether it is true that crews of first, second and third-rate ships are being maintained all winter.

If the sailors don't desert, what is their pay per month on land, and how do they spend their time before setting out?

Try and find out if there is any way of provoking haggling and discontent on this score. Get information on the number and strength of English privateers and their course. Do the same for the Dutch ones.[43]

Intelligence as to events on land was no less desirable. For instance, in January 1692 Pontchartrain sent Renaudot to see Simpson in the Bastille with the following instructions:

You must try especially to discover from him the present mood in England, of the merchants, of the people; the behaviour of the Prince of Orange towards private persons; the losses and the claims which might induce them to act; who are the friends of the King of England, whether there is any concert between them and what is to be expected from them; whether he believes that the supply bills are no longer being held up; how many troops will there be left in the three Kingdoms once the militia is called out and where will they be stationed; what are the inclinations of people in London; has he seen the stretches of the river where ships are being built and whether, if he has, he noticed how many there were . . . whether seamen are being paid . . . has the Prince of Orange given out that a descent in France was intended and what preparations has he made to ensure its success; at what time is he proposing to return to Holland?[44]

While these blueprints represented what it was desirable to discover, it was also necessary to consolidate what was known for certain, or at least what Louis XIV was told as established facts. Midway between business letters and spy reports are such letters as those addressed in 1689 to Monsieur Pierret in the rue des Victoires in Paris,[45] or a letter such as that sent by Berkenhead to Renaudot on 3/13 January 1693:

I advised you in my last as to what had been done about the fleet designed to convoy those of our ships which are ready to sail. There is no embargo on them. They will have to pick up fresh supplies, having practically run out . . . I don't doubt they will get through with such convoys despite the French. I received a letter from Portsmouth last night. The convoy from Lisbon will consist of two third-rate ships, three fourth-rate and one fifth-rate. That from Bilbao will have a third and a fifth-rate, while that from the Canaries will consist of one third-rate, one fourth-rate and one fifth-rate ships. That from the Islands [the West Indies] will be the same as I have told you already. They will sail together to go through the Canal when another three third-rate ships will watch them as they go through before returning to their stations.

Several frigates have returned . . . ready to sail as soon as the weather is good . . . work is going on with the greatest possible speed on third-rate ships to get them ready. It is well advanced.[46]

Matters relating to communications occasioned much friction between the servants of King Louis and those of King James, but this was a symptom rather than a cause of a more general misunderstanding. Copies of Melfort's letters to French agents in Calais were usually forwarded to Versailles. There again Renaudot took a copy of one of Melfort's letters to Simpson (Jones) and marked it 'Lord Melfort his letter to M.J. 30 May 1693'.[47] The idea behind these procedures was that, in its dealings with England, the court of St. Germain should not rely on its own channels of communication but should have to depend on those provided by the French. Thus the Jacobites were constrained not only by financial dependence but by strict surveillance.

Before leaving the world of spies, it may be mentioned that the whole business of intercepting mail and seizing trunkfuls of letters could harm persons who were quite innocent. Thus on 18 October one Livier, a Paris merchant, on 26 October Arthus the banker[48] and on 14 December 1695 'several private persons' all complained to Pontchartrain that their business papers had been seized, causing them great injury. These incidents were distasteful to Renaudot, who wrote, 'the case of Mr. Arthus is particularly embarrassing to me as he is the banker of the King of England and it would be a kindness to return them', adding, 'I admit that I am not speaking in terms of present-day statecraft, but in the past, it seems to me, war was not waged on workers and merchants, and I believe it would be generous not to do harm to Dutch merchants unnecessarily . . . for my part, I would prefer to be reading Arab manuscripts than foreign mail.[49] These reflections, which may have been the effect of weariness at years spent with spies and double agents, show the more pleasing side of Eusèbe Renaudot. The historian can only rejoice at this lapse in the rule against comment.

Renaudot was also a man of propaganda. It has been noted that he brought out each week the *Gazette* he had inherited from his father and grandfather. One may assume it was this ready outlet which encouraged him to become a propagandist. He was then a man at the height of his powers, between forty and fifty, well versed in printing techniques and in supervising an experienced and old-established staff. His work-table was only a few steps from his presses and he could write quickly if not always clearly or elegantly. This had, of course, been his family's task since the days of Richelieu, one of the functions of the *Gazette* being to print intercepted letters. As regards Renaudot himself, his involvement in propaganda for English consumption goes back to 1683 at least, to two pamphlets about the Rye House Plot published in Paris. Here can be seen the beginnings of Renaudot's work as a propagandist: it was a short step from the weekly *Gazette* to the special 'supplements', similar in every way to the newspaper. Most of the time propaganda was put out in the news published in the newspaper, and this is not the place to discuss how this was manipulated to give a gloss favourable to France. One example will suffice: Croissy wrote to Renaudot on 2 November 1693, 'I have read out to the King your memorandum on what you believe should be included in the *Gazette* and I am returning it to you with a "no" against the points the King does not want to be inserted and "good" against the others'. Here we see the very core of the famous *travail du Roi* and how faithfully Louis performed it.[50]

Besides these publications closely related to the *Gazette*, Renaudot wrote short pamphlets to suit the occasion, which may be ascribed to him from the evidence of his papers. It is not suggested, however, that he alone was involved in their production. In February 1689 La Reynie reported:

> Messrs Martin and Boudot, the printers selected by Lord Melfort . . . brought me this afternoon an English text with a French translation . . . I told these two men that I could not allow it [the translation] to place before the public views, even though condemned therein, which horrify all the King's subjects and which Frenchmen cannot listen to or allow to be expressed . . . It seems to me that the words used imply the tenet that the Pope may excommunicate or depose Kings not of the same religion as the Pope's or contrary to the interests of that religion, which proposition is false and has been refuted, is destructive to royal power and authority and dangerous to the life and persons of monarchs.

In June 1689 Melfort wrote from Dublin, 'the King's servants who have managed the printing and distribution in England of papers written against the Prince of Orange have spent £10,000 of their funds already and ask for more'.[51]

Though but one writer among several, Renaudot has left a document, which can be dated about 1693, describing the effects of propaganda as he saw them. After drawing a picture of an England on the edge of the abyss, in a state of the greatest disorder as regards its coinage and finances generally, with its troops unpaid, he noted:

> doubts began to be expressed as to whether French affairs were in such a bad way after a rather unusual event . . . They [the Jacobites] having received from France a copy of the King's letter to the archbishop relating to a *Te Deum* on the peace with Savoy and finding therein noble expressions worthy of a King, translated it into English, had it printed and distributed a large number of copies. This gave untold encouragement to the Jacobites and discomfiture to the other side.[52]

This is not the place to investigate the Fenwick plot nor the separate Assassination Plot of 1696.[53] It should suffice to publish the material in the Renaudot papers relating to the conspiracy (Appendices I and II) and two reports on English affairs dealing with its aftermath (Appendices III and IV). Nevertheless, a more general question may be asked as to how far the causes of the Jacobite setback in the Nine Years War may be discerned from the Renaudot papers? It has been seen that the abbé was a bitter opponent of Melfort, and this may have led him into error. His own superior, Pontchartrain, was somewhat sceptical about Renaudot's assurances. For instance, when Renaudot boasted that in his dealings with the Quaker Bromfield he had taken 'precautions which would prevent mishaps', Pontchartrain wrote a note on the letter: 'God willing, as you are rather prone to be deceived'. He was presumably speaking from experience! Some of the suggestions made by Renaudot to supporters of the Stuarts in England, such as that made in November 1692, might have produced mixed reactions:

The King's friends have taken judicious measures as to their conduct in Parliament, so as not to show their hand, but to content themselves with opposing the Court's proposals on grounds of national interest. To this end, they will support some bills designed to curb the royal power, without, however, any intention of enforcing them once the King returns.[54]

Difficulties about religion led Renaudot to similar inconsistencies a year later:

The object must be that the most zealous Protestants should find nothing to object to in His Majesty's zeal for the Catholic religion, but they have been so alarmed by the false rumours which have been circulated in England about the plans to destroy the Protestant religion that, provided they can be given assurances that the King had no part in them . . . they will be satisfied.[55]

The troubles and uncertainties which affected the court of St. Germain are so well depicted in an anonymous, undated, memorandum by an Englishman that it is worth quoting at length:

To heap abuse on all Whigs, Protestants and patriots will, in the end, so distort the whole controversy that it will no longer be a question of whether King James or the Prince of Orange but whether Catholics or Protestants get the upper hand, which will turn the whole thing into a war of religion. For the issue will then be whether the Roman or the Reformed religion will be the religion of the kingdom with, on one side King William, the Protestant religion and liberty, all arrayed against King James, the Roman religion and slavery . . . My God! What a crowd of ignorant, arrogant, rash, jealous people, without judgment, without heart, without soul, has the King round him at St Germain! People incapable of the breadth of mind required for dealing with the affairs of a King and three kingdoms; people who have no notion of the kind of generous self-denial which sacrifices private interests for public good and the service of a master; people of little talent, narrow minds and narrower souls, who yet engross all business, be it far above their knowledge and competence, and who either by ill-conduct or by slanders, spoil everything; people who sacrifice the glory, the interest and the reputation of their master to their own interests and ideas and who chance and will chance his very restoration rather than fail to obtain credit for it and places for which God has not given them the gifts or talents required . . . I realize that there are some real patriots at St Germain, who stand out clear and pure amidst all this contamination, but the description I have just given fits most of them there. It is not, therefore, surprising that so many false steps are taken, so many shocking measures adopted, and that the King's reputation suffers for the favourable reception he grants to those sorts of people. If only he would grant access to his person or to knowledge of his affairs only to those worthy of it by their devotion and talents, his fame would shine forth once more . . . ill-founded distrust would disappear, his friends would be able to help him, and everyone would be ready to receive him . . .[56]

By 1696 Renaudot was being gradually edged out of English business, and in June of that year he complained that he was losing contact with England. His fast sloops no longer ran and he gradually lost touch with his old friends across the Channel. By June 1699 he had to admit that he knew no more of English affairs than did anyone else in France, adding that all he could say was that some very bad books were being produced in that country.[57] Nevertheless, Renaudot remained devoted to James II. From the evidence of his papers, it appears to have been he who drew up James's protest at the Peace of Ryswick with a view to getting it printed.[58] The irony of it was that Renaudot, the faithful servant of Louis XIV, was now helping James II, the guest of Louis XIV, to protest against a treaty negotiated on behalf of Louis by Renaudot's own friend and collaborator on the *Gazette*, François de Callière. In 1709 the abbé was called in to help with the interrogation of Lord Lovat, then a prisoner in France. Ill-health, which had dogged him all his life, now forced him, in any case, to restrict himself to management of the *Gazette* and scholarly pursuits. On his death on 8 February 1720 his manuscripts passed into the hands of his nephew Monsieur de Verneuil and eventually found their way to the Bibliothèque Nationale where they were bound as the 'Collection Renaudot' in 1852.[59]

NOTES

1. The text of this paper and the quotations within it have been translated into English, and punctuation altered, to make for greater clarity. The appendices are printed as in the original.

2. H. Omont, *Inventaire sommaire des manuscrits de la collection Renaudot* (Bibliothèque de l'Ecole des chartres), Paris 1690.

3. *Lettres inédites de l'abbé E. Renaudot au ministre J.-B. Colbert* (1692-1706), ed. Abbé F. Duffo, Paris 1931.

4. The volumes of the Renaudot papers concerned with English affairs are in Bibliothèque Nationale nouvelles acquisitions francaises (BN n.ac.fr.) 7487-7492 and BN Clairambault 1057. These should be supplemented by the letters and papers in Archives Etrangères Correspondance Politique, Angleterre (AECP Ang.) 171-173, by the material in the Marine archives. There are Renaudot papers in the Bastille archives in the Bibliothèque de l'Arsenal, some of which are published by F. Ravaisson, *Archives de la Bastille*, 17 vols., Paris 1866, not always entirely accurately.

5. See A. Villien, *L'Abbe Eusèbe Renaudot, Essais sur sa vie et sur son oeuvre liturgique*, Paris 1904.

6. Archives Nationales (Arch. Nat.) L6 No. 13, Renaudot to Cardinal de Noailles.

7. BN n.ac.fr. 7487 ff. 260-61.

8. On Montgomerie see P. Riley *King William and the Scottish Politicians*, Edinburgh, 1979, 30-1, 39-41.

9. BN n.ac.fr. 7487 ff. 89-101.

10. BN n.ac.fr. 7492 ff. 288-93, 355.

11. *State Trials*, ed. T. B. Howell, 33 vols. 1816-26, xii. 711-2.

12. See *Correspondance de Bossuet*, ed. Urbain et Levesque, v. 526-40 (from BN n.ac.fr. 22388 ff. 108-20 and *ibid.* ff. 255-94 for letters of Cardinal Gualterio to Lord Middleton. See also A. Joly, *Un converti de Bossuet, James Drummond, duc de Perth 1648-1716*, Lille 1942.

13. BN n.ac.fr. 7490 ff. 380-81; AECP Ang. 172 f. 283.

14. John Miller, *James II, a study in Kingship*, Hove 1978, 336.

15. BN n.ac.fr. 7492 ff. 288-93.

16. BN n.ac.fr. 7491 ff. 227-28.

17. BN n.ac.fr. 7491 ff. 197-8.

18. A. Debans, 'Une affaire d'espionnage maritime à Marseille en 1696', *Revue Maritime*, 1906.

19. BN MS fr. 5845.

20. Renaudot to Croissy, 6 February 1694, BN n.ac.fr. 7487 ff. 310-11.

21. Arch. Nat. Marine B^7 499 f. 139.

22. Renaudot to Pontchartrain, 9 November 1692, BN n.ac.fr. 7487 f. 81.

23. Renaudot to Pontchartrain, 7 November 1692, BN n.ac.fr. 7487 f. 57.

24. Renaudot to Pontchartrain, 8 January 1694, Ravaisson, ix. 438-9.

25. Croissy to Renaudot, 30 November 1692, AECP Ang. 172 f. 390.

26. Letter from Croissy, 1689, AECP Ang. 171 f. 462.

27. April 1702, Archives de la Préfecture de Police AA/4m f. 922.

28. Renaudot to Pontchartrain, 23 October 1693, BN n.ac.fr. 7490 f. 378.

29. Renaudot to Pontchartrain, 28 October 1693, *ibid.* f. 379.

30. BN n.ac.fr. 7487 ff. 14-15.

31. 23 January 1694, Marine B^2 96 f. 22.

32. Renaudot to Bromfield, 6 May 1695, Bibliothèque de l'Arsenal, MS 10533 (unfoliated). For the delivery on 16 October see Marine B^2 109 f. 191.

33. Renaudot to Pontchartrain, 14 June 1696, Arch. Nat. KK 601, partly published by G. Servois, 'Lettre de l'abbé Renaudot à Jerome Phélypeaux de Pontchartrain', in *Annuaire-bulletin de la societé de l'histoire de France*, 1868, Pt. II, pp. 157-68.

34. Bibliothèque de l'Arsenal MS 10533.

35. *Ibid.*

36. BN n.ac.fr. 7488 f. 42.

37. Marine B^4 12 f. 340.

38. Melfort to Thosse, BN n.ac.fr. 7492 f. 167.

39. Pigault to Renaudot, Calais 29 April 1693, BN n.ac.fr. 7487 f. 217.

40. BN n.ac.fr. 7487 ff. 195-6.

41. Renaudot to Croissy, 3 January 1694, BN n.ac.fr. 7492 f. 309.

42. BN Clairambault 1057 ff. 13-14.

43. 'Mémoire pour le sieur de Birkenhead, à Versailles le 3 Novembre 1692', in Marine B^2 86 f. 255. It is the Berkenhead whose arrest was called for in the proclamation of 31 March 1696 o.s., '*alias* Fish, West, South and Baker', in Steele, *Proclamations* No. 4191.

44. Pontchartrain to Renaudot, 25 February 1692, Marine B^2 87 f. 137.

45. Letters to Pierret, Arch. Nat. Stuart K 1351/48-59.

46. Berkenhead to Renaudot, BN n.ac.fr. 7487 f. 180.

47. Marine B^2 109 f. 194.

48. A banker of this name in the rue Mauconseil in 1692, specialising in remittances to England, Scotland, Ireland, Holland and Flanders is mentioned in Lüthy *La banque protestante en France*, Paris 1959-61.

49. Marine B^2 286 f. 686.

50. BN Clairambault 506 ff. 271-6.

51. AECP Ang. 170 f. 98.

52. Renaudot to Croissy, AECP Ang. 172 ff. 262-3.

53. See G. H. Jones, *Main Stream of Jacobitism*, Cambridge, Mass. 1954, 44 *et seq.* and J. Garrett, *The Triumphs of Providence, the Association Plot 1696*, Cambridge. 1980.

54. Report on English affairs in Renaudot's hand dated November 1692, BN n.ac.fr. 7487 f. 85.

55. BN n.ac.fr. 7487 ff. 263-64.

56. Anonymous memorandum, BN n.ac.fr. 7489 ff. 375-78. Note that this had been translated into French by Renaudot and is now re-translated here.

57. BN n.ac.fr. 7491 f. 393.

58. AECP Ang. 173 ff. 249-50.

59. Villien, 60-155.

Appendix I

AECP Ang. 173 ff. 104-106

3 Mars 1696, Renaudot to Croissy

LA Reine d'Angleterre que j'ay eu l'honneur de voir ce matin a Chaliot m'a d'abord chargé de vous temoigner qu'elle auroit eté fort aise de vous voir si votre sante l'avoit permis, et qu'elle souhaitoit que vous fussiez promtement soulagé. S. M. m'a donne le copie cy jointe de la Declaration que le Roy d'Angleterre a fait durer, parce qu'a ce qu'elle m'a dit, on avoit trouvé quelque chose a dire de l'autre et qu'on avoit jugé a propos de n'y pas parler du Test, a cause des difficultez de conscience qu'on a faites au Roy d'Angleterre sur ce sujet. On y a aussi inseré quelques autres articles qui avoient eté oubliez dans les premiers entre autres un qui regarde la confirmation des Actes qui regardoit les affaires particulieres cette addition a etté faite fort prudemment.

Je vous envoye aussi un extrait de divers memoires recus depuis peu touchant les serviteurs du Roy d'Angleterre, la plupart ettant depuis long temps engages a faire pour luy, n'ont point quitté ses interests.

Il y en a certainement un plus grand nombre. Mylord Berwick n'en a veu que peu, vous pouvez vous souvenir Monseigneur, que depuis long temps, il y en a deux on trois qui font tout au nom des autres pour une plus grande sureté.

Mylord Griffin avoit aussi aporté des listes plus amples qu'il a données au Roy son Maistre . . .

Dans le Gloucestershire les habitants et la noblesse sont bien disposés. On y a pour chefs . . .	Le Duc de Beaufort Le marq. de Worcester son fils Mylord Neubourg
Dans le Lincolnshire, presque de même	Le Comte de Lindsey, Grand Chambellan d'Angleterre Mylord Macklesfield
Dans le Cheshire et Galles beaucoup de gentilhommes bien intentionnés	Mylord Pawlet Mylord Mohun Ch. Haswell Tent
En Somerset et Devonshire de même Exeter un grand nombre	Mylord Arundel de Trerice Ch. Jean Trelawny L'évêque etc.

Dans le pays de Cornouailles
il y a 8 à 10 mille mineurs
prêts à marcher dès qu'on leur
enverra des officiers. Le pays
est dans des dispositions
très favorables.

M. Kempe gouverne
cette affaire

Bristol est presque
entièrement au Roi

Le Ch. Thomas Knight qui a une
grande autorité dans la ville est
demeuré fidele et attaché aux
premiers projets depuis 4 ans.
Le Ch. Richard Hart
Le doct. Levet Doyen

Nord et Southwalles bien
disposé

Le Duc de Beaufort, son fils,
Mylord Chandois Mylord Buckley

Dans le Lancashire
et le Cheshire: il y a un
grand nombre de soldats et
gens de main enrôlés et tenus
chez des gentilhommes, les uns
comme jardiniers etc d'autres
sous la livrée.

Le colonel Parker y a beaucoup
avancé les affaires du Roi et en
sait le détail.

Whiltshire

Mylord Weymouth
Mylord Aylesbury
L'évêque de Bath et Wels se doit
mettre à la tête du clergé.

Northhampton Shire

Mylord Exeter
Mylord Chesterfield
Le fils du Mylord Griffin

Norfolk

Mylord Huntington
Mylord Yarmouth, son frère etc.

La ville d'Yarmouth
Très bien disposée, prête à se déclarer si le Roi débarque de ce côté la. Norwich suivra son exemple.

Mylord Cornwallis Lieutenant Gouverneur est dans les intérêts du Roi. A Londres, il y a beaucoup d'officiers réformés qui ne sont pas connus, et plusieurs autres qui servaient autrefois le Roy: qu'on assure prêts à se déclarer si le Roi d'Angleterre marche de ce côté là. On prétend aussi avoir des intelligences parmi la lieutenance ou officiers de la milice de la Ville.

Seigneurs sur lesquels on croit aussi pouvoir compter certainement:

Duc de Northumberland	Evêques de Norwich
Marq. d'Halifax	Bath et Wells
Comtes de Thanet	Exeter
de Clarendon	St David
de Rochester	Peterborough
Mylords Litchfield	et d'autres que connait l'évêque
Scarsdale Clare	de Norwich
Ferrers Fanshaw	Oxford
Forbes Brudenel	Plusieurs doyens et Dignitaires des
Montgomery, Mordant, Geffreys,	Eglises
Ashley, Castleton, Lansdown	Et grand nombre de ministres non
Fairfax, Clifford.	conformistes.

Appendix II
AECP Ang. 172 ff. 108-9

4 Mars 1696

ON croit qu'il peut être de quelque utilité de faire par avance quelques réflexions sur ce qui peut arriver en Angleterre lorqu'on y sera, ou que le Roi est débarqué ou qu'il est sur les côtes de France prêt à le faire. Car il n'y a pas lieu de s'imagine que d'abord le Parlement et ceux qui en ont le Gouvernement en main ne feront pas des démonstrations d'attachement au Prince d'Orange. Il faut donc s'attendre que le premier bruit s'étant répandu, que des troupes françaises seraient entrées dans le Royaume, on en donnera part au Parlement, comme d'une invasion faite par les Etrangers. Les députés, surtout ceux de la Chambre des Communes, quand il n'y en aurait qu'un fort petit nombre, ne manqueront pas de faire une délibération par laquelle il sera dit que chacun se mettra en état de repousser l'invasion, que tous ceux qui sont entrés dans le Royaume à main armée seront réputés traîtres, qu'il sera défendu de leur donner assistance ou retraite sous peine de haute Trahison. Ces déclarations sont de style et pourraient se faire sans qu'on en dût craindre aucun inconvénient. Car plusieurs députés bien intentionnés pour le Roy pourront être de cet avis afin de mieux couvrir leurs bonnes intentions, au lieu que s'ils se retiraient d'abord ils ne seraient pas en état de le servir, ou dans la même séance, s'il arrive qu'elle continue, ou dans les suivantes, si le dessein était retardé par quelque contretemps.

Mais il y a apparence que le Parlement quelque chose qui arrive se séparera au moins pour quelques jours et il n'y en a aucune que dans ce premier mouvement, on puisse faire conclure les textes pécuniaires qui sont sur le tapis à cause que la matière des fonds qui ont été proposés est trop embrouillée.

C'est encore par cette raison qu'il est important que les députés bien intentionnés ne quittent point l'Assemblée de peur que s'ils s'étaient retirés le Prince d'Orange qui a compté sur environ deux cents députés qui lui sont dévoués, ne fît passer quelque délibération tumultuaire au préjudice de celles qui ont été faites jusqu'à présent contre ses intérêts et son autorité.

Car ces députés paraissant demeurer attachés au Prince d'Orange auront des postes de confiance et d'autorité qui les mettront bien plus en état de servir que s'ils se déclaraient d'abord. On espère que M. Seymour, M. Musgrave et quelques autres des meilleures têtes de la Chambre des Communes qui ont rendu de grands services, quant on était presque sans espérance d'être promptement délivré de l'Usurpation, prendront en cette rencontre le parti le plus sage, qui paraît être de faire proroger le Parlement. Car comme il n'y a encore aucun fond de réglé que la taxe de quatre schelins par livre, qui ne doit se payer que par quartier, on est comme certain que par la prorogation du Parlement, tout l'argent est arrêté. On ne doute pas non plus, que dès le premier bruit de la descente, les Anglais selon leur coutume ordinaire dans les temps turbulents ne cessent de payer toute sorte de droits: Et si M. Foxe et Mylord Ranelagh gardent comme on l'a dit une somme considérable pour la mettre entre les mains du Roi d'Angleterre le Gouvernement pourrait manquer tout d'un coup, parce que selon toute vraisemblance les receveurs particuliers pour avoir occasion de détourner quelque somme, ne manqueront pas d'en faire autant.

Il aurait semblé que dans la Déclaration du Roi d'Angleterre ou au moins dans les billets que l'on faisait répandre dans le public, il fut marqué bien positivement que S. M. B. défend à tous et quelconque sous quelque prétexte que ce soit (particulièment des prétendus Actes du Parlement tenus sous l'autorité de l'Usurpateur) de lever aucuns deniers, sur le peuple, à peine dêtre puni selon la rigueur des lois comme concussionnaires. Car quoique les Anglais savent bien que tous les impôts présents doivent finir avec l'Usurpation, néanmoins comme cet article est capital, à l'égard d'une nation qui aime autant son interêt que celle-là, il semble qu'on ne peut trop leur faire envisager la délivrance de ces taxes insupportables, qui serviront plus à leur faire recevoir leur Roi légitime, que tous les remords de conscience et les sentiments de leur devoir. Cette pensée mérite d'autant plus de réflexion qu'on ne manquera pas de faire craindre que le Roi, s'il se trouvait d'abord fortifié par la jonction d'un grand nombre de ses sujets, ne voulût faire lever les mêmes impôts établis sous le Prince d'Orange. Car on n'a pas oublie qu'il fit ainsi, par une Proclamation continuer la levée du Droit de Tonnage et de Pondage, aussitôt après la mort du Roi Charles II, qui n'en jouissait que pour sa vie, ce qui fut un des premiers motifs dont on se servit pour faire craindre l'usage immense du pouvoir arbitraire, qui le rendit suspect à la Nation.

On proposera aussi une pensée qui peut avoir de grands effets, si elle convenait au service de S.M. Ce serait de promettre par avance une chose qu'on accordera dans la suite, en cas que l'entreprise ait le succès qu'on en doit espérer C'est de faire déclarer que ceux qui se soumettront au Roi d'Angleterre dans un certain terme, obtiendront aussitôt la main levée de leurs vaisseaux qui pourraient être pris depuis ce temps-là par les Armateurs français. Comme il y a un grand nombre de vaisseaux marchands en mer, et que l'interêt du commerce se répand dans toute la nation, cette promesse pourrait engager un grand nombre de personnes indifférentes à se déclarer plus tôt.

Si le Prince d'Orange avait à espérer quelque chose de son Parlement, en cas qu'il en fût absolument le maître, ce qui certainement n'est pas, ce serait qu'on fît comme au temps de l'invasion du Duc de Monmouth: c'est à dire que le Parlement prononça sur le champ une sentence contre les Invaseurs et les déclara Traîtres etc. Mais on peut croire qu'il est impossible que cela se fasse. Car le Roi étant à la tête, il n'y a pas la moindre apparence qu'on prononce rien contre lui. Le parricide de Charles I fait encore horreur. On obligea le Prince d'Orange dans la première fureur de la Rebellion, de chasser Ludlow, un des juges de ce Roi, qui était venu en Angleterre sous sa protection. On peut juger que puisqu'il n'a pu obtenir qu'on passât le serment d'abjuration du Roi Jacques, il aurait moins de facilité à obtenir une sentence qui ne peut être fondée en aucun exemple même du temps des rébellions.

Ainsi ce qui pourrait arriver de meilleur est que le Parlement se sépare, et que les Députés soient chargés de veiller chacun dans les comtés de leur Députation, à la sûreté publique. Car certainement ceux qui sont attachés à le Cour n'ont presque aucun crédit dans les Provinces: et tous ceux qui y sont opposés dont la plupart sont disposés favorablement pour le Roi, y en ont beaucoup. De sorte qu'ayant cette occasion de se joindre à ceux qui se déclareraient en même temps pour le Roi, les Provinces entières seraient soumises en fort peu de temps.

Appendix III
AECP Ang. 173 ff. 129-34

8 Octobre 1696

Rapport sur l'Angleterre

POUR donner une idée plus juste de l'état des affaires d'Angleterre, on commencera par un récit sommaire de celui où elles étaient au commencement de cette année, parce qu'il peut beaucoup servir à faire voir qu'au lieu qu'elles paraissaient avoir pris une nouvelle face, à l'avantage du Prince d'Orange, elles semblent être pour lui dans une situation plus mauvaise qu'elles n'étaient à la fin de l'année dernière.

On peut se souvenir que par les mémoires qui furent donnés, en ce temps-là, on fit voir que le Prince d'Orange avait été obligé de casser son Parlement, par la grande opposition qu'il y trouvait à diverses propositions, auxquelles le Parti de l'Eglise anglicane s'opposait toujours. Ce fut ce qui le détermina à tâcher de faire élire autant de Presbytériens, qu'il lui serait possible. Il ne put pas entièrement réussir dans ces élections, quoi qu'il y eût employé tant de mauvais moyens, que le Parlement même crut devoir en prévenir les conséquences, par un acte qui en a réglé la forme et empêché les dépenses excessives qui se faisaient à cette occasion.

Le Parlement quoi que composé en partie de ses créatures, lui fut néammoins si peu soumis, que nonobstant ses instances et ses harangues réitérées, 1) il y eut près de trois mois employés à écouter des plaintes, et à réformer les abus, avant que de terminer l'affaire du subside. 2) On lui assigna de très mauvais fonds; et on ôta des impôts onéreux au public, qui produisaient un argent prompt et certain. 3) On n'égala pas le subside à la demande, faite selon les états donnés par ses ministres; et il s'en fallait de quelques millions. 4) On appropria la plupart des fonds. 5) On ne voulut pas se charger de l'affaire de la monnaie: mais on le chargea d'une grande partie de la perte. 6) On rejeta long-temps la demande de quelque somme extraordinaire pour le paiement de ses dettes. 7) On rejeta l'Acte d'abjuration proposé par quelques-unes de ses créatures. 8) On passa malgré lui l'Acte pour la procédure criminelle: celui du Conseil de Commerce et divers autres qui donnaient des bornes fort étroites à son autorité. Enfin on peut dire sans témérité qu'il y avait tout sujet de croire, que ce Parlement seul travaillait à le détruire, d'une manière si efficace, que sans le malheur de la découverte du dessein qu'on avait, de faire passer le Roi d'Angleterre, et le fracas de la conspiration, le Prince d'Orange, n'était pas en état de soutenir la guerre, et son usurpation, encore une année.

Cette découverte fut alors son salut, et le trouble qu'elle répandit, lui donne moyen de finir toutes ses affaires plus heureusement qu'il n'aurait osé espérer. Il obtint l'argent qu'il avait demandé pour sa maison, et quelques autres fonds extraordinaires il n'eut plus de peine à faire recevoir sous le nom d'Association, ce même serment d'Abjuration qui avait été rejeté: et l'autorité qui lui fut accordée au préjudice des Lois pour rechercher la conspiration le mit en état d'exercer toutes les violences imaginables contre les serviteurs du Roi d'Angleterre.

Il est très certain que la rigueur avec laquelle il les a traités lui a fort aliéné les esprits de la nation, surtout en ce qu'il en a fait juger à mort quelques uns, peu de jours avant que l'Acte paru la nouvelle procédure criminelle fut en vigueur: qu'il a fait emprisonner plus de dix mille personnes en même temps: que les vexations arbitraires ont été sans mesure: que les prisonniers ont été traités avec une extrême barbarie, et enfin parce que contre l'avis de ses plus zélés partisans, il n'a pas jusqu'à présent accordé l'amnestie à tous ceux contre lesquels on n'avait pas de preuves positives, comme tous les Rois légitimes avaient fait en pareilles circonstances. Ainsi la terreur générale s'est changée en haine puis on a reconnu qu'il n'était pas capable de modération, dans les occasions qu'il avait d'entreprendre contre la liberté publique.

La découverte n'a pas été fort loin: et on peut dire sans exagération, qu'elle a plutôt fortifié que détruit le parti du Roi. Il faut se souvenir pour le comprendre que les serviteurs de S.M. Britannique étaient divisés en deux partis, dont on n'a que trop ouï parler: dont l'un avait eu correspondance avec la Cour de Saint Germain, par le canal de Mylord Melfort; l'autre n'avait point voulu avoir de commerce avec lui, et encore moins avec ceux qu'il employait, du nombre desquels étaient Porter, Goodman et les autres témoins, dont on s'est servi contre ceux qui ont été exécutés à mort. Tous ceux de ce dernier parti se sont trouvés accableés et parmi ceux là, on n'a trouvé de preuves positives que contre Mylord Aylesbury, qui était comme leur chef. Les autres personnes de qualité accusées par les dépositions de ces témoins, ou ont déjà été mis en liberté faute de preuves, ou y seront mis certainement dans un mois. Les autres qui n'ont jamais voulu avoir de commerce avec les traîtres, n'ont point été découverts: et si M. Berkenhead qui est échappé de prison par le moyen de deux milles guinées qu'ils ont données, et une fois en secret il ne craindront plus rien, puisque Peter Cooke, et le Ch. Fenwike, ne peuvent les accuser, et que le premier a tant de fois varié dans ses dépositions, soit que la tête lui ait tourné, comme on le dit, soit qu'il en fasse semblant, comme d'autres croyent, qu'on n'en peut presque plus rien craindre.

Ainsi ce parti subsiste entièrement, puisqu'on peut vérifier par les listes qu'on en donna au mois de mars dernier, que la plupart des personnes les plus considérables sont en pleine liberté, et n'ont pas été découvertes. Mais de plus on le sait positivement par le témoignage de M. Lee qui revint il y a environ six semaines, et qui en a vu la plupart: aussi bien que par Madame Philips revenue depuis peu, et par plusieurs lettres. Le Roi d'Angleterre a su par ces personnes et par d'autres voies très sûres, que ses serviteurs étaient toujours dans la même disposition à son égard.

Il faut même que le Gouvernement s'en aperçoive, parce que depuis quelque temps, on répand le bruit de la publication d'un pardon général, qui venant trop tard, et quand la suspension de l'Habeas Corpus sera expirée, ou prête à expirer, n'aura plus le même effet. On se sert de toutes les voies pour décourager les serviteurs du Roi, entre autres de l'espérance de la paix, à l'exclusion de S.M.B. même on a répandu avec soin toute sorte de faux bruits sur l'état de la santé du Roi: et cependant on n'oublie pas de jeter dans l'esprit des Parlementaires, tout ce qui peut les disposer à accorder encore des subsides, pour la continuation de la guerre.

Cet embarras du Gouvernement paraît encore plus, en ce qu'on apprend de bons endroits que le Prince d'Orange a fait aller plusieurs personnes de confiance dans les Provinces pour découvrir s'il y aurait quelque sûreté à choisir de nouveaux députés, et casser le Parlement présent pour en avoir un autre dont il fût maître.

On est persuadé que celui-ci ne sera pas plutôt rassemblé qu'il reprendra les délibérations sur toutes les matières odieuses à la Cour que la prétendue conspiration avait fait interrompre. L'idée d'un assassinat concerté par les serviteurs du Roi en avait trompé plusieurs, que la Déclaration faite en mourant par le S Charnock, par les Ch. Perkins et Freind, et par quelques autres a entièrement dissipée. On voit qu'il n'y a que le Parlement qui puisse remédier aux abus infinis qui augmentent plutôt que de diminuer. Ainsi, sans trop se flatter, on peut croire que ce Parlement-ci sera un des plus difficiles que le Prince d'Orange ait eu à essuyer depuis son usurpation.

De plus quand le Parlement serait bien disposé pour lui, les moyens ne sont plus les mêmes. Tous les fonds des subsides sont épuisés: la plupart des impôts et des taxes sont déjà accordés pour plusieurs années: celle des terres qui était la plus certaine et la plus claire, outre qu' elle est fort diminuée, se trouve engagée à payer des intérêts de sommes avancées. La banque qui devait avancer deux millions et demi, sur ce fond, perd tous les jours son crédit, et n'a pu fournir cette somme. Ainsi il n'y a qu'une seule ressource que craignent les serviteurs du Roi d'Angleterre qui est l'Excise generale. Mais il y a lieu d'espérer que puisqu'on n'a pas pu y parvenir depuis six ans qu'on en parle, il y aura encore plus de difficulté présentement, dans la crainte qu'elle ne fût proposée ce qui donnerait trop d'autorité au Gouvernement, et ne pourrait être que fort à charge aux peuples, accablé déjà par toutes sortes d'impôts.

Pour faire voir clairement que le Parlement, supposé même qu'il voulût tout accorder au Prince d'Orange, ne le peut faire, il faut se souvenir des années dernières. Afin de lui faire un subside d'environ six millions de livres sterlings, il a fallu depuis trois ans, contre l'ancien usage, accorder les impôts et les taxes pour plusieurs années, même quelques uns pour vingt ans, les doubler et tripler, comme entre autres les impôts sur les liqueurs, sur le sel etc., de sorte qu'on n'en peut rien tirer présentement. Il y a beaucoup de non valeurs dans d'autres recettes: les banques ont perdu presque tout crédit, les particuliers pécunieux sont hors d'état de faire des avances, à cause des sommes qui leur sont dues par le Prince d'Orange. Ainsi tous les fonds sont généralement épuisés ou extrêmement diminués, et la crédit de l'Echiquier, Du Corps de Ville de Londres et des Compagnies entièrement tombé. Si donc lors que les choses étaient dans un autre état et que l'argent roulait, il a fallu toute sorte d'impôts et de taxes pour fournir cinq ou six millions de livres sterlings, que depuis trois ans il faut engager les fonds et qu'on a peine à trouver de quoi payer les intérêts, et cela avant le désordre prodigieux de la monnaie, on peut juger que les difficultés de trouver de l'argent pour la continuation de la guerre doivent être infiniment plus grandes au prochain Parlement et la preuve en est aisée.

Il ne faudrait pas moins pour le subside de terre et de mer la campagne prochaine, que pour les précédentes, ce qui a été ordinairement à cinq millions sterlings.

Le secours extraordinaire pour la maison du Prince d'Orange appelé la Liste civile, qui lui fut accordé l'année dernière, et dont il fera apparemment la demande, parce qu'il en a autant de besoin que jamais, fut de pareille somme de 500 000 livres sterling.

Il faut ajouter à cela 2 500 000 livres sterling, que la banque des terres n'a pu fournir, et qu'il faut remplacer.

On avait accordé 1200 mille livres sterling pour le renouvellement de la monnaie. Il s'est trouvé que sur quatre millions que l'on a réformés, il y a eu plus de la moitié de perte. Ainsi il reste plus de 800 000 livres sterling qu'il faut que le Parlement trouve, ou que le Prince d'Orange perde.

Il reste par une estimation générale plus de cinq millions d'espèces rognées à réformer. Il ne faut pas douter que les meilleurs fonds ne soient employés à cela; et la perte estimée sur le pied de la première réforme ira à plus de 2 500 000 livres sterling.

Il n'y a point presque de fond qui ne se trouve fort diminué, et celui des douanes est réduit à moins de la moitié: mais le Parlement n'entre pas en connaissance de cet article.

En supputant tous les autres, il se trouve que si le Parlement accorde au Prince d'Orange tout ce qu'il peut lui demander, il faut trouver 12 000 000 ou environ de livres sterling, et c'est ce qui excède la possibilité de l'Angleterre, comme on voit clairement par la difficulté qu'il ya eu à en trouver la moitié avant le désordre de la monnaie.

Mais quand on pourrait accorder cette somme, on peut être assuré que selon l'état où sont les finances, le Prince d'Orange n'aurait pas le tiers en argent, mais en assignations et en billets sur l'Echiquier, qui sont autant de dettes, et par conséquent, ce secours pourrait servir à l'acquitter en partie, mais ne peut lui produire l'argent comptant dont il a besoin.

Ces dettes sont à des sommes immenses, et les amis mandent qu'elles sont au moins de 9 000 000 de livres sterling. (Apostille en marge: Une lettre très particulière marque que par le compte rendu depuis peu à la Trésorerie, les dettes montaient à 8 750 000 livres sterling, sans y comprendre la perte sur la banque des terres.) On peut juger qu'il n'y a pas d'exagération, par les faits suivants qui sont certains. Le jeudi 9 d'août dernier, on porta au Sceau Privé l'état de ce qui avait été ordonné par les commissaires de la Trésorerie, pour le paiement de ce qui était dû pour la campagne dernière. Il y avait trois millions sterling pour les troupes de terre et pour l'armée navale. Deux cent mille livres pour l'artillerie et 50 mille livres sterling pour l'armée d'Irlande. De toutes ces sommes, il n'y a pas eu un sol de payé, puisque M. de Benting étant venu en même temps ne put en faisant les derniers efforts, trouver 200 mille livres sterling que par voie d'emprunt dont les trois quarts furent en billets.

On fait état que tout l'argent qu'on a tiré jusqu'environ le mois d'août a été en espèces rognées, qu'on a prises dans les bureaux de recette pour leur valeur entière, et le moins qu'on y ait perdu a été plus de cinquante pour cent.

Depuis qu'on n'a plus reçu les espèces rognées que pour leur juste valeur, on a été obligé de se servir de cet expédient pour attirer l'argent à l'Echiquier. On donne un billet de cent livres sterling payable en un an, pour 88 1. et on paie les intérêts à raison de sept pour cent, de sorte que sans sortir d'Angleterre, il en a coûté dix neuf pour cent. Et les frais des remises ont été si grands, que quoiqu'on n'en puisse faire une estimation juste, on peut croire qu'ils ont été souvent depuis 30 jusqu'à 40 pour cent. Car on a négocié communément les billets de la banque et de l'Echiquier à 30 pour cent de perte, dans Londres. Les négociants hollandais qui avaient pris de ces billets, et qui n'avaient pu être payés sur leurs lettres de change, qui leur étaient revenues protestées, ont fait condamner les Anglais à payer le principal, les dommages et intérêts, le change et le rechange. C'est ce qui a causé en partie la ruine du crédit de toutes les banques.

On ne croit pas qu'il soit possible de le rétablir avant le rétablissement de la monnaie, qui selon l'avis des personnes les plus éclairées ne peut être fait durant la guerre; at même on ne peut le faire durant la paix que dans l'espace de six ou sept ans.

On avait estimé la perte pour le royaume à 1200 mille livres sterling: on reconnait présentement qu'elle ira à plus de quatre millions. On a cru que l'or n'était pas diminué, et qu'il n'en était pas beaucoup sorti du royaume: mais comme tout ce qu'on a emporté pour les armées a presque été en guinées, et que les Hollandais en ont beaucoup tiré, on ne doute pas qu'on en sente bientôt la diminution.

Le désordre est si grand faut d'espèces que plusieurs hommes de qualité ont quitté Londres, n'y pouvant vivre, quoique riches de six à sept mille livres de rente, parce qu'on ne peut tirer davantage des provinces.

On a été obligé de prendre depuis peu les obligations des merchands pour les douanes dues par les vaisseaux arrivés en Angleterre de Virginie et d'ailleurs, ce qui s'était toujours payé en argent comptant, et de leur donner six mois pour les acquitter. Si cet exemple continue comme il y a quelque apparence, c'est encore une des plus claires ressources du Gouvernement présent qui manquera au Prince d'Orange.

Il y a encore une autre affaire qui peut achever d'ôter au Prince d'Orange le secours qu'il pourrait espérer des banques établies ou à établir, et des emprunts extraordinaires. C'est que les banques, du Million, ou rentes viagères, celle des Terres, et celle qu'on appelle Royale ont demandé que les billets de banque fussent pris en paiement dans les comptes qu'ils auront à rendre pour les droits dont ils font la recette. Cette proposition, quoique très raisonnable a été rejettée: et cela a produit une telle défiance que la compagnie est divisée; les uns en plus grand nombre veulent retirer leur argent; les autres continuer. Mais tous conviennent qu'il est impossible de soutenir la banque, si l'Echiquier ne reçoit plus leurs billets. Ainsi ou elle tombera complètement comme il y a beaucoup d'apparence, ou cette affaire sera portée au Parlement. Si elle est jugée en faveur de l'Echiquier, les intéressés seront minés et hors de tout pouvoir de faire des avances: s'ils obtiennent ce qu'ils demandent, le Prince d'Orange ne tirera pas la moitié de ce qu'il en pouvait espérer; mais quantité de billets qu'on negociera avec les intéressés; ce qui ne pourra lui servir qu'à s'acquitter chose qui ne le presse pas beaucoup.

Il est déjà arrivé tant de désordres sur le refus de payer les billets à l'Echiquier à leur échéance, que les banques particulières s'en sentent, entre autres on en marque deux, celles de Brisco, et du docteur Chamberlaine prêtes à faillir. Les billets des orfèvres seraient soutenus, mais ils commencent à tomber comme les autres.

Un des moyens qu'on avait employé depuis peu pour faire valoir les billets de l'Echiquier, était de publier que ceux qui les recevraient une fois en paiement pourraient après cela les rapporter à l'Echiquier, où ils seraient reçus en déduction des taxes dues par les particuliers. Cela a eu quelque effet, mais si médiocre qu'à peine on l'a senti: parce qu'en refusant de recevoir en paiement les billets de banque et deux des orfèvres, tout le dommage est retombé sur les marchands, qui ne pouvant convertir leurs billets en argent, ni payer les lettres de change tirées sur eux, ont fait de grandes pertes. Dans les lettres du 21 qui viennent d'une personne très sûre, on marque qu'il y a eu dix ou douze banqueroutes considérables en huit jours.

Tel est l'état présent des affaires du Prince d'Orange en Angleterre, particulièrement pour ce qui regarde les finances, dont le désordre n'a jamais été si loin.

Il n'est pas moindre en tous les autres articles. Les troupes et la flotte n'ont reçu depuis fort longtemps qu'une partie de ce qu'ils appellent subsistance money, ou argent de subsistance: et ou il faut les laisser périr, ou les satisfaire avec le premier argent qu'on pourra tirer. Le voyage de M. de Benting et tout ce qu'on a su de divers endroits touchant la misère des troupes de Flandres en est une preuve bien certaine. En Angleterre les soldats qui sont réduits à 12 000 hommes de troupes réglées vivent presque partout à discrétion, ce qui va être un grand sujet de plainte au Parlement, où il y en aura beaucoup d'autres. On ne peut presque douter qu'il ne soit aussi difficile à gouverner en cette séance prochaine, qu'il ne l'a été en la dernière. Le Gouvernement a déja pris des measures pour tâcher d'en exclure environ soixante députés des meilleures têtes, et qui avaient plus fait naître d'opposition aux volontés du Prince d'Orange. Le moyen qu'on a résolu d'employer pour y parvenir est d'en faire exclure ceux qui n'ont pas signé l'Association, ce que la plupart ont refusé de faire. Mais on apprend que plusieurs ont résolu de la signer en cas qu'ils ne puissent empêcher cette résolution, ne se souciant pas de faire un faux serment, comme ils ne s'en sont pas souciés en faisant celui de soumission au Prince d'Orange, disant que ce serment ne les oblige point, et que sans cela ils ne seraient pas en état de servir le Roi.

On peut juger par ce qui a été dit jusqu'à présent que les affaires du Prince d'Orange ne le mettent pas en état de donner la loi, mais plutôt de la recevoir, même qu'il lui est presque impossible de soutenir encore la guerre, quand tous les alliés lui demeureraient attachés: et que si quelqu'un l'abandonne encore, comme a fait M. le duc de Savoie, sa perte est inévitable. Il paraît qu'il le sent assez, puisque selon son artifice ordinaire de répandre dans le public ce qui peut servir à ses intérêts, ses créatures font courir en Angleterre des nouvelles fort opposées. Car on répand que la paix est certaine, et qu'il dépend de lui d'y être compris à l'exclusion du Roi d'Angleterre: et on dit en même temps que les choses ne sont pas si avancées, et qu'il faut penser aux moyens de continuer encore la guerre une campagne pour réduire la France, à des conditions plus dures que celles qui ont été proposées. On prétend en persuadant que la paix est certaine déconcerter les mesures des serviteurs du Roi et les décourager de telle manière qu'ils ne puissent ou ne veuillent rien faire au prochain Parlement, flatter la nation qui souhaite la fin de la guerre et durant ce temps-là fortifier le parti de la Cour, afin que si on peut obtenir un grand subside, le Prince d'Orange soit en état de renverser toutes les négociations et d'obliger les Hollandais de donner encore de l'argent ce qu'ils ont toujours fait quand le Parlement en accorde. Ce qu'on apprend sur ce sujet par l'Angleterre est bien aussi sûr que ce qu'on peut savoir par la Hollande.

On voit un grand désordre dans le Conseil. Mylord Sunderland a perdu son crédit, depuis l'avis qu'il donna l'année passée de casser le Parlement. Les Régents ont passé la moitié de l'été à leurs maisons de campagne, laissant faire à Summers Garde du Grand Sceau, à l'arch. de Cantorbury, et à ceux qui se trouvent par hasard en ville les ordonnances de police et des proclamations sur des bagatelles. Un des secrétaires d'Etat qui est Trumball, n'a guère plus de part aux affaires qu'un commis: le mécontentement est général, la misère s'étend jusque sur les personnes les plus riches, on ne peut vivre avec beaucoup de bien, le commerce n'a jamais été dans un tel état. Les Compagnies des Indes Orientales et autres ont perdu l'année dernière plus de cinq millions sterling en capital, sans compter la perte du profit sur les marchandises perdues. La liberté publique est opprimée, l'Eglise anglicane mécontente, en un mot depuis l'usurpation les choses n'ont jamais été dans un si mauvais état, de sorte qu'il n'y a que la paix qui puisse empêcher le Prince d'Orange de périr.

On croit donc qu'il est du service du Roi, que cet état de l'Angleterre soit mis en considération, puisque selon toute apparence, il dépend du Parlement prochain de mettre le Prince d'Orange en état de pouvoir troubler les négociations, d'affermir la Ligue au moins pour quelque temps, et de faire naître des obstacles qui retarderaient la paix ou la rendraient moins sûre et moins glorieuse. Car si dans un mois ou six semaines on voit seulement que le Parlement ait voté un subside, les alliés qui voudraient s'opiniâtrer à la guerre n'examineront pas si ce sera de l'argent comptant ou des billets, ou si cela achève de ruiner l'Angleterre, dont il ne se soucie guère. Ils en deviendront plus intraitables et plus orgueilleux, et ils continueront la guerre. Au lieu que si on prend des mesures pour ne se pas tellement fier à ce qu'on peut promettre de la part du Prince d'Orange, qu'on ne le laisse pas tirer tous les avantages qu'il tâchera de tirer de son Parlement, en cas qu'il n'y trouve aucune contradiction, il se trouvera nécessairement obligé à rechercher la paix et sera moins en état de la troubler dans la suite. Peut être même que s'il se trouvait entièrement dépourvu des moyens de continuer la guerre l'année prochaine, quelques alliés ouvriraient les yeux par nécessité et seraient touchés des motifs de religion, d'humanité, de respect pour les têtes couronnées, et d'autres semblables qu'ils ont mis en oubli pour élever un usurpateur sur le trône et le mettre à la tête des ennemis de la France. S'ils en étaient une fois détachés, il ne serait pas alors difficile de rétablir par une paix plus sûre, plus stable et plus glorieuse qu'aucune qui ait jamais été faite, l'Angleterre et toute l'Europe dans son état naturel, à quoi on n'a pu jusqu'à présent parvenir par la continuation de la guerre.

K

Appendix IV

BN n.ac.fr. 7488 ff. 35-8

Mémoire sur les affaires d'Angleterre   2 Janvier 1698

DANS la situation presente des affaires d'Angleterre, on peut supposer comme certain qu'elles n'ont pas moins changé de face au dedans, qu'au dehors, et ainsi tout ce qu'on pourroit avoir observé des Regnes passez, ne peut servir presentement a donner aucune regle de conduite a ceux qui sont en charge des affaires du Roy en ce païs la. Ceux qui estoient autrefois en place n'y sont plus. Il en est mort un grand nombre, de ceux dont on avoit pu autrefois se servir utilement. En un mot tout y est changé, et mesme les Loix ont receu tant d'atteintes depuis le revolution, qu'a moins qu'elles ne reprennent leur ancienne force par la fermete du Parlement, tous les jugements qu'on pourroit faire sur la forme que prendra dans la suite le Gouvernement par rapport aux Loix, se trouveroient aussi faux, que ceux qu'on avoit fait avant le revolution, pour croire qu'elle ne pourroit pas avoir les suites que nous avons veües.

A l'egard du nouveau Roy, ses qualités personnelles sont connües: et apres ce qu'il a fait, on peut juger quel fondement on peut faire sur sa parole, et sur tous les engagements qu'on peut avoir avec luy.

Son caractere est une grande defiance, en sorte que tres peu de persones, mesme de celles qui sont en place ont son secret. Les secretaires d'Estat qu'il a eus, si on excepte, Mylord Shrewsbury n'ont esté que des Commis renforcez, qui n'avoient que des expeditions d'affaires courantes dans les Bureaux, et aucune part a son secret, qui est tout entre les mains des Hollandois.

M. de Sunderland avoit il y a plus d'un an, repris un entier credit par le soin qu'il avoit eu de se lier auec Mylord Portland, et on assure qu'il l'a encore.

Mylord Ranelagh, M. Foxe, et quelques autres qu'il est aisé de connoistre, en ont beaucoup dans les affaires de Finances, ou ils l'ont beaucoup servi. Le Conseil d'Estat et mesme celuy qu'on appelle du Cabinet, n'est a proprement parler, que pour la forme, et la plupart de ceux qui le composent sont des gens assez mediocres, et qui avant ces derniers temps, n'avoient eu aucuns emplois, qui ayent pu leur donner une experience des affaires, sinon fort mediocre.

Ils n'ont veu la Nation que dans cette espece d'yvresse qui leur a fait oublier toutes les anciennes maximes de Liberté et de Proprieté dont elle estoit autrefois si jalouse. Aucun n'a esté en place dans les Parlements turbulens, ou les Rois ont tout a souffrir et a risquer le tout pour le tout: Ainsi il n'y en a aucun qu'on puisse regarder comme un homme de ressource, puisque tout l'artifice avec lequel on a mené les Parlements depuis dix ans, a esté de corrompre des Deputez par argent ou par des emplois lucratifs, ou d'intimider ceux qu'on ne pouvoit corrompre. Or comme le principal moyen estoit des accusations vagues d'intelligence avec la France, qui cessent presentement, et que les Parlements sont toujours beaucoup plus traitables quand la guerre est ouverte avec la France qu'en d'autres temps, si ce Parlement cy entreprend de contredire, et de remettre les affaires sur l'ancien pied, il ne paroist pas que le nouveau Roy puisse trouver dans ses Ministres les secours dont il auroit besoin en pareilles affaires.

Car parmy les Seigneurs qui sont brouillez avec la Cour comme le Duc de Leeds, alias Mylord Danby, ou qui n'y sont ny bien ny mal, on peut conter que se trouvent les meilleures testes de la Nation et les personnes les plus accreditées dans les deux Chambres. Il ne faut pas juger de ce qu'ils peuvent faire, par le peu qu'ils ont fait, particulierement ceux qui ont conservé quelque affection pour leur Roy legitime. Car il est certain que les divisions qui ont esté continuelles dans le parti opposé a la Cour, en ont esté la seule cause. Presentement les choses estant changées, et l'esperance du retablissement du Roy d'Angleterre perdüe entierement, ils n'ont plus les mesmes mesures a garder, et ils peuvent parler et agir plus hardiment pour la Liberté, et pour la conservation des Loix qu'ils ne faisoient autrefois.

Si on en croid le raport des persones qui sont venües depuis peu d'Angleterre, et les amis qui en viennent, le nombre des Seigneurs Mecontents est fort grand. La Cour n'est plus la mesme et le nouveau Roy n'ayant pas ces manieres familieres des Rois precedents, se laissant voir rarement, et a un petit nombre, n'a pas gagné leur affection. La plupart de ceux qui ont le plus contribüé a l'execution de ses desseins ont perdu ses bonnes graces et plusieurs sont morts. Mylords Danby, Monmouth et divers autres qui se declarerent assez fortement contre le parti de la Cour, dans l'affaire du Ch. Fenwick, sont en estat de former un parti assez puissant dans le Parlement et c'est ce qu'on verra en celuy cy. Plusieurs conservent le ressentiment de la dureté, avec laquelle on refusa la grace au Ch. Fenwick, qui estant d'une tres ancienne Maison, quoique non titrée et ayant épousé la fille du comte de Carlile, estoit allié a un grand nombre de seigneurs. Il y a aussi parmy eux, ceux qu'on appeloit les Rochesteriens, a cause du comte de Rochester, qui en estoit le chef qui ont toujours soutenu fortement les interests de l'Eglise Anglicane, et qui l'ont toujours jusqu'a present maintenüe superieure aux Presbyteriens. Ces differents motifs generaux joints aux mecontentements particuliers, ont partagé le corps des Seigneurs en diverses factions, dont il sera necessaire d'estre exactement informé sur les lieux, et ont produit une espece de jalousie entre le nouveau Roy et la Chambre Haute, qui parut en plusieurs rencontres au dernier Parlement et dans les precedents. C'est ce qui l'obligea pour maintenir l'egalité des suffrages et gagner s'il estoit possible la superiorité, de faire entrer par Writs ou Brevets des fils de seigneurs dans la Chambre et qui luy en a fait augmenter le nombre. Le premier moyen a esté depuis long temps regardé comme odieux et mis au nombre des griefs de la Nation.

Les Seigneurs en ont plusieurs semblables, et quand on songe que dans tous les Regnes deux ou trois malintentionnez ont suffi pour troubler les Parlements, et obliger les Rois de les casser, on jugera que les Mecontents qui restent sont tout aussi capables, de faire dans les occasions, autant d'affaires a celuy cy qu'a aucun de ses predecesseurs, d'autant plus qu'on conviendra que le duc de Leeds, Monmouth et quelques autres, n'ont pas moins d'esprit et de hardiesse, que les plus grands acteurs des regnes precedents.

Il ne faut pas se laisser surprendre par l'opinion commune que le Roy Guillaume est adoré par les Anglois, qu'il est aimé universellement, et qu'il est le maistre. La facilité qu'on a eüe de le croire a plus contribué qu'aucune autre chose a affermir son usurpation.

Les Seigneurs communement parlant, ne l'aiment point et ne l'estiment gueres. Les autres sont partagez; car tout ce qui est attaché a l'Eglise Anglicane a de fortes preventions qu'il l'a voulu detruire, et le veut encore s'il peut. Les Presbyteriens ne font pas un parti assez fort pour le soutenir dans un temps turbulent. Mais tous en general si on peut juger de l'avenir par le passé commenceront a ne le pas plus menager qu'ils ont toujours fait leurs Rois legitimes, quand ils ont eu autant besoin des Parlements qu'il en a presentement, a cause de ses dettes immenses, ausquelles il ne peut satisfaire que par la continuation de tres grands subsides.

Il n'y a pas d'apparence qu'estant delivrez de la crainte qu'on avoit eu soin de repandre parmy eux, de la puissance du Roy, ils accordent tout, aussi facilement qu'ils ont fait durant la guerre. On ne peut encore former de jugement sur cela, que fort incertain. Mais il est de la derniere importance pour le service du Roy, qu'avant la fin de ce Parlement, ceux qui seront chargez de ses affaires, sachent exactement l'estat de la nation, ce qui est tres facile, parce que tous les Estats de recepte et de depense, se presentent au Parlement pour estre examinez par les Commitez. Ainsi on n'a pas besoin d'avoir des intrigues a la Cour pour estre informé de ce detail: il n'y a qu'a avoir quelque amy secret dans la Chambre des Communes: et c'est par ces sortes de pieces qu'on peut mieux juger de l'Estat de l'Angleterre que par toutes les intelligences, qu'on pourroit etablir avec les Ministres.

On scaura par cette mesme voye l'estat du Commerce, des armées, des flotes, du revenu de la Couronne, et de tout ce qui a raport aux finances.

On pourra aussi juger suivant les Estats de recepte et de depense ce que pourront produire les nouveaux fonds qui seront accordez: et sur cet article, ainsi que sur plusieurs autres semblables, un Ministre du Roy doit avoir plus d'attention a ce qu'il apprendra par des voyes simples et publiques, comme sont toutes les pièces communiquées au Parlement, que par tout ce qui luy pourroit venir par des amis secrets, dont il doit fort se defier.

Il paroist du service du Roy que son Ambassadeur ait des agents secrets dans le Parlement, qui n'ayent aucun commerce avec luy que par tiers, mais qui puissent non seulement luy conner des avis de ce qui se passe; mais dans les cafe houses, ou les Deputez se rendent, repandre adroitement tout ce qui peut servir a leur oter la pensée que le Roy songe ou ait jamais songé a contribuer a l'oppression de leur Religion et de leur liberté: qui leur fasse connoistre qu'on les a grossierement abusez, sous pretexte de Traitez Secrets par raport a de pareils desseins, que jamais on n'a pensé icy a retablir le Roy d'Angleterre que de concert avec le Nation, et que quand on a veu qu'elle n'y entroit pas on n'a pas porté la chose plus loin. Il sera bon aussi de detruire toutes les faussetez qu'on a persuadées aux peuples durant la guerre, touchant les pretendues conspirations: enfin de travailler a mettre en usage tout ce qui peut oster a la nation la crainte d'aucune entreprise du costé de la France, parce qu'il n'y a que ce seul motif, dont on se servira toujours pour engager les Parlements a donner des subsides pour l'entretien de plus de troupes qu'il n'en faut pour la sureté de l'Angleterre.

Il paroist important que l'Ambassadeur de Sa Majesté se conduise de telle maniere que sans se livrer trop a la Cour, il ne se rende pas suspect a ceux qui n'y sont pas devoüez: ny a la Cour, ayant commerce avec des mecontents, ou des Jacobites. Le commerce qu'on doit avoir avec les uns et les autres ne se peut mieux faire que par tiers. Mais il se doit defier des Refugiés François plus que tous les autres, et ne pas souffrir que ses domestiques les frequentent, ny qu'ils aient trop libre accez dans sa maison. Cela ne peut faire aucun tort par raport aux Anglois, tous ceux qui sont attachez a l'Eglise Anglicane ne les aimant point: et les Jacobites les ayant en horreur comme les premiers instruments de la trahison faite a leur Roy legitime.

M. l'Amb. doit avoir presque les mesmes precautions a l'egard de plusieurs Catholiques, sur tout les Religieux. Car la plupart sont plus Autrichiens que Catholiques: Ceux qui ont temoigné quelque zele pour le Roy comme quelques Benedictin Anglois ont plus fait de mal que de bien par leur imprudence. Les autres sont devoüez au nouveau Roy, et l'ont toujours fort bien servi. Ainsi pour ce qui concerne les Catholiques, la principale confiance doit estre dans Ceux du Clergé seculier, particulierement Mrs. les Evesques Layborne et Giffard, personages de vertu et de merite qui ont la confiance des honestes gens, et qui ne sont pas suspects au gouvernement. Ils scavent mieux que les autres ce qui convient au bien des Catholiques, au lieu que les Religieux ont toujours leurs interests particuliers. Ils pourront proposer les moyens les plus convenables de procurer quelque soulagement aux Catholiques et de remettre peu a peu les choses en l'estat ou elles estoient a leur egard sous le regne de Charles I.

Il paroitroit mesme important que M. l'Amb. ne menât avec luy aucun Religieux: car on peut conter qu'il en peut arriver de grands (? in conveniens) aucun n'ayant communement point d'interests plus chers que ceux de sa robe. L'experience du Roy d'Angleterre doit estre une grande leçon sur cet article: car le Clerge Seculier a eu autant a souffrir et plus sous son regne que sous celuy de Charles I, et la derniere cause de sa ruine fut la confiance qu'il eut pour le P. Peter, qui se livra a Mylord Sunderland.

De plus comme on ne peut pas douter que l'intention de S.M. ne soit de contribuer autant qu'il luy sera possible a l'avancement de la Religion, il est certain que le Clerge Seculier y contribue beaucoup plus que les Reguliers, qui la pluspart ayant etudié chez les Espagnols, et esté elevez par des Superieurs qui leur sont devoüez sont ennemis de la France: outre que la plupart sont egalement haïs et meprisez par les Protestants.

Pour ce qui regarde l'Eglise Anglicane, on peut croire que ce Parlement ne finira pas sans qu'il y ait plusieurs affaires qui ont raport a ses interests. Il est important de les suivre avec exactitude: car elles ont toujours eu des suites en ce païs la. Les Presbyteriens ayant un Roy de leur secte sont devenus insolents, ils ont cru pouvoir opprimer d'autorité l'Eglise Anglicane dans les commencements, mais ils n'ont pu y reussir. Ils ont tasché d'y parvenir, par divers moyens de reünion qui ont aussi esté rejettez.

Il n'est pas mauvais que ces contestations subsistent, et il ne les faut pas regarder comme indifferentes. Mylord Leeds, Rochester, Clarendon et autres sont les zelez defenseurs de cette Eglise et y ont beaucoup plus de credit que les Evesques, qui la plupart sont Presbyteriens dans l'ame, et ne trouvent rien de bon dans l'Eglise Anglicane que leur dignité et leur revenu. Il n'y en a presque aucun qui merite qu'on le cultive et la plupart n'ont pas grand credit. Mais parmy ceux qui ont esté deposez pour n'avoir pas voulu reconnoitre le Prince d'Orange, il y en a de qui on pourroit quelques fois recevoir de bons avis, et avec lesquels on peut utilement faire connaissance, par persones tierces. Un des principaux est l'Evesque de Bath et Wells.

Quoy qu'il n'y ait presentement aucune apparence a quelque changement favorable pour le legitime Souverain, on peut neantmoins supposer qu'il a encore beaucoup de serviteurs dans tous les Estats. Il ne paroist pas du service du Roy presentement de faire seulement semblant de le scavoir: mais il est fort important de les connoistre par des voyes secretes: quand ce ne seroit qu'en cas de mort du Roy present. Mais sans l'attendre: quiconque fera reflexion aux frequentes revolutions d'Angleterre, conviendra, qu'il faut estre touiours prest pour en profiter quand il plaira a Dieu qu'elles arrivent. Si le Parlement refuse comme il a commencé de consentir a la conservation d'une armée sur pied, et qu'il s'obstine a faire congedier les troupes etrangeres, il en viendra a bout, parce qu'il refusera de l'argent: quoy qu'il en accorde par d'autres fonds, s'il continue comme il a fait deja en un article a transferer les dettes sur ces fonds, c'est comme si on ne luy en donnoit point. Il veut faire fortifier des places, si on ne luy donne pas de quoy, il ne le pourra faire. Si on fait appercevoir la nation qu'elle est assez defendüe par la mer; et que c'est un pretexte pour avoir une armee preste en tirant des garnisons de ces places fortifiées elle s'y opposera. Si ensuite le Parlement veut reformer l'Estat et attaquer les Ministres sur tout les Hollandois, le nouveau Roy avec tout son scavoir faire se trouvera peut estre aussi embarassé qu'un autre. Car les dettes immenses dont il est chargé le mettent dans la necessité de convoquer des Parlements: et on remarque qu'en tems de paix, quand ils voyent qu'un Roy a besoin d'eux, c'est alors qu'ils portent la hardiesse jusqu'à l'extremité.

Voilà les principales remarques qu'on peut faire sur l'estat present des affaires d'Angleterre, ausquelles on en pourra ajouter quelques autres si Mg. le Marquis de Torcy croid pouvoir faire usage de celles cy.

7

A Contribution to an Inventory of Jacobite Sources

Bruno Neveu

LONG regarded as a lesser discipline, of marginal significance, historiography to-day has so far re-asserted itself that one wonders if history as such is not about to be replaced by the introspective study which constitutes the history of history.

This history at one remove, so to speak, careful to note the prejudices, aspirations and fashions which inspired and influenced historical works in the past, finds an exceptionally fertile and varied field in publications dealing with the Jacobites. There are few subjects in which two centuries or more of research have seen so many successive works so clearly reflecting the political and religious beliefs of their authors. In Great Britain, and in a lesser degree in the rest of Europe, the rivalry between the House of Stuart and the holders of the British Crown has given rise since 1689 to a voluminous literature in which flourish, more often than not unbeknownst to their authors, the passions which collective memory keeps alive from generation to generation and which finally achieve the status of national myths.

If this political and religious history of Britain from 1689 to 1807 or thereabouts never has been really looked at for its own sake as knowledge of the past, apart from its philosophical and political implications for the present, is it surprising that historiography, growing ever more ambitious and penetrating in exposing at every point the enormous part played by imagination and prejudice in the consideration of facts and documents, throws doubts on nearly all historical interpretations? This re-examination of the case can result in a positive contribution. If all claim to objectivity is chimerical, as one admits nowadays, the striving for impartiality which ever historian must seek is not. Thus only the original texts, without 'speaking for themselves' as was believed rather naively when positivism was in fashion, can provide solid foundations for such an impartial attitude by imposing the corrections, additions and new insights which lead in the end to a revision of the accepted version and one which has been hitherto too easily accepted.

The intention here is to reach specialists more aware than oneself of the depths of the questions covered too conveniently by the description of 'Jacobitism', to stress the need for historiographical revision and with this end in view to call for the compilation of a corpus of extant sources, or at least for an analytical inventory of their contents. The few samples of unpublished texts presented here are drawn from research in various archives or manuscript collections and can claim nothing more than to draw attention to sources which still lie forgotten or neglected. May I be allowed to plead, as an archivist as well as an historian, for a closer collaboration in dealing with these original documents between the custodians of archives and librarians on the one hand and historians and specialist researchers on the other? At present this methodological approach does not in fact exist, since other and ever heavier professional duties tend to divert archivists and librarians from what I believe to be their main task, the drawing up of catalogues and inventories as an essential tool of research. When it comes to a phenomenon such as Jacobitism involving a cats-cradle of negotiations and intrigues stretching across the whole of Europe, and an heterogenous collection of people — no progress is possible without the compilation of a summary calendar of all surviving documents. Some works which are doubly inadequate, both from the scientific point of view and from their remaining unfinished — such as those of the Marchesa Campana de Cavelli published in 1871 and of Falconer Madan published in 1889[1] — dreamt of this goal but it is one that collective research alone can bring about.

It is surprising, however, that work on this 'corpus' was not further advanced in the flourishing era of scholarship just before and after the First World War, especially in the United Kingdom, home of the Historical Manuscripts Commission, of the Calendars of State Papers, and of the monumental calendar of the Stuart Papers at Windsor, all of which laid a solid foundation for a future expansion. The prolonged stay of pioneer researchers in Spain or in Venice, where H. F. Brown worked so diligently, should have led, for instance, to a systematic study of the Roman archives as soon as the Vatican archives, whose historical importance as well as political and religious significance has recently been appointed out by Owen Chadwick,[2] were opened to serious scholars. Thus the dispatch to Rome of W. H. Bliss resulted in the very valuable Roman Transcripts — of less use to-day since the pressmarks and foliation of the originals have been changed — even though a very small portion of them cover the seventeenth and more particularly the eighteenth century.[3] H. E. Bell's brief *Report on the proposed continuation of the Calendar of Roman State Papers relating to English affairs,* drawn up in 1939,[4] is inadequate in scope, and since then no one seems to have considered tackling this work in earnest, even with the more rapid techniques of microfilming. Yet the historical value of the documents preserved in the Vatican Archives, as well as those in the Vatican Library (whose collections have been accessible for far longer), offers a unique opportunity for the study of the period following the reign of James II. His fall appears in collections as well as in the Calendars as an unbridgeable divide. No doubt this is due in great part to the increasing accumulation of documents which marks the triumph of the age of absolutism and its administrative techniques. It may, however, stem from indifference, nay repugnance, on the part of English historical interpretation (seen as a whole, with the exception of isolated figures such as Lord Acton) towards foreign documents reconstructing in an unconventional way the development of a very critical period and one more dangerous for the new dynasty than has been generally recognised by official national historiography. Whatever the reason for this comparative neglect, many continental documents have not been consulted to the extent which might have been expected, let alone edited or calendared.

In order to present an overall picture of Jacobite sources in Europe, the experience of a lifetime, and indeed of several, spent in travelling from Sweden or Russia to Malta would be necessary. I shall be content here to skim the surface, without aiming to cover all the separate *membra disjecta* of a story which was written, in the course of a century, in Rome, Paris, Vienna, Madrid, The Hague and London. At the present time, in any case, the curiousity of historians is turned not so much towards the unfolding of diplomatic negotiations and secret intrigues between European chanceries as towards the political weight to be attached to Jacobitism in Great Britain, an approach illustrated by the recent book of Dr. E. Cruickshanks, *Political Untouchables*.[5] Similarly there has been intensive study of refugee groups of Jacobite exiles whose emigration made a notable contribution to the religious, intellectual and social life of their host states, and earlier in England of that élite of the refugees, the Huguenots. In many cases, this emigration cut across or reinforced the catholic 'diaspora' settled on the Continent since the Reformation, from whose history much can be learned.[6] Thus it is that the Jacobite colony in the Holy Roman Empire has been the subject of articles and monographs[7] which have far from exhausted the considerable resources of the State Archives of Vienna.[8]

The wealth of Roman sources is even more considerable, since the Holy See had offered protection and hospitality to the Stuarts after their departure from France, and the more so as it had to organise the survival and the development of catholic missions in England, Scotland and Ireland. This was done mainly through the Congregation *de Propaganda fide* which was responsible for these territories. The purely religious aspect dominates clearly from the year 1717 to 1720, when a certain lessening of tension took place on a local basis, as is shown by the negotiations associated with the names of Mgr. Stonor and of the Abbé Strickland. In the period before 1689, political overtones are more marked, and it would be particularly interesting to clarify the real attitude of the papacy or more exactly of successive pontiffs, such as Innocent XI, Alexander VIII, Innocent XII and Clement XI, towards the House of Stuart during the reign of James II and after his fall. Some time ago, I endeavoured to show that Innocent XI did not approve of the ways in which the religious zeal of James II and his entourage manifested itself and regarded that King as too deeply compromised with the Jesuits and Louis XIV to be of any real use to the catholic religion[9] A close study is needed of all the evidence which may survive of the efforts — perforce secret and leaving little outward trace — of William of Orange before 1689 to reassure the Papacy about his intentions once his power was established in Great Britain.[10]

The Apostolic Library in the Vatican contains a wealth of manuscripts of very differing historical importance, from the correspondence of Lorenzo Casoni, the closest adviser to Innocent XI in 1688-9, to those stray or official papers whose contents are known from other sources. As progress in cataloguing each archive group has been very slow, it is till very difficult to proceed to an analysis of their contents, a most time-consuming task, even before going on to make an historical assessment in depth of the historical value of documents which are merely noted in old lists under the extremely vague heading *Angliae regnum*.

Only for Irish history has any accurate and conscientious analysis of documents been undertaken. This covers part of the archive groups and can be referred to in a number of studies published in *Archivium hibernicum*.[11] The riches of an archive actually formed from the seventeenth to the eighteenth centuries, the *Fondo Ottoboni* (the family of Alexander VIII), have yet to be used.[12] The same sounding could be made with the most important collection, that of the *Vatican latini* manuscripts, fortunately catalogued in detail for certain periods, but in which lie hidden important correspondence, such as that of Cardinal Cibo with Ferdinando D'Adda, Papal Nuncio in London,[13] or the papers of Cardinal Passionei,[14] an active diplomat at the time of the Peace of Utrecht. Other groups well worth consulting are the *Borgiani latini* manuscripts, formed from papers issued by the Propaganda, one of which I shall quote in a moment.

Research is less disjointed in the Vatican archives, since they consist basically of homogeneous archive groups each with an internal unity. Although the various groups deriving from the secretaryship of state *Principi, Cardinali, Vescovi, Particolari, Brevi, Epistolae* are well calendared, piece by piece in chronological order, it is not the case for a much more substantial series, whose importance for the modern period is underestimated in Great Britain.[15]

First of all the *Fondo Inghilterra* (cf. Indice 1071), namely 32 volumes covering the period 1555-1856, and containing on one hand diplomatic correspondence, such as that of the nuncio D'Adda and, on the other, some *Varia* and some *Avvisi* which can be useful.[16]

The *Fondo Francia* and the *Fondo Fiandra,* containing the correspondence of the nuncios in France and of the internuncios in Brussels are also very rewarding, since those two diplomats dealt with British affairs, from 1592 in the case of the nuncio in France and from 1596 in the case of the internuncio in Flanders.[17] A wealth of despatches, letters, reports, memoranda, and printed matter relating to English policy towards Catholics and also to the relations between the Holy See and the Stuarts can be found in this series. It is worth noting, for instance, that it is in the *Fondo Fiandra,* among the papers of Monsignor Santini, internuncio, that are to be found the few documents about the plan to allow Catholics to take the oaths of loyalty to the Government brought forward by the Abbé Strickland in 1716-7.[18] As regards the records of the nunciature in France (the most important part of which are on microfilm in the Archives Nationales), the treasures which they contain are well known, for instance the correspondence of Cardinal Gualterio, nuncio in France from 1700 to 1706, which will be touched upon again. It is worth pointing out that for this crucial period, from 1700 to 1721, a major source is provided by the private papers of Pope Clement XI (Albani), first-hand material with numerous papers in the Pope's own hand. This *Fondo Albani* comprising over 200 volumes contains five volumes (nos. 163-168), an old inventory of which (Appendix I) is in any case the only one in existence (Indice 144, fol. 26-41v) and deserves to be republished. Subordinate to the Holy See like the other congregations, but having always kept its archives separately in its palace on the *Piazza di Spagna, the Sacred Congregation of* Propaganda Fide supplies an important reserve of additional information relating to other than purely religious matters. Recent studies, published to mark the three hundred and fiftieth centenary of the Propaganda (1622-1972) have defined its methods as well as its organisation.[19] An excellent summary list published in 1961[20] which condenses a number of old inventories enables one to find one's way in the major series, be it the *Acta* ('Atti delle congregazioni generali') (in Italian since 1657), the 'Scritture originali riferite nelle congregazioni generali' (in geographical and in chronological order), the 'Congregationi Particolari', the 'Scritture riferite nei congressi', and lastly the 'Fondi minori', which contain a *Collegi vari* archive group concerning the English, Irish and Scottish seculars and regulars and the training given to missionaries in the Collegio Urbano in Rome.

Clearly this survey should be extended in several ways to take in the separate archives of the colleges which still exist in Rome, the Venerable English College, the Pontifical Scots College, and the Irish College in Rome, as well as the records of the great international religious orders, such as the Society of Jesus, the Dominicans (to which Cardinal Norfolk belonged), the Carmelites, the Franciscans, and the Augustinians. These archives, which for some series go back to the Middle Ages, are better known to British historians and were consulted by Englishmen as far back as the days of the Grand Tour.

As a relief from a somewhat abstract and dry catalogue made from a distance, let us listen for a moment to a forgotten witness, François Foucquet, whose autograph and unpublished day-book is in the Vatican Library: *Fondo Borgia* Latin ms. 565. A French Jesuit and a missionary to China, Foucquet arrived in the Celestial Empire in 1699 and had to leave in 1722 as a result of being recalled by his Society, by then loath to see him expound any longer, at a particularly delicate point, his views on Chinese rites and cults. These were contrary to the policy of the Jesuit mission in China, then bent on a cultural conciliation and an intellectual apostolate. After a short stay in Paris, Foucquet made for Rome and succeeded in evading the control of his Society thanks to the interest taken in him by the Congregation of the Propaganda, who provided him with lodgings at its headquarters on the Piazza di Spagna, and the patronage of Cardinal Gualterio, who had befriended him on the recommendation of the duc de Saint-Simon. Thus Gualterio received him in his Roman palace, famous for its library and its museum, and even in his country retreat, and sometimes confided to him some secrets of high politics during his nunciature in France, his relations with Louis XIV and Madame de Maintenon, with le Tellier the Father Confessor and with Cardinal de Noailles. He had introduced Foucquet (whom Benedict XIII made a bishop in 1725 by raising him to the see of Eleutheropolis *in partibus* and thus freeing him from any dependence on the Society of Jesus), to the Cardinal de Polignac, who had represented French interests in Rome since 1724, and above all to the little Stuart court at the Muti Palace. Foucquet was warmly welcomed by James III, whom he had met and dined with as early as 8 October 1723, and by his Queen. He also came into contact with another eccentric character, the Chevalier Ramsay who was, for a short time only, the tutor to the young prince. At once, the two men became close friends, discussing their very similar historico-religious theories on pagan and exotic mythology interpreted as a survival and misinterpretation of original revelation. To this relationship, which continued after Ramsay's departure for Paris, we owe the existence of the day-book which Foucquet kept with meticulous care during these years (copying the text of the letters received and sent out by him), including diverse and precise details about life at the Muti Palace during the matrimonial crisis which saw the departure of Clementina for the convent and deepening rivalries between the factions there. It is enough here to recall two controversial conversations, one with James III, the other with Gualterio, about the views of Louis XIV on religion and politics. On 10 April 1725, calling on the royal couple after his consecration as a bishop, Foucquet recorded the following conversation with the King:

> Je suis resté seul avec le Roy, qui m'a dit bien des choses dignes de mémoire.
> 1° Que le roy Louis 14 estoit un prince plein de religion, que quand luy, roy d'Angleterre, le quitta pour la dernière fois, il se trouva avec la reyne sa mère et Me de Maintenon chez le roy Louis 14, qui dit à la reyne qu'il estoit bien aise de dire un mot à son fils en particulier. La reyne se retira, laissant là Me de Maintenon (luy disant, si je ne me trompe, qu'il n'y avoit point de secret pour elle). Me de Maintenon ne laissa pas de se retirer aussi, et alors Louis 14 s'adressant au jeune roy d'Angleterre luy recommanda de n'estre jamais janséniste. Le jeune roy qui s'attendoit que Louis 14 alloit luy confier quelque grand secret fut surpris de ce que tout se terminoit à ce mot, et dit au roy Louis que s'il estoit capable de s'oublier jusqu'à abandonner la foy, il se feroit protestant plustost que janséniste.
> 2° Que quand le roy Jacques II mourut, Louis XIV contre l'avis de ses conseillers et M^r le duc de Bourgogne le reconnurent pour roy. C'est ce que m'expliqua il y a quelque temps M. le c[ardinal] G[ualterio] qui estoit alors présent et comme le roy Louis ayant fait demander s'il pourroit voir le roy mourant fut d'abord prié par la reyne de ne point entrer, qu'il entra néanmoins, ensuitte M. le c[ardinal] G[ualterio] alors nonce, ayant dit à la reyne que le roy vouloit dire une parole qui ne luy déplairoit pas, alors voyant le roy mourant mais qui avoit encore l'esprit plein de connoissance, il luy dit qu'il reconnoissoit son fils pour roy d'Angleterre si Dieu l'appelloit et qu'il partît de ce monde avec cette consolation. Il parla ensuitte au jeune roy, auquel il assura qu'il seroit toujours son défenseur s'il estoit fidelle à la religion mais son adversairee déclaré s'il y manquoit.[21]

It is well worth comparing the account given by Cardinal Gualterio nearly a quarter of a century after the event with that he made at the time as nuncio, two days after the death of James II, for the benefit of Cardinal Paolucci the secretary of state. At this point the value of this document makes it necessary to say something about the state of preservation of the papers of Cardinal Gualterio in Rome and in London.

Following the custom universal among statesmen and diplomats, especially at the court of Rome and despite the rule of 'spoglio' (*jus spolii*) which should have secured the return to the Holy See of part of the inheritance of a dead cardinal, Gualterio, once his nunciature in France was over, had kept for himself a multitude of original documents: first of all correspondence, including original letters from the king, the royal family and from ministers, minute of most of his letters and dispatches to the Roman secretaryship of state, as well as registers of outgoing correspondence and a great part of his direct correspondence with his master, Clement XI, consisting of minutes of his own letters and the Pope's originals, sometimes in his own hand.

Thus, while the Vatican archives inherited the official correspondence, in theory in its entirety — and it is still preserved in the archive group *Nunziatura de Francia*

— the Gualterio family which produced many prelates, one of whom Filippo's nephew was also a cardinal and nuncio in France, kept the precious legacy of the private papers (in fact state papers for the most part). This sizeable portion. acquired by the British Government in 1856, was deposited in the British Museum (now the British Library), where it can be consulted. It is odd that this purchase, which showed the importance attached by Great Britain to what was the obvious complement to the Stuart Papers at Windsor, has produced no edition or general survey of them and that the opening of the Vatican archives did not set in motion either a general inventory of the Gualterio archives comprising both the papers in the Vatican and those in London. The result of this neglect is that twentieth-century scholars (and perhaps those of the twenty-first century!) are forced one after the other and time after time to go over the same volumes to establish some sort of order, if they have been fortunate enough to retain a sufficiently exact recollection of these two widely separated collections to be able to compare them. Yet, as early as 1871 the Marchesa Campana de Cavelli had stressed, in the wake of G. Masson, the importance of the 'Gualterio Papers' and had intended to make use of them.[22] Several historians have followed this advice, but always in a very limited way and for a few documents only, the most thorough, as far as I know, being still the Rev. Frederick Waldegrave Head, in *The Fallen Stuarts* in 1901.[23]

I am engaged on a study of Gualterio's nunciature in France based on a thorough search of his papers in Rome and in London for the years 1700-1706, devoting part of it to British affairs, from the time of the visit of that prelate of St. Germain in early December 1700 to convey to James II the new Pope's letter of compliment and to discuss with him the possibility of regaining his throne.[24]

Once again, I shall give only one proof out of a hundred possible ones of the importance of bringing together both collections — that in London and that in the Vatican — to obtain a fuller picture of one or other particular incident.

At last in September 1701, the event took place which had long been expected by all the chanceries and which was to be so minutely described in their memoirs of the court of France by Dangeau and Saint-Simon. Gualterio, whose recollections of James II to Foucquet I have just related, sent to Paolucci, secretary of state to Clement XI, on 18 September a brief despatch devoted mainly to the political and religious consequences of the death of the exiled King and the recognition which the Holy See should make every effort to secure from other states. We shall see from the text itself (Appendix II), preserved in the *Fondo Nunziatura di Francia*,[25] that the nuncio states that he included with it a 'diary' ranging over four days of the illness and death of the King, whose bedside he never left during that time. Now nothing remains today in the Vatican volume except *Avvisi* from France, and it is in the letter-book kept and preserved by Gualterio which is now in the British Library that this very interesting 'diary' is to be found. This diary is rendered even more valuable by the known efforts of the Jacobites to draw a parallel between the death of Charles II and that of James II. To this text we join another dispatch by Gualterio sent from Paris on 21 March 1702 in which must be noted the ambiguity of the recognition accorded by Louis XIV, which could be applied either to the legitimacy of James III's title as King, or to his right to rule effectively over Great

Britain. Also remarkable is the strong interest in British affairs shown by the representatives of the Holy See which foreshadowed the imminent death of the Prince of Orange (Appendix III): England will remain without a head, the legitimacy of the succession will be disputed; opposition from the Tories is predicted to the accession of the Princess of Denmark who lacks health and intelligence; the Netherlands will regain a certain freedom of movement which will mean a revival of its two traditional conflicting policies; with this death the Emperor will lose the sympathy of Protestants and their financial assistance in the war of the Spanish succession. The reply of Clement XI on 4 April 1702 and the Gualterio dispatches of 27 March and 3 April[26] confirm the historical importance of these papers for diplomatic history during the war of the Spanish succession. With the return to Italy in 1706 of Gualterio as a cardinal and his becoming the agent of French policy in Rome as well as the declared champion of the Stuarts, his correspondence assumes an even greater importance for Jacobite history: the papers in the British Library, with the *Correspondance Politique* in the archives of the ministry of foreign affairs in Paris as well as the documents contained in the Albani deposit already mentioned, together form a very coherent documentary source and one which has yet to be tapped (Appendix III).

The unity of the collection I wish to turn to next is of a different kind: the papers of the Scottish Catholic refugees on the Continent, in Paris and in Rome especially. Since they were regular and very full, their correspondence forms a rich source for the seventeenth and eighteenth centuries. Part of them, after heavy losses during the French Revolution, has found a safe haven in Scotland itself, first at Blairs near Aberdeen and then in the Scottish Catholic Archives in Edinburgh which have been open to serious scholars only in the last few years. The late lamented keeper of these archives, Mgr. David McRoberts, gave in the *Innes Review* in 1977 an excellent summary of the troubled history of the papers of the Scots College in Paris before and since the Revolutions of 1689 and 1789. What should be stressed here is the great number of these papers — thousands of letters — and the virtual inaccessibility of this precious salvage from the time of its return to Scotland thanks to the abbé MacPherson at the turn of the eighteenth and nineteenth centuries until the years 1972-4, which saw the setting up of Columba House in Edinburgh to enable them to be consulted. Only the works, in many ways polemical, of Major Malcolm Hay of Seaton (1887-1962), *The Blairs papers, 1603-1660* (1929), *The Jesuits and the Popish Plot* (1934), *The Enigma of James II* (1938) and *Failure in the Far East* (1957) skimmed or rather despoiled this collection. I shall not examine here its key documents — the problems raised by the manuscript life of James II still call for specialist attention — and I shall not dwell either on the archival reconstruction needed by way of comparison with the archives of the Propaganda in Rome, and in particular with the papers there of the *Missione di Scozia* from 1653 to 1709. I shall call upon only two eye-witness accounts, as far as I know unpublished, chosen out of hundreds of others, because of their date and subject.

One consists of two letters sent by the Duke of Perth from Saint-Germain to the Scots College concerning the last hours and death of James II. The texts printed here (Appendix IV i and ii) convey the kind of emotions which stirred those intimate with the Stuart Court at the edifying end of their sovereign and at the recognition of their young master.

Let us also, for an instant, allow a less well-known figure to speak for himself and one to whom I intend to devote a much wider study under the title of 'A Scotsman in Rome': William Leslie (or Lesley). Numerous letters sent by him between 1677 and 1707 to his correspondents at the Scots College in Paris, mainly the two Innes brothers, Lewis and Thomas, reflect the hopes and fears of a catholic priest, haunted by the persecution of his faith and by the fall of his legitimate king whom he thought badly advised in his refuge at Saint-Germain. Born in 1620 in the diocese of Moray, William Leslie, a pupil at the Scots College in Paris c. 1637, then of the Collegio Scozzese c. 1641, lived permanently in Rome from 1649 until his death in 1707. To gain a quick but striking notion of his character and of his political and religious views, one should read a few extracts of his letters to Lewis Innes, the principal of the Scots College in Paris from 1682 until 1714 and one of the chaplains at the court of Saint-Germain since 1689. In 1688 William Leslie had deplored the diplomatic blunder committed by James II and Mary of Modena in insisting that the court of Rome should pass over Cardinal Norfolk, who in everything — birth, temper and experience — was highly suitable as Protector of English affairs, in favour of the insignificant Rinaldo d'Este, whose sole merit was his being a near relation of the Queen, and who, moreover, belonged to the Imperial 'faction' and was thus out of favour with the French. The fall of the Stuarts seemed to Leslie due in very large part to the excessive and culpable favour shown by the British sovereigns to the Jesuits at the expense of the secular clergy. It is very true, as I have tried to show by the diplomatic correspondence, that the court of Rome and Pope Innocent XI, who in particular did not like the Jesuits, were outraged as much by this support of the Society of Jesus as by the close alliance with Louis XIV, then the Pope's most ferocious adversary. 'Tempo perdo: lost tyme,' exclaimed Leslie on 1 March 1689 at the arrival of James Porter, dispatched to Rome by James II to ask for help and plead for a mediation between France and Rome. The Stuarts did not understand that the desire for revenge against Louis XIV would carry it over every other consideration, as Walter Leslie, William's brother, put it bluntly on 26 April 1689: 'Assure yourself they (the Romans) would crucifie Christ again to be revenged of the French'.

Leslie never ceased to criticise bitterly the leading part played at Saint-Germain by the King's confessor and the influence of the council of conscience: 'In a word, the less that ecclesiastiques middles with secular affairs, the better they will goe on; and on the other syde, the more they middle with the same affairs, the worst will they succeed,'[27] he wrote to Lord Melfort on 26 November 1692.

Powerless, the procurator witnesses the eclipse of the Royal House in the choice of bishops and in overall church policy, which Rome takes over entirely, He urges firmness and, to begin with, a better choice of advisers: 'Be warre, I tell you. And above all lett not your court bacchettoni, in France you call them bigots, in their true name call them des francs hipocrits, lett them not Italy deceave you, for they will smouth the barke and the skinne for more than the Romans themselfs. They enter in your court under the pretext of ghostly fathers, pietie, devotion, learning and understanding and last as politicyoni, des maistres politiques, *sed intrinsecus sunt lupi rapaces* ' . . O how well you doe never to lett ecclesiastiques compeare at court nor put their nose in state affairs . . . But who is the cause, rout and origin of this your mistake at the court of Saint-Germains? Who other but your bacchettoni, your bigots and other hypocrites, *qui veniunt ad vos in vestimentis ovium*, true emissaries of this court, nothing in ther mouth but the Holy Sea, the zeall of His Holyness, the obedience dew to the vicairs of Jesus Christ on earth, the head of the Church, all most true but come to practise and you will find que l'Eglise de Rome et la cour de Rome sont *deux*. But your bacchettoni either out of simplicitie our out of malice wold and will that the two are but one.'[28]

The conclusion is that: 'It was plaine simplicitie to imagine that Rome wold doe anything for us . . . The Romans looke upon with a most different eye in the beginning, and afterwards cared so little for us, when they saw that wee wold not joine with the rest against France, that they sacrized us and our souverain to ther rage against the French. And this is the very truth palpable now to all the worlde.'

On 28 September 1694 Leslie, with the fruitless sojourn of Lord Castlemaine in Rome in mind, who, to crown everything, had immediately surrounded himself with Jesuits, wrote even more openly: 'You cannot imagine nor dream what prejudice it brings to His Majestie the fals (I grant you) opinion that ther Italians have, to witt that all the secrets of S. Germain are knowen to weemen and jesuits . . . Dear Mr. Nairne, you will not have mee to believe as ghospell all the Romans fancy's: God almightie forbids that I hold such men for Evangelists. You say that at S. Germans you know better then they dispositions and humours of the English and the obstacles of the King's restauration. Its most true. And I made great use oftymes of this your argument for to excuse the proceedings of the court, when heer they were prognosticating all the ensueing calamities before the King quited England blameing his favors to F. Peters and the Jesuits; ther answear was then: "Staremo a vedere". When now I make use of the same argument, they laught at me and says: "Così dicevate in tempo del Padre Peters; già havevamo credute quello che n'è arrivato". What shall I answear to them . . . The staying of ecclesiastiques, especially Jesuits, at the court is sufficient to make the English rebell when soever they take the fancy in ther brain.'

And Leslie specified on 31 August 1694: 'I have ofthymes discourses both with prelats and cardinals besydes others and declamed against this court in ther face to ther coldness and ther indifferency and unconcernment in our King's affairs, and allways ther excuse was and is: "Quel principe non vuole seguitare buoni consegli". I contradict this as much as I can and gives very sharp replies, but I could never convince them nor persuade the contrary.'

According to the letters of the procurator of the Scottish mission, we see in the bosom of the court of Rome those faithful to James II and his cause arrayed against those he calls 'Our Roman Orangistes', who number among them many Jesuits who joined forces with the imperial faction, henceforth allied to William. The influence of this anti-Jacobite party makes itself felt in the circle of Pope Innocent XII. 'Our Romans,' wrote Leslie on 6 December 1695, 'are persuaded daily by the ligueurs that ther is no persecution at all in these kingdoms', and further on: 'Ther maximes is che quanto più uno è scottato, tanto più forte strilla, out of which they conclude that since our King makes no noise heer about his affaires, its taken ther is no great need from Rome as wee, privat men, pretends'. What Leslie is criticising and what he would like to see modified is the clumsiness of the whole policy of the Stuarts towards the court of Rome. Instead of always asking for money, of begging, 'les affaires vraiment et proprement royales' should be put forward. For the want of this Rome will finally abandon the Stuart cause, henceforth separated from the interests and the very survival of the church in the Three Kingdoms: 'I must tell you a great secret. Rome is half convinced that all our persecutions will end, if anie regulars be banished and sent forth of those thrie kingdoms and that govern them how so ever please, thir will be a toleration for bishops, and clergie priests depend on bishops.'

Other specialists could easily draw upon several other examples of unpublished texts, or others printed in older works even more neglected than manuscripts. I am thinking of those who search through the 'Correspondance Politique' in the archives of the ministry of foreign affairs in Paris, with the loss of time and duplication there more than elsewhere, owing to absence of a systematic inventory, or of those who consult the archives of the British Parliament. Besides producing monographs, syntheses and essays, the historical world should turn anew to the promotion on an international scale of publications and inventories of sources with scholars of the future in mind. This is the only way of getting the better of prejudices and gaps so glaringly exposed by historiography and the only way of tearing historians away from the twofold and dangerous temptation of the computer and Romance.

NOTES

1. Marchesa Campana de Cavelli, *Les derniers Stuarts à Saint-Germain-en-Laye. Documents inédits et authentiques puisés aux archives publiques et privées*, Paris 1871, 2 vols. (1672-1689); *Stuart Papers relating chiefly to Queen Mary of Modena and the exiled court of King James II, printed from official copies of the original, with facsimiles, under the superintendance of Falconer Madan*, London, for the Roxburghe Club, 1889, 2 vols.

2. Owen William Chadwick, *Catholicism and History, the opening of the Vatican Archives* (Herbert Hensley Henson lectures, 1976), Cambridge, 1978.

3. PRO 3/68, 'Transcripts from Rome sent by Mr. Bliss', 124 ff. (1877-1896) XVIIth century, ff. 94 *et seq.* (Avvisi, Nunziature varie), XVIIIth century, ff. 120v-121r. PRO 3/69, 'Additional list of Roman transcripts sent to the Public Record Office, 1897-1900, for the use of the Public', 254 ff. for the year 1685 *et seq;* f. 181 for 1689; f. 202 v. for 1701 *et seq.*

4. PRO 3/67, 8 ff. of typescript.

5. London, 1979.

6. See, for instance, the work of Dom Mark Dilworth, *The Scots in Franconia. A centenary of Monastic Life.* Edinburgh and London, 1974.

7. Ernst Schmidhofer, 'Das irische, schottische und englische Element im kaiserlichen Heer', phil. Diss. Wien 1971, an extract of which is published under the title 'Das irische Element im kaiserlichen Heer', *Österreich in Geschichte und Literatur* 19, 1975, pp. 81-90;

Wilhelm Kraus, 'Irländer im kaiserlichen Heer' (in manuscript form), Kriegsarchiv Wien; L. C. Cavanagh, 'Irish Colonels Proprietors of Imperial Regiments', *The Journal of the Royal Society of Antiquaries of Ireland* (ser. 7), xvi., 1926; 'Irish Knights of the Imperial Military Order of Maria Theresa', *ibid.*; M. Walsh, 'Further Notes on some Irishmen in the Imperial Service', *The Irish Sword* vi., 1963-4; C. Duffy, 'The Irish in the Imperial Service', *The Irish Sword* v. 1962.

8. See, for instance, the reports of Own O Rourke (or Eugène d'O'Rowerke), ambassador from James III to the court of Vienna (England, varia, box 8, bdle. 1727-1742, ff. 98-496); See also Brian de Breffury, 'Letters from Connaught to a wild goose', *The Irish Ancestor*, x. 1978, pp. 81-98; copies of letters of James and his mother (England, varia box 7); the reports and instructions concerning the return of James III to England, from 1726 and the memorandum of the envoy of James III to Vienna, J. Graeme (England, Varia, box 7, ff. 592-603); the marriage of James III in 1718 (Polen, Varia, 1718). These documents should be complemented by the material in the Archives départementales de Nancy (letters from James III to Duke Leopold, and the reports from Stainville). I owe these references, as well as those in the preceding note, to Dr. Leopold Auer, Keeper of the State Archives in Vienna, to whom I am most grateful.

9. Bruno Neveu, *Jacques II médiateur entre Louis XIV et Innocent XI* (*Mélanges d'archéologie et d'histoire publies par l'Ecole française de Rome*, lxxix (1967), 699-764.

10. See, for instance, the story told by Carte (Bodleian Lib. Carte ms, 231 f. 31a verso) about the mission of the prince de Vaudemont in the name of the Prince of Orange to the Catholic princes and the Pope: ' . . . in case they would favour and promote this attempt upon England, he would undertake to procure a toleration for the R. Catholiks. P. Vaudemont went to Rome and with this argument engaged the Pope, Emperor and King of Spain to come into P. O.'s scheme and favour his attempt. The first thing therefore attempted by P.O. after the Revolution was a toleration, wich he carried for the Dissenters and though not for the R.C. yet all his reign he gave them a connivence equivalent to a toleration . . .'

11. See especially in *Archivium hibernicum, Irish historical records*, xviii. 1955, pp. 66-144; Cathaldus Giblin, O.F.M., 'Vatican Library: MSS Barberini latini. A guide to the Material of Irish Interest on microfilm in the National Library, Dublin, mainly on the XVIIth century', pp. 145-149; Rev. Couleth Kearns, O.P., *Archives of the Irish American College, San Clemente, Rome. A summary report*, xxiii. 1960, pp. 1-147 and xxiv., 1961, pp. 31-102; Dominic Conway, Guide to documents of Irish and British interest in Fondo Borghese, (ser. 1) ii-iv; xxvii., 1964, pp. 13-75: John Hanly, 'Records of Irish Colleges in Rome'.

12. For instance, mss. Ottob. lat. 579 on the projected marriage of the Prince of Wales with Maria, the Spanish Infanta.

13. Vat. lat. 10881 (for 1686, 1688 and 1689).

14. Among the Passionei mss: Vat. lat. 3175, 13: Persecuzione mossa contro cattolici per opera del principe di Oranges; Vat lat. 3179, 9 and 63: documents concerning Lord Portland; Vat. lat. 9804 f. 15: 'extract from the House of Commons, 20 March 1712' (translated into Italian), f. 77 'Conference of 27 June 1712: offers made by France to the allies at the instance of Her Majesty the Queen of Great Britain; f. 81 'memorandum by Passionei concerning the Queen of England's declarations on the treaty of Utrecht'; f. 109 'Denzil Hollis, lord. Thoughts on the British Constitution, court and Parliament 1716. With a preface of March 1712'; f. 135 'Subsidies of English Parliament for the year 1712'; f. 141 'Methods of the Dublin justices and those in Ireland to examine Papists (order of late September 1712)'; ff. 149, 181, 185, 'Sundry papers concerning Queen's Anne's policy' (29 Oct. 1709, 7 Jan. 1712/3, 14 March 1712/3; 10738 f. 124 v. 'Proceedings of the House of

Lords' (on Queen Anne's speech on the peace of Utrecht). See also Vat. lat. 7472, 'Discorso di Gio Francesco Albani in lode di Giacomo II (the famous speech delivered at the entertainment given by Queen Christina)'; Vat. lat. 10227, 'Accademia di Cristina, 9 Febr. 1687, in onore del Re d'Inghilterra, presente lord Castelmaine'; Vat. lat. 7494, 47 'Allocatio habita in consistorio, in obitu Jacobi II'; see also Angliae regnum, mss. 8137, 8512, 8641, 8833-8834, 9008, 9027, 9212, 9415, 9447, 9712, 9732, 9834. I am obliged to Madame Jeanne Bignami Odier for the information she has kindly given me.

15. See Leslie Macfarlane, 'The Vatican Archives, with Special reference to sources for British Medieval history', in *Archives*, iv. 1959, No. 21, pp. 29-44; No. 22, 84-98 (the modern period is touched upon, pp. 95-101).

16. The original collection comprised 18 volumes, covering the period 1566-1704, to which were added in 1920-1922 some volumes of 'Varia'.

17. See Bernard Barbiche, 'La nonciature de France et les affaires d'Angleterre au début du XVIIᵉ siècle', in *Bibliothèque de l'Ecole des chartes*, cxxv., 1967, pp. 399-429.

18. See Martin Haile (Marie Hallé), *James Francis Edward, The Old Chevalier*, London 1907, pp. 232-35 and p. 463 from the Roman Transcripts and the Gualterio Papers. The question should be entirely re-examined, notwithstanding the perhaps excessive accusations of Alec Mellor, in his various works on Freemasonry, that Strickland was a Hanoverian agent in the pay of the English Government and an anti-Jacobite mason.

19. See *Sacrae Congregationis De Propaganda fide Memoria rerum . . . 1622-1972*, vol. I/1: 1622-1700, Rome 1971 (Index pp. 733-766).

20. Nikolaus Kowalsky, O.M.I., 'Inventario dell' archivio storico della S.C. 'de Propaganda Fide', in *Neue Zeitschrift für Missionswissenschaft*, xvii. 1961, pp. 9-23, 191-200, and a complementary study by Josef Metzler, O.M.I., 'Indici dell' Archivio Storico della S.C. 'de Propaganda Fide', in *Euntes docete*, xxi, 1968, pp. 109-130, which gives a list of inventories.

21. Bibl. Vaticane, Ms Borgia lat. 565 ff. 322v-323r.

22. *Les derniers Stuarts à Saint-Germain-en-Laye. Documents inédits et authentiques puisés aux archives publiques et privées*, Paris 1871, i.

23. *Cambridge Historical Essays*, xii. See the extracts from some of the Gualterio papers, pp. 337-343, and some quotes, *passim*. 'The chief authority upon which the Essay is based is the Gualterio Manuscripts at the British Museum.'

24. I would ask readers to consult my remarks in the *Annuaire de la IVᵉ section de l'Ecole pratique des Hautes Etudes*, for the years 1974 *et seq.*, 'Rapport . . . sur les conférences d'Histoire des relations diplomatiques en Europe aux XVIIᵉ et XVIIIᵉ siècles', *passim*.

25. Add. Ms. 20241 f. 40; 20242 ff. 142v-143r, 144v-145r.

26. Vol. XXII. No. 2.

27. To Lord Melfort, 26 November 1692.

28. To the same(?), 24 March 1693.

Appendix I

Archivio Segreto Vaticano: Indice 144

'INDICE delle scritture de negozj trattati nel pontificato di Papa Clemente XI, disposte distintamente secondo l'ordine de paesi e le materie degli affari. In duecento sessanta cinque volumi.'

	Inghilterra	
Gran Bretagna	Scozia	= Vol. 163-168
	Ibernia	

Ff. 26-41v = *Inghilterra, Scozia et Ibernia.*

Tomo I = 163.

Scritture spettanti agli affari d'Inghilterra, Scozia et Ibernia, trattati nel pontificato d'Innocenzo XII, mentr'era Segretario dei Brevi il card. Gio. Franc. Albani, poi Sommo Pontefice Clemente XI, che in essi ebbe notabil parte e maneggio.

Scritture spettanti alla persecuzione mossa dagli eretici d'Inghilterra contra la Religione Cattolica e suoi seguaci. Scritture spettanti alli Vicarii Apostolici d'Inghilterra, alle cose giurisdizionali ecclesiastiche, stato della Religione e della Diocesi.

Controversia nata in Inghilterra tra li PP. Benedettini e li Vicarii Apostolici per causa delli Privileggi.

Cause di matrimonio

Disciplina ecclesiastica

Lettere del Duca di Berwick al Card. Albani.

Tomo II = 164.

Scritture spettanti agli affari di questi regni del tempo del pontificato di Clemente XI dall'anno 1700 fino all'anno 1712.

Alcune memorie delli Re Cattolici et Eretici che hanno dominato nella Gran Bretagna, essendo Pontefice Clemente XI, cioè di Giacomo II, con una relazione francese di certa guarizione miracolosa ottenuta per sua intercessione nell'anno 1703.

Di Guglielmo III e Maria.

Di Giacomo III.

e di Anna I.

Memorie Miscellanee delle cose spettanti alla Religione Cattolica nelli regni medesimi.

Notizie spettanti alla spedizione e sbarco di Giacomo III tentato nel regno di Scozia con infelice successo nel mese di Marzo dell'anno mille sette cento otto.

Tome III = 165.

Scritture spettanti alle cose della Religione, al nuovo tentativo fatto dal Re Giacomo in Scozia, et altri particolari delli detti tre regni dall'anno 1712 fin'all'anno 1717. Sollevamen to de Scozzesi a favore del Re Giacomo e nuovo tentativo fatto da lui per impadronirsi di quel regno. Scritture spettanti al trattato d'alleanza tra la Francia, la Gran Bretagna e le Provincie Unite dell'Olanda.

Scritture spettanti alle cose dell'Isole Britanne et al Re Giacomo dopo il fatto di Scozia passato a risedere in Avignone.

Documenti della persecuzione contro li Cattolici d'Inghilterra rinnovata dopo il fatto di Scozia.

Tomo IV = 166.

Scritture concernenti la venuta del Re Giacomo d'Inghilterra nello Stato della S. Sede Apostolica in Italia, con altri affari spettanti al re medesimo, alli regni sudetti, et alle cose della Religione dall'anno 1717 fin'all'anno 1720. Passaggio del Re in Urbino e sua dimora nella stessa città e in Pesaro.

Scritture spettanti al sospetto concepito dal Re Giacomo sopra il Milord Peterboroug.

Arresto del medesimo in Bologna: transporto alla fortezza di Forte Urbano e ciò che seguì in appresso.

Scritture concernenti il matrimonio del Re Giacomo. Palazzo Apostolico di Castel Candolfo richiesto per sua abitazione dal Re Giacomo.

Scritture spettanti all'arresto e custodia della Principessa Clementina in Ispruch.

Tomo V = 167.

Sieguono le scritture spettanti alla custodia della Principessa Clementina.

Partenza improvisa del Re Giacomo da Roma e sua andata in Spagna.

Affare gravissimo del giuramento da darsi in Inghilterra dalli Cattolici a richiesta del magistrato eretico. Collegi d'Inglesi.

Se in Inghilterra dura la vera successione de Vescovi e Sacerdoti tra gli eretici, dopo lo scisma et il regno di Elisabetta.

Tomo VI = 168.

Raccolta d'altre scritture spettanti alle cose d'Inghilterra, Scozia et Ibernia dall'anno 1675 al 1720, con altre aggiunte concernenti la persona del Re Giacomo III e sua real Famiglia.

Appendix II
Gualterio to Paolucci

B.L., Add. MS. 20268, f° 337v-342, registre
Paris, 18 Septembre 1701
Relazione della morte del Re Britannico
[Death of James II, recognition by Louis XIV of his son as king]

Sù l'avviso che giunse la notte de 12 del corrente dello stato pericolosissimo in cui si trovava il Re Britannico stimò il nunzio a proposito di traferirsi la matina seguente alla corte de San Germano. Vi trovò S.M.tà con febre, che gli ripligliava per fino a tre volte il giorno con una prostratione totale di forze, e con una sonnolenza gravissima, la quale lo faceva continuamente dormire senza però impedirgli di riscuotersi ogni volta che volevano dirgli qualche cosa e di rispondere adattatamente con uso di ragione che ha conservato sempre intierissimo per fino all'ultimo. I medici lo facevano fino d'allora disperato, onde il nunzio predetto credette che per edificazione delle due corti e per dimostratione di riconoscenza ad un prencipe ch'era stato cosi fedele alla Chiesa gli corresse debito di assistergli per fino all' ultimo respiro, si come ha fatto in effetti non abbandonandolo né giorno né notte dal martedi matina perfino al venerdi sera in cui rese l'anima a Dio. Continuo è stato altresì il concorso de' prencipi della case reale e de gran signori che sono andati a sapere di mano in mano lo stato della sua salute, mà tra gli altri si è distinto con particolari marche d'affetto il sig. prencipe di Conti che per essere cugino germano della Regina ha voluto usare con essa particolari finezze restendo tutti que' giorni dalla matina per fino alla sera in San Germano. Il Re ha mandato ogni giorno più signori della prima sfera ad informarsi dello stato delle cose, et il mercordi dopo desinare vi venne egli stesso in persona. Il nunzio si ritrovava nella stanza della Regina quando fù portato l'avviso della sua venuta. S.M.tà gli disse che non haverebbe voluto che il Re Christianissimo passasse per la stanza dell'infermo, dubitando che si come s'erano sempre teneramente amati così potesse seguire una vicendevole commotione in vedersi, e lo incaricò di procurare d'indure S.M.tà a passare per un picciolo balcone al di fuori. Il nunzio pregò il sig. duca di Lauson [Lauzun] ad insinuarlo a S.M.tà, il quale non fece difficoltà di prendere quella strada mà trovato poi esso nunzio sul medesimo balcone gl'espresse un sommo desiderio di vedere onninamente il Re Britannico, in maniera che si concertò che ciò sarebbe seguito appresso la visita della Regina. Entrata S.M.tà nella di lei stanza, fece instanza che si chiamasse il prencipe di Galles. Venuto questi rimasero tutti tre soli, mà si è poi saputo per bocca del Re medesimo che il picciolo prencipe si come era stato un tempo considerabile senza vedere la madre così subito che fù entrato nella camera senza riguardo del Re presente gli si gettò al collo e ivi con molte lagrime s'abbracciarono così teneramente che il Re dice d'havere havuto della pena a distaccarli l'uno dell'altra. La Regina a cui tratanto il. Re haveva communicato la propria intentione notificò al prencipe la risoluzione presa da S.M.tà di riconoscerlo e trattarlo da Re ogni volte che venisse a mancare il Re suo Padre. Il fanciullo che non havea notizia alcuna dell'avvenimento e che non poteva havere ne tampoco speranza nientedimeno riceve tal avviso come se vi fosse stato preparato, e gettandosi a i piedi del Re gli disse queste precise parole: Io non mi scorderò mai che sete [sic] voi che mi fate Re, e qualsivolglia cosa che mi succeda impiegarò questa dignità a farvi conoscere la mia riconoscenza. Il Re gli disse che lo faceva volontieri mà sotto conditione che conservasse sempre immutabile il religione cattolica, in cui era stato educato, mentre se fosse stato mai possibile ch'egli l'abandonnasse o volesse anche solamente nasconderla non solo perderebbe affatto la sua amicitia mà sarebbe risguardato con horrore di tutti gl'huomini da bene che sono nel mondo e come l'ultimo e il più vile degl'huomini. A che il prencipe rispose con le proteste della maggiore costanza. Più altre cose furono dette vicendevolmente sopra lo stesso argomento; dopo di che il prencipe si ritirò e essendo uscito dalla camera dirottamente piangendo dette motivo a milord Perth suo governatore di dimandargli che cosa gl'havesse detto il Re di Francia: mà gli rispose che ne haveva promesso il segreto a S.M.tà e che non poteva violarlo. In effetti non vole dirle cosa alcuna. Bensì tornato al suo appartamento si rinchiuse nel gabinetto e si pose a scrivere e domandatogli dal governatore medesimo ciò che notasse disse senz' altro ch'era il discorso tenutogli dal Re Christianissimo, il quale voleva poter rileggere tutti i giorni della sua vita.

S.M.tà finì tratando la visita della Regina et accostandosi al letto del Re infermo gli fece i più cordiali complimenti. L'altro assopito nella sua sonnolenza habbe sul principio qualche difficoltà a riconoscerlo e l'andava ricercando quasi sospeso con gl'occhi, mà rivoltosi finalmente alla parte ove il Re era, tosto che l'hebbe veduto pose la bocca al riso e dimostrò un estremo piacere. La ringratiò poi di tutte le finezze le quali gl'usava e singolarmente d'havergli mandato il giorno antecedente il suo primo medico. Dopo varie espressioni d'affetto il Re Christianissimo disse che haverebbe voluto parlare di qualche negozio a S.M.tà Britannica. Ciascheduno volea ritirarsi per rispetto mà il Re comandò che tutti si fermassero e alzando la voce disse che voleva assicurarlo che quando Dio havesse fatto altro di lui, haverebbe presa cura particolare del principe di Galles, e non minore di quella che potesse haverne esso stesso se fosse vivo; che dopo la sua morte lo riconoscerebbe per Re e lo trattarebbe nella medesima forma con cui haveva trattato lui medesimo. Ciò che gli rispondesse il Re Britannico non pote udirsi perchè gl'Inglesi, de' quali era piena la camera e che non solamente non s'attendevano ad una tale dichiaratione mà per il contrario haveano probabilità tali da credere tutto l'opposto dettero tutti un'alto grido di Viva il Re di Francia, e gettandosi a i piedi di S.M.tà gli testimoniarono la loro gratitudine d'una maniera che quanto era più viva et in un certo modo lontana dal rispetto ordinario tanto maggiormente mostrava i sentimenti de loro cuori. Il nunzio dopo haver dato luogo a tal trasporto di gioia in quelle genti s'accostò ancor'egli a S.M.tà e gli disse che lo ringratiava a nome di tutta la Chiesa dell'atto eroïco il qual veniva di fare, pregando Dio a volerglielo ricompenzare con altretante felicità. S.M.tà gli rispose allora con somma benignità e poi esso nunzio essendo andato servendolo per fino alla carrozza lo richiamò per strada e gli soggiunse ch'egli ben sapeva di quale importanza poteva essere tale risoluzione e conosceva le difficoltà che potevano esservi state mà che il rispetto della religione havea sorpassato ogni cosa e ve lo havea unicamente determinato. Si sa poi S.M.tà haver detto in appresso che ben conosceva tutti gli pregiuditij che poteva recargli una così fatta determinazione, la quale haverebbe dato pretesto al Prencipe d'Oranges di fare de' strepiti in Inghilterra di suscitargli contro il Parlemento e forse di caggionargli la guerra mà che havea voluto che gl'interessi della religione passassero innanzi a tutte le altre cose, lasciando a Dio la cura del resto. In effetti si penetra che la maggior parte del Consiglio fosse di contraria opinione e che l'operato si debbia al solo arbitrio del Re. E'vero che i prencipi della casa reale erano stati di tal desiderio et hanno dimostrato una somma sodisfazione del successo; il duca di Borgogna particolarmente, che se n'espresse ne' termini più forti che possino imaginarsi.

Ritornando al Re defonto è certo che questa è stata la maggiore consolazione che potesse havere morendo, mentre altro affare temporale non gl'occupava la mente. Ne ha dati altresi gli contrassegni maggiori mentre ordinò subito che il prencipe si traferisse a Marli per ringraziarne S.M.tà se bene la Regina non giudicò poi d'inviarvelo havendosi mandato in sua vece milord Midleton suo primo ministro. La matina seguente si fece chiamare di bel nuovo esso prencipe e parlandogli del medesimo affare gli ricordò la fedeltà a Dio, l'ubidienza alla madre e la riconoscenza al Re Christianissimo. Né poi ha parlato con alcun prencipe o signore della corte di Francia che non gl'habbia tenuto ragionamento sopra di ciò et espressegli le grandi obligazioni che sentiva sù tale sogetto. Queste sono state le sole parole ch'egli habbia impiegate negl'affari del mondo. Tutto il rimanente non ha risguardato che il Cielo, eccitando di tempo in tempo i preti e i religiosi che l'assistevano a dire delle orazioni, scegliendo esso stesso quelle che maggiormente desiderava e sopra tutto mostrando un sommo desiderio et una somma divozione della messa, recitandosi la quale egli che nel rimanente del tempo soleva essere addormentato si è sempre tenuto con gl'occhi aperti e facendo con la testa tutti que' segni di venerazione che la sua positione e la sua debolezza potevano permettergli all'elevazione. Fino agl'ultimi respiri è stato udito recitare delle preghiere e allorché gli mancò la voce fù veduto movere a tal ogetto le labra. Oltre di ciò ha dimostrata una tranquillità d'animo infinita e una rassegnatione eroica al divino volere: consolando egli stesso la Regina del dolore che dimostrava per la sua perdita. Ha finalmente esercitata una somma patienza non essendosi mai doluto di cosa alcuna nel corso dell'infermità et havendo sempre risposto che stava bene. Ha havuto una esatta ubidienza alle ordinationi de' medici e ha preso senza replica tutto quello che hanno voluto dargli benche vi havesse per altro ripugnanza. Finalmente ha havuto sempre il giuditio sanissimo e la mente etiandio più pronta e più libera di quella che l'havesse per molti mesi antecedenti. Gli è durato de lunedi fino al venerdi sempre in una specie d'agonia patendo varij accidenti che di tanto in tanto facevano crederlo vicino a morire e risorgendo un momento appresso. Gl'ultimi singulti della morte furono brevi e non durarono lo spatio d'un hora e mezza ancor'essi assai miti e che per quanto pote osservarsi non gl'erano un gran tormento. Spirò venerdi alle tre e mezza della sera pianto con caldissime lagrime da suoi tanto cattolici che protestanti, i quali l'hanno tutti per tanti giorni servito con un'amore e attenzione indicibile. Le Regina non ha fatto in tutto questo tempo che piangere mà senza però abandonare la cura degl'affari correnti. Morto il Re hebbe le più grandi angoscie mà persuasa alla fine di lasciarsi mettere in carrozza si è trasferita ad un convento delle monache della Visitatione posto in un villaggio vicino a Parigi per nome Challiot ove si tratterrà fino lunedi sera. Il Re s'era offerto di accompagnarvela in persona mà non ha voluto permetterglielo. Si ritroverà bene a S.Germano nel ritorno che S.M.tà vi farà per riporla nel suo appartamento, et allora si crede che visitarà la prima volta il successore in qualità di Re.

Il nunzio credette di non dover frapporre indugio alcuno a far questa parte per dare un'esempio autentico agl' altri ministri e per dimostrare tanto maggiormente al nuovo Re la benevolenza della Sede Apostolica, onde passò subito a complimentarlo nel suo appartamento, dicendogli che nel gravissimo dolore che la Chiesa sentiva per la perdita d'un membro cosi principale qual era il Re defunto non poteva invenire maggiore consolazione di quella che gli proveniva dal riconoscerne S.M.tà per successore, non dubitando che dovesse essere herede ugualmente delle virtù che delle corone del Padre e particolarmente in ciò che risguarda la costanza nella religione per cui quel prencipe era stato cotanto glorioso. Rispose che S.S.tà poteva essere certa di haverlo sempre altretanto ubidiente quanto sia stato suo padre. Le disposizioni venture di quella corte non sono per ancora note mà si avviseranno in appresso. In quanto alle ossequie S.M.tà Christianissima voleva fargliela fare reali a sue spese mà il Re defonto raccommandò d'essere sepolto senza pompa e la Regina ha poi talmente insistito sopra la medesima istanza che si è rimasto di far trasportare il cadevere senza pompa alle benedittine inglesi per tenervelo in deposito per fino a tanto che piaccia a Dio di disporre le cose in maniera da poterlo riportare nel sepolcro de suoi maggiori in Inghilterra. Ha bensì S.M.tà fatto fare un cuore d'argento dorato coronato alla reale per rinchiudervi quello del del defonto già trasferito segretamente a Challiot per essere risposto vicino a quello della Regina sua madre che si conserva nel medesimo luogo. Pensa inoltre a tutto ciò che possa essere di sollievo, di conforto e di commodità alla Regina e procura d'usargli tutte le finezze possibili per consolarla. Il che si rende tanto più necessario quanto l'afflittione dell'animo reca alla medesima pregiudizio anche nel corpo, trovandosi hoggi travagliata da mali di stomaco e da una straordinaria debolezza benche speri che le cose non siano per passare più oltre.

Appendix III
Gualterio to Paolucci
A.V., Nunziatura di Francia 203, fo. 438-439, dépêche
Paris, 21 mars 1702
[Death of William III]

NEL mentre che uniformemente al solito eravamo questa mattina tutti in Versaigles, è capitato un corriero di Londra spedito dal ministro di Portogallo all'inviato che qui risiede in questa corte di quella stessa corona, portando lettere a lui et a più altri ministri con avviso che il prencipe d'Oranges soprapeso da nuovi accidenti si trovi vicino alla morte. Senza stendermi di vantaggio, l'E.V. si degnarà di raccogliere il vero suo stato dell'annesse due relazioni che contengono tutto ciò che fin'ora si sa. Secondo tutte le probabilità non puo sopravivere e deve essere morto a quest'ora. Ciò che sia per produrre la sua morte non puo per ancora sapersi, perché dipende dal movimento de popoli, di cui alcuno non puo giudicare preventivamente ma non puo essere a meno che cagioni delle grandi rivoluzioni non solamente nel paese in cui chiude i suoi giorni e nella Republica che ha governata, ma in tutta universalmente l'Europa, atteso che l'abbraciasse intieramente co' suoi maneggi e che non vi sia corte nella quale non habbia havuti grandi interessi, sia di confederazione o vero d'inimicitia.

L'Inghilterra, quando ciò siegua restarà senza capo in un tempo che disponendosi ad una guerra considerabilie ne tiene maggiore bisogno. La successione dubiosa tra il Re legitimo e la principessa di Danimarca partegiarà l'inclinazione de popoli, e se bene la presenza, il rispetto della religione e le ultime leggi passate nel Parlamento siano per rendere la condizione della principessa più vantagiosa, non mancanno verisimilmente molti che tocchi dalla sinderesi delle cose passate e mossi degl'instinti naturali della giustizia propenderanno al herede naturale dell'antico signore. D'altronde l'havere detta principessa due zij materni che sono i conti de Clarendone e di Rochester, capi della fattione anglicana, e l'essere altresi della medesima Milord Malboroug con altro nome Churchil, la di cui moglie ha fama di governarla, puo concitargli contro la fattione avversa de Vigh et universalmente tutti quelli che sogliono chiamare non conformisti, si che quando anche gli riesca di salire sul trono, non puo verisimilmente promettersi che un regno turbolento et infausto, forsi né tampoco durevole, massime essendo essa senza figliuoli, trovandosi congiunta ad un marito debole che non ha né la stima né l'amore degl'Inglesi, et essendo essa stessa di poco spirito e di nessuna salute, a segno che puo difficilmente invitare alcuno a sposare gli suoi interessi. Tutte disposizioni che possono incaminare ugualmente le cose al riconoscimento del Re legitimo o vero portarle ad un governo di Republica popolare secondo che si rivolgerà la fortuna, rimanendo fin'ore di questo o di quello altretanto ignoti gl'effetti futuri quanto sono certe e costanti le cose antidette.

L'Olanda che fin'ora ha goduto più tosto l'apparenza che l'essenziale della libertà puo hora cangiare di sorte se ardirà di governarsi senza un nuovo stadhouder e nella forma che già i fratelli Wict haveano a tempo loro disposta. Combatterano cola le due fattioni degl'antichi cittadini, a cui la Republica è debitrice della sua fondazione ma rimasti esclusi quasi che intieramente del governo dal prencipe d'Oranges perché gli ha riputati poco affetti al suo dominio, e de nuovi che hanno ottenuto da lui le cariche a prezzo della più abietta servitù. I primi non potranno restituirsi all'antico possesso degl'onori senza mutatione sensibile nello Stato I secondi non sono bastanti a continuarvisi se non prendono un nuovo padrone; et in questo caso i loro voti saranno divisi in più prencipi, tra gl'altri nel prencipe di Nassau, che vi haverà facilmente la maggior parte, in quello di Baden, e forsi anche nell' elettore di Brandeburgo, che sembra aspirarvi da lungo tempo. L'antica forma di governo sarà propensa alla pace, quest'ultima continuarà ne sentimenti di guerra.

Nessuno perderà maggiormente in tale accidente che l'Imperatore si per il grand credito che il prencipe d'Oranges ha sempre havuto con i protestanti, ad effetto d'interessarli nella sua causa, si per essere egli l'unico, il qual potesse tenere concordi nella mede sima gl'Inglesi e gl'Olandesi, non ostante la naturale contrarietà degl'interessi, si perché difficilmente si troverà altro sogetto capace di mettere alla testa degli eserciti collegati in sua vece, si finalmente perché la sua morte quando succeda lasciando le cose in una grande confusione è quasi impossibile che per questa campagna la casa d'Austria riceva più que sussidij e quelle diversioni che s'era con fondamento promessi, e dall'altro canto sembra difficile che possa senza di ciò continuare vigorosamente le guerra.

Questa corona e la Spagna potranno al contrario raccoglierne frutti considerabilissimi e forsi d'una pace stabile e vantagiosa.

Ho creduto mio debito nel dare l'avviso soggiungere queste deboli riflessioni che la presenza e la pratica degli affari m'inspirano, riservandomi a rettificarle secondo che gl'accidenti o le notizie mi renderanno meglio avvertito [. . .]

Appendix IV

(i)

James, duke of Perth, to Mr Wallace
Edinburgh, S.C.A., Blairs Papers, autogr.
Saint-Germain, 5 septembre 1701
[King James' seackness]

'Alas Mr Wallace, Dom Mabillon's visite must be put off until his return, for our confusion is very great. Yesterday we thought the K[ing] dead but by a great evacuation by vomiting of blood, he gott out of the fitt. He called for the sacraments, spoke to all his servants in general and particular, exhorted the Protestants to mind their souls and become Catholics, that they might feel the consolation at their deaths. He now did exhorted the P[rince] to obey God and the Q[ueen], to depend upon the K[ing] of Fr[ance] to live and dye a good catholic, cost what it wold and to be a good man. He recommended his son to me again and again and said he had a good governor, and when the curate bro[ught] the Blessed Sacrament he cried out: "Ha! Voycy l'heureux temps venue" and receaved with the devotion of a dying saint. He answered to the prayers at the receaving of the Extreme Unction distinctly and to the litanies and other prayers of the recommendation of his soul. And in all things disposed himself for dying with the greatest tranquillity and courage imaginable. He called me and expecting to dye immediatly charged me to tell the K[ing] of Fr[ance] somewhat from him. But now I hope he wil see him himself for he is lyke to last some time longer. All they fear for his dying soon at least a gangrene gett into his bowels for the blood he voyds by stool has a cadaverous smell and he voyds a great quantity that way.

'This account immediatly to Mr Whitf[or]d send it to Fa[the]r Fordyce too. I have not leisure to write all in detaille but do you send the substance of this to Monsieur le Ministre, for I have not time to write to himself.'

Adieu

Send me out as soon as ever you can conveniently *The Life of Saint Louis* done by the abbé Choisie.

Saint — Germain, 5 septembre
A Monsieur, Monsieur Wallace, au Collège des Escossois sur le fossé Saint-Victor, à Paris.

Appendix IV

(ii)

James, duke of Perth, to a member of the Scots College
Edinburgh, S.C.A., Blairs Papers, autogr.
Saint-Germain, 24 octobre 1701
[Miracles wrought by King James' intercession]

'Very Reverend Sir,

Our blessed King's death and all that has followed upon it has so taken up all our court and yet more particularly my self that I had not a moment to employ in writing. Other ways you had had a full account of the King's death being shortly to be printed and sent to Rome, it is but to have a little patience and you shall be fully satisfyed. The K[ing James III] has writt to the Pope and by this post to all the cardinals at Rome. The Pope's speech upon the occasion of our late King's death is here and is mighty fine and pleases both this court and that of Fr[ance] to a wonder. The troubles at Naples we hope will have no bad consequence for the King of Spain affaires, and if the Imperialists there put from taking winter quarters in Italy, things would look well; but the P[rince] of O[range] is raising all the devils in parliament against us. But God is master. The King behaves to a miracle and if he lives wil be a great prince. His father dyed a saint and it seems Almighty God intends to have him considered as such for wee hear of miraculous effects of his intercession every day and the people of Paris already have canonised him by the publick voyce. I wish our poor had some relief. They say there is a certain sum out of everie dispense and composition for bulls for pious uses called the componenda. Could it be better bestowed than in preserving the lives of so many poor people as wee have here actually starving? Pray for me, dear Sir, and believe I am while I breath'.

Yours Intirely

24 oct[ober] [1]701

8

Spain and the Jacobites, 1715–16[1]

L. B. Smith

AT the end of the War of the Spanish Succession Spain's relations with Britain were renewed by the Anglo-Spanish Peace Treaty signed at Utrecht on 13 July 1713, followed in December by a Commercial Treaty between the two countries. By the former, Spain recognised the Protestant Succession to the English throne, namely that Queen Anne was to be succeeded, not by her brother, James Edward Stuart, a Roman Catholic, but by the nearest Protestant heir, the Dowager Electress Sophia of Hanover or, should she die before Anne, her son George, the Elector. The Anglo-Spanish Peace Treaty also confirmed Britain's retention of Gibraltar and Minorca, captured during the War of Succession; moreover, Spain was compelled to award to Britain for thirty years the Asiento contract for the supply of African slaves to Spanish America. There were also three secret articles to the treaty of July 1713: in the first, Britain promised to try and prevent the dismemberment of Spain's Empire, and in the second, to help Philip secure the sovereignty of Limburg for the Princess des Ursins, *camerara mayor* (chief lady in waiting) to his first wife, Maria Luisa. Of chief importance to the Spanish government was, as Professor Miguel Martin has shown,[2] the third secret clause by which the Tory administration of Queen Anne had supported the continuation of Spain's sovereignty over the territory of Siena (then ruled by Cosimo III de Medici, Duke of Florence); in addition, Anne had promised to act with Philip to preserve what was vaguely referred to as '. . . the equilibrium (and) . . . liberty of Italy'.[3]

For Spain this, not her abjuration of the Catholic Stuarts (despite the fact that James Edward, the son of James II, was a second cousin of Maria Luisa, Philip's first wife),[4] was the most important point in the Anglo-Spanish Peace Treaty. By the terms of the Utrecht settlement Spain's Italian Empire had been dismembered. Milan, Sardinia, Naples and the Tuscan ports (known as the *stato dei presidii*) went to the Emperor Charles VI, and Sicily to Victor Amadeus II of Savoy, although it was to revert to Spain if the Savoyard male line became extinct. Philip was not prepared to accept the loss of these Italian territories and therefore made no peace treaty with Charles VI renouncing his claim to Spain's territories in Italy ceded to the Emperor, with the exception of Milan.[5] In this context the third secret article to the Anglo-Spanish Treaty was viewed as encompassing not only a recognition by London of Spain's claim to Siena, but also to the Tuscan ports (which had been Sienese territory prior to their annexation by Spain in the mid-sixteenth century);[6] in addition Philip believed in the period immediately following the signature of this secret article that the reference it contained to the need to preserve an equilibrium in Italy might be interpreted as a recognition by the British government of Spain's claim to recover Naples and Sardinia.[7]

Philip V therefore ignored the ties of religion and family which might have inclined him to James, and allowed a broader concept of Spain's national interest to dictate his relations with Britain. The death of Anne in August 1714 and the accession of George I with the replacement of a Tory administration by one composed of Whigs, however, posed a question mark over Britain's relations with Spain, since there could be no certainty that the new government in London would honour the treaty commitments of its predecessor.

Differing Tory and Whig attitudes towards Majorca demonstrated the changed attitude of the new Hanoverian administration.[8] The island's inhabitants, like those of Catalonia, had supported the Habsburgs during the War of Succession, and refused to accept the Convention for the Evacuation of Catalonia signed at Utrecht by Britain and France on 14 March 1713 introducing a ceasefire in Catalonia and the Balearics to enable their Imperial garrisons to be evacuated to Italy. Bolingbroke was prepared to assist Philip V in reducing the Catalonians and Majorcans to submission by blockading Barcelona and Palma with a British fleet.[9] The Whig government, mindful of the Majorcans' loyalty to the allied cause during the war, was less ready to collaborate with Spain. Although George I's Ministry turned down an Austrian request to support the islanders (on the grounds that Britain was a guarantor of the 1713 convention), the government in London hoped to act as a mediator between Philip V and the Majorcans. Under pressure from Louis XIV, in April 1715 Philip accepted Britain's planned mediation;[10] however, the following June Spain dispatched an expedition to Majorca which overcame the rising and compelled the inhabitants to accept Philip.

The significance of Philip V's Italian policy — and the need to obtain British backing for it — was emphasised by his second marriage in December 1714 to Elisabeth Farnese, niece of Francesco Farnese, Duke of Parma. Since the duke and his younger brother Antonio were childless, she was the heiress to the Duchy of Parma-Piacenza, and through her great grandmother, Margherita de Medici, she had the best claim to suceed to Tuscany should the Medici become extinct. If Philip died before her, Elisabeth hoped to move back to Italy along with any children she might have who would appear to stand little chance of succeeding to the Spanish throne since there were three sons surviving from their father's first marriage. Elisabeth, supported by her husband, was therefore determined to secure Parma-Piacenza and Tuscany — to which she believed she was the rightful heir — to provide for herself in widowhood and her children.[11]

Against this background Spain had to clarify the attitude of the new regime in Britain to the treaty commitments of its predecessor concerning the recognition of Spain's claim to Siena as laid down in the third secret clause.

George I's government for its part wanted to preserve good relations with Spain: its concern, however, lay not in any desire on the part of the new administration to support Spanish policy towards Italy but in the need to renegotiate Britain's commercial relations with Spain. There was widespread dissatisfaction among the British merchant community at the fact that the Asiento had failed to open the door to a substantial illicit trade with the Spanish Empire, and with a clause in the Anglo-Spanish Commercial Treaty of December 1713 which had inadvertently resulted in a substantial increase in the duties payable on British goods entering Spain.[12] In February 1715, therefore, the Whig government sent Paul Methuen, a Minister Plenipotentiary, to Spain to persuade Madrid to consent to a renegotiation of the trading agreements on lines more favourable to Britain.[13]

At the time that relations between Madrid and London were in an uncertain state, the Jacobite leadership in the British Isles and on the Continent was working out a strategy to overthrow George I and his government. Against this background it was, perhaps, surprising that the Stuart high command made no request for Spanish support. The only approaches to Madrid on James's behalf consisted of vague appeals for aid made by the Duke of Berwick, James's half-brother (a naturalised Frenchman),[14] and by Sir John Forester, a Jacobite courier whom the Stuart leadership dispatched to Madrid in March 1715.[15] This act of omission on the part of James and his chief advisers reflected the belief among Jacobite circles that their best hopes of obtaining foreign support lay in France and Sweden (due to the enmity between her king, Charles XII, and George I as Elector of Hanover),[16] and the possibility of Spain being asked to back the forthcoming rebellion, either directly or indirectly, was not seriously considered.

The catalyst which initiated the process of bringing James and Philip V together was the flight from Britain to France of the Duke of Ormonde. The Jacobites had intended that he should head the planned attempt to overthrow George I. The British government was prepared to impeach Ormonde, but because of his popularity preferred to remove him indirectly: the Ministry therefore used the Spanish ambassador in London, Monteleón, a close friend of the Duke, to persuade him to make his peace with George I by retiring to the continent.[17] In the absence of any formal Jacobite approach to Spain, Monteleón readily acted as the Whig administration had hoped. On 31 July Ormonde fled to France and arrived in Paris on 7 August.[18]

Soon after his arrival in the French capital Ormonde passed a request to Louis XIV through his foreign minister, the Marquis de Torcy, for troops, arms and £100,000. In his reply Louis avoided a definite commitment to either side in the Hanoverian-Stuart conflict. He agreed to supply Jacobite activists in Britain with arms (thus ensuring that in the event of a victory for James, France had assisted the winning side), provided this could be kept secret, but refused the requests for troops and money[19] because of a combination of reluctance to risk a war with George I by openly assisting James and a suspicion that the Jacobite threat was losing momentum.[20] However, Louis saw a source of finance for the Jacobites which would enable France to avoid the risk of conflict with Britain inherent in any direct involvement in the preparations for a rebellion against George I. To this end Louis decided to write to his grandson, Philip V, asking him to supply the money requested by Ormonde.[21]

This proposition was put to the Prince of Cellamare, the Spanish ambasador in Paris, by Torcy (accompanied by Berwick) on 11 August.[22] Torcy skilfully exploited Spanish uncertainty over the attitude of the Whig administration in London to

Spain's Italian claims by arguing that a Jacobite rebellion would effectively prevent George I's government from executing a policy opposed to that of Spain in (for instance) Italy,[23] and implying that assistance for such a rebellion was therefore in Philip V's interest. This argument aroused an immediate response from Cellamare who suggested a secret offensive and defensive alliance between Philip V, Louis XIV and James in support of Spain's claims to territory in Italy. Torcy naturally refused to consider this proposition (since it could embroil France in a new European war), but on Louis' behalf he promised French recognition and diplomatic support for Philip V's claim to Naples and Sicily and that of Elisabeth Farnese to Parma and Tuscany'[24]

On 12 August Cellamare wrote to Grimaldo, the Spanish minister for foreign affairs, describing this interview:[25] his dispatch was accompanied by letters from Louis, Torcy and Berwick requesting a sizeable Spanish financial contribution to the forthcoming Jacobite rebellion, to be handed over to a representative of the Stuart cause in Paris.[26]

These reached Madrid at six o'clock on the evening on 20 August.[27] Philip's reaction was swift. The following day (21 August) Grimaldo informed Cellamare that the Spanish king agreed to supply James with 400,000 *pesos* (the equivalent in Spanish money of the £100,000 requested by Ormonde) in return for an offensive and defensive alliance between Spain and the Catholic Stuarts in support of Spanish claims in Italy.[28] If the French government was prepared to participate, then France was to be included; if Louis would only offer diplomatic support, Cellamare was to conclude an alliance with James alone.[29]

Philip's willingness to assist the Stuarts indicated that Spain, like France, wished to see how the Jacobite rising progressed before deciding whether to declare openly for James. The Spanish government intended the aid to the Stuarts to be dependent on two conditions, an offensive and defensive alliance with James plus French diplomatic support. This would allow Madrid time to see how the Jacobites' fortunes fared: if, when the negotiations between Cellamare and the Stuart leadership were completed, the rebellion seemed set to fail, Spain could withdraw from the plan without jeopardising her relations with George I; on the other hand, if the rebellion then appeared successful, Spain hoped that the alliance with James, cemented by financial backing for his cause, would ensure the support of a Stuart Britain for her policy in Italy.

The government in Madrid therefore immediately began to calculate how the money promised to James might be conveyed to Paris with the maximum possible secrecy so that it escaped the surveillance of the British government's network of spies and informers.[30] Philip V decided that diversification was the best solution: rather than send Spain's financial contribution to James all in one denomination (entirely in bullion, or in bills of exchange), Spain's financial contribution to James was to be dispatched to Paris in a combination of gold specie and bills of exchange'[31]

On 26 August Grimaldo informed Cellamare that the Bishop of Cadiz, secretary of the Spanish Department of Finance (*Hacienda*), was sending bills of exchange worth 9,000 *doblones* (approximately £6,000) to be handed over to the Jacobites.[32] The Stuarts were also to receive a sum of 100,000 *pesos* (£25,000) in a mixture of gold and silver bullion and coinage which was already in Cellamare's custody in Paris.[33] It had been sent from Spanish South America earlier that year to be used, according to Cellamare, as a payment by Philip V to his uncle Maximilian Emanuel, Elector of Bavaria;[34] but it was instead to be handed over to a representative of the Jacobite movement in Paris if the two conditions which Spain intended to impose were satisfied.

The first of these was the offensive and defensive alliance between Philip V and James. Grimaldo sent Cellamare the draft of this on 16 September.[35] The Spanish government demanded two things of James as the price of its financial assistance: firstly, the aforementioned alliance in support of Spain's Italian policy, and secondly, an undertaking to restore the Catholic religion in Ireland and subsequently in the rest of the British Isles.[36] The draft had originally referred to the restoration of Catholicism in Ireland and then in England (Scotland and Wales were not mentioned), but the omission was spotted and the phraseology altered to include the whole of the British Isles.

This treaty neatly combined Spain's need to obtain support from Britain for her policy of recovering territory in Italy with a statement of the tie of religion binding Philip V to James. In the first article Spain was trying to secure the backing of a Stuart Britain in a future attempt to expel the Habsburgs from the Italian territories which Philip had been compelled to cede to the Emperor at the end of the War of Succession. The second article emphasised the importance to Spain of assisting a Catholic monarch to regain his throne. From the draft of this treaty, it appears that Spain was primarily concerned with obtaining British support for her policy towards Italy; thus it contained no mention of the restitution of Gibraltar and Minorca in the event of a Jacobite success. Bolingbroke, nominally James's chief adviser or 'Secretary of State', who knew of the approach to Spain but was excluded from the negotiations since James's representative in these was Berwick, feared (wrongly) that James would be tempted to promise anything in return for Spanish support and would be prepared to sign away Gibraltar and Minorca irrespective of the future consequences upon British public opinion.[37]

The other condition insisted on by Spain related to the attitude of France. Philip realised that Louis XIV was not prepared to enter into a formal alliance with Spain and the Stuarts: France would only adopt an attitude of benevolent neutrality towards the rebellion itself and Spain's part in the financial preparations for it, along with diplomatic support for the claims of Philip and Elisabeth to territory in Italy.[38]

On 1 September Louis XIV died. He was succeeded by his five-year-old great grandson, also named Louis. The post of Regent during the ensuing minority was occupied by the Duke of Orléans, nephew of the deceased king. The France of Orléans, because of the strained relationship between Orléans and Philip V, was unlikely to continue, at least for the time being, Louis XIV's policy of conniving with Spain to assist James. As Louis XV's uncle, Philip had hoped to become Regent of France himself and, despite having twice (in 1700 and 1712) renounced all claim to this and to the throne of France, he still hoped to succeed Louis if he died in infancy, even if this meant forsaking the throne of Spain. The animosity between Philip and Orléans had also been fuelled by an attempt made by the latter in 1708 to approach the British military leadership proposing that he might replace Philip as the Bourbon candidate for the Spanish throne.[39]

Against this background Cellamare had to discover to what extent (if any) the new French government would keep to the understanding between its predecessor and Madrid to connive at the Jacobite rebellion and Spain's indirect participation in it. As soon as Louis' death became known, Cellamare realized that Orléans was unlikely to collaborate with Philip V as Louis XIV might have done,[40] and that the second of the two conditions laid down by Spain — benevolent neutrality on the part of France — was unlikely to be fulfilled. He therefore began to play for time.

Cellamare strongly hinted to Berwick that some delay in the implementation of Spain's plan to subsidise the Jacobite rebellion was inevitable because of the changed political situation in France. He reminded Berwick that the receipt of Spanish finance was dependent on two conditions (the treaty with James and assurances of a favourable attitude on the part of the French government) and, by way of an excuse, alluded to what the Marshal described as 'the difficultys of the bankers'.[41] There was some truth in this. The Bishop of Cadiz had inadvertently sent the bills of exchange worth 8,000 *doblones* to Monteleón in London,[42] not to Cellamare as instructed: rather than risk handing over the cash equivalent of these to Jacobite sympathisers in Britain, Monteléon had to have them converted into bills exchangeable in Paris so that the transaction could take place in France.[43] Cellamare's reference to difficulties in providing the money was, however, used as a smokescreen to cover the political obstacles facing the plan to supply James with money. This can be shown by the fact that a portion of Spain's intended contribution to the Jacobites — the 100,000 *pesos* previously intended for Maximilian Emanuel — was already in Paris, and its existance reported in Jacobite circles,[44] and there was in theory no reason why this could not have been handed over once an alliance between Philip and James had been concluded.

The non-appearance of the subsidy which the Jacobites had expected from Spain was a particularly serious setback to them. On 26 August Old Style (6 September N.S.) the Earl of Mar, leader of James's supporters in Scotland, had precipitately raised the Stuart standard at Braemar. The Jacobite rebellion had begun before Spain's financial involvement was assured. Bolingbroke was acutely aware that the money promised by Philip V could be decisive in tilting the scales in James's favour — he even suggested that James should go to Spain himself in the hope of persuading Philip V to hand over the money.[45] Unfortunately for the Jacobites, however, the circumstances which had prompted Philip's decision to support their cause were rapidly changing: whereas late in August action in support of James on the lines suggested by Louis XIV had seemed feasible, a month later it appeared a very dubious proposition.

Two separate sources pointed out to the Spanish government the political wisdom of abandoning James for the time being. The first was Orléans. His position towards the Jacobite rebellion was equivocal: in the words of Bolingbroke, '[The Regent] has all the irresolution of temper possible, and is, perhaps, the man in the world the least capable of saying no to your face'.[46] Orléans needed to obtain foreign backing for his position as Regent to counteract Philip V's challenge: he therefore tried to improve France's relations with George I, who was his second cousin.[47] The Regent lost little time in assuring the Earl of Stair, George I's Envoy Extraordinary at the French Court, of his desire for good relations with Britain, and demonstrated this by ordering the confiscation of arms and ammunition intended for use by Jacobite rebels in the British Isles which were on board ship in Le Havre.[48] However, Orléans also needed to win internal French support and could not therefore afford to alienate the Jacobites, whose cause enjoyed considerable sympathy in France.[49] While the rising in Britain continued, Orléans thus aimed to conciliate both parties involved in order to be on the side of the eventual victor.

In September, when the rebellion was in its early stages and its outcome uncertain, the French Regent tended to caution and support of the status quo in Britain. Thus when, on the 29th of the month, Cellamare approached Orléans with the proposition that France should collaborate with Spain in assisting James, the Regent responded coolly.[50] Instead, he suggested that Spain should act similarly toward France and seek to improve its relations with the Hanoverian regime in order to obtain the support for Spanish policy towards Italy desired by Philip V. In support of this, Orléans cited intimations he had recently received through diplomatic channels to the effect that Stanhope, Secretary for the Southern Department, had hinted to Monteleón that London wished to renegotiate the commercial treaty of 1713 with Spain.[51]

A more decisive argument on these lines was put forward in Madrid by Giulio Alberoni, the Parmesan envoy to the Spanish court, who, due to the support of Elisabeth Farnese, the niece of his master, the Duke of Parma, had become extremely influential.[52] Although Alberoni saw that, in certain circumstances, Jacobitism could serve Spain's interests as a tool against George I if Britain opposed the Spanish policy for recovering the disputed territories in Italy, he had little faith in the effectiveness of the Jacobites' plans for a rebellion in 1715. Acting upon a hint passed by the Duke of Parma,[53] he argued that an agreement with George I was more in the interests of Spain and Parma than collaboration with James. Alberoni's strategy was to try to conciliate London by offering to smooth out the commercial differences between the two countries, and in return hope for British support — or at least benevolent neutrality towards Spain's Italian claims.

This policy which appeared to benefit both Spain and Parma won the support of the Queen: Alberoni was therefore able to proceed. On the night of 30 September he sent Ripperda, a Dutch agent, to George Bubb, Methuen's successor as British ambassador in Madrid, offering to settle the British merchant community's commercial grievances with Spain.[54] This approach to Britain reflected Spain's determination not to be diplomatically isolated when the outcome of the 1715 Jacobite rebellion became clear. After having previously contemplated supporting James, Spain was now improving her relations with George I in the light of the changed political situation in France and Britain. Philip V had not completely abandoned the Stuart cause: Alberoni's negotiations with Bubb for a new Commercial Treaty between England and Spain were a form of insurance for the Spaniards which also camouflaged any involvement between Philip V and James.

M.

Confirmation of the Spanish government's temporary abandonment of James came in a dispatch from Grimaldo to Cellamare dated 7 October.[55] This superseded Philip's directive of 21 August (his affirmative response to Louis XIV's request to provide the Jacobites with money) and the planned alliance between Spain and the Stuarts. Cellamare was now instructed to cease all involvement with the Jacobite leadership in Paris, and inform Orléans that although Philip had been willing to agree to Louis XIV's proposition, he now had no intention of conniving with the Jacobites in their plan to overthrow George I.[56] This instruction reflected Madrid's fear that Orléans might try to drive a wedge between Britain and Spain by informing the British government of Philip's previous intention to back James. Later in October Cellamare was told to hand over the sum of 100,000 *pesos* in his custody to Ferdinand-Augustin de Solar, comte de Monasterol, the Elector of Bavaria's representative in Paris,[57] as had been Spain's original intention, although as will be seen, this directive too was later countermanded.

While Spain was turning away from the Stuart cause, the Jacobites themselves were attempting to revive the rebellion. Their original strategy had been to mount an uprising centred upon the West Country headed by Ormonde.[58] The latter's flight to France along with the arrests of other Jacobite leaders involved — Lord Lansdowne and Sir William Wyndham — had destroyed this plan of campaign. In the changed circumstances, the Jacobites intended Ormonde to sail from Normandy to the West Country in the hope that his appearance would spark off an insurrection there, and thus confront the British government with three risings — that in the South-West joining Mar's in Scotland and a smaller uprising in the Border country. News of Ormonde's intended departure persuaded Orléans that the rebellion might yet succeed: he therefore allowed James to cross France from his refuge at Bar in the Duchy of Lorraine, and sail to join the rebels in Britain from any part of the French coast except Normandy and Picardy[59]

Ormonde's intention to return to Britain to head a Jacobite uprising in the West Country had a twofold effect on the question of Spanish backing for the Stuart cause. Queen Mary, James's mother, tried to impart this news to Cellamare at the earliest opportunity in the hope that the possibility of a widespread rebellion against George I might persuade Spain to hand over the money initially promised in August. In accordance with Grimaldo's instructions of 7 October, the Spanish ambassador managed to avoid her until 27 October when she obtained an interview, ostensibly to express her condolences at the recent death of his wife.[60]

Mary told Cellamare about Ormonde's departure and assured him that he was the first person outside the ranks of the Jacobites to be told this news:[61] this was incorrect, since Orléans had received full details from Ormonde when the two secretly met on 17 October, the night before the Duke left Paris for the French coast to sail to the West Country.[62] Nevertheless, Mary's supposedly confidential information made a great impact on Cellamare. He appeared convinced that under Ormonde's leadership the Jacobite rebellion stood a good chance of success provided that it had the finances to sustain it, and he stressed this in a dispatch of 28 October to Grimaldo reporting Mary's news.[63]

This dispatch did not arrive in Madrid until 11 November.[64] Its impact was considerable, and led to another shift in Spanish policy. On 18 November Grimaldo wrote to Cellamare that the 100,000 *pesos* initially intended for Maximilian Emanuel were to be handed over to a representative of the Jacobite leadership if they had not already been supplied to the Elector of Bavaria. James was also to receive 20,000 *pesos* (approximately £5,000) in bills of exchange which were enclosed along with the dispatch, plus the equivalent in French money of the 8,000 *doblones* initially sent from Madrid to Monteleón in August once they had been converted into bills of exchange redeemable in Paris.[65] Grimaldo instructed Cellamare to hand these sums over with the greatest secrecy: in particular, not to tell Orléans.[66] In this Philip V was clearly hoping to steal a march over the French Regent in the belief that James could be installed on the English throne without France's support.

This hope was not to be realised. Ormonde's attempt to resuscitate the rising (along with wildly optimistic accounts of its progress)[67] had persuaded Orléans that the rebellion stood a good chance of success, thereby meriting a gesture of support from France. However, until a clear result emerged, the Regent was not prepared to give any firm commitment to the Jacobites. Instead, he revived Louis XIV's plan whereby Spain would provide James with finance while France restricted her support to that which could be disavowed if the Jacobites' fortunes deteriorated.

On 14 November Orléans secretly saw Cellamare.[68] He told the Spanish ambassador that since the Jacobite rebellion appeared to stand a good chance of success, both Spain and France should collaborate on the lines envisaged by Louis XIV; namely, Madrid was to supply the Jacobites with money while France remained benevolently neutral.[69] In keeping with his policy of avoiding a definite commitment to either George I or James, the Regent was vague as to the nature of France's neutral stance — Cellamare gained the impression that this would be restricted to connivance at Jacobite attempts to smuggle arms to the rebels through French ports.[70] Orléans was placing the responsibility for deciding whether to resurrect the scheme for backing the Stuarts fairly and squarely upon Spain.

News of Orléans' about turn reached Madrid on 30 November.[71] The need for a speedy decision gave Philip V little option but to act on the lines suggested by the Regent. On 2 December, therefore, Grimaldo confirmed to Cellamare the instructions of 18 November, and enclosed a further nineteen bills of exchange worth 42,840 *pesos* (approximately £11,000), but for security reasons referred to as a mere 24,000, for Cellamare to hand over to the Stuarts.[72]

Spain's decision to supply James with comparatively large amounts of money caused Cellamare some confusion; in particular, he feared that too large a transfer of cash, bullion and bills of exchange would reach the ears of Stair, the British ambassador in Paris, through his network of Jacobite informers.[73] After Cellamare discussed the security aspect with Queen Mary (whom James had placed in change of the disposal of any money supplied by Spain during his absence in Britain),[74] it was decided to hand over the gold specie, money and some of the bills of exchange. The silver bullion which had been sent from South America was, however, to be supplied to the Jacobites at a later date,[75] thus enabling Spain to withhold payment if the prospects of success for the rebellion had by then lessened.

In the second week of December Cellamare handed over 100,000 *pesos* to Mary. This comprised gold bullion (worth approximately £15,000 at current values), about 19,000 *pesos* in coinage and 20,000 in bills of exchange.[76] In return, he obtained a receipt in Mary's handwriting.[77] At the end of December he handed over the bills worth 42,840 *pesos*[78] which Grimaldo had sent for the Jacobites' use at the beginning of the month following news of Orléans' apparent willingness to connive with Spain in supporting James's cause.

Of this financial succour which Cellamare handed over, it is only possible to trace the fate of the gold bullion. Mary ordered this to be sent to her son who was believed to be in Scotland* in the custody of Mar's cousin, Sir John Erskine of Alva,[79] Berwick's son, the Earl of Tynemouth (better known by the Spanish title of Duke of Liria which he later acquired),[80] and Berwick's brother-in-law, Francis Bulkeley.[81] For reasons of speed, the gold was rather unwisely carried on board one small vessel. This struck a sandbank off St Andrews early in January 1716 and, although the crew survived, its valuable cargo was lost.[82] This loss was undoubtedly a severe blow to Jacobite morale, but its longer-term impact was less since it reached Scottish waters too late (had it been handed over to James) to halt the decline in the fortunes of the Jacobites following the decisive check to their progress administered by British government forces at Preston and at Sheriffmuir the previous November.

Spain's decision to supply James with money was followed by an apparent *volte face*. On 14 December — at the time that Cellamare was distributing Philip V's financial support to Mary — Spain concluded a Commercial Treaty with George I,[83] the culmination of the negotiations between Alberoni and Bubb which had begun at the end of September. Ironically, this treaty was widely viewed as a declaration of confidence by Spain in the Hanoverian regime. This diplomatic move was not solely the result of Madrid's attempts to back both parties in the Jacobite rebellion in the hope of Spain's benefiting irrespective of the victor. It rather reflected a power struggle being waged between Philip V's nominal chief minister, the Inquisitor General, Cardinal del Giudice, and Alberoni.[84] The signature of the commercial treaty with Britain was the first example of the success of Alberoni's policy of offering England commercial concessions in the hope that George I would reciprocate by supporting — either directly or indirectly — Philip V's policy of recovering Spain's lost territories in Italy and securing Parma-Piacenza and Tuscany for his wife.

For Spain, the signature of this commercial treaty was particularly timely. The Jacobite rising was about to collapse. Ormonde had never reached the West Country because the Jacobites' plans were betrayed to the British authorities by his secretary, Sir John Maclean, and the slow progress of the rebels elsewhere in Britain had been checked at Preston and at Sheriffmuir. Spain's commitment to James had run the risk of involving her with the Jacobite cause, with serious consequences for her relations with the Hanoverian regime in Britain.

By signing the Anglo-Spanish Commercial Treaty Philip V opened an escape

---

* James was still crossing Northern France in search of a port from which to sail undetected by British agents, and did not reach Scotland until the beginning of January.

route. At the beginning of January 1716 Spanish government sources passed Bubb the message that Philip had halted a project by which Spain would assist James.[85] This report was vague as to the extent of the alleged plot and the stage at which it had been stopped. The Spanish 'inspired leak' paid off, however. The British government had no wish to jeopardise its relations with Spain so soon after the signature of the Commercial Treaty by allegations of Spanish-Jacobite contacts which now, according to Bubb's information, no longer existed. This was the message passed to Orléans when, piqued by Spain's rapprochement with Britain, he intimated to Stair the extent of Madrid's involvement with James.[86] George I's government was willing to trade off the British desire for an improvement in commercial links with Spain against Philip V's wish to abandon his flirtation with Jacobitism.

The Anglo-Spanish Commercial Treaty also removed for the time being the political reason for Spain's having supported James. Philip could not rely on the Stuarts whose attempt to overthrow George I had failed, and instead had to hope to obtain support for his territorial ambitions in Italy from the established regime in London. The supply of Spanish finance was therefore gradually discontinued. It could not be halted immediately, partly because of the delay in communicating between Madrid and Paris, and also because of the confusion resulting from the different instructions relating to the disposal of Spain's financial contribution to James which had been received by Cellamare. Due to this general confusion and delay, Cellamare supplied the Jacobites with almost 11,000 *pesos* in silver coinage, part of the consignment sent from South America in 1715, in the second half of January 1716,[87] a month after the signature of the Anglo-Spanish Commercial Treaty. Indeed, until 30 January[88] the Spanish government remained unsure of how much the Jacobites had actually received through Cellamare. Only when this information reached Madrid did Philip V order a halt to his financial support of James.[89] By this time Spain had contributed 153,734 *pesos*[90] (at current values approximately £38,000) towards the Jacobite rising.

When Spain was trying to cut her links with the Stuarts following the signature of the Commercial Treaty, Grimaldo instructed Cellamare to supply the equivalent in French currency of the 8,000 *doblones* (which had been inadvertently sent to Monteléon the previous August) to Monasterol, the Elector of Bavaria's representative in Paris.[91] It transpired, however, that due to a combination of confusion and fear that the Bavarians would discover the fact that money initially destined for them had been passed to the Jacobites, Cellamare had begun to supply Monasterol with money: between 21 December 1715 and 9 January 1716 the Spanish ambassador supplied the Bavarian representative with 58,248 *livres* (approximately £5,000) in all.[92]

Following the improvement in relations between Spain and Britain after the Commercial Treaty, the British government was determined to ensure that no assistance reached James from Spain, either with or without the connivance of the government in Madrid. Late in January Stair reported to Bubb alleged attempts by Jacobite supporters in the Basque provinces of Northern Spain to ship arms and ammunition to Britain through Pasajes, the port for San Sebastian.[93] Bubb used this item of intelligence to present the Spanish government with a memorandum, requesting that Philip V halt this particular Jacobite intrigue, forbid all officers in his army from assisting the Stuart cause in any way and, finally, declare publicly that Spain would not support James.[94] In view of the improved relations between Madrid and London, Philip had little option but to issue (on 23 March) the required disavowal of Jacobitism.[95] The effect of this, however, was chiefly psychological since the rebellion was over — James had arrived back in France from Scotland on 27 February — and Philip therefore had no reason to refuse to declare that Spain was disavowing the Stuarts.

The Jacobite rising of 1715-16 may have been over. Spain's association with Jacobitism was not. Philip V had become involved with James. This was arguably a mistake, but it had made Spain the Stuarts' leading backer. James himself urgently needed a pension and a place of asylum. He could not stay on in France, nor, due to British diplomatic pressure, could he return to Bar.[96] For similar reasons most of continental Europe — the Empire, Portugal, the Dutch Republic — was closed to him. George I's government aimed at compelling James to seek asylum in Papal territory in Italy, thereby strengthening the identification of the Stuart cause with Catholicism. In an attempt to escape this trap, James wrote to Philip V on 29 February requesting asylum in Spain along with a pension,[97] and he repeated these requests when he secretly saw Cellamare in a house in the Bois de Boulogne on 5 March.[98] Spain's reaction to both requests was negative. At the end of March Cellamare passed this message to James (who had been compelled to seek temporary asylum in the Papal enclave of Avignon) via the Marquis de Magny, *introducteur des ambassadeurs* at the French court,[99] whom James used as his intermediary with the Spanish ambassador.[100]

However, Spain had not completely deserted the Stuart cause. Alberoni saw that James was of potential use as a tool against Britain in the future (if, for instance, George I's government failed to support Spain's territorial claims in Italy as a *quid pro quo* for Alberoni's commercial concessions). In April Cellamare forwarded a small amount of money — two bills of exchange worth 28,000 *livres* (approximately £2,200) in French currency, the denomination in which they were payable, to James[101] via Magny and Fr. Lewis Innes, principal of the Scots College in Paris.[102] Though no regular pension was awarded, this shows the Spanish government's desire to sustain James at a time when his political prospects appeared to have little chance of success.

Furthermore, in October 1716 James received 37,113 *livres* (£3,100) more from Spain.[103] This money came into Cellamare's hands as a result of floating exchange rates. Due to the continuing depreciation of the French currency against those of England and Spain, it represented the final instalment in French money of the 8,000 *doblones* which the government in Madrid had inadvertently sent to Monteléon in London rather than to Cellamare in August 1715.[104]

Philip V's decision to supply James with this money (which could have been put to some other use) was political. Spain was displeased by the Treaty of Westminster between George I and the Emperor Charles VI, signed on 5 June 1716.[105] This was a treaty of mutual guarantee of the titles and possessions of each signatory and the first stage in a policy adopted by Stanhope of partially satisfying Imperial territorial aims in Italy in return for Charles's abandonment of all claims to the throne of Spain. Being purely defensive, this did not conflict with the Anglo-Spanish Commercial Treaty of the previous December. However, the Treaty of Westminster was signed a mere ten days after a new Asiento: it thus became clear that Alberoni's hope of using commercial concessions to the British merchant community to obtain George I's backing for Spain's territorial claims in Italy was not viable. The Treaty of Westminster acted as a warning to Madrid that Britain's acquiescence in Spanish plans for expansion in Italy could not be bought as Alberoni had intended; it also drew attention to James's future potential as a tool against George I — to paraphrase Alberoni's own words: 'the scarecrow that lived at Avignon [James] might one day be used to frighten . . . [George I]'.[106]

In conclusion, there are three points to be made. Firstly, Philip V was the largest individual contributor to James's cause in 1715-16. Between December 1715 and the following October Spain supplied the Stuarts with an assortment of bullion, coinage and bills of exchange equivalent in value to £43,500. According to William Dicconson, treasurer to the Stuart Court, the second largest amount to reach James at this time (approximately £26,000) came from Pope Clement XI; the third largest contributor was the Duke of Lorraine, whose contribution equalled £25,700 when converted into sterling.[107]

Secondly, Spain had no prearranged plan for supporting James. The money was sent in response to the pressure of external events, with the result that when supplied this was done unconditionally. Spain's finance was, to say the least, unevenly distributed among the Jacobites, and arrived too late to be of any use.

Thirdly, the principal beneficiary in Spain of Philip V's involvement with Jacobitism in 1715-16, at least in the short term, was Alberoni. He saw that James's political usefulness to Spain was limited. Rather than Philip relying on a treaty with the Stuarts to obtain British support for Spain's territorial claims in Italy, Alberoni believed that Madrid's interests would be better served by an accommodation with the Hanoverian regime in Britain; in other words, his strategy was to offer commercial concessions to Britain in the hope that George I would make diplomatic concessions in return by recognising the claims of Philip and Elisabeth Farnese to territory in Italy. This partly bore fruit in the Quadruple Alliance (1718) which provided for Parma-Piacenza and Tuscany to pass to the offspring of Elisabeth when the male lines of the Farnese and Medici became extinct. After Philip V refused to accept its terms, Alberoni, faced with war between Spain and Britain, had little option but to strike at George I by backing a Jacobite attempt to overthrow him (1719). This, like the 1715 rebellion, ended in defeat for the Stuart cause. Alberoni had made the mistake (which he had avoided four years previously) of making Spain the principal backer of the Jacobite cause' Alberoni was dismissed; Philip V had to accept the terms of the Quadruple Alliance.

NOTES

1. I should like to thank Professor Ragnhild Hatton and Dr Derek McKay of the International History Department, London School of Economics for their suggestions and advice on the previous draft of this article.
Unless otherwise stated, all dates are in the New Style.

2. For the significance of Spain's territorial ambitions in her relations with Britain after the Anglo-Spanish Peace Treaty of 1713, see Professor Miguel A Martin's PhD thesis, 'Diplomatic Relations between Great Britain and Spain 1711-1714' (London University, 1962), published in Spanish as *España entre Inglaterra y Francia* (Panama, 1964), and 'The Secret Clause: Britain and Spanish Ambitions in Italy 1712-31', *European Studies Review* (henceforth abbreviated *E.S.R.*), 6 (1976), 407-25.

3. Martin 'Secret Clause', *E.S.R.* 76, 411.

4. Her mother, Anne-Marie of Orléans (1669-1728), wife of Victor Amadeus II of Savoy, was a cousin of James's.

5. This was because the Milanese had been an Imperial fief which Charles V gave to his son Philip II. When in 1703 the Archduke Charles (later the Emperor Charles VI), the Habsburg claimant to the Spanish throne, went to Spain, he signed a secret treaty with the Emperor Leopold I by which Milan was to revert to the House of Habsburg.

6. In 1713 the *stato dei presidii* (Orbetello, Piombino, Porto Ercole, Porto Santo Stefano, Monte Argentario, L'Ausedonois and Talamone plus Porto Longone on the island of Elba) had been ceded to Austria as dependencies of Naples. Researches carried out on behalf of the Spanish government revealed, however, that Spain's claim to the *presidii* was unconnected with that to Naples: the Tuscan Ports had been annexed to the Spanish crown after the capitulation of the Republic of Siena to Cosimo I Duke of Florence, an ally of Spain, in 1555 — Martin 'Secret Clause', *E.S.R.* 76, 404.

7. *Ibid.*, 410-11.

8. For an analysis of Tory and Whig policies towards Majorca between 1713-15, see Derek McKay, 'Diplomatic Relations between George I and the Emperor Charles VI, 1714-19' (London University, unpublished PhD thesis, 1971), 43-44 and William Roth, 'L'affaire de Majorque (1715)', *Revue d'Histoire Diplomatique* (henceforth *R.H.D.*) 86 (1972), 21-53.

9. McKay, 'Diplomatic Relations', 20.

10. *Ibid.*, 43-44; Roth, 31-39. The mediation proposals put forward by the British government provided for the evacuation of the Imperial troops on Majorca, while Philip V was to grant an amnesty for the islanders and recognise their rights and privileges.

11. For Elisabeth Farnese's influence upon Spanish policy towards Italy, see Edward Armstrong, *Elisabeth Farnese 'The Termagant of Spain'* (London, 1892); Emile Bourgeois, *Le Secret des Farnèse* (vol II, of *La Diplomatie Secrète au XVIIIe siècle: Ses Débuts* (Paris, 1909-10)); the first example of her influence in Spain, the expulsion of the Princess des Ursins, is treated in Maria Esther Bertoli, 'Elisabetta Farnese e la Principessa Orsini', *Hispania* XV (1955), 582-99.

12. The most detailed study of Anglo-Spanish commercial relations in the first half of the eighteenth century is Jean O. McLachlan, *Trade and Peace with Old Spain 1667-1750* (Cambridge, 1940), 3-29, 46-67.

13. *Ibid.*, 66; A D Francis, *The Methuens and Portugal, 1691-1708* (Cambridge, 1966), 348.

14. Berwick to James, 22 June 1714, Historic Manuscripts Commission, Stuart Papers (abbreviated H.M.C. *Stuart*), vol. I, 328; same to same, 18 June 1715, *ibid.*, 368.
James Fitzjames, 1st Duke of Berwick (1670-1733), son of James II by Arabella Churchill, sister of the Duke of Marlborough, was a Marshal in the French army.

15. Berwick to James, 10 March 1715, H.M.C. *Stuart* I. 351.

16. For Swedish motives for assisting the Jacobites in 1715-16, see R M Hatton, *Charles XII* (London, 1968), 416-17. In October 1715 George I, as Elector of Hanover, declared war on Sweden.

17. Maria Josefa Carpio, *España y los ultimos Estuardos* (Madrid, 1954), 12-14.

Isidoro Casado Avezada de Rozales, marqués de Monteléon (1664-1733) was Spanish ambassador in London from 1712-18. The British government's use of him in bringing about Ormonde's flight is discussed by J. H. & Margaret Shennan, 'The Protestant Succession in English Politics, April 1713-September 1715', in *William III and Louis XIV: Essays 1680-1720 by and for Mark A. Thomson,* edited by Ragnhild Hatton and J. S. Bromley (Liverpool, 1968), 267-68, and Claude J. Nordmann, 'Louis XIV and the Jacobites', in *Louis XIV and Europe,* ed. Ragnhild Hatton (London, 1976), 100-01.

18. George Hilton Jones, *The Mainstream of Jacobitism* (Cambridge, Mass., 1954), 106.

19. Memorial enclosed in Ormonde's letter to the Earl of Mar, 27 Dec 1715, H.M.C. *Stuart* I, 534; Jones, 107; Edward Gregg, 'The Protestant Succession in International Politics 1710-1716' (London University, unpublished PhD thesis, 1972), 284.

20. Torcy to D'Iberville, French Ambassador in London, 4 July 1715, Archives Affaires Etrangères, Correspondence Politique (A.A.E.C.P.) Angleterre, 268 ff. 386-87, and Louis XIV to d'Iberville, 4 July 1715, *ibid.,* f. 385; both cited by Gregg, 278 n. 171.

21. Memorial enclosed in Ormonde's letter to Mar, 27 Dec 1715, H.M.C. *Stuart* I, 534.

22. Cellamare to Grimaldo, 12 August 1715, Archivo Historico Nacional, Madrid (A.H.N.), Estado, legajo 3494; cited by Carpio, 18-20 & Gregg, 286 n. 242.

Antonio de Giudice, Duke of Giovenazzo and Prince of Cellamare (1657-1733), was Spanish ambassador in Paris from 1715-18; José Grimaldo (1660-1733), created a marqués in 1714, was secretary of state for foreign affairs (*secretario de estado*) to Philip V from 1714-24.

23. Cellamare to Grimaldo, 12 August 1715, A.H.N. Est. leg. 3494.

24. *Ibid.,* cited by Carpio, 18 n. 17.

25. Carpio, 19.

26. P. E. Lémontey, *Histoire de la Régence et de la Minorité de Louis XV* (Paris, 1832), I, 89.

27. Grimaldo to Cellamare, 27 Aug 1715, A.H.N. Est. leg. 3494.

28. *Ibid.,* cited by Carpio, 20-21 & Gregg, 286 n. 244.

The Spanish *peso* of eight *reales* corresponded to the crown (five shillings) in English currency and to the *écu* (three livres) in that of France. In their subsequent financial negotiations with the Jacobites, the Spaniards also used the *doblone* or *pistole* (4 *pesos*), worth approximately one pound.

29. Grimaldo to Cellamare, 21 Aug 1715, A.H.N. Est. leg. 3494, cited by Carpio, 20-21.

30. Grimaldo to Cellamare, 21 Aug 1715, A.H.N. Est. leg. 3494.

31. Postscript to the above.

32. Information contained in Cellamare's account of expenditure for the period 18 June 1715 — 31 July 1716 submitted on 7 Sept 1716 and enclosed with a dispatch of that date to Grimaldo, Archivo General de Simancas (A.G.S.) Est. leg. 4323.

33. I have found no trace of the Bishop's original order to Cellamare to supply this money to the Jacobites; however, Cellamare, in his dispatch to Grimaldo dated 9 Sept 1715 (A.H.N. Est. leg. 3494), confirmed that he had received these instructions, and further details of the transaction may be found in Cellamare's account, A.G.S. Est. leg. 4323.

34. Cellamare's account (Sept 1716), A.G.S. Est. leg. 4323. Further details of the bullion and coinage sent from South America are found in A.G.S. Secretaria y Superintendencia de Hacienda (abbreviated S.S.H.), leg. 1 f.2 'Dinero rezivido por el senor Principe de Chelamar del que vino de Indias'.

Maximilian II Emanuel, born 1662, Elector of Bavaria 1679-1726, was the brother of Philip V's mother, Maria Anna (1660-90).

35. 'Poder y Plenipotenzia al Principe de Chelamar para volver al trono de Inglat [err] a al Rey Jacobo'. (Power and plenipotentiary to the Prince of Cellamare to return King James to the throne of England); instructions and draft treaty enclosed with Grimaldo's dispatch to Cellamare, 16 Sept 1715, A.H.N. Est. leg. 3494.

36. 'Poder y plenipotenzia . . .', A.H.N. Est. leg. 3494.

37. Bolingbroke to James, 3 Sept 1715, H.M.C. *Stuart* I, 411.

38. Grimaldo to Cellamare, 21 Aug 1715, A.H.N. Est. leg. 3494.

39. Franco-Spanish relations during the minority of Louis XV are extensively explored by Lémontey; Alfred Baudrillart, *Philippe V et la Cour de France*, vols, I & II (Paris, 1890); Louis Wiesener, *Le Regent, l'abbé Dubois et les Anglais d'après les sources Britanniques)*, 3 vols. (Paris, 1891-99); P. Bliard, *Dubois Cardinal et Premier Ministre (1656-1723)* (2 vols., Paris, 1901); Emile Bourgeois, *Le Secret du Regent & Le Secret de Dubois*, vols. I & III of *La Diplomatie Secrète* (full title in note 11 above); Dom H. Leclercq. *Histoire de la Régence pendant la minorité de Louis XV* (vols. I & II, Paris, 1921-22).

There is a useful summary in English of the incident in 1708 referred to in the text in A.F.B. (Basil) Williams, *Stanhope, a Study in Eighteenth Century War and Diplomacy* (Oxford, 1932), 89-91.

40. Cellamare to Grimaldo, 2 Sept 1715, A.H.N. Est. leg. 3494.

41. Berwick to James, 1 Sept 1715, H.M.C. *Stuart* I, 412.

42. Cellamare to Grimaldo, 9 Sept 1715, A.H.N. Est. leg. 3494; Cellamare's Account, A.G.S. Est. leg. 4323. It transpired that the Bishop of Cadiz had sent bills of exchange worth 8,000 *doblones*, not 9,000 as Cellamare had been led to believe.

43. Cellamare's Account, A.G.S. Est. leg. 4323.

44. For evidence of this, see Bolingbroke's letter to James of 15 August, H.M.C. *Stuart* I, 390: '(Philip V) has actually 100,000 crowns in this city (Paris) . . .''

45. Bolingbroke to James, 21 Sept 1715; printed in Lord Mahon, *History of England from the Peace of Utrecht to the Peace of Versailles, 1713-1783*, vol. I (London, 1858), appendix, xxiv.

46. Bolingbroke, Letter to Sir William Windham, printed in Bolingbroke's *Works* (London, 1809), I, 78. Leclercq I, 258 n. 44 cites a similar verdict on Orléans made by Saint Simon (*Mémoires*, ed. Chéruel, VIII, 307): 'avec addresse, nageoit entre deux eaux'.

47. Orléans' mother, Charlotte-Elizabeth, was the niece of the Electress Sophia, mother of George I.

48. Wolfgang Michael, *England under George I: The Beginnings of the Hanoverian Dynasty*, translated from German by Annemarie & George E. MacGregor, vol. I (London, 1936), 165-67.

John Dalrymple, 2nd Earl of Stair (1673-1747), Envoy Extraordinary (1715) and Ambassador Extraordinary to the King of France, Oct 1715-June 1720.

49. Wiesener I, 28; Leclercq I, 246.

50. Cellamare to Grimaldo, 30 Sept 1715, A.H.N. Est. leg. 3494.

51. *Ibid.*

52. The policy pursued by Alberoni during his period of influence in Spain is dealt with in Joaquin Maldonado Macanaz' series of articles entitled 'El Cardenal Alberoni', *Revista de Espana* 83 (1881), 5-27, 145-64, 296-317, 433-60 & 84 (1882), 5-23; Armstrong; Bourgeois; Pietro Castagnoli, Il Cardinale Giulio Alberoni, vol. I (Piacenza-Rome, 1929); Simon Harcourt Smith, *Alberoni or the Spanish Conspiracy* (London, 1943).

53. Armstrong, 56 n.2: Duke of Parma to Alberoni, 12 Mar 1715 & Alberoni to the Duke of Parma, 15 Apr 1715; Archivi di Stato, Naples, Carte Farnesiane 58.

54. Bubb to Stanhope, 30 Sept 1715, Public Record Office, State Papers (abbreviated P.R.O. S.P.) 94/84; cited by Michael, I, 275 n'3; also see Armstrong, 71-73; Williams, *Stanhope*, 207 & McLachlan, 67-69.

Jan Willem, Baron van Ripperda (1680-1737) was Dutch envoy extraordinary to Spain from 1715-1718. He later gained the favour of Philip V and became chief minister of Spain, but was disgraced in 1726 and fled to Morocco.

55. Grimaldo to Cellamare, 7 Oct 1715, A.H.N. Est. leg. 3494.

56. *Ibid.*

57. A.G.S. S.S.H. leg l, f.2 (Details of the bullion and coinage sent to Cellamare from South America in 1715) refers to the Spanish ambassador's receipt of instructions for the disposal of the 100,000 *pesos* to Monasterol sent by Grimaldo on 28 Oct.

58. Elizabeth Handasyde, *Granville the Polite* (Oxford, 1933), 145; Sir Charles Petrie, 'The Jacobite Activities in South and West England in the summer of 1715', *Transactions of the Royal Historical Society*, 4th series, 18 (1935) 95-96; Gregg, 279-80.

59. Berwick to James, 3 Nov 1715, printed in P. Thornton, *The Stuart Dynasty* (London, 1890), 409, cited by Wiesener I, 124 n.l & Leclercq I, 258 n.45; Berwick to James, 4 Nov 1715, H.M.C. *Stuart* I, 452, cited by Gregg, 293 n.323.

60. Cellamare to Grimaldo, 28 Oct 1715, A.H.N. Est. leg. 3494. Carpio 41 n.49 gives a résumé of this meeting between the Spanish ambassador and Mary.

Journal du Marquis de Dangeau avec les Additions inédites du Duc de Saint Simon, edited by Soulié & Dussieux, vol. XVI (Paris, 1860), 207 (entry for 9 Oct 1715) noted that Cellamare's wife had recently died in Rome.

61. Cellamare to Grimaldo, 28 Oct 1715, A.H.N. Est. leg. 3494.

62. Ormonde to James, 21 Oct 1715, H.M.C. *Stuart* I, 442, cited by Wiesener I, 116; Leclercq I, 253 n.26 & Claude Nordmann, *La Crise du Nord au début du XVIIIe siècle* (Paris, 1962), 48 n.73.

63. Cellamare to Grimaldo, 28 Oct 1715, A.H.N. Est. leg. 3494.

64. Date of receipt in Madrid, marked on the cover of the above.

65. Grimaldo to Cellamare, 18 Nov 1715, A.H.N. Est. leg. 3494; Cellamare's Account (Sept 1716), A.G.S. Est. leg. 4323.

66. Grimaldo to Cellamare, 18 Nov 1715, A.H.N. Est. leg. 3494.

67. Even Stair, the British ambassador in Paris, believed a report that James himself had joined the rebels in Scotland — Thomas Crawford, Secretary at the British Embassy in Paris, to Robert Pringle, Under Secretary to the Southern Department, 27 & 28 Nov & 11 Dec 1715, S.P. 78/160, ff. 142, 144, 159; Gregg, 293.

68. For reasons of secrecy, Orléans' request to see Cellamare was passed to the Spanish ambassador through Marshal Villeroy, Governor of Louis XV — Cellamare to Grimaldo, 18 Nov 1715, A.H.N. Est. leg. 3493, cited by Carpio 42 & Nordmann, *Crise*, 48 n.73. The latter states that Cellamare met Orléans at the château of Vincennes in Villeroy's presence; the Spanish ambassador's dispatch of 18 November makes it clear that he saw the French Regent privately at the latter's residence on 14 November, the day following his meeting with Villeroy.

69. Cellamare to Grimaldo, 18 Nov 1715, A.H.N. Est. leg. 3494. Bliard I, 123 n.4 cites a letter from Cellamare to Grimaldo of that date relating Orléans' suggestion that Spain should financially support in the Archives Affaires Etrangères, C.P. Espagne, vol 282 f.48 — this may be a copy of that in the A.H.N.

70. Cellamare to Grimaldo, 18 Nov 1715, A.H.N. Est. leg. 3494.

71. Date of receipt of Cellamare's dispatch of 18 November (marked on the reverse), A.H.N. Est. leg. 3494.

72. Grimaldo to Cellamare, 2 Dec 1715, A.H.N. Est. leg. 3494; cited by Carpio 44 n.52; Cellamare's account (Sept 1716), A.G.S. Est. leg. 4323.

73. Cellamare to Grimaldo, 2 & 9 Dec 1715, A.H.N. Est. leg. 3494.

Penetration of the ranks of the Jacobite movement by Stair's agents is dealt with by Paul S Fritz, 'The Anti-Jacobite Intelligence System of the English Ministers, 1715-1745', *Historical Journal* XVI (1973), 279-80. Stair's principal informant at Saint-Germain-en-Laye, Queen Mary's residence and the Stuarts' headquarters in France, was George Higgons, brother of Thomas Higgons, James's chief adviser before the appointment of Bolingbroke — Martin Haile, *Queen Mary of Modena: Her Life and Letters* (London, 1905), 515, app. D (an extract from Stair's dispatch to James Craggs the Younger, Secretary for the Southern Department, dated 18 June 1718, S.P. 78/161 f.328).

74. Instructions issued by James, 10 Oct 1715, H.M.C. *Stuart* I, 531.

75. Cellamare to Grimaldo, 16 Dec 1715, A.H.N. Est. leg. 3494; cited by Carpio 48 n.56. Cellamare contacted Mary through Berwick — Cellamare to Grimaldo, 9 Dec 1715, A.H.N. Est. leg. 3494.

76. Cellamare's account (Sept 1716), A.G.S. Est. leg. 4323; this is corroborated by William Dicconson, treasurer to the Stuart court at Saint-Germain, in an account of money supplied to the Jacobites in 1715-17 [Royal Archives, Windsor Castle, Stuart Papers (unpublished); (abbreviated W.S.P.) 44 f.80]: 'From the King of Spain in Ingots of gold piastres and bills, 2 [/13] Dec 1715, 300,000 *livres*, (the equivalent in French currency of 100,000 *pesos*)'.

77. Mary's receipt of 13 December was enclosed with Cellamare's dispatch to Grimaldo of 16 Dec, A.H.N. Est. leg. 3494.

78. Cellamare to Grimaldo, 30 Dec 1715, A.G.S. Est. leg. 4323; Cellamare's account (Sept 1716), A.G.S. Est. leg. 4323. Dicconson described this amount as 128,520 *livres*, the equivalent in French currency of 42,840 *pesos* — W.S.P.44 f.80.

Mary's receipt, dated 20 Dec 1715, was enclosed with Cellamare's dispatch to Grimaldo, 6 Jan 1716, A.G.S. Est. leg. 4323; the transaction is also noted in Cellamare's account. Dicconson (W.S.P. 44 f.80) states that this, Spain's second contribution to the Jacobites in 1715-16, was received at Saint-Germain on 6 Jan.

79. Bolingbroke, *Works* I, 75. Erskine (c.1673-1739), a cousin once removed to Mar, had been Member of Parliament for Clackmannanshire, 1713-15. He was married to Catherine, sister of John Sinclair, Master of Sinclair, another of the Jacobite rebels.

80. James Fitzjames, Earl of Tynemouth (Tinmouth) (1696-1738). After returning to the continent from Scotland in 1716, British government pressure compelled him to leave France so, by arrangement with Philip V, he was allowed to adopt his father Berwick's Spanish title of Duke of Liria and associated lands.

81. From later correspondence in H.M.C. *Stuart* (II, 117 & VI, 584) Bulkeley can be identified as Berwick's brother-in-law, the brother of Anna Bulkeley, Liria's stepmother, whom the Marshal had married in 1700.

82. Berwick, *Memoirs of the Marshall Duke of Berwick written by Himself* (London, 1779), II, 244-45; John Sinclair, *Memoirs of the Insurrection in Scotland in 1715* (Edinburgh, 1858), 356; Ninian Hull, 'A Side Light on the 1715', *Scottish Historical Review* XVII (1920), 232; Duncan Warrand, *More Culloden Papers* (Inverness, 1925), 87; Berwick y Alba, Duque de, *El Marischal de Berwick* (Madrid, 1925), 84 (cited by Carpio, 74); Alistair & Henrietta Tayler, *1715: the story of the Rising* (London, 1936), 144 relate the story of the lost Spanish gold using papers in the P.R.O., S.P. Domestic, Scotland, 54/11, nos. 33 & 38.

Further references are to be found in H.M.C. *Stuart* I, 487, 490; IV, 26-27.

83. For the negotiations leading to the Anglo-Spanish Commercial Treaty see Michael I, 277-80; McLachlan, 68-70. The main provisions of the treaty were

a — the removal of the offending articles of the 1713 treaty;

b — British merchants became liable for the same rate of duty as Spanish subjects;

c — Both Britain and Spain agreed to accord the other the status of 'most favoured nation' in commercial affairs;

d — Duties payable by British merchants were lowered to the rates prevailing in 1700.

84. For the antagonism between Alberoni and Giudice, see Bourgeois, *Farnese*, 175-79.

85. Bubb to Stanhope, 13 Jan 1715, S.P. 94/85; copy in British Library, Department of Manuscripts (abbreviated B.M.), Egerton MSS. 2171 f.5.

86. Stanhope to Bubb, 6/17 Feb 1716, S.P. 104/136; Carpio, 83 n.26; Monteleón to Grimaldo, 20 Feb 1716, A.G.S. Est. leg. 6834.

87. Cellamare to Grimaldo, 27 Jan 1716, A.G.S. Est. leg. 4323, cited by Carpio, 69; Cellamare's Account (Sept 1716), A.G.S. Est. leg. 4323.

Dicconson (W.S.P. 44 f.80) describes this transaction as consisting of '7 piggs of silver which made 10893½ piastres when produced at the mint'. A receipt for this amount signed by Queen Mary and dated 2 March 1716 was enclosed with Cellamare's dispatch of 9 March to Grimaldo, A.G.S. Est. leg. 4323.

88. Date of arrival in Madrid of Cellamare's dispatch of 13 January, A.G.S. Est. leg. 4323.

89. Cellamare to Grimaldo, 17 Feb 1716, A.G.S. Est. leg. 4323 refers to a dispatch from the latter dated 3 February as having contained this order.

90. This comprised the 100,000 *pesos* and the 42,840 which Cellamare handed over to Queen Mary in December 1715 plus the 10,893½ *pesos/piastres* supplied the following month.

91. Grimaldo to Cellamare, 30 Dec 1715, A.G.S. Est. leg. 4323.

92. Cellamare to Grimaldo, 13 Jan 1716 & Cellamare's Account, A.G.S. Est. leg. 4323.

93. Stair to Bubb, 27 Jan 1716, B.M. Eg. 2171 f. 79b.

94. Bubb to Stanhope, 9 March 1716, S.P. 94/85. Bubb submitted the request to Philip on 5 March — see B.M. Eg. MSS. 2171 ff. 228-29.

95. Grimaldo to Bubb, 23 March 1716, B.M. Eg. MSS. 2171 ff. 234-35; there are two copies of this document, one in Spanish and the other in French, in S.P. 94/85, ff. 91 & 93. A further copy is in A.G.S. Est. leg. 6836; this is cited by Carpio, 85 n. 28, but incorrectly dated 23 May.

96. Stair to Bubb, 9 March 1716, B.M. Eg. MSS. 2171 f. 159.

97. James to Philip V, 29 Feb 1716, H.M.C. *Stuart* I, 514-15. Bolingbroke handed this to Cellamare on the night of 1 March to be forwarded to Madrid — Cellamare to Grimaldo, 2 March 1716, A.G.S. Est. leg. 4323; cited by Carpio, 85 n.29 (but incorrectly dated 2 May).

98. Cellamare to Grimaldo, 9 March 1716, A.G.S. Est. leg. 4323; cited by Carpio, 91; Saint-Simon, *Mémoires*, ed. A. Boislisle (Paris, 1879-1928), XXX, 41-43; Haile, 476; Leclercq I, 265; Nordmann, *Crise*, 53.

99. Cellamare to Grimaldo, 30 March 1716, A.G.S. Est. leg. 4323; (cited — with the month incorrectly given as May — by Carpio, 94 n.40).

Nicholas-Joseph Foucault, 2nd Marquis de Magny (1677-1772) was also used by James as his intermediary with Orléans — Gregg, 289 n. 271: H.M.C. *Stuart* I, 463-65, 471.

100. Cellamare to Grimaldo, 9 March 1716, A.G.S. Est. leg. 4323.

101. Cellamare's Account (Sept 1716), A.G.S. Est. leg. 4323. Mary's receipt for this, dated 27 April 1716, was enclosed with Cellamare's dispatch to Grimaldo of 4 May — A.G.S. Est. leg. 4323. Dicconson (W.S.P. 44 f.80) dates this amount as having been received by the Stuarts on 1 July 1717 — the date may have been incorrectly written down.

102. Magny to James, 18 & 25 Apr. 1716, H.M.C. *Stuart* II, 98 & 118. For Fr. Innes (1651-1738), see V. M. Montagu, 'The Scottish College in Paris', *Scottish Historical Review* IV (1907), 399-416.

103. Draft reply by Grimaldo to Cellamare's letter of 7 Sept 1716, A.G.S. Est. leg. 4323. Cellamare noted that the instructions to supply this money to James were dated 12 Oct — Cellamare to Grimaldo, 26 Oct 1716, A.G.S. Est. leg. 4323.

Mary's receipt for this, dated 27 Oct 1716, was enclosed with Cellamare's dispatch to Grimaldo of 2 Nov 1716, A.G.S. Est. leg. 4323.

104. Cellamare to Grimaldo, 7 Sept 1716; Cellamare's Account, A.G.S. Est. leg. 4323.

105. For the background to the Treaty of Westminster, see Wiesener I, 210 & Michael I, 252-62.

106. Armstrong 78 n. 1: letter dated 20 Apr 1716; Neapolitan Archives, Carte Farnesiane.

107. W.S.P. 44 f. 80. It should be noted that Dicconson, the treasurer to the Stuart court, omitted Spain's donation of 37,113 *livres* in the autumn of 1716 and thus understates the total value of Philip V's contributions to the Jacobites in 1715-16.

9

The Jacobite Career of John, Earl of Mar

Edward Gregg

John Erskine, eleventh Earl of Mar and eighteenth Lord Erskine in the Scottish peerage, has hitherto received attention from historians of Jacobitism largely for his leadership of the Fifteen rebellion and his controversial role vis-a-vis Francis Atterbury, Bishop of Rochester, during the 1722 Plot.[1] The purpose of this essay is to examine Mar's actions within the wider context of Jacobitism from 1715 to 1725 and to illuminate the personal plight of one eighteenth-century aristocratic refugee.

Mar was born in 1675 and succeeded to his father's title in 1690. Throughout his life, he retained immense pride in his rank as one of the senior peers of Scotland and in his family's traditional association with the fortunes of the House of Stuart. He early acquired a reputation as a sentimental Jacobite, but for the young Earl, who took his seat in the Scottish Parliament in 1696, material considerations precluded any open support for the exiled dynasty. The estate which Mar inherited was 'extremely involved, but which by good management, he in great measure retrieved';[2] his brother-in-law was later to claim that Mar's annual income did not exceed £1,500 *per annum*.[3] Mar's artistic tastes, and particularly his absorption in architecture, required more than this to support an increasingly expensive existence. For Mar, the financial rewards of governmental office early became imperative.[4]

To his pursuit of office, Mar brought only a small political base (even in Scottish terms) of support from Highland clans, but more important personal characteristics: he possessed considerable administrative ability and a charm, persuasiveness and address, both in person and in writing, by which he managed to convey the impression of absolute sincerity. His keen intelligence was marred by his unoriginality (his first action in exile was to send for a copy of Clarendon's *History*),[5] his overly high opinion of his own intelligence, and his exaggerated sense of self-importance. Finally, while anxious to play a leading political role, Mar was exceptionally thin-skinned about any criticism, whether friendly or not, of his conduct. From first to last throughout his life, Mar was motivated by personal rather than ideological considerations, and his ambition led to his famous nickname, 'Bobbing John'.

Constant governmental employment was what he sought, and what he achieved. From his first appointment in 1699, to his family's hereditary position as Keeper of Stirling Castle, Mar acted as a lieutenant or adjunct to a more powerful political figure. In the first instance, his mentor was James Douglass, second Duke of Queensberry. Like Queensberry and other aspiring Scottish politicians before him, Mar regarded England as the land of milk and honey and, acting under

Queensberry, Mar consistently supported the Act of Union until its ratification in 1707. Thereafter, Mar's career must be viewed in English rather than purely Scottish terms. During the latter years of Queen Anne's reign, Mar thought of himself — and we should think of him — more as an English Tory than in terms of any Scottish political grouping.[6]

Mar's advancement in English politics was largely due to the friendship and alliance which he struck up with Robert Harley, Secretary of State from 1704 until his forced resignation in 1708. Harley carefully maintained his contacts with Mar during his period in the wilderness until his overthrow of the Marlborough-Godolphin ministry and Harley's triumphant return to office in 1710. The connection between the two men was strengthened by the fact that, in September 1709, Harley's eldest daughter, Abigail, married Mar's brother-in-law, George Hay, Lord Dupplin, the son and heir of the sixth Earl of Kinnoul. As well as being a political ally, Mar enjoyed an entrée into Harley's family circle through Dupplin and his younger brother, John Hay, who came to London at the age of eighteen as Mar's especial friend and protégé.

Queen Anne's last ministry from 1710 to 1714 was dominated by the completion of the Treaty of Utrecht, which ended the War of the Spanish Succession and alienated Great Britain from her erstwhile allies (including the heir presumptive, Georg Ludwig, Elector of Hanover), and by the growing divisions between the principal minister, Robert Harley (created Earl of Oxford in 1711) and the Secretary of State, Henry St. John, Viscount Bolingbroke. While the personal and political quarrel between Oxford and Bolingbroke grew more heated and violent, a third group within the Tory party emerged, the titular leader of which was the great 'Tory hero', James Butler, second Duke of Ormonde, but whose guiding genius was Francis Atterbury, Bishop of Rochester. Geoffrey Holmes has analyzed the effects of this internal struggle which divided the Tory party irrevocably,[7] and laid the basis for quarrels and factions which were to plague and ultimately destroy the Jacobite movement as well.

Mar belonged firmly to the Oxford camp. It was Oxford who, in 1708, procured Mar's £3,000 *per annum* pension from Queen Anne for her lifetime, it was Oxford who awarded Mar the lucrative position as Secretary of State for Scotland after Queensberry's death in 1711; furthermore, Mar conceived a bitter hatred for Bolingbroke, with whom he quarrelled over the privileges of their respective secretaryships.[8] Indeed, as long as Oxford remained in the saddle, Mar, as his closest Scottish advisor, continued to ride high. He was careful, however, to maintain his personal friendships with his own countrymen, including John Dalrymple, second Earl of Stair, who remained a staunch Whig.[9] On 26 July 1714, only six days before Queen Anne's death, the Earl of Mar completed an important new alliance: he married Frances Pierrepoint, daughter of the Earl of Kingston, a staunch Whig who was to hold Cabinet office throughout the greater part of George I's reign. Although we lack the direct evidence of their correspondence, Mar's later tributes to his wife make it clear that she was his most important political advisor.[10] The new Countess of Mar brought with her marriage settlement a jointure of £1,500 *per annum*.

The death of Queen Anne on 1 August 1714, although not unexpected, was a disaster for the Earl of Mar. He appeared to accept stoically the political changes which the Hanoverian succession heralded and boasted to his brother, James Erskine (commonly known as Lord Grange), that 'I can make as good terms with the other side for myself as any of them'.[11] The failure of any Hanoverian minister to call on him during the Queen's reign had indicated to Mar that he was suspect at the Electoral court: Mar participated on 31 July in the Privy Council which summoned the Elector to England posthaste and, the next day, in the Accession Council which proclaimed George I as King.[12] He also took care to arrange for the heads of twelve Highland clans to write to him, pledging loyalty to King George.[13] Despite this attempt to ingratiate himself with the new regime, Mar was dismissed from office when George I arrived in England. One of his severest critics, the Master of Sinclair, commented on Mar's conduct: 'It's evident he was not acted of late by his zeale for his Countrie or the Royalle Familie, but his ambition to be again Secretarie of State, and all that his best friends can say for him is, that he was a creature of my Lord Oxford's.'[14] Not only did Mar's £3,000 annual pension cease with the Queen's death, but he also left office with £6,500 in arrears due to him,[15] which the new Whig government made clear they were in no hurry to pay.

Indeed, Mar was suspected of being a Jacobite by both Hanover and France,[16] but there is little hard evidence of close connections between him and the exiled court before 1714. There can be little doubt that Mar began his correspondence with James III sometime in 1710,[17] but Mar himself dated his entry into the service of James III from the middle of 1713,[18] a time when Oxford was inducing his other close associates, including Earl Poulet,[19] to establish Jacobite contacts to press for the Pretender's conversion from Roman Catholicism to Anglicanism. Mar duly followed this line,[20] although both James III and his advisers clearly considered the Scottish earl to be of secondary importance, compared to their separate negotiations with Oxford, Bolingbroke and Ormonde. Immediately after Queen Anne's death, Mar paid a special visit to the French envoy, Charles d'Iberville, to lament that the Pretender's positive refusal ever to consider conversion had tied the hands of those who wished to help James.[21]

The first Whig administration of George I made it clear that it intended to avenge the Treaty of Utrecht through the destruction of the Tory party. In March 1715, Bolingbroke fled to France, joining the Pretender four months later as his Secretary of State and chief advisor. In April 1715, the House of Commons appointed a Committee of Secrecy to investigate the mismanagements of the previous four years and to prepare articles of impeachment against Oxford and Ormonde. In July, Oxford was arrested and sent to the Tower. Faced by this systematic, relentless campaign, the Tory leaders managed to bury their hatchets — albeit temporarily — and to concert measures of resistance to brute Whig force. The role of the Earl of Mar in planning the 1715 rebellion remains obscure, for he is rarely mentioned either in the Jacobite reports or in the dispatches of d'Iberville. By December 1714, Mar had reversed himself on the Union and now called for its dissolution ('All agree that 'tis better to be disunited than continue under the hardshipes they have put us', he informed his brother),[22] and in March 1715 Mar boycotted the election of

Scottish peers in Edinburgh.[23] It seems that Mar spent most of 1715 in London and that he attended separate planning sessions with Ormonde, Ormonde's brother the Earl of Arran, Bishop Atterbury, and George Granville, Lord Lansdowne. In these meetings, Mar acted largely as Oxford's surrogate, with whom he apparently communicated through Erasmus Lewis, Oxford's former secretary.[24] The first plan which the Jacobite leaders conceived, for simultaneous rebellions in England and Scotland, was foiled when the Earl of Stair, now George I's envoy to France, discovered the details and relayed them to London. With the arrest of the major Jacobite leaders, the Duke of Ormonde — knowing the real weakness of English support for the Stuart cause — fled to France on 28 July (Old Style).

Mar himself left London on 9/20 August[25] to sail for Scotland to raise the Highlands against the Union and for the House of Stuart, apparently in the belief that Louis XIV would send French troops in support of James III. Only on 18/29 August did a memorial reach London in which Bolingbroke and Ormonde informed their colleagues that there would be 'no troops, no money, no officers, no appearance which may not be disavowed on the part of France',[26] a message which Lansdowne did not know how to communicate to Mar.[27]

In the event, Mar, who had no military experience, raised the Jacobite standard at Braemar on 26 August/6 Semptember 1715.[28] Mar certainly knew of the postponement of the first plan and of the suggestion that 15 September (New Style) should be the date of the rebellion.[29] Furthermore, Mar himself had previously advised James that nothing should be undertaken while Parliament remained in session.[30] It was later suggested that Mar's precipitate action was inspired by Oxford, who wished to prevent his impeachment coming to an immediate trial: this was certainly the explanation which Bolingbroke accepted. Much later in discussing the failure of the '15 with a Jacobite, Bolingbroke 'immediately fell on the subject of the late business in Scotland, and instantly fell upon Oxford with a thousand curses, calling him the ruin of all'.[31]

We need not be concerned with the military campaign of the '15, which proved to be a disaster, in part because of Mar's inability and inexperience but more importantly because the Scottish rebellion — which was supposed to be secondary — became the principal arena of struggle against the Hanoverian dynasty. There are, however, three factors which should be noted. First, after the indecisive battle of Sheriffmuir in November 1715, and foreshadowing his future policy, Mar proposed to the government, through George I's commander in Scotland, James Campbell, second Duke of Argyll, that the Jacobite rebels be allowed to lay down their arms and retire peacefully to their homes without further governmental retribution. This proposal was rejected out of hand and served only to lay the basis within Jacobite ranks for future charges that Mar was in fact a traitor to 'the Cause'.[32] Second, in December 1715, James III and VIII arrived in his ancient kingdom and Mar met the monarch with whom his future political career was to be inextricably intertwined. James III, thirteen years Mar's junior, had been reared in the habit of dependence on older and stronger advisors (an attitude which Jacobites were later to criticize as 'rule by favourites') and amidst continual exhortations for caution and patience from his followers in Great Britain. His gratitude to the man who had actually risked taking up the cudgels on his behalf was unbounded: even before he arrived in Scotland, James had elevated Mar to a dukedom in the Jacobite peerage[33] and Mar automatically assumed the role of the King's principal advisor once he arrived in the northern kingdom. Mar, for his part, discovered that his intellectual superiority and wider political experience gave him an easy domination over his titular monarch. During the latter part of his Jacobite career, Mar's letters to the King were to take on a hectoring tone which could scarcely conceal the contempt Mar felt for James's weaker intellect.

Finally, by the time of James III's arrival in Scotland in late December 1715, it was clear that government reinforcements would soon easily suppress Mar's rebel army, which had already reached its peak of 12,000 men and was rapidly declining in numbers. It was Mar who convinced the King that the wisest course was to abandon his supporters and, on 4 February, James, with the Duke of Mar and a handful of other leaders, sailed from Montrose while the remainder of the Jacobite army was retreating from Perth to Inverness. This unexpected disappearance of the King and his leading advisor caused consternation and understandable bitterness among those Jacobites who had been left in Scotland and had not been forewarned of the King's departure. When the leaders managed to escape from Scotland by various routes and to converge upon Paris in April and May 1716, their complaints against Mar were loud and bitter; Stair, the British envoy, believed that the majority of Scottish exiles were permanently estranged from Mar.[34] The loudest condemnation came from the young George Keith, eleventh Earl Marischal, who was always to remain Mar's bitterest Scottish enemy,[35] but the Duke had already undertaken to publish his *Journal*,[36] in reality an *apologia* for his conduct and a statement of his favourite theme, that Bolingbroke's failure to supply the Scottish rebels had fatally undermined their campaign.[37] Significantly, Mar felt the need to begin proclaiming of himself that 'he will never serve another interest'.[38]

Despite the bitter complaints from his erstwhile followers, Mar still kept his hold on the King. James had an implicit faith in Mar's probity and refused to listen to anything against him, ultimately with fatal results. In March 1716, Mar exercised his influence by inducing the titular King to humiliate Bolingbroke by dismissing him from office. After allowing for a 'decent' interval of a month,[39] Mar agreed to replace his rival and the arch-enemy of Mar's patron, Oxford, as Secretary of State, a position which Mar was to retain until 1719. Although in 1716 there were few Jacobites who were willing to defend Bolingbroke, Mar immediately assumed an attitude of implacable hostility to those who had earlier been associated with the former Secretary, including Lord Marischal and James Murray,[40] second son of Viscount Stormont and the brother-in-law of Mar's protégé, Colonel John Hay.[41]

Denied refuge in France and in Lorraine, the Jacobite exiles converged on Avignon — still a papal enclave — where James III's court was to reside for almost one year. In the small Provençal city, all the enmity between the three nations and the various Tory factions found ample breeding grounds. Theoretically, the Dukes of Mar and Ormonde held equal rank as James's principal councillors, but in reality Ormonde possessed neither the intelligence nor the drive of Mar, and tension quickly developed between the Cavalier hero and the high-handed Scot. Ormonde, from loyalty to James, suppressed his resentment that Mar was monopolising the King's favour, but his followers were vociferous in their complaints that Mar was ruling the roost, and this in turn exacerbated the latent tensions between the Oxford faction and the Ormonde group in England. Furthermore, despite the optimism of Mar's official letters that a new invasion of Great Britain would soon be undertaken, disaster continued to stalk the Jacobite cause. Mar and his chief agent in Paris, General Arthur Dillon, an Irish officer in the French armies of great probity but no diplomatic experience, placed their chief hopes for the future in what ultimately proved to be the non-existent willingness of Charles XII of Sweden to mount an invasion against George I on behalf of the Pretender; as a consequence, Mar and Dillon induced the English Jacobites — principally Bishop Atterbury and his associates — to raise £10,000 in gold, which was transferred into the hands of Swedish diplomats. Only in February 1717, after the arrest of Görtz and Gyllenborg, did the English Jacobites realise that Sweden had never intended to sponsor the Jacobite cause; thereafter, Atterbury regarded anything proposed by Mar and Dillon with a highly critical eye.[42]

By the autumn of 1716, news of the secret Anglo-French negotiations which were to culminate in the Triple Alliance of January 1717 had reached Avignon, and in October the French government formally notified the Jacobites that among the agreed-upon terms was the expulsion of the Pretender 'beyond the Alps' to the Papal States. In November, James III — unmarried and without direct heirs of his body — underwent a severe operation for anal fistula and his always delicate constitution seemed to foreshadow an early death. It was small wonder that by the beginning of 1717, Mar was looking for a way out of the Jacobite camp and for some means to return with honour to Great Britain.

The events of 1717, in retrospect, may be viewed as a dress rehearsal for what occurred in 1719-1720. Bolingbroke was the only previous example of a major Jacobite rebel who had attempted to make his peace with the government; Bolingbroke, however, had carried no followers with him and was now languishing in exile, scorned by Jacobite and Hanoverian alike' The lesson was not lost on Mar: it was of the utmost importance that he be able to deliver a significant number of Jacobites with him when he returned to Great Britain. Early in February 1717, James III, accompanied by his principal followers, left Avignon for the Papal States, but hardly were they in Italy when Mar left James — ostensibly to return to Paris to take in hand the continuing Jacobite negotiations with both Charles XII and Peter the Great of Russia —[43] and Ormonde soon joined him. In reality, the object of Mar's journey was also to establish contact with the British government. In December 1716, he had notified Stair of his intention to make a short journey to Flanders to visit his wife there[44] and, on his arrival in Paris on 12 March, he immediately wrote to Stair asking for an audience. Stair, however, was in London at the time, and Mar carefully kept these letters secret. On Stair's return to Paris in late May, Mar again applied for an audience,[45] informing James III that he had done so with Dillon's concurrence, but stressing that Ormonde had not been informed.[46] The meeting between Mar and Stair took place on 5 June, ostensibly to discuss Mar's formal request to the French government for permission to retire to Bourbon to drink the waters there.[47] Mar promised Stair that he and Lady Mar would 'live privately and give no manner of trouble'.[48] Mar's approach to his old friend produced no results, other than further British demands that Ormonde and Mar be removed from France in conformity with the provisions of the Triple Alliance,[49] and Stair — careful of his own reputation — did not even report Mar's visit to his superiors in London.

Undeterred, Mar retired to Flanders in July to meet Lady Mar[50] and, presumably, to hear what were his political prospects in England from his father-in-law, now Duke of Kingston and Lord Privy Seal. On 15 September, Mar wrote a remarkable letter to the effective head of the English ministry, Charles Spencer, third Earl of Sunderland: ostensibly a proposal (which Mar could not have imagined would be seriously considered) that George I should voluntarily relinquish the British crown to James III in return for British help in expanding his German territories. Mar's letter was in fact a carefully constructed invitation to Sunderland to initiate a correspondence with him. Mar gratuitously informed Sunderland that James was negotiating a marriage, revealed to the minister one of the many Parisian postal addresses the Jacobites were using, and invited Sunderland to name an intermediary to conduct their negotiations, asking Sunderland to acknowledge the letter 'whether you be resolved to listen to any thing of this kind or not'.[51] At the same time, Mar also wrote a similar appeal to William, Lord Cadogan, the British envoy at The Hague: Mar only revealed this letter to the Jacobites later, when Cadogan publicly boasted of receiving the letter, attributing his action to the advice of Charles Talbot, Duke of Shrewsbury, who was by this time dead.[52] No answer arrived from either Cadogan or Sunderland, but when Mar returned to Paris in October 1717, he made his third approach to the government,[53] again meeting for four or five hours with Stair. 'By his way,' Stair reported to James Craggs, the Secretary of State, Mar 'looked at that time upon their affairs to be desperate. He flung out several things as I thought with a design to try whether there was any hopes of treating. Because I did not think it was fair to give false hopes to an old friend . . . we did not dip deep into particulars'.[54]

Several factors prompted the government's lack of interest in Mar's approaches. First, the Whig party had been seriously split when Charles, Lord Townshend, and Robert Walpole had gone into opposition to the government, and the Sunderland administration could not risk the slightest appearance of negotiating with any attainted rebel for fear of parliamentary retribution; secondly, the government was regularly receiving copies of Mar's intimate political correspondence with his brother-in-law, Sir Hugh Patterson, from the postmaster of Leyden, where Sir Hugh was living.[55] Finally, the government did not consider Mar sufficiently important as a political prize: British forces stationed in the Austrian Netherlands could have seized Mar during his stay at Namur, Jean de Robethon, George I's private secretary, informed Stair, but the government did not consider such an action worth the trouble.[56]

Mar's return to the exiled court at Urbino in November 1717 began yet another year of political disappointment for him. He discovered that his brother-in-law, Colonel John Hay, had become a personal favourite of James's, but apparently this did not bother Mar, regarding Hay as he did as an extension of himself. Mar attempted to set himself up as the head of the 'Protestant party' by inducing James to dismiss prominent Catholics, including the Queen Mother and Father Lewis Innes, principal of the Scots College in Paris, from the conduct of his political affairs,[57] but nothing could stem the decline in Mar's own political position. When James Murray returned from London to the Jacobite court in July 1718 as the representative of the party in England (including what remained of the former Bolingbroke faction and that headed by Bishop Atterbury), it was clear that Mar's mentor, the Earl of Oxford, was acting a highly equivocal part and, in Mar's description, allying himself to people 'who he knew were very farr from being friends to me'.[58] Criticism of Mar burst into print in the form of a pamphlet entitled *A Letter from a Gentleman in Rome,* which accused Mar of monopolising the King, surrounding him with a small group of Scottish favourites, insulting and abusing the best of his own countrymen (including the Earl Marischal) and sending the 'good Englishman', the Duke of Ormonde, on a wild goose chase to the Baltic (where Ormonde was waiting disconsolately for an opportunity to negotiate a joint treaty on behalf of the Jacobites with Sweden and Russia).[59] The crowning blow, as far as Mar was concerned, came in the autumn of 1718, when Giulio, Cardinal Alberoni, invited Ormonde to Spain to command a Spanish expedition against England. The court in Rome was kept completely in the dark until Ormonde had actually arrived in Spain and had nominated Mar's enemy, the Earl Marischal, to head a separate attempt against Scotland.[60]

James III, always eager to seize any chance for armed action, immediately responded to Alberoni's invitation, but it is clear that Mar disagreed with the proposal and had no intention of involving himself in a second rebellion, a decision which may have been influenced by the fact that Lady Mar had joined him in Rome in November 1718. After James, accompanied by Colonel Hay, set out for Spain in February 1719, Mar penned his letter of resignation as Secretary of State and, in his valedictory advice to James, suggested that after the Restoration, the King should rely largely on those politicians whose co-operation with Oxford had been notable.[61] Mar himself, accompanied by James Drummond, second Duke of Perth, set out from Rome at the same time as the King, ostensibly to join him in Spain; instead of taking the agreed-upon route to Genoa, they crossed into the territory of the Milanese, under the control of George I's ally, the Emperor, and were arrested and imprisoned at Milan. Both Stair and James Murray, who had been left in charge of the Jacobite court during James's absence, suspected that Mar had deliberately induced his own arrest in order to have an excuse not to participate in the Spanish invasion attempt.[62] When Mar, released from his Imperial captivity, returned to Rome in March, he and Murray quarrelled bitterly.[63] On 24 March, Mar applied to James for permission to ask France for leave to retire to Bourbon[64] (a letter which he knew James could not receive for weeks), and on 9 April, leaving his wife in Rome, Mar set off yet again, this time with Geneva as his goal. There was little doubt in the minds of the British government that Mar virtually invited a second arrest in the Swiss capital:[65] the first person he notified of his arrival there was the Earl of Stair[66] and, on 22 May, immediately after his arrest, Mar again wrote to Stair, renewing his request to go to Bourbon, telling Stair that he had resigned the Jacobite seals and insinuating that he wished to make proposals to the British government through Stair, 'if it will be thought worth the while to be lissened to'.[67] Stair, believing that 'there is nothing more likely to hurt ye Pretender's interest than that ye chief of ye Protestant party leaves his side',[68] dispatched Mar's letter to Hanover, where George I, Sunderland and Stanhope then were. He later added his personal belief that Mar would never sever his ties with the Pretender without being promised something concrete — a pension and an eventual pardon — by the government. Through this means, Stair advised Stanhope, 'vous serez toujours maitre de sa conduite, et insensiblement il se detachera du Pretendant, et deviendra suspect à luy et à son parti, et vous tirerez de luy insensiblement ce qu'il refuseroit de faire, si l'on l'exigeroit de luy par une capitulation'.[69] Proferring the baits of a pension and a pardon, Stair relentlessly drew Mar out: on 30 June, Mar informed him that 'I have had a mind some time to retire from all kind of business' and suggested that he might be allowed to live quietly in France, not 'giving any disturbance nor hurting the interest you serve'.[70] On 8 July, Mar became more explicit, hoping 'that there would be some difference made betwixt him & a certain abandon'd rake [i.e., Bolingbroke], who being without principle never acted by any & who . . . was contented to do anything how durty soever'. Mar's goal was to gain his pardon by stages while keeping face with his followers. He told Stair he hoped to live peacefully 'without making a confession of his faith'; he promised not to disturb George I's government, 'but further than that he can at this time do or say nothing; a time may come when it may be otherwayes, but of that it is needless to say anything just now'.[71]

Mar now embarked on an elaborate double game, determined to extract what he could from the British government without sacrificing his ties with the Jacobites until the most propitious moment for himself personally. His brother-in-law, John Hay, later reviewed Mar's letters to James III and concluded that Mar 'was resolved not to lose what he had from the Government of England, without he saw a visible certainty of the King's Restoration, and this is the most favourable Construction can be put upon them'.[72] Mar (as always, only after he had made his advances to the government) informed James in general terms of what he was doing, but without going into details of his negotiations with the British ministers.[73] Neither James nor Hay suspected Mar's fundamental sincerity, and the King always loyally provided an *ex post facto* approval for the actions of his erstwhile Secretary of State.[74] Mar was, however, less successful in persuading the British government of his sincerity. By the late summer of 1719 it was being widely rumoured in Jacobite circles that Mar was negotiating with the government[75] and Mar hotly denied this charge — labelling such suspicions 'the ordinary & never failing custome of Torys'[76] — in letters of his closest associates including Sir Hugh Patterson. Copies of these letters were soon on the desk of Craggs.[77] Indeed, neither Craggs nor Sunderland was willing to promise Mar anything unless he declared openly that he had deserted the Jacobite cause.[78] 'I don't find he is willing to be a Spy there for us,' Craggs complained to Stair, '& what are we to pay him for unless he gives us at least ye appearance of having abandoned that cause . . . If by any rules of cunning, he would keep well there without letting us know what he transacts, & avoid declaring for us, I understand his meaning, but who will be able to guess at ours in doing any thing for him?'[79] In any case, given the continuing split in the Whig party and the administration's precarious majority in the House of Commons, the British ministers refused to ask Geneva for Mar's release from his imprisonment;[80] in October 1719 the Hanoverian ministry asked Geneva to continue to keep Mar under arrest.[81] In December, Craggs made it clear to Stair that the ministry had determined, if any parliamentary pardons were granted, that Bolingbroke stood first in line.[82] By February 1720, Mar was exasperated by the continued delay of his release and threatened to Stair to 'go on in his old way . . . He believes now that thers nothing intended in his affair by his Creditors [i.e., the British government], if he will not do something that may expose him, which he thinks is all they design'.[83] By the time Mar was released in June 1720 and was allowed to proceed to Bourbon, he had apparently been assured that Lady Mar's jointure of £1,500 would be regularly paid and had been given a promise of a future pension, as well as £1,000 in ready money supplied by Stair.

By this time, Lady Mar had joined her husband in Geneva, full of stories of the high-handed behaviour of James Murray and his sister, the wife of John Hay, during the Pretender's absence from Rome and the arrival there of his new Queen, Clementina Sobieska. Although Mar's standard excuse for refusing James's reiterated pleas that he rejoin him in Italy was the state of his health (for which he finally visited Bourbon in the late summer of 1720),[84] he also made it clear that he would never return to the exiled court as long as the despised Murray was there.[85] In October 1720, Mar and his wife returned to Paris and he immediately complained to the new British envoy, Sir Robert Sutton, that the hoped-for pension had not yet been paid[86] and gratuitously warned Sutton of the arrival in Paris of Colonel Hay 'on private business'.[87] At the same time, through experience, force of personality and on James's insistence, Mar seized control of James's business in Paris and of his communications with England through his influence over both General Dillon and George Granville, Lord Lansdowne (who had settled in Paris in July 1720). Mar, Dillon, and Lansdowne henceforth operated as 'the Triumvirate',[88] although it is clear that the major decisions were made by Mar, and the other men unwittingly served as his dupes to cover his actions with their approval.

Despite Mar's assurances to Sir Robert Sutton that Hay came to Paris in November 1720 on 'private business', he in fact had been sent by James to try to induce Mar to return to Rome. Unaware of the fact that Mar had ignored James's positive order a year earlier not to hold further communication with British diplomats,[89] James felt aggrieved by Mar's demands that James Murray be sent away from Rome, believing that Mar was trying 'to force me to receive him on his own terms'.[90] Hay, defending his brother-in-law against James's suspicions by assuring the King that Mar was 'Very sincere',[91] fell in with the Triumvirate by strongly recommending Murray's dismissal and praising Mar's contacts with the French court.[92] Even though James agreed with his new favourite that Murray must be dismissed to preserve peace within the movement, James remained bitter at Mar's refusal to return to Rome, particularly 'after all the pains I have been at to support his [Mar's] caracter & reputation, that he should not so much as thank me for it', and warning Hay 'not to be carryed away with appearances'.[93] As yet, however, the King and Hay suspected that Mar was actuated against Murray by a desire for personal vengeance, and did not consider that his political loyalty was in any doubt.

In fact, Mar had no intention of returning to Rome, for the political vistas in England were now more attractive to him than they had been since the death of Queen Anne. The Whig reunion of April 1720 and the reintroduction of Walpole and Townshend into high office had been quickly followed by the bursting of the South Sea Bubble in August, for which Sunderland as First Lord of the Treasury received the greatest blame. In February 1721, Sunderland's principal ministerial colleagues, Stanhope and Craggs, both died suddenly and — although Sunderland still retained George I's confidence — he was left isolated within his own administration. G. V. Bennett has examined the ways and means Sunderland used to acquire Jacobite support during the last sessions of the first Hanoverian parliament in order to prepare for the general elections which were mandated by law for 1722.[94] Part and parcel of this policy was the government's sudden offer to Mar of a pension of £2,000 per annum in January 1721, to be paid in addition to Lady Mar's jointure of £1,500. Mar, informing James III of his acceptance of this pension, claimed that the government had also offered him a pardon but that he had held out for a general indemnity for all Jacobite rebels and that the pension was merely a stop-gap; he justified his acceptance 'for which there was a necessity for me to make an immediat answer', claiming that he had consulted Dillon,[95] but failing to add what Dillon later admitted: the offer was based on the British government's expectation that Mar would maintain a 'correspondence' with their representatives in Paris.[96] Incredibly, not even Mar's admitted acceptance of a government pension alerted either James or Hay to the danger of such a step, or to the thought that the government might demand value for money. In his reply to Mar's letter, James said that 'what it contains appears so clear to me that I did not need to take much time to consider on the matter' and gave Mar a warm and enthusiastic endorsement of his step, an approval which was later to haunt the King.[97]

Mar, with the government's money safely in his pocket (he claimed to James in September 1721 that he had only received £400),[98] could see that he needed for his ultimate goal — the granting of a parliamentary pardon — a sufficient degree of control over the Jacobite movement to be able to draw large numbers of Jacobite followers into accepting a general indemnity if and when the government should offer it. His easy control of the Triumvirate[99] led Mar to believe that he could render the King a political cypher by removing John Hay from Rome, the last remaining Briton there capable of giving James sound political advice. In August 1721, in his private correspondence with Hay which Mar maintained separately from that with the King, Mar initiated a theme which was to become more pronounced and more frequent through the years to come: Mrs. Hay (the sister of the snubbed James Murray) had thoroughly alienated Queen Clementina and should be removed from the court in Rome, preferably to be sent back to Scotland.[100] Of course, Mar added, Hay must remain at the King's side but, knowing the trouble and expense to which Hay had been to have his wife join him in exile, Mar could not have believed that Hay would settle for a permanent separation from her. At the same time, Mar was busily proposing to the King various articles for a new constitution for Scotland, which were eventually to figure in his 'Legacies'.[101] His major goal, he later assured Hay, was not to return Scotland to her pre-Revolution position as a technically independent kingdom actually governed from London, but to establish Scotland as a fully sovereign nation which merely shared the same monarch with her neighbouring kingdoms.[102] Without demur, James III dutifully approved Mar's proposals,[103] an approval which Mar used widely in Jacobite circles in Paris to demonstrate his *bona fides* to dubious Scottish exiles as a true patriot and statesman. Indeed, the docility with which James accepted all of Mar's suggestions must be attributed largely to the influence of Hay over the King. It was only after October 1721, when James Murray finally arrived in Paris from Rome and a series of running quarrels began between him and Mar, that chinks in the alliance between Mar and Hay began to appear.[104] At the beginning of 1722, James III and Hay appeared to ignore warnings from their agents in London of widespread rumours that Mar was relying upon Sunderland to procure his pardon,[105] and information from John Sempill, Sir Robert Sutton's butler in Paris, that Mar was paying secret visits in disguise to the British embassy.[106] The association of Lord and Lady Mar with at least one British diplomat, Alexander Hume-Campbell, Lord Polwarth, was quite public: in March 1722, again after the fact, Mar notified James that he would be 'drinking a bottle with Pol[warth] & speaking pritty freely to him of the miserable situation of their country',[107] and Hay conveyed the King's warm approval of Mar's plans.[108]

For Mar, the bubble burst with the unexpected death of Sunderland on 19/30 April 1722. Dr. Bennett elsewhere has brilliantly set out Mar's role in the 'Atterbury Plot': how the government, receiving intelligence warnings from Cardinal Dubois and others of an imminent Jacobite uprising, dispatched Marlborough's bastard nephew, Colonel Charles Churchill, to Paris with a letter signed by Walpole, Townshend and Carteret, demanding that Mar co-operate with the government by writing an incriminating letter to Atterbury, or risk the loss of his pension and public exposure as a traitor to 'the Cause'.[109] This Mar did, although Carteret suspected 'à present qu'il se soit rangé avec l'ennemy'.[110] The only thing to add to Bennett's account is a recital of the hypocrisy of Mar, who three months earlier had complained bitterly to Hay of some Jacobites 'for proposing to make applications to the Elector of Hanover'.[111] On 11 May, the day he penned his incriminating letter to Atterbury, Mar informed James that the government had received information from Rome of an imminent Jacobite rising[112] and assured Hay that he had done everything possible to lull the government's suspicions.[113] Very quickly, despite the continued insistence of the Triumvirate,[114] it became clear that the vital leak of information had occurred in Paris rather than Rome. On 8 June, Mar reported to Hay the rumours in England that Mar had revealed the plot to the government, but dismissed them as a Whig attempt to discredit him, saying it was 'scarsly to be believed that he could find his account in it'.[115] As the rumours continued to circulate and to grow in force, Dillon and Lansdowne[116] were pressed in service, writing to James that Mar had been unfairly traduced and libelled.[117] On 31 August, James responded to Lansdowne's appeal with a warm endorsement of all Mar's actions[118], a letter which was subsequently shown widely in Paris to demonstrate James's complete approval of Mar's conduct.[119]

James's letter to Lansdowne was written before he could receive one written from Paris on 22 August by Lucius Cary, sixth Viscount Falkland, who had been dispatched from England by Atterbury to warn James that Mar had betrayed Jacobite secrets in return for a secret pension.[120] This seems to have been the first moment when James began to suspect that Mar had been less than completely honest with him. The receipt of Falkland's warning in Rome was quickly followed by the arrival there of John Sempill, who was able to provide James and Hay with detailed evidence of Mar's meetings with Sir Robert Sutton and other British diplomats. James was now trapped: his past approval of everything Mar had written could easily be used by the Duke in his own self-justification. James began quietly but firmly to withdraw his confidence from Mar, but he naturally hoped to avoid a public *éclat* which might expose his own naïveté. He consequently did everything possible to appease Mar and, in December 1722, granted Mar's request (to be kept strictly secret) for an Irish dukedom in the Jacobite peerage.[121]

The publication of the Commons' report on the Atterbury Plot provided the final proof of Mar's complicity in writing the incriminating letter to Atterbury, although the government did not print all the details of Mar's co-operation with Churchill. Mar's actions, however, had not gained him new credit in Whitehall and the government was not edified by his continued close association with the Jacobites: 'The indulgence My Lord Mar has received from the King,' an agent of George I reported to Horatio Walpole, 'deserves a better return than what he makes; but I perceive the Character his own Countreymen give of him truly confirm'd, that he can be no more just to any one than gratefull, & a double part is his master piece.'[122]

Bishop Atterbury, banished from Britain for life under a bill of pains and penalties, arrived in Brussels in the summer of 1723, and James immediately dispatched Hay to consult with him. Hay, by this time, was thoroughly distrustful of his brother-in-law's motives, particularly as Mar escalated his demands that Hay send his wife away and had brought in Lansdowne and Dillon to advise Hay himself to retire from court;[123] in addition, Mar had advised the appointment of his close friend, Andrew Michael Ramsay, the famous disciple of Fénélon, as tutor to the young Prince Charles Edward, and both James and Hay suspected that Mar intended Ramsay to replace Hay as James's *de facto* Secretary of State.[124] During his journey to Paris, Hay met Lord Falkland on the road, who assured him that Mar was still receiving his government pension of £2,000 per year. When Hay asked Mar about this in Paris, Mar replied, 'he wished the particular was true, for then he would not be so much in debt as he is'. At the same time, Mar showed Hay a copy of a memorial[125] which he had written, Ramsay had translated into French, and Dillon had presented to the Regent, the duc d'Orléans, two weeks earlier, without any consultation with the court in Rome: significantly, Mar kept the memorial secret from Lansdowne, the English member of the Triumvirate. The memorial in effect proposed that France should support a Jacobite restoration, which would completely remove all English control over both Scotland and Ireland and result in French troops being permanently stationed in the two kingdoms. Mar could not possibly have believed that any English politician would have supported such a proposal, nor could he have believed that Orléans would have seen fit to sever his close alliance with George I. Hay who was still attempting to defend Mar in his letters to James, called the memorial a 'ticklish business',[126] but James — who now saw Mar's game — clearly suspected that Mar had given Orléans the memorial with the hope that it would be handed in turn to the Brtish government and published in England with the hope of discrediting the Pretender there. James even feared that Mar might arrange to have Hay arrested in Flanders when he went there to confer with Atterbury.[127]

When he met Atterbury in Brussels in November 1723, the Bishop soon convinced Hay of Mar's guilt and also that he should accept the King's repeated offers to make him Secretary of State in name as well as in fact. When Hay passed through Paris on his return to Rome, he had a final interview with his former patron, which turned into an angry quarrel,[128] which Mar finished by saying, 'we'll see whose Arse is blackest'.[129] Mar began to send a steady stream of letters to James in Rome, accusing Hay of personal jealousy and of having biased Atterbury against him; this met with no direct response from the King, nor did James acknowledge the receipt of the memorial which Mar had sent to him only two months after it had been presented to the Regent.[130] James was now convinced that 'had he [Mar] all the mind in the world to breed disturbance in my family & to strip me of all honest & capable men devoted to me, hee could not act otherways than he doth'.[131] On 24 April 1724 Mar wrote a long letter to James, accusing him of neglecting his faithful servants exiled in France and of allowing his Highlanders to starve;[132] this struck a sour note at a court which was begging for the payment of the small pensions allotted by France and Spain, and Hay suspected that Mar wished to encourage some clan leaders to accept pardons, so that he could follow in their wake.[133] Indeed, Mar later admitted to James that he had shown a copy of his letter to some of the Highlanders in self-justification and to prove that he advocated their interests.[134]

In June 1724, Lady Mar returned from Paris to London and it was widely suspected that she went over to negotiate her husband's pardon: James Murray warned the King that when Mar 'finds he can no longer support the double part he has undertaken on this side, he will suggest measures to the English government in order to divide those who suffer for you abroad and carry as many of them as he can to accept terms'.[135] In a threatening letter to Rome on 3 July, Mar mentioned the possibility that Parliament might enact a general amnesty during the coming year.[136]

By this time, Bishop Atterbury had arrived in Paris and, in a fatal mistake, Mar volunteered to let Atterbury examine his personal papers in order to remove his suspicions. Atterbury found positive proof that Mar had co-operated with Churchill in 1722 and, from that moment, Mar's Jacobite career was ruined. Mar wrote to James on 19 July, furiously denying everything and blaming Hay and Atterbury — whom he later styled 'the Vizer & Mufty' — for plotting his ruin and, for the first time, he threatened to publish his case if the King did not issue him a clean bill of health.[137] James's response to this was publicly to withdraw his confidence from

Dillon and Lansdowne (who, in Hay's contemptuous phrase, 'acts the part of the Duke of Mar's Scribbler')[138] in November 1724, when it became clear that they would not sever their close connections with Mar.[139] Mar, who was now loudly bemoaning the fact that Lady Mar's jointure was 'all we have', presented a full-scale defence of his actions to the King on 15 January 1725 and, when he received no response whatsoever, sent a second letter on 18 March, threatening to publish the King's letters and the memorial to the Regent,[140] which he did in a handwritten justification which was sent to London and Scotland in the summer of 1725.[141]

Mar's enemies were now triumphant at the court in Rome. In March 1725, Hay was named Secretary of State and Earl of Inverness; during the summer, James summoned James Murray to return to Rome, gave him the title of Earl of Dunbar, and created him 'the Protestant governor' for the Prince of Wales, Charles Edward. Mar now played what he hoped would be his trump card: the Queen, Clementina Sobieska. Confident, as he had informed Hay in 1721, that 'Andrew [Clementina] cannot well fail of getting the better of every body with Peter [James] in time',[142] Mar had always carefully maintained his contacts with Queen Clementina, both through the Duchess of Mar, who maintained a friendly correspondence with the Queen,[143] and through Mrs. Dorothy Sheldon, Dillon's sister-in-law, who had been brought from France to Rome as the Prince's governess[144] and who was now displaced by the new Earl of Dunbar. In November 1725, inspired and encouraged by her close confidante, Mrs. Sheldon, Clementina demanded that her husband dismiss Lord and Lady Inverness; Clementina's religious advisers, including Pope Benedict XIII, demanded that Dunbar also be discharged. When James refused to dismiss Protestants from his court, Clementina fled the Muti Palace for a Roman convent, beginning a separation which was to last over two years and to divide the whole Jacobite movement into a King's Party and a Queen's Party. The Triumvirate led the Queen's supporters in Paris and John Sempill assured Bishop Atterbury 'that none doubted but those of Marr's faction but that he, Marr, was the Person by the assistance of Dillon and Mrs. Sheldon, that . . . Projected & Spirited up the Lady [Clementina] to act as She has done'.[145]

By this time, Mar's Jacobite career was largely finished. He dropped his regular correspondence with James III in December 1725,[146] and was shunned by most Jacobites, other than Dillon and Lansdowne. In May 1727 Mar wrote to James for the last time 'to show & make plain to you the uprightness & sincerity of all my actions & intentions towards you',[147] but at the same time Mar's brother, Lord Grange, was appealing to Sir Robert Walpole for a pardon for Mar and the re-establishment of his estates and title;[148] Grange renewed his instances to the leading ministers after George I's sudden death in June 1727.[149] In October, Mar himself appealed to Horatio Walpole for the support of his brother,[150] but the chief minister casually dismissed Mar's appeal: 'What passed in that affair in the late King's time was an application from Lord Grange,' Robert Walpole reported in forwarding Mar's letter to the Duke of Newcastle, 'which I allways understood to have been given very little encouragement, nor can I see any reason for altering my opinion at present.'[151]

In November 1727, Lady Mar first displayed the symptoms which were later to lead to her declaration as a lunatic in 1730 and the awarding of legal custody (and control of her marital jointure) to her sister, Lady Mary Wortley Montagu. In October 1729 Mar was forced to flee France to avoid his creditors, taking up residence in the Austrian Netherlands,[152] and Lewis Innes concluded of Mar that 'no man ever had a more glorious game to play & play'd it worse than he has done from first to last'.[153] When Mar died in Aix la Chapelle in May 1732, his death passed almost unnoticed in Jacobite circles.

From the Revolution of 1688, it was always the policy of successive British governments to render the probity and honesty of various Jacobite prime ministers suspect, both to the Jacobites themselves and to their foreign allies. In the case of John Erskine, Earl of Mar, the government found an eager and effective collaborator, whose duplicity in exile did as much, if not more, to weaken the Jacobite movement than had his military incapacity in the Fifteen.

NOTES

1. The exception has been Maurice Bruce, 'The Duke of Mar in Exile', *Transactions of the Royal Historical Society (TRHS)*, 4th series, XX (1937), 61-82, with whom I disagree in almost all my conclusions.

2. Hon. Stuart Erskine, ed., *The Earl of Mar's Legacies to Scotland and to his son, Lord Erskine, 1722-1727, Publications of the Scottish History Society* XXVI (Edinburgh, 1896), 141.

3. Royal Archives (RA), Stuart Papers (SP) 74/95: John Hay to James Murray, 23 May 1724, Rome; I acknowledge the gracious permission of Her Majesty the Queen to quote from the Windsor archives. It would appear that Hay underestimated Mar's worth; in 1710, a Whig agent who labelled Mar as a 'Court Tory', put his estate at 'not £3,000': Christ Church, Oxford, Wake MSS 17, f. 269v: Richard Dongworth to Bishop William Wake, 11 November 1710, Edinburgh. I am grateful to Clyve Jones of the Institute of Historical Research who called this reference to my attention and provided me with a copy of it.

4. P. W. J. Riley, *The English Ministers and Scotland, 1707-1727* (London, 1964), 25-6.

5. HMC *Stuart* II, 77: Mar to Robert Leslie, 12 April 1716, Avignon.

6. Riley, *English Ministers and Scotland,* 239.

7. Geoffrey Holmes, 'Harley, St. John, and the Death of the Tory Party', *Britain after the Glorious Revolution,* ed. G. S. Holmes (London, 1969), 216-237.

8. Mark Thomson, *The Secretaries of State, 1681-1782* (London, 1932), 32-3.

9. Riley, *English Ministers and Scotland,* 160.

10. Erskine, *Earl of Mar's Legacies,* 176-8.

11. HMC *Mar & Kellie,* 505: Mar to Lord Grange, 7 August 1714, Whitehall.

12. Niedersächsisches Staatsarchiv (NSA), Hannover 93, 12A, II-11, vol. 1, ff. 380-1: British Privy Council to Georg Ludwig, Saturday, 31 July/11 August 1714, 11 a.m., Kensington; vol. 2, ff. 100-01: Original Proclamation of George I, 1/12 August 1714, St. James's.

13. John Nichols, ed. *The Epistolary Correspondence, Visitation Charges, Speeches, and Miscellanies of the Rt. Rvd. Francis Atterbury, Bishop of Rochester,* V, (London, 1798), 215-217: Mar to George I, 30 August 1714 OS; cf. James Browne, *A History of the Highlands and of the Highland Clans,* II (Glasgow, 1834), 258-9.

14. John, Master of Sinclair, *Memoirs of the Rebellion* (Edinburgh, 1858), 60.

15. Scottish Record Office (SRO), G.D. 135/145: [Mar to Stair], 8 July 1719 [Geneva]; cf. Erskine, *Legacies of the Earl of Mar*, 176.

16. For Hanoverian suspicions, see Riley, *English Ministers and Scotland*, 254-5; for French suspicions, Archive des Affaires Étrangères (AAE), Correspondence Politique (CP) Angleterre 246, ff. 205-7: duc d'Aumont to Torcy, 29 September 1713 NS, London.

17. Mar himself dated the beginning of his correspondence from 1710 (Erskine, *Legacies of the Earl of Mar*, 163), which is supported by a cypher (RA, SP Box 5/16) annotated '1710' by the Pretender; James Drummond, first Duke of Perth, later claimed that Mar was 'toujours en Correspondance avec le Roy' throughout Mar's tenure as Secretary of State: British Library (BL), Add. MSS 31, 256, ff. 164-6: Perth to Cardinal Gualterio, 23 October 1715, St. Germain.

18. Erskine, *Legacies of the Earl of Mar*, 163.

19. Felix Salomon, *Geschichte des letzten Ministeriums Königin Annas von England und der englischen Thronfolgefrage* (Gotha, 1894), 339-41; cf. AAE, CP Angleterre 261, pp. 206-7: François Gaultier to James III, 19 February 1714 NS, London; 254, f. 74: [Gaultier to James], 22 February 1714 NS, London.

20. HMC *Stuart* I, 314: Berwick to James, 8 April 1714, St. Germain.

21. AAE, CP Angleterre 257, f. 312: d'Iberville's Memoire [to Torcy], 14 August 1714 NS, London, quoting Mar.

22. National Library of Scotland, MSS 5072, No. 26: [Mar] to 'Dear Pap' [Lord Grange?], 23 December 1714 OS, London: again, I must thank Dr. Jones for providing me with a copy of this reference. For Mar's equivocal attitude towards the Union after 1707, see W. L. Burn, 'The Scottish Policy of John, sixth Earl of Mar, 1707-1715', *Huntington Library Quarterly (HLQ)* II (1938-9), 439-48.

23. NSA, Cal. Br. 24, England 123, ff. 70-1: Robethon's newsletter to Hanoverian council, 8/19 March 1715, St. James's.

24. *The Collected Works of Henry St. John, Viscount Bolingbroke* (London, 1809), I, 69; as late as August 1721, James III was corresponding with Oxford through Mar: RA, SP 54/88: James III to Oxford, 8 August 1721, Albano.

25. NSA, Cal. Br. 24, England 123, ff. 199-201: Robethon's newsletter to Hanoverian council, 19/30 August 1715; cf. AAE, CP Angleterre 269, ff. 347-51: d'Iberville to Torcy, 29 August 1715 NS, London.

26. HMC *Stuart* I, 528-9: Bolingbroke's Memorial 'to be sent to the King's friends in England', 13 August 1715.

27. AAE, CP Angleterre 274, ff. 132-5: d'Iberville to Torcy, 30 August 1715 NS, London, quoting Lansdowne.

28. G. H. Jones, *The Mainstream of Jacobitism* (Cambridge, Mass., 1954), 108-9; cf. John Baynes, *The Jacobite Rising of 1715* (London, 1970), 32-35.

29. BL, Add. MSS 31, 256, ff. 190-2: Perth to Gualterio, 29 March 1716, St. Germain.

30. HMC *Stuart* I, 523: Mar's Memorial to James, 5/16 July 1715, London.

31. HMC *Stuart* II, 389: Earl of Southesk to Mar, 2 January 1717, Paris, misdated '1716' by editor; cf. Claude Nordmann, *La crise du Nord au début de XVIIIe siècle* (Paris, 1962), 47.

32. HMC *Stuart* II, 169: Lewis Innes to Mar, 20 May 1716 St Germain; 292-3: Mar to Harry Straiton, 19 July 1716, Avignon.

33. HMC *Stuart* I, 443: James to Bolingbroke, 21 October 1715, Commercy; see p. 445 for the warrant, dated 22 October.

34. BL, Stowe MSS 228, ff. 284-6: Stair to Robethon, 26 May 1716, Paris.

35. HMC *Stuart* II, 150: Earl of Southesk to Mar, 14 May 1716, Paris; 169; Lewis Innes to Mar, 20 May 1716, St. Germain.

36. HMC *Stuart* II, 99: Mar to Lewis Innes, 20 April 1716, Avignon; cf 107: Mar to Robert Arbuthnot, 22 April 1716.

37. For 'The earl of Mar's Journal, printed at Paris', see Robert Patten, *The History of the late Rebellion* (London, 1717), 241-271; for a study of how Mar's *Journal* was transformed by Defoe into a telling piece of anti-Jacobite propaganda, see John Robert Moore, 'Defoe's Hand in *A Journal of the Earl of Marr's Proceedings* (1716)', *Huntington Library Quarterly (HLQ)* XVII (1953-4), 209-228.

38. HMC *Stuart* II, 165-6: Mar to Innes, 19 May 1716, Avignon.

39. HMC *Stuart* II, 12: Mar to Harry Straiton, 11 March 1716, Paris.

40. HMC *Stuart* II, 285: Mar to John Menzies, 16 July 1716, Avignon; 292: Mar to Harry Straiton, 19 July 1716, Avignon; 330: Mar to Sir John Erskine, 7 August 1716.

41. Colonel Hay married Stormont's daughter, Margery Murray, in June 1715.

42. G. V. Bennett, *The Tory Crisis in Church and State, 1688-1730: The career of Francis Atterbury, Bishop of Rochester* (Oxford, 1975), 207-12.

43. Public Record Office (PRO), State Papers (SP) 78/161, f. 81: Thomas Crawford to Addison, 8 May 1717, Paris.

44. SRO, G.D. 135/145: 'John Murray' [Mar] to 'Captain John Brown' [Stair], 30 December 1716. 'Frank' was Mar's code name for Frances, Countess of Mar.

45. SRO, G.D. 135/145: Mar to Stair, 12 March, 30 May 1717, Paris.

46. HMC *Stuart* IV, 315: Mar to James III, 4 June 1717 [Paris].

47. BL, Stowe MSS 230, ff. 136-9: Dubois to Robethon, 9 June [1717], Paris.

48. SRO, G.D. 135/145: Mar to Stair, 30 May 1717, Paris.

49. BL, Stowe MSS 230, ff. 143-4: Dubois to Robethon, 13 June 1717, Paris.

50. BL. Stowe MSS 230, ff. 160-1: Stair to Robethon, 14 July 1717, Paris.

51. BL, Add. MSS 9129, ff. 41v-46: Mar to Sunderland [transcript by William Coxe], 15 September 1717; the letter is extensively quoted in Stuart J. Reid's MSS 'Report and Classification of the Blenheim Palace Archives' (1891), I, 60-1, dated '17 September'; in the summer of 1974, the original was not in D I 33, although it may be discovered among the Blenheim Papers now in the British Library. I am grateful to His Grace, the Duke of Marlborough, and the Trustees of the British Library for permission to quote from the Blenheim Papers.

52. HMC *Stuart* V, 50-2: Mar to Cadogan, 17 September 1717; cf. VI, 299: John Menzies to Mar, 31 March/11 April 1718. [London].

53. SRO, G.D. 135/145: Mar to Stair, 9 October 1717 [Paris].

54. Philip Yorke, Earl of Hardwicke, *Miscellaneous State Papers* II (London, 1778), 561: Stair to Craggs, 25 October 1717, Paris; cf' BL, Stowe MSS 230, ff. 249-50: Stair to Robethon, 12 October 1717, Paris.

55. This intercepted Jacobite correspondence is found in BL, Stowe MSS 232 *passim*; the letters were intercepted in Leyden and transmitted to London by William Leathes, British resident in Brussels: PRO, SP 77/67, ff. 220-1: Leathes to Townshend, 3 October 1716, Brussels.

56. SRO, G.D. 135/141, vol. 12: Robethon to Stair, 10 September 1717 NS, Hampton Court.

57. BL, Stowe MSS 231, f. 79: Stair to Robethon, 4 May 1718, Paris; cf. HMC *Polwarth* I, 496, 497: Robethon to Polwarth, 10, 13 May 1718 NS, London.

58. RA, SP 45/108: Mar to James, 8 December 1719 [Geneva]; cf. BL, Stowe MSS 232, ff. 164-5; Walkinshaw to Sir Hugh Patterson, 22 December 1718, Paris.

59. See *A Letter from a gentleman in R[ome] dated 15 September 1718. To a friend at London* (London, W. Jones, 1718). Mar and his family attributed the authorship to Abbé Thomas John Strickland: RA, SP 42/59: Sir Hugh Patterson to Mar, 24 February 1719. cf. BL, Stowe MSS 231, ff. 245-6: Stair to Robethon, 30 NoVember 1718, Paris; cf. 232, f. 130: [James] Hamilton to Sir Hugh Patterson, 30 July 1718 OS, London.

60. For Stair's suspicions that Mar's later actions were motivated by the fact that Ormonde's party now had the upper hand within the Jacobite movement, see SRO, G.D. 135/141, vol. 19A: Stair to Stanhope (Private), 27 May 1719, Paris.

61. The excerpts from Mar's letters to James III of 4 and 5 February, 1719, printed by Henrietta Tayler, *The Jacobite Court at Rome in 1719, Publications of the Scottish History Society*, third series, XXXI, (Edinburgh, 1938), 143-146, are misleading: see the originals, RA, SP 41/128, 129. The politicians Mar recommended included Henry Boyle, Lord Carleton, and Robert Benson, Lord Bingley.

62. PRO, SP 78/163, ff. 171-2: Stair to Craggs, 11 March 1719, Paris; cf. RA, SP 42/76: James Murray to James III, 6 March 1719, Rome.

63. RA, SP 42/94: Mar to James III, 18 March 1719, Rome.

64. RA, SP 43/1: Mar to James III, 24 March 1719, Rome.

65. SRO, G.D. 135/141, vol. 23: Robethon to Stair, 9 June 1719, Hanover.

66. Hardwicke, *Miscellaneous State Papers*, II, 566-7: Mar to Stair, 6 May 1719, Geneva.

67. Hardwicke, *Miscellaneous State Papers*, II, 567-9: Mar to Stair, 22 May 1719, Geneva.

68. PRO, SP 78/164, f. 51: Stair to Stanhope (Private), 28 May 1719, Paris.

69. PRO, SP 78/164, ff. 179-80: Stair to Stanhope (Private), 17 June 1719, Paris: 'you will always be the master of his conduct, and insensibly he will detach himself from the Pretender and become suspect to him and his party, and you will lead him into doing things which he would refuse to do if extorted of him as a surrender'; cf. BL, Stowe MSS 231, ff. 326-7; Stair to Robethon, 1 October 1719, Paris.

70. SRO, G.D. 135/145: Mar to Stair, 30 June 1719, Geneva.

71. SRO, G.D. 135/145: [Mar to Stair], 8 July 1719 [Geneva].

72. RA, SP 79/91: Hay to Earl of Orrery, 24 January 1725, Rome.

73. RA, SP 43/82: Mar to James III, 9 May 1719, from near Geneva; 44/8, 9: Mar to James III, 3 July 1719, Geneva, partly printed, Tayler, *Jacobite Court*, 170-2; 45/8, 13: Mar to James III, 26, 29 September 1719, Geneva.

74. RA, SP 44/15: James III to Mar, 15 July 1719.

75. SRO G.D. 135/141, vol. 19A: Craggs to Stair, 18/29 June 1719; cf. 135/141: [Mar to Stair]; 9 July 1719, [Geneva]; BL, Stowe MSS 232, ff. 210, 213: [William] Maule to David Patterson, 20 June, 4 July 1719 [Leyden].

76. RA, SP 45/52: Mar to James III, 19 October 1719, Geneva.

77. SRO G.D. 135/141, vol. 19B: Craggs to Stair, 5/16 October 1719, Cockpit.

78. SRO, G.D. 135/141, vol. 19B: Craggs to Stair (Private), 23 July/3 August 1719, Whitehall.

79. SRO, G.D. 135/141, vol. 19B: Craggs to Stair 18/29 August 1719, Cockpit.

80. SRO, G.D. 135/141, vol. 19B: Craggs to Stair, 10/21, 18/29 August, 24 September/5 October, 1719.

81. RA, SP 45/63: Mar to James III, 21 October 1719, Geneva.

82. SRO, G.D. 135/141, vol. 19B: Craggs to Stair, 18/29 December 1719, Cockpit.

83. SRO, G.D. 135/145: [Mar to Stair], 15 February, 1720, [Geneva].

84. PRO, SP 78/167, f. 240: Mar to Sir Robert Sutton, 28 July 1720, near to Paris.

85. RA, SP 49/34: Colin Campbell of Glendaruel to Hay, 8 October 1720, Paris; 49/42: Dillon to James III, 8 October 1720, Paris, quoting Mar.

86. PRO, SP 78/169, ff. 87-92: Sutton to Craggs, 30 October 1720, Paris.

87. PRO, SP 78/169, ff. 118: Mar to Sutton, 2 November 1720, Paris.

88. RA, SP 49/98, 100: Dillon to James III, 28 October 1720, Paris; cf. 48/106: James III to Mar, 17 August 1720, Rome.

89. RA, SP 45/82: James III to Mar, 4 November 1719, Rome.

90. RA, SP 49/114, 50/47: James III to John Hay, 4, 24 November 1720, Rome.

91. RA, SP 50/50: Hay to James III, 26 November 1720, Paris.

92. RA, SP 49/119, 50/20, 35, 74: Hay to James III, 5, 12, 18 November, 3 December 1720 [Paris].

93. RA, SP 50/57: James III to John Hay, 29 November 1720, Rome.

94. G. V. Bennett, 'Jacobitism and the Rise of Walpole', *Historical Perspectives: Studies in English Thought and Society in honour of J. H. Plumb,* ed. Neil McKendrick (London, 1974), 70-92.

95. RA, SP 51/135: Mar to James III, 3 February 1721, Paris.

96. Bodleian, Carte MSS 231, ff. 51-2: Thomas Carte's Memorandum Book, entry for 14 November 1724, quoting Dillon.

97. RA, SP 52/54: James III to Mar, 22 February 1721, Rome. Although the King, in this letter to Mar, said he had discussed the matter with Hay the latter later denied knowledge of James's approval of Mar's actions, although he had by this time reviewed the King's correspondence: *ibid.,* 74/95: Hay to James Murray, 23 May 1724, Rome. In addition, Mar twice wrote to his brother-in-law concerning the government's offers: *ibid.,* 50/16: Mar to [John Hay], 23 December 1720, Paris; 51/17: Mar to Hay, 20 January 1721, Paris.

98. RA, SP 54/141: Mar to James III, 1 September 1721 [Paris].

99. As late as July 1721, James III expressed his complete confidence in the Triumvirate: RA, SP 54/21: James III to John Menzies, 14 July 1721, Rome.

100. RA, SP 54/117, 175, 56/58: Mar to Hay, 18 August, 22 September, 15 December 1721 [Paris].

101. Erskine, *Earl of Mar's Legacies,* 194-205; cf. RA, SP 55/115: Mar to James III, 'Memorial Concerning Scotland', 17 November 1721, Paris.

102. RA, SP 58/6: Mar to Hay, 16 February 1722, Paris.

103. Erskine, *Earl of Mar's Legacies,* 206-12: James III to Mar, 1 January 1722, Rome.

104. RA, SP 56/1, 5: Mar, James Murray to Hay, 1 December 1721, Paris; for Mar's later claims that Hay favoured Murray, see 58/42, 61/12: Mar to Hay, 2 March, 17 August 1722, Paris.

105. RA, SP 56/78: Robert Freebairne to Hay, 20 December 1721 NS, London; for Freebairne's career, see W. J. Couper, 'The Pretender's Printer', *Scottish Historical Review* XV (1918), 103-23.

106. RA, SP 57/100: John Sempill to James III, 27 January 1722 [Paris]; for Sempill, see Paul Fritz, *The English Ministers and Jacobitism between the Rebellions of 1715 and 1745* (Toronto, 1975), 141-2; Bennett, *Tory Crisis,* 283: in June 1721, James Murray reported Mar's 'conferences with Sir Robert Sutton' to Rome: RA, SP 53/159: Murray to Hay, 4 June 1721, Nancy.

107. RA, SP 58/41: Mar to James III, 2 March 1722 [Paris]; for the Mars' social connections with British diplomats, see HMC *Polwarth* III, 79-80, 86, 89: Polwarth's journal entries for 1, 7, 9, 17 March 1722, Paris.

108. RA, SP 58/110: Hay to Mar, 24 March 1722 [Rome].

109. Bennett, *Tory Crisis,* 244-9; according to James Murray, Churchill was 'a great partisan of Walpole's and lyes with his wife': RA, SP 52/161: James Murray to Hay, 26 March 1721, Munich.

110. BL, Add. MSS 22, 517, f. 116: Carteret to Sir Luke Schaub, 7/18 June 1722, Whitehall.

111. RA, SP 58/8: Mar to Hay, 16 February 1722, Paris.

112. RA, SP 59/104: Mar to James III, 11 May 1722 [Paris], written in the hand of Colin Campbell of Glendaruel.

113. RA, SP 59/107: Mar to Hay, 11 May 1722, Paris.

114. RA, SP 61/15: Lansdowne to James III, 20 July 1722 [Paris]; 62/14: Mar to James III, 7 September 1722, Paris; 63/169: Dillon to Hay, 14 December 1722, Paris.

115. RA, SP 60/7: Mar to Hay, 8 June 1722 [Paris].

116. In June 1722, Thomas Crawford reported that Mar had completely lost his reputation with the lower members of the Jacobite party but continued to visit the chiefs regularly: BL, Add. MSS 22, 522, ff. 284-5: Thomas Crawford to Carteret, 13 June 1722, Paris.

117. RA, SP 61/15: Lansdowne to James III, 20 July 1722 [Paris]; 62/14: Mar to James III, 7 September 1722, Paris.

118. This letter was written despite the receipt of one from the Earl of Orrery which cast doubt on Mar's 'zeal for your interest': RA, SP 47/35: Orrery to James, 31 May 1722 NS, London.

119. Bodleian, Carte MSS 231, ff. 51-52: Thomas Carte's Memorandum Book, entry for 14 November 1724, citing the letter of '31 August 1722', no copy of which survives in RA, SP. Lansdowne later quoted part of it to James: 'Is anything more to be lamented than [Mar's] Case? . . . whatever steps he has taken have been with my authority & approbation': RA, SP 75/35: Lansdowne to James III, 26 June 1724 [Paris].

120. RA, SP 61/151: Falkland to James III, 29 August 1722, Paris.

121. RA, SP 63/54, 170: Mar to James III, to John Hay, 23 November, 14 December 1722, Paris; the title was granted on 13 December: see Marquis de Ruvigny and Raineval, *The Jacobite Peerage, Baronetage, Knightage and Grants of Honour* (Edinburgh 1904), 114.

122. PRO, SP 78/179, ff. 328-9: [Westcombe to Horatio Walpole], 24 December 1723, Paris.

123. RA, SP 66/4, 5, 6: Lansdowne, Mar, Dillon to Hay, 25 January 1723 [Paris].

124. RA, SP 69/42: James III to Hay, 20 September 1723 [Albano]; for Ramsay as Mar's agent in Rome, see BL, Add. MSS 32,741, ff. 108-16: [John Sempill to Horatio Walpole], 27 October 1724, Fontainebleau; 32, 746, ff. 472-5: [Sempill to Horatio Walpole], n.d.; for Ramsay's career, see George D. Henderson, *The Chevalier Ramsay* (London, 1952). In 1726, Mar lauded Ramsay's friendship: Erskine, *Legacies of the Earl of Mar*, 161-2.

125. RA, SP 69/85: Hay to James III, 4 October 1723, Paris; Falkland claimed Dillon as his authority concerning Mar's pension.

126. RA, SP 69/115: Hay to James III, 18 October 1723, Paris; Hay later described the memorial as 'a too [sic] edged tool and cutts on all sides': RA, SP 74/142: Hay to James Murray, 13 June 1724, Rome.

127. RA, SP 69/128: James III to Hay, 25 October 1723 [Albano].

128. RA, SP 72/31: Mar to James III, 10 January 1724, Paris.

129. RA, SP 79/98: Hay to Ezeckial Hamilton, 27 January 1725, Rome, quoting Mar; cf. 100/54: Mar to Lord B[almerin]o, 29 September 1724 [Paris].

130. RA, SP 70/14: James III to Hay, 7 November 1723; on 15 November, James wrote to the duc d'Orléans, but did not mention Mar's memorial: 70/56: James III to Orléans, 16 November 1723, Rome.

131. RA, SP 69/98: James III to Hay, 11 October 1723, Albano.

132. RA, SP 73/151: Mar to James III, 24 April 1724, Paris.

p*

133. RA, SP 74/79: Hay to Murray, 16 May 1724 [Rome].

134. SP 74/136: Mar to James III, 12 June 1724 [Paris]; cf. 73/101: Murray to Hay, 9 April 1724, Paris.

135. RA, SP 74/130: Murray to James III, 10 June 1724, Rheims.

136. RA, SP 75/49: Mar to Sir David Nairne, 3 July 1724, Paris.

137. RA, SP 75/115: Mar to James III, 19 July 1724, Paris; for 'Vizer & Mufty', 81/5: Mar to James III, 18 March 1725, Paris.

138. RA, SP 78/8: Hay to Atterbury, 21 November 1724, Rome.

139. RA, SP 77/142: James III to Ormonde, 4 November 1724, Albano; cf. 77/134, 135: Hay to Murray, to Atterbury, 31 October 1724, Albano.

140. RA, SP 79/46: Mar to James III, 15 January 1725, Paris; 81/5; Mar to James III, 18 March 1725, Paris.

141. RA, SP 85/128: James Hamilton to Inverness, 2/13 September 1725, London; 86/8: Peter Smith to Inverness, 10 September 1725 [Boulogne]; for Mar's 'Letter to Scotland', 10 March 1725, and his key for the cant names therein, see SRO, G.D. 124/15, No. 1256/1 and 2.

142. RA, SP 56/58: Mar to Hay, 15 December 1721 [Paris].

143. SRO, G.D. 124/15, No. 1230: Clementina to [Lady Mar], 3 November 1722, Rome: cf. HMC *Mar & Kellie*, 520-1, 528: Clementina to [Lady Mar], 23 September [1719], 9 March 1721, 16 January 1725, Rome; RA, SP 80/90: Frances, Duchess of Mar, to Clementina, 26 February 1725, Paris.

144. Mrs. Sheldon was summoned by James III personally: RA, SP 48/36: James to Dillon, 13 July 1720, Rome.

145. BL, Add. MSS 32/745, ff. 539-40: [John Sempill to Horatio Walpole], 4 May 1726, Paris; for James's suspicions of Mar's role in the separation, see RA, SP 87/97: James III to Atterbury, 19 November 1725, Rome.

146. RA, SP 101/18: Mar to James III, 30 December 1725, Chatou near Paris.

147. RA, SP 106/88: Mar to James III, 5 May 1727, Chatou.

148. SRO, G.D. 124/15, no. 1298/1: James Erskine, Lord Grange, to Sir Robert Walpole, 18 May 1727, London.

149. *Ibid.*, 1298/2, 1302/2: Grange to Robert Walpole, to Townshend, 29 June 1727, Edinburgh.

150. SP 36/3/195: Mar to [Horatio Walpole], 26 October 1727, Chalton.

151. PRO, SP 36/4/13: Robert Walpole to [Newcastle], 6 November 1727, Lynford.

152. RA, SP 131/131: Daniel O'Brien to James III, 31 October 1729, Paris.

153. RA, SP 131/174: Lewis Innes to James III, 7 November 1729, Paris.

10

Choiseul and The Last Jacobite Attempt of 1759

Claude Nordmann

WHEN Robert Nugent, an Irishman and M.P. for Bristol, declared in the House of Commons in November 1754 that there were no Jacobites left in the country, he met with a sharp rebuke from William Pitt. Aiming at William Murray (later Earl of Mansfield), the new solicitor-general, whose family had been connected with the Stuarts, Pitt warned Parliament against the University of Oxford and 'begged the House not to be sure that all the chickens she hatched would ever entirely forget what she had taught them'.[1] Yet the Great Commoner was not ignorant of the progressive disintegration of the Jacobite party. Economic and social changes in Britain had contributed materially to the weakening of the Stuart cause, which now seemed to belong to another age. This decline is the main reason why most historians of the Jacobite movement have deliberately neglected the period I shall try to elucidate. For them, Jacobitism was finished as a political force after the defeat at Culloden in 1746, even in the Highlands of Scotland, not only because of the Acts abolishing the heritable jurisdictions of the clan chiefs and the forfeitures there,[2] but also because of the depopulation of the region.[3]

This is to forget that the descendants of those who rose in the '45 were old enough to take up arms fourteen years later, and was this not what Cumberland himself had feared after his merciless punitive expedition?[4] Moreover, the 'Jacobite Diaspora' had not ceased to grow since the Stuart defeat, forming a pressure group or lobby with many ramifications.[5] It was true that the Anglican clergy had for the most part given in, and even the famous Dr. William King of St. Mary's Hall, Oxford, was soon to rally to the Hanoverian dynasty,[6] but Jacobitism could still revive and even rally some of the Tories,[7] in as much as it represented a kind of nationalism or regionalism, and not only a 'consoling legend' as Christopher Hill has put it.[8] Ireland, 'the frontier of Catholicism', might be expected to take up arms again, the Scottish Highlands remained a threat and there were still supporters of the Stuart cause in Wales.[9] In England Jacobitism could provide a focal point for the discontent over enclosures as well as for the strikes by apprentices and London clothworkers, when continental wars, often regarded as dictated by Hanoverian policies and interests, resulted in higher taxes and impositions on the British people.[10]

These underground and counter-revolutionary forces could act only with the support of foreign powers, the chief of whom was France, one of the principal refuges of the Jacobite Diaspora. The part played by the Duc de Choiseul, still little known as a political figure, in the Jacobite projects of the 1750s has been questioned and pretty well denied in the now superseded works of Coquelle and Bourguet.[11] Sources used, in order to elucidate Choiseul's role, besides the work of Peter de Polnay,[12] have been the Stuart papers at the Quai d'Orsay and at Windsor Castle,[13] the Archives de la Guerre at the château de Vincennes, the Archives Nationales, the Bibliothèque Nationale, and the archives of the château de Serrant. The aim is to set an earlier attempt at defining some aspects of Jacobite emigration[14] in the wider context of the history of international relations. After a long journey in the wilderness, this great historic discipline flourishes anew thanks largely to the energy and scholarship of Professor R. M. Hatton and that of her pupils.[15]

With the Diplomatic Revolution at the beginning of the Seven Years War, and the initial setbacks suffered by the dispirited Anglo-Hanoverian forces, Jacobite hopes reawakened. In 1757 the famous and unfortunate Comte de Lally Tolendal, who had distinguished himself at the head of the Irish brigade at Fontenoy, became governor of Boulogne, an active centre for Anglo-Irish and Jacobite smuggling, and was himself still actively plotting on behalf of the Stuarts.[16] As early as June 1755, he had presented the King's Council with a plan for a descent on England led by Prince Charles Edward Stuart to take place simultaneously with attacks in India and the West Indies. In Lunéville, Stanislas Leszcynski, Duke of Lorraine and elected King of Poland, looked favourably on the project, but his brother-in-law Louis XV and Rouillé, the secretary of state for foreign affairs, vetoed it.[17]

On 27 December 1755, the duc de Belle-Isle was made commander-in-chief of all the French coasts including the Channel and the Atlantic stretching from Dunkirk to Bayonne.[18] The grandson of Fouquet, a marshal of France, a long-standing friend of the Stuarts and allied to the Sobieskis by his second marriage, Belle-Isle became a minister of state on 16 May 1756.[19] According to a Jacobite source, at this time he even went to the château de Navarre, near Evreux, to meet the Young Pretender, who was enjoying there the hospitality of his cousin the duc de Bouillon and urged him to act, since the capture of Port Mahon in Minorca by the maréchal de Richelieu offered a favourable opportunity.[20] The Prince, however, was discouraged and did not seem disposed to listen to Belle-Isle, who was appointed minister for war on 28 February 1758, the first army officer to hold that office in France,[21] and, on 4 May the comte de Maillebois, who commanded the Flemish coasts, boldly offered to lead 25,000 men over to England.[22] He was not listened to either, for cardinal de Bernis' foreign policy was indecisive. The duc de Choiseul, however, who replaced him at the department of foreign affairs on 3 December, was to inject new energy into French policy. The disaster at Rossbach in 1757 had shown up the deficiencies in the French army, and at the same time the English had regained control of the seas and were threatening French colonies. To fight Great Britain more effectively, it was necessary to obtain from Maria Theresa's Austria the right to pull out of the war in Germany.[23] The only person capable of achieving this was Choiseul, a great nobleman, the adviser of Madame de Pompadour, the friend of the *Philosophes* and the *Parlements*, with as much pride in himself as he had in his own country, courteous, generous and bold. Choiseul was worthy of Pitt, his great opponent.[24]

As early as 1 January 1759, Sir Alexander Peter Mackenzie Douglas of Kildin presented his first memorandum to the King's council recommending a descent on England in the winter; the sooner the better, according to him, the English having only 10,000 men at home, the people being dissatisfied with the war and the English fleet being dispersed over the seas.[25] A Scottish knight and a Roman Catholic, Douglas, who had just returned from two missions to the Russian court in 1755 and 1756-7, had been initiated into the *Secret du Roi*. A protégé of the Prince de Conti, he had so far succeeded with the Tsarina Elizabeth and more especially with her vice-chancellor Michael Illarionovitch Vorontzov as to obtain on 1 May Russian accession to the treaty of Versailles concluded in 1756 between France and the House of Austria.[26] Yet the comte de Broglie, who was in charge of the *Secret*, was displeased at Douglas's indiscretions.

In February 1759 Mackenzie Douglas presented a second memorandum, claiming that a descent would be easy and inexpensive since English credit was undermined by the amount of paper money in circulation. He recommended a main landing at Bristol with 30,000 men, in the belief that the Welsh to the west would rise, together with a diversionary operation near Glasgow. Subsequently, the troops massed in Picardy would land either at Newcastle or at Dunbar near Edinburgh, to assist their comrades in the landing near Glasgow.[27]

In the end, Prince Charles Edward Stuart allowed his supporters to persuade him to seek a reconciliation with Madame de Pompadour and to approach Choiseul.[28] The French court sent him a pass and the duc de Belle-Isle arranged a meeting on 7 February 1759 with the duc de Choiseul in the garden of the *Hôtel* de Choiseul in Paris. The unfortunate prince arrived very late, carried by one of his followers and in a state of drunkenness which augured ill for his ability to lead a great enterprise.[29] Choiseul was already ill-disposed because of the rumours concerning Charles Edward's loose way of life, his affair with Clementine Walkinshaw who was accused of spying on the Stuarts for the House of Hanover, and the misunderstanding between Charles Edward and his father James III then residing in Rome.[30] Nevertheless, King Louis' ministers assured Charles Edward that their master was ready to help him to return to Britain and that the work of gathering together men and ships had begun. Once everything was ready, Charles Edward could inform his supporters on the other side of the Channel.[31] As it was, a new passport signed by Choiseul to enable him to return to Bouillon was given him on 9 February. On 14 February Choiseul wrote to Mackenzie Douglas from Marly: 'as soon as the preparations have reached such a point as to enable us to foresee the future safely, I shall make it my duty to inform His Royal Highness, so that *nothing will be done without him but by him and for him*. Until then, the King will always approve the arrangments which His Royal Highness will make with the King his father, but will not appear to influence them.'[32]

Choiseul was subject to pressure from numerous supporters of the Stuarts at Court, in the Church, the Army, the Navy, the East India Company and in Masonic circles.[33] His own brother, Antoine Cleriadus de Choiseul, cardinal archbishop of Cambrai and a friend of Lady O'Brien of Lismore, had interceded on their behalf.[34] Louis, the Dauphin, was also very favourably disposed.[35]

The supporters of the Stuarts, however, were divided not only in the British Isles but within the Jacobite Diaspora itself. Thus Dominique O'Héguerty, comte de Magnières, an Irish gentleman and a freemason, advised the French court in January and May 1759 to propose to Charles Edward that he should be content with the Crown of Ireland. Should he persist in turning it down, James III should be treated with and restored solely to the Irish throne.[36] The Scottish Jacobites were represented in France by William Stuart, Lord Blantyre,[37] called 'Leslie', who had a meeting on 15 June with the prince de Soubise, the general entrusted with the command of the main forces designed to land in England. He insisted on the necessity of getting a foothold on the western coast of Scotland provided the French commander-in-chief had obtained the necessary powers either from King James or from the royal prince his son to raise regiments there. The aim would be to set up a Scottish civil government, restore the Privy Council and Parliament of Scotland, and to re-establish the old laws, customs and privileges of that kingdom. Besides, he proposed that Lord George Murray, the commander-in-chief during the '45, then a refugee in Holland, should be called upon although he was on bad terms with Charles Edward.[38] Choiseul expressed the deep attachment of Louis XV to the Scottish nation, France's ally for centuries, and told him that the Prince's friends in Scotland would be warned in good time.[39] Leslie handed over to the ministers at Versailles a list of twenty-three peers of Scotland[40] and of sixty-five baronets, knights and gentlemen who had retained considerable property and had influence enough to enable them to raise their clans. In order to raise 20,000 Highlanders, Leslie demanded very good arms and clothing as both were lacking. A French force of 7000 — 8000 regular troops with experienced officers and army engineers with siege artillery and mortars should land at Greenock and at Montrose. Because of strong currents in the Channel, he advised going round Ireland with large privateers. In addition, a combined landing in Wales would be useful as well as, if possible, a descent on Dunbar on the eastern shores of Scotland whence French ships could proceed to Norway where they would find gentlemen well disposed towards them. On the other hand, he advised against any attempt on Plymouth and Portsmouth, the principal bases of the English navy.

A manuscript document reveals the mutual hesitations of the French ministry and of Jacobite agents.[41] As with Mackenzie Douglas, Leslie would have liked to be appointed by Choiseul as the official representative of the Jacobites and to play the role formally played by Colonel Daniel O'Brien, who was now discredited and nearing his end.[42] On his side, Charles Edward used the services of Andrew Lumisden his private secretary, and Alexander Murray, brother of Patrick Murray, 5th Lord Elibank, or those of Leslie's enemy, Robert MacCarthy, 5th Earl of Clancarty (1686-1769), (ex-governor of Nova Scotia from 1733 to 1735), who had become a vice-admiral in the French Navy.[43] He also resorted to the good offices of Waters the Paris bankers.[44]

Leslie told Choiseul of the cautious attitude of Prince Charles Edward, who feared that his supporters in the three kingdoms might be compromised and who lacked the powers necessary to act in the name of his father James III. According to Leslie, should the French be unable to maintain themselves in Scotland, Charles

Edward would be pleased to hold that kingdom, but this possibility should be kept secret from the English Jacobites.[45] In fact Charles Edward had sounded James III in Rome several times in order to obtain an abdication in his own favour.[46] Choiseul considered sending to Bouillon his secretary, Jean-Louis Favier, a diplomat and pamphleteer,[47] but since Bonnie Prince Charlie insisted on being approached by someone of higher rank, the prince's friend and kinsman the comte Joachim Casimir de Béthune, a cavalry officer, was dispatched. Charles Edward did not conceal from him his disappointment at, as he felt, being kept in the dark about the preparations hitherto, and stipulated that Choiseul and Belle-Isle be asked if the embarkation was any concern of his, in order to warn his supporters in England who were getting impatient.[48]

Choiseul, however, did not deem that he had to trust the vast diplomatic schemes he was putting in motion to foreign Jacobites whose indiscretion, moreover, as well as the number of spies infiltrated amongst them, he well knew. In this respect, the duke took up again the northern plans of the Sun King and the Duke of Berwick in 1714-15 and indeed those of the marquis d'Argenson in 1745-46, to bring Sweden into the fight against Britain.[49] Like Alberoni, Goertz or Ripperda, Choiseul meant to use combined Russo-Swedish forces for a landing in Scotland. On 21 January 1759, he informed the marquis d'Havrincourt, the French ambassador in Sweden, that joint Franco-Swedish-Russian naval operations were essential to force Great Britain to make peace and to compel her ally Frederick II of Prussia to follow suit. As yet, the battles waged by the Swedes in Pomerania had had no effect and the considerable subsidies sent by France to Sweden had been wasted.[50] He asked the Swedish Government to assemble 12,000 men in Gothenburg to be sent to Scotland. The result would be a Swedish declaration of war against the United Kingdom, but the advantage of the projected operation would be to give Stettin to the Swedes, and they as well as the Russians could use the depredations made by the English navy on their shipping as *casus belli.*[51] Anders-Johan von Höpken, the President of the Chancery, despite his longstanding ties with the Jacobite network, took fright at the scale of a project which was as bold as it would be expensive and one impossible to get through the Senate without consulting the Diet and its secret committee. Through his functions as a Hat he had contracted the deepest distrust towards the Russians and knew how highly public opinion in Sweden regarded the King of Prussia as the defender of Protestantism. Besides, Sweden was altogether too dependent on Britain as the principal customer for her iron and for Swedish-Finnish maritime products.[52] On 7 June 1759, however, Höpken pretended to agree with Choiseul's ideas provided Russia also took part in this 'grandiose scheme' and provided France increased her subsidies to Sweden substantially.[53]

Turning to Russia, Choiseul proposed to Chancellor Vorontzov that at the same time Russian forces should be sent down to the Oder to capture Stettin from the Prussians and thence to embark 10,000 — 12,000 Russians on the Swedish fleet to carry out a combined operation in the north of Scotland. The time was well chosen, he argued, because of the advanced age of George II, the divisions in the royal family and discontents among the people. Thus a complete revolution would be brought about.[54] Vorontzov did not oppose the scheme, although he showed reluctance to co-operate with the Swedes through distrust of their government and contempt for their military worth.[55] Russia concluded a defensive alliance with Sweden to close the Baltic to foreign ships.[56] Choiseul, to associate Denmark-Norway with this policy, put his friend, Baron Johan Hartvig Ernst von Bernstorff, in the picture by stressing the dangers of an English naval and commercial supremacy. The Danes were beginning to realise this and were to form with the Russians and the Swedes a league of armed neutrality in March 1760. Naturally enough, however, they would neither help to re-establish Swedish power nor take part in a crusade against powerful Albion.[57]

In the United Provinces, as in Sweden, strong alarms were felt at the news revealed by the gazette that France was working to restore the Catholic Stuarts once again.[58] In a despatch to the comte d'Affry, the French ambassador at the Hague, Choiseul denied seeking to bring about a revolution in the British Isles, adding that none better than he realised the uselessness, the danger and even the absurdity of such an idea and claimed to seek only to hurt the enemies of France as much as they had hurt her. He told him that 'Prince Edward would be informed only after the event so that, if needs be, he could enlist the help of his friends'.[59]

Despite the bonds which united Choiseul to the Court of Vienna, strengthened early in 1759 by the conclusion of a new treaty of alliance, he knew that it would be useless to ask Austria to participate openly in this affair. Kaunitz had reaffirmed the enduring hostility of the Hapsburgs towards the Stuarts and indeed had revealed to the English the moves for an understanding between Charles Edward and Frederick II in Berlin in 1751.[60] As a guarantee of the neutrality of the Low Countries, however, he had agreed to allow the French to occupy Ostend for the duration of the war against Britain. This port, a centre of Jacobitism, would provide a first-rate base for operations against England. For Choiseul, the new Franco-Austrian treaty had the advantage of lessening French expenses and keeping the war going on the continent as a drain on British resources.[61] Having learned of the French plans, many officers of Irish origin serving in the imperial army offered to fight under the banners of Louis XV.[62]

For his part, however, the Young Pretender would not agree to act as a bogey for the French in order to facilitate the opening of peace negotiations with the English. In mid-July, Alexander Murray pleaded his master's cause with Soubise, Belle-Isle and Choiseul. The latter alleged that he had been able to tell the Dutch that he would not be attacking Protestantism in Great Britain since Prince Charles Edward was an Anglican convert. As he had done to Mackenzie Douglas, he reaffirmed that nothing would be done without the Prince of Wales but with him and for him. According to Murray, Charles Edward Stuart refused to act in Ireland or in Scotland, but aimed through London to become master of the whole.[63]

On 14 July 1759, Choiseul read to the King's Council a long memorandum on the landing in Britain. Reviewing the ruin of French overseas trade, the loss of Canada, of the settlements in Africa and probably those in India too, the failure of moves towards peace with Great Britain, the uselessness of a league of neutrality against her, as well as the stalemate in operations in Germany, in agreement with Belle-Isle he proposed a landing at Portsmouth with troops starting from Le Havre under the command of maréchal de Soubise and a secondary one at Glasgow to be commanded by the duc d'Aiguillon and starting from Brest. This Armada would consist of 337 ships carrying 48,000 men; twelve Swedish *prams*, flat-bottomed cargo boats and in this case real floating batteries, would protect the convoy. He expressed his distrust of liaising with the fleet, so that the operation should take place at night and by suprise.[64] Of the ministers, Silhouette (in charge of Finances), and Berryer (in charge of the Navy) concurred, while Puysieulx and the maréchal d'Estrées objected only to points of detail. The duc de Croy noted in his Memoirs his surprise at such unanimity, seldom seen in the Council.[65]

Financing operations on what was at the time a gigantic scale raised such acute financial problems that Madame de Pompadour, who had supported the project wholeheartedly, confided to her friends the d'Aiguillons her fears that they might prove an unsurmountable obstacle.[66] As it was, Silhouette succeeded in financing the enterprise thanks to the issue of 72 millions worth of shares on the tax farms.[67] The *prams* cost 30 millions, while Jean Joseph de Laborde, a farmer-general and Court banker, supplied 4 millions in Portuguese money obtained mainly from the Court of Spain towards a secondary expedition in Ireland.[68]

True to tradition, the hopes of the Jacobites, those of the Irish especially, turned towards Madrid, where they still had supporters as well as numerous kinsmen and allies in the Peninsula generally. Héguerty had urged Louis XV to ask the Spaniards to take part in the enterprise against Great Britain 'for the glory and profit of Spain'.[69] The comte Walsh de Serrant, the great shipowner and slave-trader from Nantes, who had many contacts in Spain, especially in Cadiz and San-Domingo,[70], asked another influential Irishman and an economist, Bernard Ward, to press the Catholic King's court to assist the Stuarts. Ward, however, replied that Charles III, in Spain only since October 1759, would not intervene in Great Britain without a prior rising in favour of the Stuarts.[71] The chief minister and secretary of state for foreign affairs in Spain, Ricardo Wall, had long been well disposed towards England, although he was also of Irish and Jacobite lineage, and he remained faithful to the principles of neutrality. True enough, in 1758 he had told the French ambassador, Aubeterre, in confidence that he still had personal loyalties to the Pretender James Stuart.[72] However, on 20 June, when urged by the comte d'Aubeterre to send twenty ships to Brest to take part in the attempt against England, he had sheltered behind the new King of Spain while admitting how frightened the Spaniards were at British advances in America.[73] All this foretold the nearness of the Family Compact. Nevertheless, the Jacobites and their friends were wrong to expect the participation of the Spanish navy at this stage.[74]

While preparations on a vast scale continued and gathered momentum, particularly at Le Havre, Brest, Rochefort and Toulon, and while troops assembled in Ostend, Dunkirk, St.-Omer, Lille and Vannes,[75] the Jacobites were not always kept informed of the French plans. They were either worried or exasperated by this.[76] In his instructions dated 16 June 1759 for the duc d'Aiguillon, who was to command the corps of the King's troops detailed to go to Scotland, Choiseul told him plainly that the Pretender Charles Edward 'had not a steady enough head for a considerable undertaking to be run according to his views'.[77] The Irish regiments in the French service, the pick of the army, were not to be mixed with Scottish Highlanders, which would be disastrous to both forces. On the other hand, the Scottish battalions would provide officers for a body of men to be raised in Scotland.[78] Additional instructions were given to him in September to enable him to treat with the English government should the French troops under his orders land successfully and be able to gain a foothold in Scotland. 'It is natural to expect that, in this eventuality, the minds of the people in the British Isles would be so troubled as to lead the Court of London to thoughts of peace and, possibly, to lead it to make direct or indirect proposals for an agreement'.[79] Joined as second plenipotentiary to him was James O'Dunne, an Irishman who had entered the French diplomatic service after a long sojourn overseas, whose knowledge Choiseul valued and who 'had aroused no suspicion in England'.[80]

While Choiseul had feared leaks on the part of emissaries, double agents and Jacobite spies with their wide network stretching from the French ports to the capital, the English secret service on their side had not taken long to get wind, from several sources, of the plans for a French landing. As soon as December 1758 and the early months of 1759 many intercepted letters had revealed them to Pitt's government.[81] While Newcastle, who thought the plan dangerous and well conceived, took fright and advised William Pitt to seek peace at any price and while George, Lord Lyttelton regarded the French invasion threat as the most serious since the Spanish Armada, Pitt himself remained unmoved.[82] Working with Ligonier, he had taken all the necessary precautions to defend the United Kingdom on land and at sea.[83] For England the war at sea was the decisive war and she realised the importance of naval supremacy to her survival: 'the sea is either England's defence or her prison' (Lord Grenville).[84] Pitt was worried less by Choiseul's military preparations than by his intrigues with the Swedes, the Danes and the Batavians, as he was loath to have more enemies to cope with. He knew only too well that those states had grievances against English privateers and might listen to Choiseul's overtures. Thus they could exact revenge in the Channel by joining the French fleet and taking England by surprise.[85]

Franco-Swedish negotiations, however, got nowhere. Höpken temporised, taking advantage of the Swedish constitution. He had, however, taken into his confidence two senators, Claes Ekeblad and Charles-Otto Hamilton, the latter of Scottish origin.[86] Choiseul had informed them of the latest arrangements made with the Jacobites. Mackenzie Douglas had gone to Brussels, whence he had sent a memorandum on the resources the French commander would find in Scotland. 'Leslie', Lord Blantyre, for his part had gone back to Scotland, entrusted with the task of finding necessary pilots and sending them back to France. The French Court had tried to deal direct with the Stuart supporters and the discontented in England without going through Charles Edward, 'surrounded by suspected persons of both sexes, who were likely to betray him'. His changes of religion had cost him many supporters without winning new ones. 'It was, however, essential to have their support especially in Scotland'.[87]

Alerted by the gazettes to French naval and military preparations, as the Dutch had been, Swedish senators friendly to France such as Charles-Frederick Scheffer and Nils Palmstierna asked Havrincourt if His Most Christian Majesty really intended to invade Great Britain, in which case Sweden could not accede to the scheme.[88] The Swedish ambassador in Paris, Ulric Scheffer, also disapproved of Choiseul's plans for a landing.[89] The duke was exasperated by this opposition on the part of the Swedes, which he blamed on 'the impractical regime of Sweden' and which he hid from Louis XV's other ministers.[90] Accordingly, he confined himself to asking the Swedish Government to supply France with 250 pieces of artillery and 20,000 cannon-balls drawn from the arsenal at Karlskrona.[91] These war supplies purchased from Sweden by France were loaded on Dutch ships chartered by Grill, the banker. They were to reach Amsterdam and the southern United Provinces by way of the canals in order to be stored in French naval dockyards. This posed a threat to Dutch neutrality.[92] The Court of France also requested arms and ammunition from Denmark and Spain.[93] The threat of a Jacobite invasion backed by foreign help did not fail to raise alarms in England which were reflected on the stock market.[94] The cargo, however, was seized by the English with the complicity of the Dutch authorities.[95]

As things turned out, the Belle-Isle-Choiseul plan for landings in England and Scotland had been modified at the request of the Navy, who distrusted the use of Antoine Groignard's flat-bottomed boats with their disparate crews of fishermen and merchant seamen.[96] On 22 July, with Louis XV present, Berryer in agreement with d'Estrées had presented a report to the Council in which he stressed the necessity of a large squadron to protect so many ships. D'Estrées made no secret of the fact that the English had found out the whole thing and were cruising outside the French ports to prevent the transports from coming out. Le Havre had been bombarded and it would be necessary to crash through the blockade.[97] The Toulon squadron under La Clue was to join the Ponant fleets and act as convoy to d'Aiguillon's expedition to Scotland, the 'special expedition' as it was called. On the other hand, 20,000 men commanded by Chevert would go from Ostend to make a descent on the coast of Essex near the Blackwater estuary at Maldon, 40-odd miles from London.[98]

How the English Navy ruined Choiseul's grand design is too well known to require a detailed account here. Admiral Edward Boscawen, who was entrusted with the command of the English fleet in the Mediterranean, had fallen foul of French frigates near Toulon but had managed to get his ships repaired in Gibraltar. Seizing his opportunity, on 5 August 1759, La Clue left Toulon post-haste and even succeeded in crossing the Straits of Gibraltar (though in violation of Portugese neutrality). On 19 August his fleet was either dispersed or sunk near Lagos on the Portugese coast.[99] Of twelve ships of the line, only five were left, which had taken refuge in Cadiz, but they continued to worry Sir Edward Hawke then cruising outside Brest. By now the invasion of England was impossible, but Choiseul clung to the hope of invading Scotland.[100] Infuriated at the time already lost, he told d'Aiguillon that the Swedes were waiting for the French in order to land in Scotland.[101]

Summoned by Choiseul on 2 August, Murray was reproached with indiscretions committed by the Jacobites and even by Charles Edward. Choiseul also criticised the stupidity and brutality of the Irishmen in French ports.[102] Nevertheless, on 7 September, Choiseul informed Charles Edward that the previous arrangements remained unchanged. In turn Charles Edward reassured him that, according to his agents, there was growing impatience on the part of his friends in England. Once again, he addressed himself to Belle-Isle. Murray went on besieging the King's ministers. He begged his master to get to Paris before the departure of d'Aiguillon for Scotland, but at the same time warned Choiseul that unless there was a simultaneous landing in England, no one would rise in Scotland. Choiseul seized the opportunity of asking for a declaration from the Prince, should he not wish to take part in the Scottish descent. Murray could only counter by saying he was not empowered to reply to such a request. While reaffirming the fidelity of Louis XV and of his ministers to the Stuart cause, Choiseul admitted the difficulties experienced with transports and barges, that 24 millions had been spent already and yet not everything was ready.[103]

The decisive battle of Quiberon Bay south of the isle of Belle-Isle, in which Hawke destroyed the Brest fleet under the comte de Conflans, has remained one of the most glorious days in the annals of the English navy. It put an end, ironically enough on 25 November, to the last attempt to restore the Stuarts.[104] With it went French hopes of saving Canada and India through a descent on the British Isles. The raid carried out by Thurot in Ireland with Gothenburg and Bergen as supply bases, however, showed what could have been done with more determination and fewer delays on the part of the French command. The sincerity of Choiseul, 'a sceptic in power' on this occasion as on many others, has been questioned.[105] Was the white rose of the Stuarts a mere token for him with which to please his master and Madame de Pompadour? In the strategy of his grand design, Jacobitism was no doubt only an instrument and one difficult to use in an international context.[106]

Jacobitism has suffered from the paradox of being partly stirred up from abroad by emigrants trying to foment rebellion in Great Britain, looking to Louis XV as they had to Louis XIV before him for substantial help.[107] Yet how could the foreign Hanoverians be denounced while resorting to 'papist' powers?[108] In the long run, it could only discredit the movement and strengthen popular attachment to the Hanoverian dynasty. The 1759 attempt, moreover, had revealed not only the divisions between the Jacobites in the United Kingdom and Ireland but also the progressive integration of the Jacobite Diaspora in the host countries.

NOTES

A French version of this essay was published in the *Revue d'Histoire diplomatique*. July-December 1979, Nos. 3-4.

1. O. A. Sherrard, *Lord Chatham, A War Minister in the Making*, London 1952, pp. 278-9.

2. V. Wills, ed., *Reports on the Annexed Estates* (1755-1769), Edinburgh 1973.

3. G. Hilton Jones, *The Main Stream of Jacobitism*, Cambridge, Mass., 1954, pp. 239-41.

4. 'I tremble for fear that this vile spot may still be the ruin of this Island and our Family', in C. H. Hartmann, *The Quest forlorn. The story of the Forty five*, London 1952, pp. 247-8.

5. Besides the standard works of Sir Charles Petrie, see the brilliant but cursory article by G. Chaussinand-Nogaret, 'De l'exil religieux aux affaires: les Jacobites au XVIIIe siècle', in *Annales, Economies, Sociétés Civilisations*, September-October 1973, pp. 1087-1122; Claude Nordmann, 'Les Jacobites ècossais en France au XVIIIe siècle', in *Regards sur l'Ecosse au XVIIIe siècle*, ed. M. S. Plaisant, Publ. Univ. de Lille III 1977, pp. 81-108. Bruce Lenman, 'The Jacobite diaspora 1688–1746: from Despair to Integration', *History Today*, May 1980, pp. 7-10.

6. William King, *Political and Literary Anecdotes of his own Times*, London 1818.

7. Eveline Cruickshanks, *Political Untouchables. The Tories and the '45*, London 1979.

8. In *Reformation to Industrial Revolution*, London 1975, p. 225.

9. H. M. Vaughan, 'Welsh Jacobitism', *The Transactions of the Honourable Society of Cymmrodorion*, 1920-1921, pp. 11-39; P. D. G. Thomas, 'Jacobitism in Wales', *The Welsh History Review*, i (1962), pp. 279-300.

10. See especially the classic work of P. Mantoux, *The Industrial Revolution in the Eighteenth Century*, new and revised ed. with a preface by T. S. Ashton, London 1970, pp. 78-82, *passim;* on the question of Irish immigration in London see Dorothy M. George, *London Life in the Eighteenth Century*, London 1965, pp. 120-131; G. Rudé, *Paris and London in the 18th Century. Studies in Popular Protest*, London 1970, pp. 218-221, 304, 321.

11. P. Coquelle, *Les projets de descente en Angleterre*, Paris 1902; A. Bourguet, *Etudes sur la politique étrangère du duc de Choiseul*, Paris 1907.

12. Peter de Polnay, *Death of a Legend. The True Story of Bonnie Prince Charlie*, London 1952.

13. By gracious permission of H.M. The Queen and with the kind help of Miss V. Langton of the Royal Archives, Windsor Castle.

14. In a paper entitled 'Les Jacobites en France au XVIIe et XVIIIe siècles', given to Professor Ragnhild Hatton's seminar in the Institute of Historical Research, London 18th May 1970.

15. A comprehensive bibliography of the works of Professor Hatton cannot be given here. For a survey of research done in this field see G. Livet, 'Les Relations internationales du XVIIIe siècle', in *Dix-huitième siècle*. 'Problèmes actuels de la recherche', 1973 (No. 5) pp. 97-109.

16. E. Cruickshanks, *op.cit.*, pp. 62-63 and, for tobacco smuggling and the Jacobites, J. M. Price, *France and the Chesapeake 1694-1791. A History of the French tobacco monopoly*, Ann Arbor, Michigan 1973, i. pp. 558-60, 561-81.

17. P. A. Perrod, 'L'affaire Lally Tolendal', Paris, thèse, 1976, p. 28.

18. Camille Rousset, *Le Comte de Gisors*, new ed. Paris 1887, p. 126.

19. The maréchal de Belle-Isle married in 1729 as his second wife Emmanuelle Catherine de Béthune, the young widow of the marquis de Médavy-Grancey, and daughter of the Chamberlain of Stanislas Leszczynski, King of Poland. Through it Belle-Isle became allied with the financial party since the marquis de Béthune was Montmartel's brother-in-law and was connected with the Crozats; see A. Dussauge, *Le ministère de Belle-Isle*, Paris 1914, p. 68. For the links between the Béthunes and the Sobieskis and the Stuarts see R. Rohmer, 'Une famille limousine à la Cour de Pologne, les Baluze', *Revue d'Histoire diplomatique*, 1935 and 1936, and Hélène de Fitz-James, *Lettres de la religieuse polonaise*, Paris 1972.

20. C. d'Intraiguel, *L'Ascanius moderne ou l'illustre aventurier*, Edinburgh 1763, ii. pp. 195-6.

21. A. Corvisier, *Armées et sociétés en Europe de 1494 à 1789*, Paris 1976, p. 22.

22. C. Rousset, *op.cit.*, p. 447.

23. V. L. Tapié, *L'Europe de Marie Thérèse*, Paris 1973, pp. 163 *et seq.*

24. H. Verdier's *Le duc de Choiseul*, Paris 1969, is the best psychological portrait of Louis XV's minister. The short work of R. Soltau, *The Duke of Choiseul*, Oxford 1909, is still useful. The first volume of a massive study of Choiseul's career has just appeared: Rohan Butler, *Choiseul: Father and Son 1719-1754*, Oxford 1981.

25. P. Coquelle, *op.cit.*, p. 37.

26. See *Correspondance inédite du Comte de Broglie avec Louis XV 1756-1774* ed. D. Ozanam and M. Antoine, Paris 1961, pp. 24-5.

27. *Recueil des Instructions aux Ambassadeurs de France en Russie*, (quoted hereafter as Instr. Amb.), ii, ed. A. Rambaud, Paris 1890, pp. 5-13, 15-30.

28. Pajol, *Les guerres sous Louis XV*, Paris 1885, vi. 373 *et seq.*

29. Sir N. W. Nathaniel Wraxall in his *Historical Memoirs of my own time*, 3rd ed. revised, London 1818, i. 308-10, mentioned this meeting but places it erroneously in 1770 which has misled many historians. Charles Edward had a meeting with d'Aiguillon in 1771 about his marriage.

30. See C. Leo-Berry, *The Young Pretender's Mistress*, Edinburgh and London 1971; A. Lang, *Pickle the Spy*, London 1897, p. 80; Polnay, *op.cit.*, p. 195.

31. M. Forster, *The Rash Adventurer, the Rise and Fall of Charles Edward Stuart*, London 1973, p. 238. According to her the French would have liked the Prince to lead an expedition to Ireland on their behalf, but he was only interested in England. Choiseul then decided 'qu'on attaquera "L'Ecureuil" (l'Angleterre) par la tête et la queue , on 8 May 1759.

32. Choiseul to Mackenzie Douglas, Marly 14 February 1759 (in reply to a letter of 13 February 1759), Royal Archives, Windsor Castle Stuart ms. 390/161; Mackenzie Douglas to Charles Edward 12 April 1759, *ibid.*, 392/67; Douglas's cypher in his 1759 correspondence with Charles Edward uses an allegorical language very similar to that in the Russian correspondence, with such expressions as 'the purchases of furs'. This has made it much easier to decipher. Choiseul agreed to Douglas's cypher but demanded a duplicate on 22 February 1750 (Mackenzie Douglas to Prince Charles Edward, Paris 3 March 1759, 391/43).

33. For the part played by the Jacobites in freemasonry, see my article, 'Les Jacobites écossais en France', pp. 94-6.

34. From Paris, 23 February 1759 (Stuart mss 391/15). Thus he acted as spokesman for prelates such as Dillon and Fitzjames.

35. Mackenzie Douglas to Charles Edward, Paris 6 April 1759, Stuart mss 392/33.

36. O'Heguerty to Choiseul, Paris 25 January 1759, A.E.C.P. Angleterre 442 ff. 16-17. His advice was to get the Papacy to put pressure on James III to work towards the re-establishment of catholicism in Ireland with the support of French arms; see also P. Chevallier, *La première profanation du Temple maçonnique*, Paris, 1968, p. 127. On O'Heguerty's role in France and on the Ile Bourbon, *idem.*, *Les ducs sous l'Acacia (1725-1743)*, Paris 1964, pp. 27-8, 181-88.

37. Lord Blantyre had served as major in the 'Royal Suedois' a regiment in the French service and under the name of 'Leslie' had been sent on a secret mission to Sweden in 1745-1746 to raise troops for the Stuarts there. See Claude Nordmann, 'Jakobiterna och det svenska Hovet', *Historisk Tidskrift*, 1959, pp. 408-17.

38. Blantyre (as the comte de Leslie) to Choiseul, Paris 13 June 1759, A.E.C.P. Angleterre 442 ff. 109-111; 'Eclaircissements demandés au Duc de Choiseul', *ibid.*, ff. 119 *et seq.* On Lord George Murray, the Scottish Jacobite general, see W. Duke (1927) and K. Tomasson, *The Jacobite General*, London 1958.

39. 'Réponse du duc de Choiseul an Mémoire de M. le Comte de Leslie', 15 June 1759, A.E.C.P. Angleterre 442 ff. 123 *et seq.* Choiseul apparently considered sending the Duke of York to Scotland (Coquelle, *ante* p. 40).

40. Henry David Erskine, 10th Earl of Buchan; John Lyon (Bowes), styled Lord Glamis, later 7th Earl of Strathmore; Thomas Alexander Erskine, 6th Earl of Kellie; Charles Stewart, 5th Earl of Traquair; Charles Bruce, 5th Lord Elgin; James Lindsay, 5th Earl of Balcarres: Charles Gordon, 4th Earl of Aboyne; John Ogilvy, (but for attainder) 5th Earl of Airlie; William Maxwell, (but for attainder) 6th Earl of Nithsdale; Seton, Earl of Winton (presumably a male heir of George Seton, 5th Earl of Winton who died unmarried in 1749, though none is recorded in *Scots Peerage*, ed. Sir James Balfour Paul); Sir James Carnegie, 3rd Bt., (but for attainder) 6th Earl of Southesk; Alexander Dalzell, (but for attainder) 6th Earl of Carnwarth; George Mackenzie, 3rd Earl of Cromarty (then a prisoner in England); John Gordon, (but for attainder) 8th Viscount Kenmure; James Francis Edward Drummond (attainted 1746), 5th Viscount Strathallan; George Fraser, 15th Lord Saltoun of Abernethy; Alexander Forbes, (but for attainder) 4th Lord Forbes of Pitsligo; Eric Sutherland, (but for attainder) 4th Lord Duffus; John Nairne, (but for attainder) 3rd Lord Nairne and 1st Earl of Nairne in the Jacobite peerage; Alexander Falconer, 5th Lord Falconer of Halkertoun; Patrick Murray, 5th Lord Elibank; William Stuart, 8th Lord Blantyre; James Forbes, 16th Lord Forbes. (See the master's degree of my student Emmanuelle Durand, 'Fidelités et parentèles dans les Highlands d'Ecosse du milieu du XVIIIe siècle', Univ. de Lille III, 1978 (typescript)).

41. Bibliothèque Nationale ms. nouv. acq. fr. 23.865 ff. 1-3 entitled 'Mémoire de Charles-Edouard Stuart à Choiseul' n.d., which seems to be a project from 'Leslie' drawn from the Archives de la Marine B4 297-8.

42. On the part played by Col. Daniel O'Brien, comte de Lismore, see G. Hilton Jones, *op.cit.*, pp. 155, 165, 170 and *passim*, and E. Cruickshanks, *op.cit.*, pp. 32, 38. There was a feud between the Maréchal Charles de Thomond and his wife and the O'Briens of Lismore whom they accused of forgery. James III defended Col. O'Brien until his death and protected his widow. See Dossier bleu No. 135, Cabinet des Titres, Bib. Nat. James III to Choiseul, 9 January 1759 and 13 March 1759 in A.E.C.P. Angleterre 442 ff. 10 and 62. Testimonial in his favour by David Hennegan, principal of the Lombard (Irish) College in Paris, *ibid.*, 16 May 1759 ff. 90 *et seq.* signed by twenty Irish gentlemen.

43. A. Lang, *op.cit.*, p. 302. On the part played by Andrew Lumisden sent to Paris to restore the links between James III and Charles Edward, to whom James III wrote from Rome, the 7th October 1758: 'The Prince must be convinced by his own experience how little he has to expect from the English alone and that he has as little to hope for, in any respect, from any foreign power except France so that if he does not seriously endeavour to gain and cultivate the friendship of that Crown, it is in some respect next to renouncing all human hopes and means of restoration', and who was helped in Paris by the bankers Waters, see *The Stuart Papers at Windsor*, ed. A. and H. Tayler, London 1939, pp. 231-233. On the numerous MacCarthy family in France see Pièces originales No 17 84, Cabinet des Titres, in Bibliothèque Nationale. The Irish clan MacCarthy gave a large number of navy officers to the French navy under the Ancien Régime, many of whom were in the service of the Compagnie des Indes (Archives de la Marine C7 191, in the Archives Nationales).

44. On the Waters, George and son, see Ruvigny and Raineval, *The Jacobite Peerage*, Edinburgh 1904, p. 234; see also Etude XXXVI bdle. 468, Minutier central des Notaires parisiens. The elder George died in St.-Germain-en-Laye in 1752. His son George-Jean (1705-1771) succeeded him.

45. Bibl. Nat. Ms. fr., nouv. acq. fr., 23.865.

46. See Polnay, *op.cit.*, pp. 197-8.

47. Jean-Louis Favier is the author of 'Précis de faits sur l'Administration de M. de Choiseul', published by Flammermont in the *Révolution francaise* 1899, pp. 415-462. Many of his writings are quoted in L. Ph. de Ségur, *Politique de tous les Cabinets de l'Europe pendant les règnes de Louis XV et de Louis XVI*, Paris 1802, vol. I.

48. Mackenzie Douglas to Charles Edward, Paris 12 April 1759, Stuart ms. 392/67 and 23 April 1759, 392/103.

49. Claude Nordmann, *La Crise du Nord du début du XVIIIe siècle*, Paris 1962, pp. 35-45; R. M. Hatton, *Charles XII of Sweden*, London 1968, pp. 404-05; the essay by L. B. Smith (pp. 159-178 infra) re-opens certain possibilities, particularly on the financial side. For the policy of Ripperda towards the Jacobites, see the older works of Dureng and Syveton.

50. Choiseul to Havrincourt, Versailles 12 January 1759 and 21 January 1759, A.E.C.P. Suède 236 ff. 15, 54 *et seq.*

51. Choiseul to Havrincourt 6 February 1759, A.E.C.P. Suède 236 ff. 95-7. For the Jacobites in Göteborg, apart from the old book by A. Fischer, *The Scots in Sweden*, Edinburgh 1907, see A. Cormack, *Colin Campbell merchant, Gothenburg, Sweden. A Scoto-Swedish Study*, Aberdeen 1960.

52. Claude Nordmann, *Grandeur et Liberté de la Suède* (1660-1792), Paris-Louvain 1971, pp. 264-5.

53. Memorandum from baron Höpken to Havrincourt, 7 June 1759, A.E.C.P. Suède 236 ff. 409-422. The French had also promised that Tobago would be given to Sweden at the peace.

54. A. Vandal, *Louis XV et Elisabeth de Russie*, Paris 1896 (3rd ed.), pp. 534-6.

55. A.E.C.P. Russie 59 ff. 119 *et seq.*

56. G. Zeller, *Histoire des relations internationales*, vol III, *De Louis XIV à 1789*, Paris 1955, p. 242, who drew from R. Waddington, *La guerre de Sept Ans*, vol. III, Paris 1904.

57. Choiseul to Bernstorff, Versailles 29 July 1759, Bernstorff to Choiseul, Copenhagen 22 August 1759 in *Correspondance entre le Comte J. H. E. de Bernstorff et le Duc de Choiseul (1758-1766)*, ed. E. M. de Barthélemy, Copenhagen 1871, pp. 44-6 and 52. See also F. Bajer, 'Les entrevues de M. Hömer avec le duc de Choiseul', *Revue d'Histoire diplomatique*, 1904, pp. 406-424; *Bernstorffs Papiere (1732-1835)* ed. A. Friis, Copenhagen 1904-1907, vol I and *Correspondance ministérielle du Comte J. H. E. Bernstorff (1751-1770)* ed. P. Vedel, Copenhagen 1882, Vol. I; Danish policy is explained in S. Cedergreen Bech, *Danmarks historie*, ed. J. Danstrup and H. Koch, vol. IX, (1721-1784), Copenhagen 1964.

58. P. Coquelle, *La Hollande pendant le guerre de Sept Ans*, Paris 1899, p. 117.

59. Choiseul to Affry, 31 May 1759, A.E.C.P. Hollande, 501 f. 205.

60. Charles Edward was received by Frederick II in Berlin in February 1751 and he used the Earl Marischal, George Keith, hereditary marshal of Scotland, as Prussian ambassador to Paris to spy on the Anglo-Hanoverian government (see David Daiches, *Charles Edward Stuart*, London 1973, p. 361); Kaunitz was then Austrian ambassador in France. The British government was also warned of the Prusso-Jacobite plot and of the mission of Archibald Cameron to Scotland by Young Glengarry (Alaistar Ruadh Macdonald), 'Pickle' the spy, in the pay of Newcastle, English authorities, however, were suspicious of him, see A. Lang, *The Companions of Pickle*, London 1898, p. 236; C. E. Cuthell, *The Scottish Friend of Frederick the Great, The Last Earl Marischal*, London 1915.

61. V. L. Tapié, *op.cit.*, p. 166.

62. The Austrian general staff contained many generals and officers of Irish-Jacobite origin such as Lascy, Browne, O'Donnell, Ogilvy and Daun the generalissimo, see O. Regele, *Der österreichische Hofkreigsrat*, Wien 1949; see also *Wild Geese in Spanish Flanders*

(*1582-1700*), ed. B. Jennings, Dublin 1964; A. E. Mémoires et Documents, Angleterre 82; C. Duffy, *The wild Geese and the Eagle, a Life of Marschal von Brown* (*1705-1757*), London 1964 and 'The wild Geese in Austria', *History Today*, September 1968, pp. 646-652; E. Kotasek, *Feldmarschall Graf Lacy*, Horn 1956. There were also Scotsmen such as field-marshal Lawdon (Loudon).

63. P. de Polnay, pp. 201-2.

64. William Egerton, 'Projets d'invasion française en Angleterre' *Revue contemporaire*, January-February 1867, pp. 11-12.

65. *Journal inédit du duc de Croy*, ed. Grouchy et Cottin, Paris 1906, i. 473.

66. Madame de Pompadour to d'Aiguillon, 5 February 1759 and 25 September 1759, in *Correspondance de Mme de Pompadour*, ed. A. Poulet-Malassis, Paris 1878, pp. 137, 142-143; Paul d'Estrée and Albert Caillet, *La duchesse d'Aiguillon*, Paris 1912, p. 34.

67. Yves Durant, *Les fermiers généraux au XVIII^3 siècle*, Paris 1971, p. 166.

68. 'Mémoires de Jean-Joseph de Laborde, fermier général et banquier de la Cour', published with an intro. by Yves Durand, *Annuaire de la Société de l'Histoire de France*, 1968-1969, p. 171.

69. P. Coquelle, 'Les projets de descente', *op.cit.*, p. 39.

70. Apart from the older works of the duc de la Trémoille on his ancestors the Walshes, see Ruvigny, *The Jacobite Peerage*, *op.cit.*, 178-83; see the numerous works of Gaston, Martin on the slave-traders, that of Father Dieudonné Rinchon on van Alstein (Dakar 1964); L. Dermigny, *La Chine et l'Occident. Le commerce à Canton au XVIIIe siècle*, Paris 1964, ii. 654-655; for the banking ties of the Jacobite circles see H. Luthy, *La banque protestante en France de L'Edit de Nantes à la Révolution*, Paris 1959-1961, i. 393 *et seq.*, ii. 168-9, 304-06, 316; J. M. Price, *op.cit.*, ii. 1028-31.

71. The comte Walsh de Serrant to Ward, 27 March 1758 and B. Ward to Walsh, 15 February 1762, in Walsh's correspondence in Archives du Château de Serrant, No. 170 (Maine et Loire). On Bernard Ward, see J. Sarrailh, *l'Espagne éclairée de la seconde moitié de XVIIIe siècle*, Paris 1954, pp. 4, 28-29 and *passim*.

72. See F. Rousseau, *Règne de Charles III* (1759-1788), Paris 1907, pp. 17, 29-30; Soulange-Bodin, *Le pacte de famille*, Paris 1891, p. 23.

73. D'Aubeterre to Choiseul, Madrid 20 June 1759, A.E.C.P. Espagne, t. 525, ff. 69-71.

74. It seems that some officers counted on the intervention of the Spanish fleet to join them at Ushant, see W. Egerton, *op.cit.*, pp. 14-15.

75. 'Préparatifs pour une descente en Angleterre sous les ordres du duc d'Aiguillon', Archives de la Guerre A1 3. 538.

76. Charles Edward to Walsh de Serrant, 12 June 1759, Stuart Ms. 393/177: 'Nos armements pour la descente vont toujours très bon train, mais il n'est nulle question de notre Prince. Il est certain que si les Francais ne débarquent pas avec le Prince, et s'il n'est point à la tête de l'expedition, ils n'ont aucune chance, car les Anglais n'accepteront pas de se soumettre à leur domination'; Daniel O'Brien to the comte Walsh de Serrant, Paris 18 August 1759, in L. Ch. de la Trémoille, *A Royalist family Irish and French and Prince Charles Edouard*, (*1689-1789*), translated by A. G. Murray, Edinburgh 1904, pp. 67-68 (O'Brien of Lismore died in September 1759).

77. *Instr. Amb. Angleterre*, ed. P. Vaucher, Paris 1965, p. 370.

78. For the Irish and Scots in the French army, apart from the older works of E. Fieffé, of J. Forbes Leith, of O'Callaghan, see A. Corvisier, 'L'armée francaise de la fin du XVIIIe siècle au ministere de Choiseu'l, *Le Soldat*, Paris 1964, i. 147-148, 163, 261-263, 270-272, 545-552; ii. 961, 988. Despite the dictionary by R. Hayes published in Dublin in 1949, his other works, and those in *Irish Sword*, there remains much to do on this subject, especially on the officer class.

79. A.E.C.P. Angleterre 442 ff. 187-90; Archives de la Marine B⁴ 86 ff. 9-11.

80. P. Vaucher, *op.cit.*, p. 370. The full powers granted to the duc d'Aiguillon and to O'Dunne are dated 10 September 1759, Archives de la Marine, B⁴ 86 ff. 3-5.

81. Basil Williams, *The Life of William Pitt, Earl of Chatham*, London 1913, i. 339-400; J. S. Corbett, *England in the Seven Years' War*, London 1907, ii. 18 and 23, The Swedish envoy to Denmark informed the English envoy in Copenhagen, Goodricke, on 9 October 1759 of French attempts to involve Sweden in the plan for a descent. He was thanked with the comment that 'it was no secret to his Majesty', in *British diplomatic Instructions, Sweden (1727-1789)*, ed. J. F. Chance, London 1928, p. 137.

82. George, Lord Lyttelton, *Memoirs and Correspondence*, ed. P. Phillimore, London 1845, ii. 614.

83. R. Whitworth, *Field Marshal Lord Ligonier, a Story of the British Army, 1702-1770*, Oxford 1958.

84. P. Vaucher, *La Grande-Bretagne, l'Irlande et les colonies britanniques au XVIII ᵉ siècle*, Paris, new ed., 1978, p. 57.

85. B. Williams, *op.cit.*, pp. 400-01.

86. For the Hamiltons of Sweden, see O. Donner, *Scottish Families in Finland and Sweden*, Helsingfors 1884, p. 29 and J. Berg and B. O. Lagercrantz, *Scots in Sweden*, Stockholm 1962, *passim*. A member of the Council of State, Charles Otto Hamilton (1704-1770), was the brother of General Gustavus David Hamilton (1699-1788), commander in Pomerania.

87. A.E.C.P. Suède 237ff. 10-12; A.E.M. and D. Suède xv. ff. 13 *et seq.*

88. Havrincourt to Choiseul, 7 September 1759, A.E.C.P. Suède 237 ff. 122-130.

89. Lars Trulsson, *Ulric Scheffer som Hattpolitiker*, Lund 1947.

90. C. Nordmann, *Grandeur et Liberté de la Suède (1660-1792)*, Paris 1971, p. 265.

91. Choiseul to Havrincourt, 17 June 1759 and Havrincourt to Choiseul, 29 June 1759, A.E.C.P. Suède 236 ff. 440, 463-465.

92. Alice Carter, 'How to revise Treaties without Negotiating: Commonsense mutual fears and the Anglo-Dutch Trade Disputes of 1759', in *Studies in Diplomatic History, Essays in memory of D. B. Horn*, ed. R. Hatton and M. S. Anderson, London 1970, p. 233.

93. Choiseul asked Ogier, the French ambassador at Copenhagen on 9 June 1759 that Denmark should supply 200 cannons made out of iron of 24 to 18 *livres* with the cannonballs and to send them to Holland whence they should be transported to Dunkirk, to be paid by letters of credit drawn on M. de Laborde, A.E.C.P. Danemark 141 ff. 267-8, Aubeterre to Choisseul, 15 July 1759, A.E.C.P. Espagne 525 ff. 103-05.

94. Alice Carter, *ante* p. 234. John Calcraft, an army contractor, had caused panic in London by announcing that 26,000 men were encamped in Flanders ready to cross over in the summer and that a Swedish invasion of Scotland was also feared. Ligonier himself was worried about the worth of the militia in Britain, see R. Whitworth, *Ligonier, op.cit.*, pp. 282-4.

95. Choiseul to Havrincourt, Versailles 25 October 1759, A.E.C.P. Suède 237 f. 217. Havrincourt took heart in the thought that the cargo was safe! *Ibid.*, f. 227.

96. Conflans to Choiseul, Brest 15 August 1759, with a reminder that he had insisted on the support of his squadron, Marine B4 86 f. 185.

97. Coquelles, 'Les Projets', p. 46.

98. Correspondence of Bigot de Morogues with the maréchal de Conflans in 1759. Bigot de Morogues, a captain in the Navy and general in an artillery regiment in the Marines, was seconded to the duc d'Aiguillon. Louis XV to Bigot de Morogues, 15 August 1759, in Marine B4 87. As a large number of officers from merchant ships asked to serve, even as common seamen, one may assume that many of them belonged to the Jacobite Diaspora,

from Lannion, 25 June 1759, Marine B4 86 f. 29. For the Jacobites in Britanny see Jean Meyer, *La noblesse bretonne au XVIII ͤ siècle,* Paris 1966, ii. 1050-1. The importance of Maldon in Jacobite plans was stressed by E. Cruickshanks, *op.cit.,* pp. 42, 55, 77 and 96.

99. See the standard work of A. T. Mahan, *The Influence of Sea Power upon History (1660-1783),* new ed. London 1965, pp. 298-9.

100. Mackenzie Douglas to Charles Edward, Paris 17 October 1759, Stuart ms. 396/6.

101. Choiseul to d'Aiguillon, 3 October 1759, quoted in R. Waddington, *op.cit.,* p. 307.

102. For the divisions between the Jacobites across the Channel and those in the diaspora see M. G. Ritchings, *Le service secret de la Couronne d'Angleterre,* translated from English, Paris 1935; A. Lang, *Pickle, op.cit.,* p. 307.

103. P. de Polnay, *op.cit.,* p. 204.

104. Letter from Croisie of 21 September 1759, A.E.C.P. Angleterre 442 ff. 238-243; Mahon, *op.cit.,* pp. 300-04 (with map); G. Marcus, *Quiberon Bay,* London 1960; R. F. Mackay, *Admiral Hawke,* Oxford 1965.

105. J. Levron, *Choiseul, un sceptique au pouvoir,* Paris 1976, a brilliant work of popularisation, which endeavours to vindicate a very controversial personage. Does not deal with our subject.

106. When A. Murray wrote from Brussels on 17 July 1760 that discontent across the Channel was such that half the nation was for the Stuarts and he requested a landing in Scotland by 6000 Swedes or Russians and one in England with 20,000 French or Spaniards, Choiseul replied on 23 July 1760: 'Je vous l'ai déjà exposé plusieurs fois, qu'un concert unanime se manifeste en faveur des projets du Prince Charles Edward et S.M. ne demande qu'à les soutenir, car elle lui reste très attachée', A.E.C.P. Angleterre, 442 ff. 402-04.

107. Claude Nordmann, 'Louis XIV and the Jacobites', in *Louis XIV and Europe,* ed. R. Hatton, London 1976, pp. 82-111.

108. Roland Marx, *L'Angleterre de Révolutions,* Paris 1971, pp. 300-01.

Index